D1715386

# THE WATCHDOGS
# DIDN'T BARK

# THE WATCHDOGS DIDN'T BARK

*The CIA, NSA, and the Crimes of the War on Terror*

John Duffy

Ray Nowosielski

**HOT BOOKS**

Hot Books may be purchased in bulk at special discounts for sales promotion, corporate gifts, fund-raising, or educational purposes. Special editions can also be created to specifications. For details, contact the Special Sales Department, Skyhorse Publishing, 307 West 36th Street, 11th Floor, New York, NY 10018 or info@skyhorsepublishing.com.

Hot Books® and Skyhorse Publishing® are registered trademarks of Skyhorse Publishing, Inc., a Delaware corporation.

Visit our website at www.hotbookspress.com

10 9 8 7 6 5 4 3 2 1

Library of Congress Cataloging-in-Publication Data is available on file.

Cover design by Brian Peterson

Print ISBN: 978-1-5107-2136-4
Ebook ISBN: 978-1-5107-2137-1

Printed in the United States of America

# CONTENTS

# FOREWORD

## By David Talbot

The world is burning, and yet the firelight illuminates the way out. The times are dire, even catastrophic. Nonetheless we can sense a grand awakening, a growing realization all around the globe that "people have the power, to dream, to rule, to wrestle the world from fools" in the prophetic words of Patti Smith.

But in order to rouse ourselves from the nightmares that hold us in their grip, we need to know more about the forces that bedevil us, the structures of power that profit from humanity's exploitation and from that of the earth. That's the impetus behind Hot Books, a series that seeks to expose the dark operations of power and to light the way forward.

Skyhorse publisher Tony Lyons and I started Hot Books in 2015 because we believe that books can make a difference. Since then the Hot Books series has shined a light on the cruel reign of racism and police violence in Baltimore (D. Watkins's *The Beast Side*); the poisoning of US soldiers by their own environmentally reckless commanding officers (Joseph Hickman's *The Burn Pits*); the urgent need to hold US officials accountable for their criminal actions during the war on terror (Rachel Gordon's *American Nuremberg*); the covert manipulation of the media by intelligence agencies (Nicholas Schou's *Spooked*); the rise of a rape culture on campus (Kirby Dick and Amy Ziering's *The Hunting Ground*); the insidious demonizing of Muslims in the media and Washington (Arsalan Iftikhar's *Scapegoats*); the crackdown on whistleblowers who know the government's dirty secrets (Mark Hertsgaard's *Bravehearts*); the disastrous policies of the liberal elite that led to the triumph of Trump (Chris Hedges's *Unspeakable*); the

American wastelands that gave rise to this dark reign (Alexander Zaitchik's *The Gilded Rage*); the energy titans and their political servants who are threatening human survival (Dick Russell's *Horsemen of the Apocalypse*); the utilization of authoritarian tactics by Donald Trump that threaten to erode American democracy (Brian Klaas's *The Despot's Apprentice*); the capture, torture, and detention of the first "high-value target" captured by the CIA after 9/11 (Joseph Hickman and John Kiriakou's *The Convenient Terrorist*); the deportation of American veterans (J. Malcolm Garcia's *Without a Country*); and the ways in which our elections have failed, and continue to fail, their billing as model democracy (Steven Rosenfeld's *Democracy Betrayed*). And the series continues, going where few publishers dare.

Hot Books are more condensed than standard-length books. They're packed with provocative information and points of view that mainstream publishers usually shy from. Hot Books are meant not just to stir readers' thinking, but to stir trouble.

Hot Books authors follow the blazing path of such legendary muckrakers and troublemakers as Upton Sinclair, Lincoln Steffens, Rachel Carson, Jane Jacobs, Jessica Mitford, I. F. Stone, and Seymour Hersh. The magazines and newspapers that once provided a forum for this deep and dangerous journalism have shrunk in number and available resources. Hot Books aims to fill this crucial gap.

American journalism has become increasingly digitized and commodified. If the news isn't fake, it's usually shallow. But there's a growing hunger for information that is both credible and undiluted by corporate filters.

A publishing series with this intensity cannot keep burning in a vacuum. Hot Books needs a culture of equally passionate readers. Please spread the word about these titles—encourage your bookstores to carry them, post comments about them in online stores and forums, persuade your book clubs, schools, political groups and community organizations to read them and invite the authors to speak.

It's time to go beyond packaged news and propaganda. It's time for Hot Books . . . journalism without borders.

# DEDICATION & ACKNOWLEDGMENTS

The work you hold in your hands was never intended to be a book. It is the result of an intermittent investigation conducted over ten years by the authors, with a lot of help. In its current form, it began as an article undertaken with Emanuel Stoakes, inspired by an interview conducted by Jon Gold. Stoakes insisted we pitch it to David Talbot, who said "yes" when many others have said "no," recommending us to Tony Lyons at Skyhorse Publishing, who green-lit it as a book. Stoakes was actively involved in the writing of the first half of the first draft. We conducted a number of interviews with Stoakes, and he provided to us a couple he did on his own. Rory O'Connor also conducted several interviews with us, as he has also been investigating this topic for many years. We thank these four people from the bottom of our hearts.

This book would not exist but for the unearthing of important information by many incredible journalists. In particular, we walk a path first paved by Lawrence Wright, James Bamford, and Kevin Fenton, as well as Ali Soufan and Daniel Freedman with their own prior books, *The Looming Tower*, *The Shadow Factory*, *Disconnecting the Dots*, and *The Black Banners*, respectively. We also follow the tracks laid by Matt Apuzzo and Adam Goldman in their Associated Press article "At the CIA, Mistakes by Officers Are Often Overlooked." The first to open the door, if largely overlooked, were Michael Isikoff, Joe Trento, and Robert Schopmeyer. We would also like to acknowledge the journalism of Tyler Bass, David Fanning, Siobhan Gorman, Stephen Grey, Seymour Hersh, Douglas Jehl, Michael Kirk, Jason Leopold, Eric Lichtenblau, Jane Mayer, Mark Mazzetti, Friedrich Moser, Dana Priest, James Risen, Brian Ross, Jeremy Scahill, Philip Shenon, Ken

Silverstein, Jeff Stein, Shannon Tyler, Joby Warrick, Tim Weiner, Bob Woodward, Amrit Singh and the Open Society Foundations, and those at Human Rights Watch and the American Civil Liberties Union.

Much of the research for this book relied as a starting point on HistoryCommons.org, which acts as a kind of cheat sheet used by many national security journalists with too little acknowledgment. It is a website often struggling for funding. Its founder and sole maintainer remains Derek Mitchell, and the timelines built by Paul Thompson and later Kevin Fenton were instrumental.

There is a short list of people who came to our aid in the ways they had available to them during the scary moments in 2011 that are detailed in chapter 10, as well as those who enthusiastically supported the initial work when we didn't have many people behind us. We will forever be indebted to Sean Adl-Tabatabai, Larisa Alexandrovna, Jim Babka, Bill Bergman, Sheri Bernson, Kristina Borjesson, Patty Cassazza, Paul Church, Peter Collins, John Cook, Sibel Edmonds, Monica Gabrielle, Alex Gibney, Glenn Greenwald, Gary Griffin, Kevin Gosztola, Kyle Hence, Scott Horton, Ben Johnson, Mindy Kleinberg, Barbara Kopple, Scott Malone, Abby Martin, Robbie Martin, Betsy Metz, Ray McGovern, Michael Micklow, Jeff Morley, Alexa O'Brien, Erik Potter, Martina Radwan, Michael Ratner, Reifs, Jon Roberts, Coleen Rowley, Damian Salimeno, Danny Schechter, Anthony Summers, Patrick Thrasher, Lorie Van Auken, Marcy Wheeler, Ben Wizner, John Young, and the aforementioned Fenton, Gold, Leopold, Mayer, O'Connor, and Thompson.

We of course owe thanks to Nicholas Magliato at Skyhorse for his editorial assistance, as well as a thank-you to the rest of the editorial staff who helped us to shape this book. Going way back in the chronology, we must thank Tony and Val Nowosielski, who provided the first funds out-of-pocket way back in 2003 that allowed us to begin this journey. As parents, they and their families gave author Nowosielski an upbringing that made the matters in this book of personal importance. We also thank our spouses, Danielle Gonzales and Ruth Vaca, who put up with too little of our attentions while we wrote this and were supportive when it looked like jail was an actual possibility. We hope that is behind us.

Please support good feet-to-the-fire journalism by purchasing subscriptions. Without our country's journalists—the good, the bad, and the ugly—we would all be relying entirely on our government and corporations to tell us the truth. Support the few organizations looking out for whistle-blowers and leakers once they have been targeted by government prosecutors for telling the truth about matters of public importance, namely the Government Accountability Project and the National Whistleblower Center.

This book is dedicated to everyone who was harmed by the September 11 tragedy as well as those harmed by the US government's response, the "war on terror," which shows no end in sight. It is also dedicated to all people of conscience who risked something to leak or to blow the whistle in order to provide for us a more complete picture of the world than those in power might have desired.

# A NOTE ON SOURCES

Good journalism should see all statements of controversy backed up by a minimum of two sources and/or a bulletproof document. Ideally, no anonymous sources would be employed. However, when investigating a subject such as the US intelligence and law enforcement communities—a group actively and expertly engaged in keeping secrets, a group with the unique ability to "classify" much of their own story, a group that will not as a matter of policy confirm the identities of some of their key participants—the authors would argue that a different standard may at times be appropriate. This is particularly the case when publicly important allegations being made by a single individual would otherwise go unreported.

Journalism at its heart is an exercise in establishing fact, first and foremost, and its major responsibility is bringing to light matters of wrongdoing. Readers of journalism's end results are then able to play their own role, to the extent they wish, in righting those wrongs or in seeking justice for that which cannot be undone. There have been times in the course of reporting this story that a choice had to be made: the importance of including facts and statements for the record versus the reality that they derive solely from a single source. In some of these cases, we determined that holding back would give undue power to the US intelligence and law enforcement community to craft history through strategic withholdings of confirmations. Given the knowledge we have accumulated about how these entities use that power to keep certain potential realities outside the sphere of public debate, we have chosen in many instances to include these single-source accounts.

In the notes at the end you can consider for yourself whether or not to accept as true single-source statements that appear bold. A few individuals in particular, namely Richard Clarke, Thomas Drake, John Kiriakou, and Mark Rossini, have provided a disproportionate number of these statements. The readers must make their own judgments as to the character and motives of these individuals. If you believe these men in particular, then most everything in this book happened as described.

# PRINCIPAL CHARACTERS

## AL QAEDA AND ASSOCIATES

**Khallad bin Attash:** Saudi national who lost a leg fighting in Afghanistan against the Northern Alliance, an Al Qaeda "errand boy" who is alleged to have helped plan the US embassy bombings in Africa and the USS *Cole* attack.

**Osama Basnan:** A Saudi national who interacted with future 9/11 hijackers Nawaf al Hazmi and Khalid al Mihdhar while they were living in San Diego, California.

**Omar al Bayoumi:** A Saudi national who interacted with future 9/11 hijackers Nawaf al Hazmi and Khalid al Mihdhar while they were living in San Diego, California.

**Ahmed al Hada:** Friend of Usama Bin Laden whose house in Sana'a, Yemen, was used as an Al Qaeda terrorist plot communications center and safehouse; father-in-law of 9/11 hijacker Khalid al Mihdhar.

**Nawaf al Hazmi:** Saudi national who fought in Bosnia in the 1990s before heading to Afghanistan to fight for the Taliban; one of the 9/11 hijackers of Flight 77.

**Ibn al Libi:** Libyan national and alleged Al Qaeda training camp manager in Afghanistan, captured by the US military in 2002 and "renditioned" by the CIA to Egypt where he provided a false confession under torture.

**Khalid el Masri:** German citizen of Lebanese birth who was mistaken by the CIA's Alec Station as a member of Al Qaeda, abducted to a secret prison in early 2004.

**Khalid al Mihdhar:** Saudi national who fought in Bosnia in the 1990s before heading to Afghanistan to fight for the Taliban; son-in-law of Ahmed al Hada, the owner of a significant Al Qaeda communications hub; one of the 9/11 hijackers of Flight 77.

**Zacarious Moussaoui:** A French citizen of Moroccan descent who trained in an Al Qaeda camp in Afghanistan and was taken into custody weeks before 9/11 by the FBI in Minnesota after arousing suspicion at a flight school.

**Khalid Sheik Mohammed:** Pakistani national and high ranking Al Qaeda operations planner, alleged to be the "architect of the 9/11 attacks," captured by the United States in 2003.

**"Omar":** Al Qaeda-connected individual in Pakistan who became an informant to both the CIA and the FBI beginning in 2000.

**Fahad al Quso:** Yemeni national who met in Thailand in early 2000 with a mastermind of the USS *Cole* bombing and two future 9/11 hijackers, became a subject of FBI interrogations in the months that followed his arrest in Yemen for the *Cole* attack.

**Abu Zubaydah:** Saudi national alleged to have been involved in the US embassy bombings in Africa and the foiled "Millennium" plot, captured and turned over to the United States in Pakistan in 2002 and held in CIA secret prisons for years thereafter.


# CENTRAL INTELLIGENCE AGENCY

**Alfreda Bikowsky:** Information analyst who allegedly staffed Alec Station, the CIA's Al Qaeda office, upon its creation, where she served in various managerial positions from 1996 through 2006, her final position allegedly being chief; continued working closely with the director of the CIA's CounterTerrorist Center in the years since.

**Cofer Black:** Field spy and spy-manager who became director of the CIA's CounterTerrorist Center from 1999 through 2002.

**Rich Blee:** Son of a significant Cold War-era CIA manager, became a field spy, then replaced Mike Scheuer as chief of Alec Station from 1999 through 2000; advanced to run the Sunni Extremist Group, an entity over-seeing Alec Station, from 2000 through 2001, then positions in charge of Afghanistan, allegedly Pakistan, a CIA liaison to FBI headquarters, and the agency's Los Angeles station.

**Michael Anne Casey:** Counterterror "targeting" employee at Alec Station from 1997 through 2001, alleged to have gone to Afghanistan and Italy thereafter.

**Rep. Porter Goss:** Field spy and Florida local politician who became a US Congressman in 1989, chairing the House Intelligence Committee from 1997 through 2005, at which time he succeeded George Tenet as director of Central Intelligence.

**John Helgerson:** Information analyst and analyst-manager who became the CIA's Inspector General from 2002 through 2009.

**John Kiriakou:** Information analyst later trained in spy operations who led the capture of accused terrorist Abu Zubaydah in Pakistan in 2002.

**Jen Matthews:** Information analyst later trained in spy operations who was brought into managerial positions at Alec Station from 1997 through 2002, becoming a manager in the High Value Target Unit, a counterterror liaison in the CIA's London station and base chief in Khost, Afghanistan.

**Jose Rodriguez:** Field spy and spymaster, mostly in Latin America, who became Cofer Black's chief of staff in the CIA's CounterTerrorist Center in late 2001, replacing Black as director of CTC in 2002 and taking over the entire spies division in 2004.

**Mike Scheuer:** Information analyst and analyst-manager who described himself as the "architect" of extraordinary renditions, became the founding chief of Alec Station from 1996 through 1999 and special adviser to the station from 2001 through 2004.

**George Tenet:** US Congress staffer and a senior director for intelligence programs on the White House's National Security Council, became director of Central Intelligence in 1997, managing the CIA and other agencies and departments within agencies known collectively as "the Intelligence Community," through 2004.

**Hendrik Van Der Meulen:** CIA's station chief in Jordan who succeeded Rich Blee as the chief of Alec Station from 2000 through 2002.

**Tom Wilshere:** CIA employee with a background working with the FBI on counterterror investigations who became deputy chief of Alec Station from its founding in 1996 until 2001, when he moved to FBI headquarters as the agency's counterterror liaison from 2001 through 2003.

## THE CONGRESS

**Sen. Bob Graham:** After serving in both houses of Florida's legislature and as its governor, he was a US senator from 1986 through 2005, a member of the Senate Intelligence Committee for ten years, and its chairman from 2001 through 2003.

**Eleanor Hill:** Attorney and Defense Department Inspector General who became staff director to the Intelligence Committees of the US Senate and House of Representatives, running the investigation into 9/11 in 2002.

**Diane Roark:** Staffer on the US House of Representatives' Intelligence Committee beginning in 1985, holding responsibility for oversight of the NSA from 1997 through 2002.

## FEDERAL BUREAU OF INVESTIGATION

**Steve Bongardt:** US Navy officer who became an FBI counterterror agent for the New York office from 1996 through 2004.

**Jack Cloonan:** Agent working counterterror for the FBI's New York office from 1996 through 2002.

**Dina Corsi:** Analyst at the FBI's headquarters in Washington, DC, in 2001, where she worked with, among others, the CIA's counterterror liaison Tom Wilshere.

**Pat D'Amuro:** Agent and manager who served as John O'Neill's deputy overseeing the National Security Division from the FBI's New York office and became director of the bureau's CounterTerror Division from 2001 through 2003, where he ran the criminal investigation into 9/11.

# PRINCIPAL CHARACTERS

**Maggie Gillespie:** Analyst from the FBI's DC field office, detailed to the CIA's Alec Station from 1999 through 2002.

**Ed Goetz:** FBI manager from DC headquarters detailed to the CIA's Alec Station as a deputy chief, alongside Tom Wilshere, from 1998 through early 2000.

**Bob McFadden:** A Naval Criminal Investigative Service (NCIS) case agent who worked closely with FBI counterterror agents on the investigation into the USS *Cole* attack in Yemen.

**Robert Mueller:** US Marine Vietnam veteran and federal district attorney who served as FBI director, beginning one week before September 11, 2001, through 2013.

**Doug Miller:** DC FBI field office agent detailed to the CIA's Alec Station from 1999 through 2002.

**John O'Neill:** Agent and manager who became chief of the FBI's CounterTerror Section from 1995 through 1997, then the National Security Division out of the New York office from 1997 until his retirement in 2001.

**Mark Rossini:** FBI agent working counterterror for the New York office from 1997 through 2005, detailed to the CIA's Alec Station from 1999 through 2003, a co-founder of the National CounterTerror Center at CIA headquarters and further bureau positions.

**Ali Soufan:** FBI counterterror agent for the New York office from 1997 through 2005.

## NATIONAL SECURITY COUNCIL

**Richard Clarke:** Coordinated all US government agencies' counterterror efforts from the White House-level National Security Council, a position created for him by President Bill Clinton at a cabinet level and continued, but demoted to sub-cabinet, during the first term of President George W. Bush.

**Gen. Colin Powell:** Secretary of State under George W. Bush from 2001 through 2004.

**Col. Larry Wilkerson:** Chief of staff to Secretary of State Colin Powell, from 2002 to 2005.

## NATIONAL SECURITY AGENCY

**Maureen Baginski:** Russian language instructor who rose through various managerial positions to become director of the NSA's Signals Intelligence (SIGINT) division, the number three position at the agency, from 2000 through 2003.

**"Betsy":** Pseudonym of information analyst inside the NSA's "Al Qaeda Shop" who was responsible for monitoring their telephone communications center in Yemen.

**Bill Binney:** Analyst who became Technical Leader for Intelligence, co-founding SIGINT's Automation Research Center (SARC) and creating ThinThread.

**Bill Black:** Analyst and manager at the NSA from 1959 through 1997, returning from the private sector to be Gen. Michael Hayden's deputy from 2000 through 2005.

**"Bob":** Pseudonym of analyst in the NSA's "CounterTerror Shop" involved in the creation of a detailed 2001 report on Al Qaeda.

**Thomas Drake:** Air Force and Navy veteran who became an NSA contractor, then executive manager in the SIGINT division from 2001 through 2003, followed by other executive positions at the agency.

**Gen. Michael Hayden:** Air Force officer who became the only individual to serve as both director of the National Security Agency, from 1999 through 2005, and director of the Central Intelligence Agency, from 2006 through 2009, with a stint as deputy Director of National Intelligence in between.

**Ed Loomis:** Lead computer scientist and systems analyst in the NSA's SARC.

**Kirk Wiebe:** Business manager and analyst in the NSA's SARC.

# PREFACE

The purpose of a system is what it does. Stafford Beer coined this phrase to be used by systems theorists as a reminder to see beyond the intentions of those who design or operate a particular system, and instead to gain greater insight by observing total system behavior. When one remembers this upon noticing, say, the unintended consequences of particular system functionality, they can avoid falling into a mental trap whereby they infer that such consequences are dysfunction, atypical anomalies to be whacked at like so many moles. A simpler way of saying this is "It's not a bug; it's a feature."

When reading a chronology such as the one that follows, one can often find themselves spinning their wheels trying to find a fix for the systems that failed. Quite often, people assume that if the seemingly guilty remain unmolested, then that must mean there are gaps or lapses in the system that require rooting out. After so many government investigations into actions taken regarding 9/11 and the resulting "war on terror," with the millions and millions of dollars spent, the subpoena power, the access to documents, the hours and hours of interviews, somehow, we are left with a situation in which the names of individuals who should very well have been held to account are still mostly shrouded in secrecy.

When we take stock of the fact that several of the same names that come up in the Senate's 2014 report about torture were also highlighted by the CIA inspector general's 2005 report laying fault for 9/11, we see that a failure to hold individuals to account for earlier transgressions had later consequences for the nation, and the world. We can also track, through these reports, the rise of repeated accused wrongdoers to very high positions, and we can similarly track through news accounts the fall of those who have the appearance of having tried to expose these wrongdoers. Our knee-jerk response might again be to look for the gaps in the systems, the patchable holes that if only tended to would somehow make everything right.

That is when it helps to instead look at the system in reverse. Instead of assuming we know the purpose of the nation's massive and powerful intelligence apparatus, the law enforcement apparatus—and the federal bureaucracy that supposedly monitors and controls both—examines the outcomes. What is the purpose of a system that makes those who value truth into enemies of the state and participates in the kinds of actions detailed here? Declarations of justice and freedom are but words. They require nothing of those who bellow them. Actions speak louder.

The purpose of a system is what it *does*.

John Duffy & Ray Nowosielski
New York City, July 4, 2017

# 1

# INDEFINITE DOUBT

*Detective: "Is there any other point to which you would wish to draw my attention?"*
*Holmes: "To the curious incident of the dog in the night-time."*
*Detective: "The dog did nothing in the night-time."*
*Holmes: "That was the curious incident."*

Sir Arthur Conan Doyle, "The Adventure of Silver Blaze"

On October 14, 2009, our four-person documentary crew parked in the lot outside one of three generic brick-and-glass business towers stretching a dozen stories into the sky of Arlington, Virginia. Looking up from inside our rented minivan, we knew one of the floors above was home to Good Harbor, the start-up security consulting firm owned by Richard Clarke. He had been the National Coordinator for Counterterror, more colloquially known as the "White House counterterror adviser," working during both the Clinton and Bush administrations. By the time of our interview, he was six years out of government service.

We instructed the two camera operators to "roll" from the moment we entered until the moment we left. This would be our key interview. Clarke had been the top man in the land for countering terrorism, and he was in a unique position to answer the central question on our minds: If the CIA had been running some kind of operation regarding two 9/11 hijackers of Saudi origin, Khalid al Mihdhar and Nawaf al Hazmi, as the facts indicated, had they done it alone, or had it been green-lit by the Clinton or Bush White Houses?

Heading into the interview, we were concerned that Clarke would find the subject uncomfortable and only engage with it to a shallow degree. We had developed a stair-step strategy, first aiming to get him to confirm certain details around the edges. We then hoped to use those confirmations to build toward the heart of the matter. Unbeknownst to us, Clarke had agreed to the interview that day eager to come clean about his thoughts. What he had to say would have an impact on the counterterror community of his era. Despite four major government investigations into the attacks in the interim, many who were employed by the government had been debating internally for the past eight years over what had gone wrong. Clarke would shine a light.

Inside his conference room, a row of windows faced east, offering a view of the Washington Monument. Our lights were almost in place when we got our first glimpse of him, entering without pretense and quietly taking a seat at the head of the table. He was shorter than we had expected, balding, with white and silver hair. Wearing a blue suit and wire glasses, Clarke seemed comfortable. His face flashed moments of warmth, while his eyes, we felt, betrayed a world-weary thoughtfulness. Over the course of our discussion, his posture, his demeanor, and his precise articulation of certain points would convince us of his sincerity. It seemed he was laying his cards on the table.

"Look, the basic story about these two guys, Mihdhar and Hazmi, is that they entered the United States [in the year 2000]. The CIA didn't know about it at the time, but they discovered fairly soon thereafter. And fifty," he said, repeating it for emphasis, "*fifty* people in the CIA had access to that information, people ranging from low-level analysts all the way through the CIA director. That information was not shared with the FBI for months, and when it was shared with the FBI it was never given to the assistant director of the FBI for counterterror. And that information was absolutely never shared with the White House."[1]

"Under either Clinton or Bush?" we sought to clarify.

"No. It was the same people under Clinton and Bush," he continued. "It was me and my staff. The CIA admits they never told us. The CIA admits they never told the FBI, until [less than a month before the attacks], when they knew about it over twelve months earlier."

We noticed a glaring contradiction between what Clarke was telling us and the primary defense that CIA officials had used in the years since the attacks. The CIA's director during the years before and after, George Tenet, had painted a picture to government investigations of his bureaucracy "blinking red" during the months before, causing him to give unheeded warnings all over Washington in 2001, his "hair on fire." How did that story square with Clarke's, that of a lack of meaningful information sharing by Tenet's agency?

We asked about a spontaneous briefing that Tenet had insisted upon presenting to President George W. Bush's national security adviser Condoleezza Rice a little over two months before the attacks. We knew Clarke had been in the room as the CIA's director and two of his counterterror managers laid out their "best case" for action regarding Al Qaeda. We wanted to know whether or not they had mentioned Mihdhar or Hazmi. Clarke interrupted us.

"You cannot expect me to remember dates, but whatever meeting it was, whenever it was, if it involved those guys' [Mihdhar's and Hazmi's] names or the fact that Al Qaeda people had entered the United States, we were not informed about it at any point before 9/11. Condi didn't know, I didn't know, no one in the [Bush or Clinton] White House knew. I never heard their names until 9/11."

As we began asking a question about another detail, Clarke lost patience with our slow approach. He cut to the chase. "Look, we had about every other day a threat committee, where CIA and NSA and FBI and [Defense Department] would brief on the latest intelligence. [The CIA] never briefed us [on this]. We must have had dozens, scores of threat committee meetings over the period of time when they knew these guys were inside the country, and they never mentioned it. They were sharing vast amounts of information with me and my staff, and we had a structure, both to get their written reports, their raw reports, and to get oral briefings, and over a year goes by, and they never tell us." He came to his point, flying directly into the heart of the matter. "That means one thing to me: there was an intentional and very high-level decision in the CIA not to let the White House know."

Former cabinet-level presidential advisers, as a general rule, do not level such public accusations against America's premier spy agency. The words reached our ears and left us momentarily shocked. He must know, we thought to ourselves, that when we release the interview his words will reverberate through the halls of the CIA's Langley headquarters. We asked the obvious: "How high level?"

Clarke replied without hesitation, "I would think [that kind of decision] would have to be made by the CIA director."

Preparing for this interview, we thought we might have to assemble a barrage of admissions in order to get Clarke to, perhaps, concede such a thing could have happened. Our own investigation up to that point had left us leaning in that direction to explain a lot about the performance of the intelligence agencies in the years before the attacks. Now Clarke was deciding to go on record to indict his former colleague, and former friend, the CIA's beloved former leader George Tenet.

"So now the question is 'Why?'" Clarke asked with a tone that hinted he was about to lay out his theory. He did first make a point of letting us know that "We are now in the area of conjecture and hypothesis."

It was clear Clarke would not need our help to say what he wanted to say. We kept quiet and let him tell his story. "I have thought about this a lot, and there is only one conceivable reason that I can come up with [to explain the agency's repeated failure to share information about the hijackers]. There may be other reasons, but I've only been able to come up with one."

We leaned in. "I can understand [CIA] possibly saying, 'We need to develop "sources" inside Al Qaeda. When we do that, we can't tell anybody about it.' And I can understand them perhaps seeing these two guys show up in the United States and saying, 'Ah ha, this is our chance to "flip" them, this is our chance to get ears inside Al Qaeda.' And to do that, we can't tell anybody outside the CIA, until we got them, until they're really giving us information." He summed it up for us: "The CIA was trying to 'turn' these guys. They failed in that effort. They broke from [proper] procedures in that process, and they didn't want to be blamed after the fact."

What would otherwise be dismissed quickly as a "conspiracy theory" had within that moment become the official, though speculative, position of the former White House counterterror advisor. If he believed this, we thought, why was he only now bringing it up? And why not to the *New York Times* or CNN? Why give this to two unknown journalists? We later came to believe that we had simply been the only ones who had asked.

Clarke pushed forward, outlining his theory that he had been intentionally cut out of the loop regarding Mihdhar and Hazmi. "Tenet followed all of the information about Al Qaeda in microscopic detail. He read raw intelligence reports before analysts in the CounterTerrorist Center did. And he would pick up the phone and call me at 7:30 in the morning to talk about them.

There was no barrier between George and the CIA information machine when it came to Al Qaeda."

His account was level, thoughtful, but not without feeling. Clearly, this issue transcended politics for Clarke. "My relationship with him," he explained, referring to Tenet, "we were close friends. He called me several times a day. We shared the most trivial of information with each other." Clarke continued, "There was not a lack of information sharing. They told me everything, except this."

Toward the conclusion of our discussion with Clarke, the tone had become almost somber. We asked, "How are you left emotionally by all this? Are you pissed?"

"I am outraged," he answered, "and have been ever since I first learned that the CIA knew these guys were in the country. But I believed for the longest time that this was probably one or two low-level CIA people who made the decision not to disseminate the information. Now that I know that fifty CIA officers knew this, and they included all sorts of people who were regularly talking to me, yeah, saying 'I'm pissed' doesn't begin to describe it."

\* \* \*

Richard Clarke first worked alongside George Tenet on President Bill Clinton's National Security Council (NSC), located just west of the White House inside the stately Eisenhower Executive Office Building. The NSC had been created by the same 1947 legislation that had birthed the CIA. It tended to be run by each president's cabinet-level national security adviser, and its purpose was political, to coordinate the various government agencies toward the president's national security and foreign policy goals. Clarke served as the council's leader for counterterror objectives, while Tenet was liaison to the thirteen agencies making up "the American intelligence community."

Clarke and Tenet had a lot in common. Both had pulled themselves up from working-class backgrounds into an elite world. Both had a natural talent and instinct for navigating the Washington bureaucracy. Both had a knack for making useful DC friends. And both ended up as the only people to work at a high level in both Bill Clinton's and George W. Bush's White Houses during what turned out to be a pivotal moment in history.

One month into Clinton's new administration, a building in New York City, the World Trade Center, was bombed by terrorists. The event had helped Clarke's career, as the president began turning to him more frequently for briefings. *Newsweek* later reported, "[Clinton] got his intelligence from Clarke, who collected it from the various spy agencies. Clarke was not a 'principal' on the NSC, but he might as well have been, wandering into top-level meetings and even the Oval Office." Clarke was known to have more sway with President Clinton than the CIA did.[2]

Working side by side on the National Security Council, Clarke and Tenet were in the right place at the right time. Tenet was the senior intelligence director, a position that saw him liaising with Clinton's CIA director James Woolsey, who had a notoriously weak relationship with the president. "[Bill Clinton] wouldn't let the CIA director in his office," says former State Department chief of staff Larry Wilkerson. "That's why Woolsey quit."[3]

President Clinton decided to make Tenet his deputy CIA director in 1995 and, two years later, nominated him to lead the agency. As the "Director of Central Intelligence," George Tenet ran the CIA, but he also oversaw thirteen other bureaucracies. These included offices within the State, Treasury, and Energy departments, eight within the military, and the spying arms of both the Drug Enforcement Agency and the FBI. Tenet ultimately managed an annual budget of around twenty-five billion dollars, paying about half a million contractors and employees.[4] By comparison, the CEO of the most profitable corporation in the United States, Exxon Mobil, managed just under one hundred thousand.[5]

"The CIA loved Tenet," one spy told author Michael Allen. Known as a backslapper and a hugger, in a short period of time he earned something many previous directors had not, the willing devotion of his employees. "He walked the halls at all hours, chomping on a cigar, dropping into the offices of his senior officers to ask them what they were working on. He strolled through the cafeteria and had lunch with junior officers."[6]

The tables had turned dramatically for Clarke and Tenet under a new president in 2001, George W. Bush. Clarke found his cabinet-level position downgraded. Tenet was told by Bush himself that he was hanging on by a thread, but after a time Bush warmed to him, and kept him on as DCI.[7]

Army Colonel Larry Wilkerson says the new president took a decidedly different approach toward the CIA director than Clinton had. "Others like

George W. Bush feel it's better to co-opt [CIA directors], to 'warm hand' them." While Clarke pushed for months to get a meeting with the president, Bush and Tenet developed a close relationship. The power dynamic changed uncomfortably for Clarke, yet he still believed his pal Tenet was keeping him in the loop in his role as a demoted counterterror adviser.

* * *

We got back in touch with Richard Clarke again in August 2011. Via email we informed him that a twelve-minute piece had been edited from his interview and would soon be released on YouTube. The video was meant to create buzz for a one-off true crime podcast called *Who Is Rich Blee?* that we were planning to premiere online on the tenth anniversary of September 11.

We wanted to give Clarke the opportunity to review it to see if there were any statements he wanted to back away from upon further reflection. He had, after all, been strangely silent on the issue during the nearly two years since we had visited him. He had given no other interviews on the subject. Clarke hopped on the phone with us for a few minutes. He explained he would require no edits. He was standing behind what he had said.

It was also decided by our team that the time had come to use the forthcoming release of Clarke's statements to push out a response from George Tenet himself. Perhaps, we hoped, he might even sit down for an interview to defend himself. We sent Tenet's publisher a private web link to the Clarke interview and waited for a response.

A startling moment followed. A voice mail from Bill Harlow, a CIA writer who had coauthored Tenet's memoir, *At the Eye of the Storm*, let us know he was in receipt of our request and had sent a statement to us by email signed not only by Tenet, but also by Cofer Black, the former head of the CIA CounterTerrorism Center, and by Rich Blee, the former chief of the CIA office dedicated to Al Qaeda. Until that moment, Blee had never before publicly acknowledged his own name. His agency tended to argue in these cases that his identity was still protected by a "cover status" despite Blee's retirement. He had also never before defended his actions directly to Americans. Apparently, what Clarke told us had echoed beyond just Langley's halls and into the homes of retired CIA managers.[8]

In our in-box, Harlow's letter read, "HarperCollins relayed to us your request to interview George Tenet. Mr. Tenet does not wish to be interviewed either on camera or on background for your project. However, in light of some of the absurd and patently false statements made by Richard Clarke in the YouTube clip you shared, Mr. Tenet reached out to Cofer Black and Richard Blee. Together they are providing the attached joint statement to you. We request that you make their statement available, in its entirety, to any media organization to which you distribute your interview with Richard Clarke."

The attachment read:

Joint Statement from George J. Tenet, Cofer Black and Richard Blee
August 3, 2011

Richard Clarke was an able public servant who served his country well for many years. But his recently released comments about the run up to 9/11 are reckless and profoundly wrong.

Clarke starts with the presumption that important information on the travel of future hijackers to the United States was intentionally withheld from him in early 2000. It was not.

He wildly speculates that it must have been the CIA director who could have ordered the information withheld. There was no such order. In fact, the record shows that the Director and other senior CIA officials were unaware of the information until after 9/11.

The handling of the information in question was exhaustively looked at by the 9/11 Commission, the Congressional Joint Inquiry, the CIA Inspector General and other groups.

The 9/11 Commission quite correctly concluded that ". . . no one informed higher levels of management in either the FBI or CIA about the case."

In early 2000, a number of more junior personnel (including FBI agents on detail to CIA) did see travel information on individuals who later became hijackers but the significance of the data was not adequately recognized at the time.

Since 9/11 many systemic changes have been made to improve the watchlisting process and enhance information sharing within and across agencies.

Building on his false notion that information was intentionally withheld, Mr. Clarke went on to speculate—which he admits is based on nothing other than his imagination—that the CIA might have been trying to recruit these two future hijackers as agents. This, like much of what Mr. Clarke said in his interview, is utterly without foundation.

Many years after testifying himself at length before the 9/11 Commission and writing several books but making no mention of his wild theory, Mr. Clarke has suddenly invented baseless allegations which are belied by the record and unworthy of serious consideration.

We testified under oath about what we did, what we knew and what we didn't know. We stand by that testimony.

We forwarded this statement to Clarke as he had requested if anything like it came in. He never responded. For another four years, he would continue his previous silence on the subject, despite multiple requests from interested news outlets upon the release of our video on YouTube later that month. He would apparently let his one-time statement speak for itself.

We also sent a reply to Bill Harlow. "Thank you very much for providing that joint statement. We will make it available in its entirety to any media organization to which we distribute the Clarke interview, as requested. We are passionate about telling an accurate story, but the refusal of Mr. Tenet, Mr. Black, and Mr. Blee to discuss it even on background makes that impossible, as we are forced to rely on the info we've been provided by those who *will* talk to us. I have summarized the highlights of that information in an attached doc, including many, many issues still unaccounted for with regard to CIA's handling of Mihdhar and Hazmi, none of which have anything to do with Mr. Clarke's judgment or accuracy.

"If there are simple—even benign or admirable—explanations for those issues," we pleaded, hoping to let him know that our minds were not yet closed on the matter, "I sincerely wish Mr. Tenet, et al, would break their media silence and simply provide those answers. I want them to realize that their failure to do so only appears to give credence to speculation like that in the Clarke interview.

"Furthermore," we went on, "Mr. Clarke is not the only gov't insider who has stated to us that he/she believes these unexplained events can be explained by high-level deliberate choices within the CIA. If these folks are wrong, Mr. Tenet, et al, could easily choose to make them look foolish and set the record straight for all concerned by going through this story with us and providing explanations *in detail*, case by case. Their motivations in continuing to refuse to do so a full decade after the terrible tragedy and in the face of accusations from other gov't officials is, frankly, baffling to me."

There was no response for five days. Then, a "bing" in the in-box from Harlow. "Got your voicemail message over the weekend . . . sorry it has taken a little while to get back to you. Yes . . . the material you originally sent via HarperCollins was made available to Tenet, Black and Blee and the statement I provided to you was their response in light of that material. None of them have any plans to go beyond that statement or to respond to the additional material you sent via email on 8/4/11."

That was going to be that.

Our read on their joint statement was that it was rather carefully worded, legalistically so. Because of the language chosen, it was difficult to determine what in fact they were denying. For instance, they denied only that *important* information was *intentionally* withheld about the future hijackers' travel—and that only in early 2000. What about the rest of the year and a half prior to the attacks?

They did not say that they were unaware of the information until after 9/11. They only said that *the record shows* that they were unaware. Actually, we noticed, that statement referred to the CIA director and other senior CIA officials, so it may not have included Cofer Black and Rich Blee. They wrote that Clarke's speculation was utterly without foundation. They never denied that it was true.

This episode was one part of a long and winding investigative trail for us, the authors. We came to realize the story we were learning was an incredible case study in how power players in Washington, DC, can skirt the law with impunity—so long as they do so with the intent of furthering the aspirations of the American empire. And, as we would come to find out, anyone who attempts to fight this political apparatus is likely to find themselves subjected to the full weight and power of this machine.

* * *

In 2016, Richard Clarke broke his silence on this matter for the first time since speaking with us, a gap of seven years. The catalyst was the release of the long-withheld "28 Pages" of a congressional report about 9/11, detailing alleged Saudi facilitation of the plot behind the attacks.

Clarke's op-ed for the ABC News website detailed two major issues he felt remained unanswered. "The first," he wrote, "the subject of these twenty-eight pages, is what role Saudi government officials played in supporting Al Qaeda and the 9/11 plot. The second question, with which the 9/11 Commission struggled but was unable to answer, is why the CIA failed to tell the FBI and the White House when the agency knew about Al Qaeda terrorists in the United States.

"I believe that the two questions may be linked," he wrote further, "and that a major element of the 9/11 tragedy may remain unrevealed: a possible failed CIA-Saudi spy mission on US soil that went bad and eventually allowed 9/11 to proceed unimpeded." It is clear that Clarke still stands by his allegations even now.[9]

Back in his conference room that fall day in 2009, he offered us a concluding point, by way of a question. "Ask yourself why, after the CIA has told the FBI—but not told senior levels of the FBI—why not bring it up at the September 4th principles meeting? What am I going to say?"

We were honestly stumped. He continued, "I'm going to say, 'Wait a minute. How long have you known this? Why haven't you reported it at the daily threat briefings? Why isn't it in the daily threat matrix?' I would have had them brought up on charges *that day* for malfeasance and misfeasance. *That's* why we were not informed."

"So they put their own asses above national security?" we asked, perhaps sounding a bit naive.

Clarke replied, "If you believe all this."

Our microphones unclipped from our collars, we began packing away our gear. Clarke rose to leave the room. We smiled and joked that we would crack the case. That comment stopped him at the door frame. His back to us, without emotion, he made one more statement before walking away. He said, "If you do, watch your backs."

We stopped smiling.

# 2

# ORIGIN STORIES

*"Men have become the tools of their tools."*

Henry David Thoreau

Over the course of one year toward the end of the 1980s, three people were recruited into the CIA whose lives would change the agency, and their country: Alfreda Bikowsky, John Kiriakou, and Jen Matthews.[1] Though strangers, they shared similar backgrounds. All were in their early twenties, born at the front of the generation that would come to be called "X." The turbulent '60s and early '70s, events like Vietnam and Watergate, were memories of their youths before they came of age in Ronald Reagan's America.

They were each exceptionally smart and raised Christian by working parents. Bikowsky and Kiriakou were Catholics,[2] while Matthews was a Baptist. All three had roots in rural and suburban Pennsylvania. Kiriakou and Matthews grew up in the Keystone State, while Bikowsky was a child there, raised in Texas by native Pennsylvanians.[3]

Records indicate that the auburn-haired,[4] tough-as-nails Alfreda Bikowsky was the granddaughter of first-generation Polish Lithuanian coal miners who lived in the Shenandoah Valley. At age thirteen, their daughter Barbara apparently became pregnant, giving birth to a baby girl.[5]

An hour's drive away in a suburb of Harrisburg, the self-assured, amiable Jen Matthews was raised by English Americans. Her mother worked as a nurse and her father was a commercial printer. Matthews had an uncle who was at that time working as a CIA spy officer operating in Laos, conducting Special National Intelligence Estimates assessing North Vietnamese capabilities.[6]

Kiriakou, olive-skinned with thick black hair like his Greek ancestors, grew up at the western end of the state, an hour north of Pittsburgh in the lightly populated steel-manufacturing town of New Castle. His parents were first-generation Greek Americans, elementary school educators.[7]

Bikowsky's young mother Barbara moved to Texas in the mid 1970s, settling in the northeast suburbs of Dallas and taking a secretary job at the Great West Life Insurance Company. The course of Alfreda's life was dramatically changed at age thirteen when, at 9:17 p.m., on December 12, 1978, records indicate she lost her mother tragically in a head-on collision with another motorist. She was taken into the home of her grandmother, Frances D. Bikowsky, who had recently moved to the Dallas suburb Garland after being widowed. Frances D. appears to have raised Alfreda like a daughter.[8]

All three were honor students. John Kiriakou's classmates joked that he would be president someday,[9] while the personable Jen Matthews was voted Most Likely to Become Barbara Walters.[10] One of Bikowsky's teachers thought of her as perhaps one of the brightest students she ever had.[11] Matthews took an interest in television and reporting, was a member of the National Honor Society, and was in Youth for Christ.[12] Kiriakou was a baseball fanatic and played in the school band.[13]

Each headed out of state for their undergrad studies. Matthews attended the Christian liberal arts college of Cedarville University in Ohio. She studied broadcast journalism.[14] Kiriakou headed to George Washington University in DC, one of the top-ranking private universities in the nation, where he was drawn to Middle East studies.[15]

Bikowsky moved to Philadelphia, two hours from her grandmother's hometown, to the Ivy League University of Pennsylvania.[16] There she lived on campus in one of the Victorian homes along Locust Street.[17] She received her bachelor's degree, heading to a northern suburb of Boston to get her master's from the Fletcher School of Tufts University in Medford, a breeding ground for diplomats, government officials, and CIA employees.[18] Matthews went to graduate school in Oxford, Ohio, at Miami University, switching from broadcasting to political science.[19] Kiriakou remained at GWU and pursued his master's in legislative affairs.[20]

Near the end of their graduate school experiences, each was likely approached by someone they had known, someone secretly contracted by the CIA. John Kiriakou says that the agency's staffing department "employed pre-retirees and recent retirees" at colleges as "spotters." The spotters' jobs would entail teaching a class or two at schools around the country. "Important universities," clarifies Kiriakou, adding, "they're not going to go to University of Iowa to look for somebody—it's the top twenty-five schools." There these individuals kept their eyes open, discreetly, for people who fit the right profile.[21]

"A CIA psychiatrist told me once," imparts Kiriakou, "that the CIA is interested in hiring people with sociopathic tendencies. Not sociopaths, right, because sociopaths can easily pass a polygraph exam, which makes them impossible to control, because they have no conscience." The agency was not interested, therefore, in sociopaths, but, ideally, those who could be discerned to carry the tendencies. "The CIA wants to hire people who are comfortable working in ethical or moral gray areas. They have a conscience, they can fail a polygraph, but they're comfortable breaking the law."

"You get 'spotted' in graduate school. Then, if the person is interested, the first thing they go through is a series of tests," says Kiriakou. The first test given to Bikowsky, Kiriakou, and Matthews was on current events. It was multiple choice. Kiriakou says, "Any moron walking past the *Washington Post* newspaper box in the morning is going to pass this test." It included questions like:

Andreas Papandreou is the prime minister of
A) Greece
B) Russia
C) Burma

The second test was a big foldout map of the world, the countries blank. Bikowsky, Kiriakou, and Matthews had to write in the names of every country on Earth. The third test, the most anxiety-inducing, listed between two thousand to three thousand statements, asking the candidate to check "Yes" or "No," statements like:

I like boxing.
Yes
No

"To tell you the truth, I don't really give a shit about boxing," but, Kiriakou thought, "If Tyson is fighting and I happen to be flipping through the channels, I'll watch Tyson. So I think I said yes. But then," he adds, "485 statements later, it again says, 'I like boxing.' And I would think, 'What did I say the first time? I can't remember.' And then another eight hundred questions later, same statement."

Were they testing for memory? Honesty? Personality type? The genius to recognize the pattern in the test?

After taking his CIA entry test, Kiriakou went home to the woman he had recently married. "How'd you do?" she asked.

"I literally have no idea how I did," he told her.

Nonetheless, the three were notified they had passed. Each took their turns meeting a panel of one psychiatrist, one psychologist, and one anthropologist at a nondescript building just outside DC.

"Describe your relationship with your mother."

"Was your father the disciplinarian of the family?"

"Have you ever betrayed a friendship?"

With each answer, the panel members looked to one another, nodding, faces turning side to side. It was intimidating.

One line of questioning stood out in Kiriakou's mind.

"Let's say you meet a guy who has a document in his house, and you really need that document. In fact, you're tasked by supervisors with taking possession of that document. You work on recruiting the guy for six months, you become best friends, but eventually you realize you just can't get him to 'flip.' What do you do?"

"Oh, that's an easy question," Kiriakou remembers responding. "You just break into his house and take it."

The panel responded, "Well, that's exactly what you do."

Kiriakou admits to feeling "perfectly happy to break the law if it's for 'God and country.'" He believes the others must have given similar answers. "That's what you do for a living. You're a CIA officer," he states matter-of-factly, coyly adding that spying is "the second oldest profession." The interviews ended with each directed into a side room, where their hair, blood, and urine were collected. Six weeks later, they received phone calls telling them to come into headquarters.

For the newbies, it was the first awe-inspiring trip to the CIA complex, on the other side of the Potomac River in the suburban Langley neighborhood of McLean, Virginia.

Driving down an entrance road, through the edge of the rich surrounding forests of tall hickory, oak, black walnut, and beech trees, they turned off into the two-hundred-fifty-acre compound known as the George Bush Center for Intelligence. This, they observed, was a virtual self-sustaining city.[22]

One could see the water tower, the steam-emitting backup power plant, and a modern house serving as a day care for the employees' children. At the center of it all were two large office buildings connected by a structure. To the right stood the classic midcentury-style Old Headquarters Building, the OHB, completed in 1961, and to the left was the modern blue glass New Headquarters Building, the NHB, only recently opened to workers and still completing its construction.

Joggers could be seen circling the circumference of the buildings, a popular way for employees to clear their heads, take a break, or just get some exercise. It took at least half an hour at a brisk pace.

Once there, agency psychologists subjected Bikowsky, Kiriakou, and Matthews to polygraph tests. Passing that, a very expensive, long, and intensive investigation into each followed. A normal government background investigation goes back five years into one's neighborhood, employment, and friendships. A special background investigation is used by the CIA, and it looks back fifteen years. One month later, they received another call. *Come to work.*

* * *

The work of the CIA was split, essentially, into two primary divisions: the information acquirers and the information processors. Every capital city in the world has its own secret agency station, like the foreign bureaus of a newspaper, each made up from between a handful to a dozen or more *case officers*, depending on the importance of the region, reporting to a station "chief." Case officers recruited and ran "assets," informants, and spies who could feed useful information from inside places of interest. Assets in various countries numbered between two thousand and three thousand.[23] The station chiefs reported back to the Operations division of headquarters, called the "Directorate of Operations" or simply referred to as "the DO," home of the spies and spymasters, the information acquirers.

During the final days of the Reagan administration, the three began their work, assigned to positions inside Langley. Kiriakou noticed Matthews in his new hire class. "She was very positive, very bubbly and friendly. She was just very sweet." She arrived at CIA with lofty goals. Asked during orientation about her future plans, Matthews responded, "I'm going to be the [Director of Central Intelligence]."

"You are trained to lie all of the time. Your whole life is a lie," Kiriakou quickly came to realize. During training, the group was told there were only three lies not to tell. "Don't ever lie to your boss. Don't ever lie to security. And don't ever lie to finance. Those are the people who can end your career." But, he says, it was encouraged that "you can lie to *every*body else."

The CIA had determined their skill sets, and Bikowsky, Kiriakou, and Matthews were all assigned to a division called "Directorate of Intelligence," or "the DI," home of the information processors, referred to as analysts. "The agency had what I would guess to be only three hundred or four hundred analysts," Kiriakou says. New analysts were often assigned to groups based on their testing rather than their prior areas of study or interest. Kiriakou had to argue his way out of first being assigned to North Korea. After all, his degree was in Middle East studies and his specialization was in Islamic theology. "I'm not even sure I could pick North Korea on a map," he told them. He won. They put him in the Iraq analysis group.

Kiriakou fell in love with the place. He tended to arrive early, as most there did, by about 6 a.m. His cubicle was in the recently completed New Headquarters Building, where the most convenient parking out front was reserved for employees "GS-15 and higher." There are fifteen "grades" to climb in the government, GS-1 to GS-15, from the lowest level bureaucrat to the highest. Above GS-15 exists a different grade system, called "SES," those considered the "senior executives" of their agencies. Rather than parking on the side nearest his office, which would have displayed his obvious excitement, Kiriakou pulled his car in every day behind the Old Headquarters Building, the OHB, "way out in the north forty." He would walk the distance around the compound and through the front door of the historic first HQ, "over the big seal of the CIA," where he could "see the stars on the wall, and the flags, and the statue of Nathan Hale saying, 'I only regret that

I have but one life to lose for my country.'" He says he did that for the first six months, "maybe longer."

He could not wait to get to his desk on the first floor each morning to find out what had happened overnight in the Middle East. "I was a news junkie anyway, and to be able to walk in and log on to see 'the classified news,' what our own people in the field were reporting, or what [the] NSA or State Department or Defense Department were reporting—to this day it was the best job I have ever had."

Kiriakou took in the culture of his workplace. Raised by politically liberal Catholic parents, he noticed a higher than average number of what he describes as "ideological conservatives," evangelical Christians and Mormons. In addition to the many employees who were second- or even third-generation CIA, with parents, uncles, or siblings having paved the way for their arrivals, many on the inside had also "coupled up."

Kiriakou had a friend in the security office who told him that not a single night passed when he did not walk into a conference room to find people having sex on the table. "So we had this rule that whenever you went to a meeting, you never touched the table," Kiriakou says. He claims the CIA, as a matter of policy, was very encouraging of employees dating because it eliminated the problem of officers with "classified" knowledge becoming close with others who lack a security clearance. CIA employees dating each other can discuss whatever they want. "It's not like you have time to meet people when you're working six days a week for eighteen hours a day, so you end up hooking up with each other. Everyone's 'cleared.' You're working these ungodly hours. One thing leads to another."

He became aware of a "family dynamic" within the agency. "Like family," he adds, "those dynamics are often difficult. You might like someone and like working with them, or you might like them and not like working with them, or you might not like them at all but end up sleeping with them." He sums up, "That's just life at the agency."

In an account written by Joby Warrick, a journalist for the *Washington Post*, he revealed that Alfreda Bikowsky and Jen Matthews had bonded in their early days at the agency, along with two other recent arrivals. "The foursome quickly concluded they needed to stick together—'the only women in a sea of men,'" wrote Warrick. "When they traveled together as a pack, as they often did, they turned heads in Langley's buttoned-down corridors.

The four lunched together in the cafeteria, took group vacations, and even planned one another's weddings." Bikowsky and Matthews soon married men they had met in college, driving to work each day from their houses in nearby Virginia suburbs.[24]

"Very few women had been permitted to join the elite fraternity of case officers in those days, so Matthews and her three new CIA friends took positions that were traditionally open to women," wrote Warrick. "Matthews became an imagery analyst and spent many hours poring over satellite photos of suspected chemical weapons factories in Libya." Bikowsky was assigned to one of the offices dealing with Soviet issues. There she connected with a like-minded up-and-coming Soviet analyst-turned-terrorism specialist named Michael Scheuer.

A native of upstate New York, Scheuer possessed a round face, gray and black hair running from the edges of his buzz cut down his medium-length beard. Capable of a friendly smile, Scheuer wore glasses over his intense eyes. Thirteen years her elder, Scheuer was Catholic like Bikowsky. "Sister Virginia used to say, 'You'll be known by the company you keep,'" Scheuer liked to recount.[25]

He had only a few years more experience at the agency than Bikowsky, and would be advancing up the ladder sooner. Despite their backgrounds, they had been placed in an office that would hold little importance during the years just after the end of the Cold War.[26] It was a dead end. Both of them ambitious, Scheuer and Bikowsky would bide their time until they could make a move.

* * *

A 1,200-pound truck bomb exploded in lower Manhattan in 1993, just over a month after Bill Clinton was sworn in as president. Coming from a Ryder truck parked in the basement garage of the North Tower of the World Trade Center, it had killed six people and injured over a thousand. At a time of relative peace and stability following the end of the long Cold War, the question became: who had dared take on the Americans?

FBI investigators followed the trail and identified the plotters. Soon reports were circulating within the government connecting those men to a Saudi-born millionaire named Usama Bin Laden and an apparent network of radicalized Muslims he was supporting. Inside the White House, newly arrived counterterror specialist Richard Clarke came up with an outside-the-box idea to deal with the growing terrorist problem confronting the United States. It would become known as "extraordinary renditions."[27]

The idea must have seemed so pragmatic to Clarke, head of the National Security Council's counterterror group. Under Ronald Reagan, he remembered, FBI agents and Navy SEALs had once kidnapped an accused hijacker from a yacht on international waters.[28] Why not turn to this as an option at times, when necessary?

The "why not" was argued by the White House counsel, who protested that Clarke's suggestion would violate international law.[29] Even if the United States had not the year prior ratified the United Nations Convention Against Torture and Other Forms of Cruel, Inhuman or Degrading Treatment, he explained, extraordinary renditions would still be illegal in nearly any country in the world due to the universality of local laws prohibiting kidnapping. "[President] Clinton recapped the arguments on both sides for [Vice President Al] Gore," later wrote Clarke. "Gore laughed and said, 'That's a no-brainer. Of course it's a violation of international law. That's why it's a covert action. The guy is a terrorist. Go grab his ass.'"

To be sure, such renditions had the government dipping its toes into the murky waters of criminal behavior as official US policy. Reagan's "snatch," what might be called an *ordinary* rendition, had brought the accused hijacker back to America to stand trial, where he was convicted and served a sixteen-year sentence at a federal prison in Virginia. Clarke claimed his renditions would do the same, later writing, "All but one of the World Trade Center attackers from 1993 had been found and brought to New York," where they went to court. Clarke's kidnappings would mostly be handled by the FBI and the military in the first years.

Two years later, after Clarke's colleague on the NSC, George Tenet, became deputy to the CIA director, one of his employees, Mike Scheuer, found a way to make renditions *extraordinary*. "We were turning into voyeurs," he would later testify to Congress, explaining, "We knew where these [suspected terrorists] were, but we couldn't capture them because we had nowhere to take them." In other words, the already thin legal veneer of renditions, bringing them back to America to be presented with evidence of their crimes in court, had started to seem inconvenient in some cases. "We had to come up with a third party [outside the United States to deliver them]," Scheuer had concluded.[30]

John Kiriakou confirms that Mike Scheuer was the one who "turned the focus of renditions to Arabs." In contrast to the macho spies in the field, the "DO people," Scheuer was a thinker, an intellectual of sorts who had spent his career as an analyst. He later summarized his overriding philosophy, saying, "[T]he crux of my argument is simply that America is in a war with militant Islamists that it cannot avoid, one that it cannot talk or appease its way out of, one in which our irreconcilable Islamist foes will have to be killed, an act which unavoidably will lead to innocent deaths, and one that is motivated in large measure by the impact of US foreign policies in the Islamic world, one of which is unqualified US support for Israel."[31] A right-wing Jewish magazine, *Commentary*, later attempted to capture him as "a cross between an overwrought Buchananite and a raving Chomskyite."[32] He was a bit of a third party.

John Kiriakou says that the CIA's CounterTerrorist Center, or CTC, was such a nonentity in the thinking of the leadership at that time that Scheuer needed only to win over the one or two men with sway at the top of that little-cared-about office. Once he was close with them, "he had carte blanche to jet around the world and negotiate these deals." says Kiriakou. He adds, "And remember, in that region they love this kind of attention. They love making these deals. Because all kinds of goodies come with them. Millions in cash. Secure communications, equipment, maybe some vehicles." Getting the Egyptian spy chief Omar Suleiman to be the first to agree to receive the CIA's kidnappees, Scheuer was finally in business.[33]

Scheuer's Egyptian deal added to the international kidnappings two extra elements of illegality: indefinite detention of individuals without a trial never provided an opportunity for them to confront their jailers about their alleged crimes in a court of law, plus another, torture. Egypt was understood by those in the US government to freely employ methods of torture on those it imprisoned. Suleiman in particular was notorious for it. Scheuer was thoroughly unconcerned, later testifying about a "kind of joking up our sleeves about what would happen to those people in Cairo in Egyptian prisons."[34] Jordan and Morocco eventually also agreed to receive those kidnapped by the CIA.

"I think there's a major difference between a rendition and an extraordinary rendition," Kiriakou explains, having himself participated in the new program. "A rendition, which is what we were doing in the 1980s and '90s, is to cross the border and snatch someone who has committed a crime against Americans or against the United States. Now that's not nice, and often times the government of the country you snatched from is going to resent it and there will be a diplomatic flap.

"Extraordinary rendition is different," he clarifies, "because there's just no way you can even pretend that it's legal. You snatch somebody and take him to a third country to be interrogated-slash-tortured, without even informing the government of the country of which the guy's a citizen."

He gives a for-instance. "I'm in Pakistan. I catch a Malaysian guy. Instead of telling the Malaysians, 'Hey, I've caught your guy. We think he's a terrorist,' I send him to Egypt or Jordan or Algeria or wherever. The Malaysians have no idea where their citizen is, and this guy may never make it back out alive. I can't torture him as a CIA agent because we [the US] have laws against it, but by God, the Egyptians can, and the Jordanians can."

\* \* \*

Importance in Washington is conveyed by things like office sizes and location within a building. Alec Station, created at the end of 1995 to counter Usama Bin Laden and his organization,[35] was initially housed in a nondescript corporate tower in the suburb of Tyson's Corner, just a stretch from Langley's impressive buildings.

When one passed through the Alec Station office door, that person entered into a distinct "station," by the agency's technicalities, as if one had gone to the Rome station. Foreign stations, however, were usually led by people with spy backgrounds. As an apparent reward for cementing the "extraordinary renditions" program, Mike Scheuer, the career analyst, was given an incredible promotion and was allowed to found this station and serve as its chief. Renditions would be run by Scheuer from this office.

Code-naming his station after his adopted son, Alec, Scheuer made exactly two hires: Alfreda Bikowsky and a colleague named Tom Wilshere.[36] Wilshere, looking a bit older than his forty-five years, spectacled with skeletal features and thinning, unkempt hair, was made Scheuer's deputy.[37] He had a background working with FBI agents on Hezbollah investigations and had a lot of credibility with the Bureau.[38] "It was [Bikowsky] who staffed up [the office]. She did all the hiring," insists Kiriakou. "I have no idea why [Scheuer] gave her that authority."

By that time, Jen Matthews had left the CIA for a brief stretch, moving overseas to support a professional opportunity of her husband's and giving birth to their first child.[39] The rest of Bikowsky's group of friends were brought into Alec Station. Matthews would return the following year, training in field operations, a rare switch to the spies division. Bikowsky would soon also bring Matthews into Alec Station, one its few "staff operations officers."[40]

Scheuer was quickly gaining a reputation by some at the CIA as a hothead and an outsider to conventional agency thinking, perhaps even as an "extremist." "He was sort of marked [back in the late '90s by the players in CIA] as a person with some good skills," explains a former CIA employee, "but a person with judgment that had gotten skewed a little bit by his experiences or something, pain or something of his own."

His decision to allow his office to be staffed entirely with young female analysts, rather than experienced spies, drew skepticism from some around Langley, the few who bothered to notice the overlooked counterterror department. Some noted these young women's intense loyalty to their boss, and the group began to be known by a nickname around the agency: "the Manson Family," often interchangeable with "the Scheuer family."[41]

\* \* \*

Thirty miles northeast of the CIA's headquarters, in suburban Fort Meade, Maryland, two opaque black cubes and a large complex of shorter, tan and white office buildings served as home to the leadership of the National Security Agency. NSA headquarters was part of a US Army installation, Fort George G. Meade, reflecting its place as part of the military. The buildings were surrounded by many acres of parking lot containing the vehicles of the NSA's estimated twenty thousand employees working inside. This number apparently accounted for roughly one-third of total agency staffing worldwide.[42] It was a mix of civilians and proud former or current members of the US military.

Before the inception of the NSA, the older buildings on-site had once been used as a holding center during the Second World War for Americans of Japanese, German, and Italian descent who had been arrested as potential threats. In contrast to the human spies utilized by the CIA, the NSA had been created to develop strategies and technologies with which to find ways inside foreign communications. Their task was to collect the best information around the world for the White House and others making government policy. With the world increasingly being run via digital communications, "Signals Intelligence," or SIGINT, was sucking up more and more of the oxygen. There were around six thousand SIGINT employees at the Maryland headquarters and another four thousand worldwide.[43]

The operations involving SIGINT were essentially divided into three groups. "Data acquisition," known by various names over the years, did the work of tapping types of communications around the world. Another group handled the data that was collected, translated by a team of linguists and looked at by analysts. This group also included what was called "production," the turning of this information into useful reports for "customers." Lastly, there was a "customer relationships" group, liaising with other agencies, primarily the CIA, FBI, State Department, and others.

The NSA's top customer was, of course, the White House. The president's daily intelligence briefing (PDB), popularly associated with the CIA, was more than two-thirds built from information based primarily on the NSA's SIGINT work. Senior analysts from their respective agencies worked together on the creation of the day's briefing. As the Internet rose to prominence, and as more and more people were communicating electronically, a greater share of intelligence in the PDB was coming from the NSA. Employees bragged internally that "ninety percent of the good stuff comes from us."[44]

The NSA's CounterTerror Shop was made up of only around a dozen people; they were a very young group, fairly evenly divided between men and women. The translators who served them were mostly Arab in origin and outnumbered their team. Only six to eight people within the CT Shop came to be specifically focused on Al Qaeda. They were known as the AQ Shop, the equivalent of Alec Station. Each individual analyst became known as an "office of primary responsibility" for a subject, region, or offshoot terrorist group, the go-to persons for certain areas of interest. These included Afghanistan, Southwest Asia, Southeast Asia, a subject like "radical Islam as a worldwide movement," the Philippines, Egypt, Yemen, and so on.[45]

Their reports were put on distribution lists to the NSA's customers. Supporting military operations was their highest priority, as the agency was under the umbrella of the Defense Department. In order for NSA reports to be shared with other agencies, they had to clear what was called "the Chop Chain," a group consisting of the NSA director's top staff and other agency executives. Once approved by this group, formal reports would be sent electronically or, more often, printed and delivered by courier.

Because the growing threat from Al Qaeda had been little understood government-wide, the employees of the CT Shop later claimed they felt rather "buried" or ignored inside the agency. "They were issuing reports," recalls former NSA communications director Tom Drake, "and no one was reading them."

\* \* \*

Usama Bin Laden's group, Al Qaeda, had created a communications hub in the city of Sana'a, Yemen. Al Qaeda operatives around the world made phone calls to the hub in Yemen as a means to pass messages to each other. This was necessary because some countries blocked or monitored all calls from one country to another as possible terrorist communications. For instance, at the time, one could not call from Egypt to Afghanistan, unless one used a go-between in a third country.

Usama Bin Laden was also known to have a satellite phone at this time, which wasn't easy for him to get. In the mid-1990s, a student in Virginia bought the phone for $7,500 using a British man's credit card. The student shipped the phone to England to Al Qaeda's de facto press secretary, who then shipped it to Bin Laden in Afghanistan.

The NSA's burgeoning Al Qaeda Shop set out to intercept the calls Bin Laden made and received via this phone. Analysts took notice of where Bin Laden most frequently called. One house stood out. It was the communications hub in Sana'a, Yemen. Research indicated the house belonged to Ahmed al Hada. Hada had fought alongside Bin Laden against the Soviets in Afghanistan throughout the 1980s. It did not take long for NSA's analysts to recognize the operational significance of the house.[46]

The CT Shop made a request to the NSA's Chop Chain to surveil the Hada house. The Chop Chain had their FBI liaison petition the FISA court on the matter. The FISA court approved it, and the AQ Shop oversaw "cast iron coverage" of the house in Yemen. "Anything going into or out of the safe house was collected," says Tom Drake. "It was targeted. But remember it wasn't a priority."[47]

While still a low priority for the leadership of the NSA, for the men and women of the AQ Shop, it was their daily job. One whom we will call "Betsy" was given the ticket on the Yemen hub. Her job was to monitor the calls going into and out of Hada's house. By monitoring Bin Laden's satellite phone, the few staffers at NSA working the issue were able to create an early global phone map of the Al Qaeda network.[48]

In December 1996, a CIA employee detailed to work at the NSA learned about the Yemen house and reported it to Alec Station's Mike Scheuer. Scheuer recognized the significance of having the phone number Al Qaeda was using to plan their operations and requested that the NSA share with him and his staff the transcripts of the calls made into and out of the house. The NSA rebuffed him.

Scheuer turned directly to the NSA's then deputy director for operations. The best he could get out of her was an agreement that they would send weekly reports concerning the calls. The "raw" intelligence remained in contention.[49]

The chief of Alec Station was not going to be made the fool by the NSA. At Scheuer's behest, he claims, the CIA's Technology Division built its own listening post from the Indian Ocean, near Madagascar. The listening station was far from perfect. For the next several years, Scheuer's team was able to hear only half of what the analysts in Fort Meade heard, only one end of the phone calls. Still, they had their first significant "ear" into Al Qaeda. It was an advantage he knew his counterterror counterparts in the FBI did not have.

\* \* \*

George Tenet, freshly appointed as Director of Central Intelligence (DCI), stepped to a microphone. The banner above his head read: DOES AMERICA NEED THE CIA?

It was November 1997, the fiftieth anniversary of the bureaucracy that Tenet just officially inherited. Facing the intellectual audience inside the Gerald Ford Library at the University of Michigan, Tenet conveyed a kind of lighthearted acceptance of the absurdity of the moment, having to publicly defend his own job. It would turn out to be the first of many humiliating tasks he would have to bear with a grin. He quipped, "I think this is the first time I've ever been asked to keynote a conference where the stated objective is deciding whether I should bother coming into work in the morning."[50]

Tenet picked up the mantle of the CIA at a time when some believed the agency was on the ropes. Only weeks before his swearing in that summer, a report by the House of Representatives' intelligence committee battered them with criticisms, including a summation that stated they lacked the "depth, breadth, and expertise to monitor political, military, and economic developments worldwide." Tenet was aware of the deeply rooted struggles before him, and he knew that he had a limited amount of time, money, and resources available to turn the ship around. He sought budgetary support from Congress and received it, to the tune of 1.8 billion dollars, promising that within five years he could revitalize the agency. Again, that was 1997.[51]

It might come as a surprise to some Americans that the CIA was in such dire straits at the turn of the century. The CIA came into being in a world in which the geopolitical situation was a long grind between two imperial powers locked in a cold war. With each year that had passed since the fall of the Soviet Union, the failure of another major power to rise as an adversary of the United States was leaving the argument for a permanent civilian spy agency weaker. Tenet, master of the "soft sell," leaned into the mic and, as Gerald Ford and the crowd looked on, gave his best pitch.

"The compelling factors behind the creation of the CIA are still present in the world that America must live in today," he said. His thesis stated, Tenet turned to remind everyone of what were "the compelling factors" for its creation. "The CIA was created by President Truman as an insurance policy against the kind of surprise that caught America off guard in World War II."

The mission explained, he turned to what he called the "core function." He was not talking about the work of officers in the field, the spies. Instead, he claimed the core function was being done by the analysts, like Bikowsky and Kiriakou. "Truman wanted an agency that could pull together the relevant information from all available sources bearing upon foreign policy matters, analyze it, and provide him a timely and objective assessment, free of a policy bias. . . . In my view, the CIA's classic mission of separating fact from fiction and presenting analys[e]s objectively has become only more important." He headed toward his point. "If the CIA did not pull it together, sort it out, and present it, who would?"

Tenet knew the CIA had a sordid past, but he may have believed that the sins of the agency were seeded in good intentions. Things would be different going forward. He said as much. "For my part, I do not intend to spend a lot of time discussing the past . . . my gaze is fixed on the future." His glimpse of the future brought warning. "As I look at the world today," the new director continued inside the session, "it is clear to me that the potential for dangerous surprise is as great as ever."

The agency's mission, he reaffirmed, was "not to observe, or catalog or comment; it is to warn and protect."

\* \* \*

Tenet was accurate in his depiction of President Harry Truman's simple reason for creating the intelligence community. Truman had, in fact, wrestled with that decision. The United States, like nearly every nation in the world, had no permanent civilian intelligence bureaucracy for most of its history. Spies and spycraft were historically considered matters for wartime, not peace. Authoritarian nations tended to keep peacetime spy agencies, and they had usually ended up being used against their own populations, to suppress political opposition and ferret out potential enemies of the state.

During World War II, the Office of Special Services (OSS) was created and acted as the wartime intelligence service. The OSS was by and large a resounding failure, having been responsible for the deaths of many of its agents as well as allied troops due to sheer amateurism. As the war came to a close, the head of the OSS, "Wild Bill" Donovan, saw a need for the United States to maintain spying outside of times of conflict. He pitched the concept of a civilian intelligence agency to the president.

Truman thought the idea was akin to an American Gestapo and rejected it. The United States had just pulled off a victory against the fascists, and he was not going to emulate them. When the war ended, he disbanded the OSS.

The shadow in the East cast by the Soviet Union, however, vexed and intimidated the military men and policymakers in the United States. Their belief in a widespread communist infiltration of the country encouraged by the Soviets created concern over an information gap. The emerging enemy might know more about what we were doing than we did about what they were doing. They might gain an advantage in what political elites saw as a global chessboard. Their fear of allowing unnecessary risk won out over ideals.

Amid the gravity of a nuclear-powered Cold War, Truman essentially felt that he needed to be better informed than random readers of the daily newspaper.[52] The CIA was to be Washington's need-to-know-only news supplier. Its analysts were to be like the editors of the *New York Times*, sifting through all the best sources of information each day to figure out what the headlines would be and which stories would get page one with DC players. What did their readers most need to know? In their case, their readers were the president, a small number of his chosen advisers and cabinet, and some members of Congress. An edited version would be sent to some other agencies.

The president would not be settling for what the American public got. The US government's news collectors would need a leg up on the competition. Though journalists may at times push the line of decency and privacy, generally news outlets discourage their reporters from outright breaking the law to get a story. The devil's bargain that Truman made for good information was that crimes were going to be committed to get it. Career CIA officer Fulton Armstrong calls this "the original sin of the creation of the intelligence community in 1947."[53] Clandestine operations would be needed to get information, often violating legality.

As soon as it was understood that the CIA was going to serve as the American government's secret illegal actions specialists, the door was open to using the agency for covert actions to affect desired political outcomes in nations around the world. What made lawbreaking palatable was that, while the crimes were planned inside the United States, in Washington and Langley, the actions would take place outside our borders, breaking *somebody else's* laws. It would be, nonetheless, an acceptance of criminality as official American policy. It would thus be necessary that their work remain mostly secret from the public, somewhat contrary to the democratic philosophy at the heart of the nation's understood mission statement.

Armstrong believes the core mission, getting the best information to American leadership, was immediately corrupted by these dueling objectives, what he calls the commingling of the intelligence mission and the covert action or clandestine operational mission. "Doing clandestine operations to influence events is the 'legally political' role of the CIA," he made clear. "The president has a problem, he adopts a policy of eradicating some problem, and he then engages [the agency] in a political game of getting it done so he can take credit for it. That's the way it works."

The "sin," as Armstrong sees it, occurs when the same agency's raison d'etre, its objectivity in reporting unbiased truth to leadership, gets distorted by the political objectives. He concluded, "It takes an extraordinary human being to be put in charge of making change happen [for the president] and [then to be neutral in] evaluating whether change is happening, which is the role of the intelligence services. The moment you have a covert action, a political role on an issue, how can you [as an information analyst] then do the intelligence mission [independently and unbiased]? You can't."

By the time of the agency's sixteenth birthday, Truman was having massive cold feet about the whole thing over this very issue. Many frequently cite Dwight Eisenhower's warning to the American public just prior to John F. Kennedy's arrival in the White House about "undue influence" exerted over the workings of the nation by what he called "the military-industrial complex." Harry Truman gave an equally dire warning about the CIA to the people of the United States immediately after Kennedy's death. The headline instructed the country to "Limit CIA Role to Intelligence." Truman boldly wrote in the *Washington Post*, "I think it has become necessary to take another look at the purpose and operations of our Central Intelligence Agency. For some time I have been disturbed by the way CIA has been diverted from its original assignment. It has become an operational and at times a policy-making arm of the Government."[54]

"I never had any thought that when I set up the CIA that it would be injected into peacetime cloak-and-dagger operations," pleaded the former president. "I, therefore, would like to see the CIA be restored to its original assignment as the intelligence arm of the president . . . and that its operational duties be terminated or properly used elsewhere." He concluded darkly and clearly, writing, "There is something about the way the CIA has been functioning that is casting a shadow over our historic position, and I feel that we need to correct it."

For most Americans, their impressions of the CIA are fictions drafted in Hollywood. In the minds of many, the agency is a technological powerhouse staffed by sleek intelligentsia who also happen to be incredibly adept in martial crafts and deep-cover espionage. The reality is that reports questioning the efficacy of the agency have been around almost as long as the agency itself.

The first such report emerged in 1948 from a study by a former president, Herbert Hoover, raising concerns over the quality of the agency's products and its internal structure.[55] Another came the year after, complaining about the organization and coordination of intel activities.[56] President Dwight Eisenhower felt compelled to create the CIA's first watchdog board in 1956,[57] and President John Kennedy famously is alleged to have fumed at one of his officials after the botched invasion of Cuba that he "wanted to splinter the CIA in a thousand pieces and scatter it to the winds."[58]

After every public foible and every critical government report, citizens and their leaders settled back into a general attitude suggesting that despite the calamitous consequences of the CIA's mistakes, there are shadows lurking around the globe, and someone ought to be working to outmaneuver them. Basically, we can't live with them, can't live without them. It took a little over a decade—and a renewed spirit of accountability following the "long national nightmare" of Watergate—for Congress to take a truly active interest in the matters Truman had warned about.

Several concurrent inquiries took place during the mid- to late-1970s. The hearings before the committee of Idaho senator Frank Church made the most lasting impression on future CIA employees. George Tenet was in New York at the time, completing his master's in international affairs at Columbia. Church's investigation lasted almost a year, becoming the largest in the history of the Senate. The nightly news recaps captivated many Americans with their revelations of decades of politically motivated covert actions that had violated international laws and often basic ethics and reasonable decision-making.

The result was a six-volume report and, many hoped, a chastened CIA. Some insiders worried that "the shock effect of an exposure of the 'family jewels'" might "inflict mortal wounds on the CIA and deprive the nation of all the good the agency could do in the future." Robert Gates later wrote of the lessons learned by Congress in his memoir. "If CIA had been acting as the president's agent in many of its improper actions, then [the lesson was that] the way to control CIA was to dilute the president's heretofore nearly absolute control over the agency. And that would be done by a much more aggressive congressional oversight mechanism."[59]

Among the reforms, President Gerald Ford issued an executive order banning assassinations. The Senate created a Select Committee on

Intelligence in 1976, and the following year the House opened the Permanent Select Committee on Intelligence. Congress would no longer abdicate its responsibilities to the executive branch with regard to the intelligence community.

The yin and yang of democratic politics, and perhaps the lobbying of special interests, sent the pendulum swinging back the other way. A push-back began against the reforms. While running for president, former actor and state governor Ronald Reagan made a campaign issue out of what he characterized as the restrengthening of the intelligence services in the post-Church era. Upon winning the Republican nomination, he chose a former political rival—and a former CIA director—as his vice president: George H. W. Bush.

Increasingly, the debate over the intelligence community took on a political nature within America's two-party system. It had, after all, been Democrats like Truman and Kennedy who had first voiced concerns, and it had been the Democrat-led committees that aired "the family jewels" and insisted on reforms. During the GOP convention, the party added to their platform language claiming Democrats had impaired agencies like the CIA and underestimated the Soviet Union's military threat.

The incoming president, Reagan, then elevated the DCI to a cabinet-level position, and his CIA director used his new power to seek and receive higher budgets, setting off the greatest period of staffing expansion in the agency's history.[60] Most of the future staff of the CIA's dedicated Bin Laden unit, Alec Station, was hired as part of this initiative.

Early in the Reagan era, George Tenet entered the US government via an assistant job to a Republican senator from Pennsylvania.[61] His boss was one of eighty-one senators to vote for the passage of the Intelligence Identities Protection Act.[62] No longer would it be solely the job of the CIA's management to keep the agency's secrets. The law inferred that the protection of classified undercover officers might legally be the duty of all.

Tenet made the jump to the staff of the Senate intelligence committee in 1985. The following year Congress learned the White House had received assistance from the CIA in secretly selling arms to the government of Iran in exchange for its help in the release of US hostages held in Lebanon. It was immediately understood to be a violation of known government policy that had been hidden from the new intelligence committees.

Less than a decade after the Church hearings, Iran-Contra caused some to speculate as to the true impact of the earlier investigation on accountability within the agencies. The national scandal gave the appearance that Langley had simply learned to operate in a more off-the-books fashion to avoid oversight. Tenet, having been promoted to staff director, had a front-row seat for his committee's investigation into the matter.

More attempts at reform resulted. Congress created a statutory inspector general (IG) for the CIA, reporting to the DCI but able to be removed from his post only by the president. The IG was bound by law to submit regular reports to the intelligence committees of Congress summarizing problems discovered. The IG would serve, essentially, as Congress's spy within the CIA.

Accountability for Iran-Contra would, however, prove illusive, as it usually did in Washington. The first CIA director to have risen to the highest position in the land, President George H. W. Bush, pardoned six accused conspirators, including three former agency officials, ending the ongoing investigation of a special prosecutor recommended by Tenet's committee. Simultaneously, the sudden and largely unforeseen collapse of the Soviet Union saw the CIA, for the first time in its history, operating outside of a Cold War. George Tenet would take the CIA's reins less than a decade later.

# 3

# SHAKE UP

*"If you're going to bluff, bluff big."*

Amarillo Slim

It had not been a last-minute bloom of cowardice that led Mohammed Al Owhali to run away from the truck bomb he helped deliver to the American embassy in Kenya. He was supposed to hold the gate guards at gunpoint but had left his pistol in his jacket, which was in the cab of the truck when he jumped out the passenger door. Once he saw the box truck move into place, he had a choice. He could run toward the truck and die in the explosion, or run away. In those frantic seconds, he thought running toward the truck would be an act of suicide, not martyrdom, which according to his deeply held religious beliefs would have been a sin.[1]

On August 7, 1998, at 10:35 a.m., the US embassies in Nairobi, Kenya, and Dar es Salaam, Tanzania, were bombed within four minutes of each other. The Nairobi bombing killed 213 people, including twelve American nationals, and injured more than 4,500. The Dar es Salaam explosion killed eleven and injured eighty-five. That death toll was low because, despite five years of Al Qaeda planning, the date chosen for the bombing was a national holiday in Tanzania, so the US embassy there was closed. The CIA director's prediction the year before that the post–Cold War world was still filled with "dangerous surprise[s]" had been fulfilled. It was also clear his agency had missed it, the first major failure of Tenet's short career at the helm.

The night of the attack, a hotel manager was working a shift in a high-crime section of Nairobi, when through the window of the Ramada he

35

watched a man make a phone call at a kiosk across the street. A strange detail struck him. The man on the phone was wearing clothing that was burned all down his back. The manager picked up his own phone and contacted the FBI command center in Kenya that had been established in the Canadian embassy.[2]

The Federal Bureau of Investigation is the United States' principal law enforcement agency. Soon, one its agents, John Anticev, was in an interrogation room with Owhali. The FBI's approach to interrogations was as old as detective work itself. "When you look at the information that they give you, you understand the reasons they are cooperating with you, then mutual respect develops," explains Jack Cloonan, Anticev's colleague from the New York office of the FBI. "The interrogation approach that we used proved out to be quite successful—and frankly, it's not that unique, it's done all the time. The Bureau, say what you will, is governed by the federal rules of criminal procedure. We know what we are supposed to do when we have a suspect in custody. It's not difficult."

Anticev presented to Owhali a piece of evidence that could not be denied: a set of phone records demonstrating that the FBI had traced his call from the pay phone in front of the Ramada. The phone records showed that Owhali had called a house in Yemen. Faced with proof, unable to lie his way out, Owhali explained the significance of the number.

"I mean, if you got one of the guys who was supposed to blow himself up," continued Cloonan, "and he fails, and he's calling this number in Sana'a, Yemen, that's a hot number. That's a great lead. It's arguably to me one of the most important leads *ever*."

Cloonan noted, with a touch of pride, that this essential lead was passed immediately to the CIA's Alec Station and to the NSA who, he believed, then began monitoring Hada's house. "Everything we ever got from one of our counterterror interrogations was given to the broader intelligence community," he claims. "It's as a result of that interrogation, that phone number, that we learn about the critical meeting [that will later happen] in Kuala Lumpur."

Our conversation with Cloonan concerning these events took place eleven years after they had happened. Seated in his den, at his home in rural New Jersey in 2009, we informed him that the lead about which his Bureau remained so proud had in fact been known for some time prior by the CIA.

They seemingly never shared their monitoring of the house or any intelligence coming out of it with the FBI. We knew this because Mike Scheuer had quietly come clean about it only earlier that year to journalist James Bamford.

"So you didn't know about the Yemen phone number until '98, until the embassy bombings?" we asked.

Cloonan responded, confused, "Well, that's when we get the telephone number."

"Because the CIA knew about it before that. Scheuer says they had it since '96."

"I don't know that," Cloonan replied, flabbergasted. "I'm told by the agents that they get this telephone number and give it to the CIA and NSA. It's the first time we know about it."

Taking a moment to process the implications of this information, Cloonan continued. "If that's the case, it's pretty difficult to understand it. It wouldn't be the first time [the CIA has done this kind of thing]. I would think that would have been pretty significant though, because obviously they are getting data mining off this phone number. Because the telephone number is Khalid al Mihdhar's telephone number. That's pretty significant. If they were working on that number for two years prior to the embassy bombings, that information, I would assume, would have been shared with those of us building the case against Bin Laden."

It would emerge that at the start of the summer, Owhali had dropped by the house of Ahmed al Hada, the Al Qaeda communications "hub" monitored by the NSA. It was the same house for which Mike Scheuer had the CIA build a satellite station to keep tabs on. Owhali had stayed there for several days.

At the start of August, Owhali then flew to Kenya and met up with other men connected to Al Qaeda. He began frequently calling Ahmed al Hada at his house. These calls continued until about 9:20 a.m. local time on the day of the embassy bombings. Bin Laden himself called Hada dozens of times between November 1996 and late August 1998, including two as late as the first week of August. Later investigations concluded that Hada had not just been providing the home for a communications switchboard, but was fully involved in plotting this attack.[3]

All of the above must have looked really bad to George Tenet when, or if, he learned the details of Alec Station's and the NSA's failures to make good use of their surveillance. He was, after all, technically the top man overseeing both. It was also understood by Richard Clarke inside the White House that a change was needed in the management.

Cloonan began to get angry as he thought about it all. "The reason why we had people at Alec Station, the reason the CIA had people back at FBI headquarters, was to *eliminate* the 'turf battles,' was to get beyond this historical tension that existed. And I thought we had done that. I thought we had matured as organizations."

\* \* \*

George Tenet did not know General Michael Hayden very well. Their first meeting was when Hayden interviewed for his job as head of the NSA.[4] A three-star Air Force general, Hayden would be an "outside hire."

Hayden grew up the son of an Irish welder in Pittsburgh, Pennsylvania. He attended an all-boys private high school and worked a part-time job that his former coach had landed him as equipment manager for the Pittsburgh Steelers. Hayden stayed near home for college, getting his bachelor's and master's at the Catholic Duquesne University. At the time, he was trained in the Air Force Reserve Officer Training Corp program, entering active military service in 1969, as the nation was radically split over war. Hayden served in Nebraska at Offutt Air Base as an analyst for the Strategic Air Command, focused on the Soviet Union and the war in Vietnam, and a mere two years later became head of the Air Force's Current Intelligence Division, taking his first overseas assignment in Guam. Hayden returned to the United States, to Vermont, to train future officers in the reserves.[5]

Michael Hayden was in South Korea, then Bulgaria, and finally made a big jump to the Pentagon as political and military affairs officer for Air Force HQ. He joined George H. W. Bush's National Security Council in the White House as director for defense policy and arms control, then leader of the Air Force staff group.

Under Bill Clinton's government, he became the intelligence leader to America's European command, then commander of the Air Intelligence Agency, based in Texas. In his memoir he noted, "since I had never served [at the NSA], I relied a lot on what I had learned at the Air Force component of the NSA."

Bald except for the silver crown of short hair that cradled the back of his head, and sporting thin wire glasses, Hayden has the look of a square government man. After taking the helm of the NSA, Hayden made a dramatic move by going on CNN to beat back rising public resentment toward the secretive agency sparked by the film *Enemy of the State*. Hayden would say, "We're trying to explain what it is we do for America, how it is we follow the law. Could there be abuses? Of course. Would there be? I am looking you and the American people in the eye and saying: there are not."[6]

\* \* \*

Mark Rossini, then in his late thirties, was one of Jack Cloonan's office mates inside the New York City FBI office. That office had been assigned to prepare the embassy bombings case for prosecution in the Southern District of New York, and Rossini was among the agents working the case.

He grew up in the Bronx, and then moved farther north to Rye in Westchester County. The son of an Italian American blacksmith father and an Armenian American social worker mother, he says his mother instilled a strong sense of justice in him. "Never give up the fight," she told him. "Never."[7]

He was raised Presbyterian, and as a child he marched with his mother in sixties peace rallies and with Cesar Chavez's farm workers. He had worked summers with the Rye police force and attended the nearby State University of New York at Purchase where he got his bachelor's degree in political science. One day as he was finishing school in 1984, working part-time as a limo driver, he received a call to pick up one of his regulars for a run to the airport: Jules Kroll, founder of the private security firm Kroll Associates.

Kroll, who knew Rossini through mutual friends in Rye, asked him what he was planning to do after graduation. "I don't know. Become a cop?" Rossini responded.

"Okay, be in my office two o'clock Tuesday." Kroll was offering him a job.

"I don't even own a suit," was all Rossini could say.

"Here's the deal," continued Kroll, unfazed, "you live in Rye. I live in Rye. You take me to work in the morning, take me back home at night, learn the business in the day." It sounded like the best plan Rossini had heard. For seven years he would work for Kroll learning how to be a detective.

After the first World Trade Center bombing in 1993, the trial of four of the six people indicted for their involvement had commenced in a courtroom in lower Manhattan by year's end. The investigation was led by the nearest FBI office at 26 Federal Plaza in lower Manhattan, and by the NYPD. The federal prosecutors of the Southern District of New York mounted the case and secured conviction of all four in early 1994. The convicted were sentenced to prison terms of 240 years each.

As further terror plots emerged and were prevented over the next couple years, a Joint Terrorism Task Force and several counterterror offices developed inside the FBI's New York building to assist federal prosecutors in something that seemed pie-in-the-sky at the time: creating a prosecutable case against the child of a wealthy Saudi family, Usama Bin Laden. Intelligence and law enforcement investigations had led again and again to evidence that the backing for these plots had originated with the man that precious few voices believed was, in fact, a terror mastermind.

Mark Rossini had a cousin in the FBI. The year after the World Trade Center was first bombed, that cousin moved to New York's Joint Terrorism Task Force and tipped Rossini off that the Bureau was looking for people. Rossini approached Tom Pickard, then head of the National Security Division, whom he had become close with when Pickard had been his cousin's supervisor. Pickard told him, "Look, I only want people with experienced criminal investigative backgrounds. Someone like you." However, Rossini couldn't jump right into counterterror. His first years with the FBI would be working "white collar," dealing with matters like pill trafficking and Medicare fraud.

A man named John O'Neill took over the FBI's CounterTerror Section in 1995 from FBI headquarters in Washington, DC. O'Neill had grown up dreaming of being an FBI agent. His favorite TV show as a kid was *The F.B.I.* He had been with the Bureau since 1971, working as a fingerprint clerk during college. He had taken his first major position as head of the Chicago office in '91. On his first day as head of counterterror, he got a call from a man in Bill Clinton's White House, Richard Clarke.[8]

Clarke was a fan of law enforcement. His call to John O'Neill was to let him know that the fugitive mastermind of the WTC bombing, one of the two indicted but not yet brought to court, had been located in Pakistan.

O'Neill worked with Clarke at the White House, his FBI team, and agents in the DEA and State Department. Within days, they had successfully apprehended their target, a man named Ramzi Yousef, and flown him back to the United States where he was later tried and convicted.

O'Neill and Clarke bonded over the experience and remained close. Mark Rossini saw his opportunity to move into counterterror when John O'Neill arrived at the New York office. Rossini's cousin soon introduced him to O'Neill. They hit it off immediately.

"I want to come over," Rossini told him.

"Yeah, you should work for me," replied O'Neill.

That was it. Rossini began his career in counterterror in May 1997. He was struck by O'Neill and by his deputy Pat D'Amuro's insistence on strong professional ethics from their team, and he believes the philosophy filtered down throughout the office. A colleague later wrote of his first meeting with O'Neill's deputy D'Amuro, at which he was instructed, "We should never forget about the endgame—disrupting terrorist plots while keeping all options on the table, including prosecutions in a court of law," and reminded the new agent of "the importance of agents remembering that they are bound by the Constitution."

O'Neill did not know many people in New York yet, and he liked Rossini's style. "Our personalities, the way we dressed." Rossini laughs. "I knew a lot of people in New York. I was single. I liked to go out." The two began regularly hitting the town together after hours. At the start of the New Year, 1999, O'Neill called Rossini into his corner office.

"I'm pulling Dan Coleman out of the CIA's Bin Laden office," O'Neill explained. Rossini did not know it, but he was witnessing among the first of the post-embassy counterterror shake-ups that Richard Clarke was pushing for from the White House. "Coleman's going to work our Nairobi investigation full time."

An employee-exchange program of sorts had been worked out since the founding of Mike Scheuer's Alec Station in 1995. The CIA had people inside FBI headquarters, and the FBI's New York office had one of their own inside Scheuer's office. Created out of a tacit acknowledgement of the long historical competitive relationship between the two agencies, the initiative was meant to ensure that information was shared when it came to preventing terrorism.

"I want to send you to Langley," O'Neill informed Rossini. "You're going to be my eyes and ears."

Rossini agreed.

* * *

"I remember like it was yesterday. It was surreal," says Mark Rossini of first entering the CIA's compound. In his first days as an FBI agent working among the spies, Rossini's clearances had not yet come through, so he had to be walked around the Langley building "like a child."[9]

Inside the Old Headquarters Building, on the second floor, he walked down a nondescript hallway and found a door marked 2G00. They called it "two-goo." Alec Station's second office, this one finally at Langley, had a staff of no more than fifty people working in open cubicles in an 1,800-square-foot room.

Rossini and the (by then) nearly fifty analysts reported to Alfreda Bikowsky and Jen Matthews, who in turn reported to deputy chief Tom Wilshere, who finally reported to Mike Scheuer. The group understood what they were getting in their new arrival. One member of the station later told their inspector general that Rossini "was there to 'spy' for [John O'Neill], who did not trust [Alec] Station."[10] Rossini seconded this assessment to CIA's IG, telling him he "felt like a 'pariah' because he was considered New York's 'spy.'"

There was certainly some truth to it. O'Neill never trusted Scheuer or the larger agency. If O'Neill didn't trust Scheuer, Scheuer outright *hated* his FBI counterpart O'Neill. The origin of their mutual dislike is still not known, but it was widely understood by their staffs. One former CIA employee described on background "Scheuer's unprofessionally strident obsession with criticizing the Clinton administration and certain individuals inside the Clinton administration, such as Dick Clarke."

Perhaps Scheuer was jealous of O'Neill's relationship with the Clinton White House, via Richard Clarke. Or perhaps he resented that O'Neill was able to show off his FBI accomplishments through public trials and convictions of terrorists, while Scheuer's victories in that arena remained closely guarded, the downside of a career in espionage. Maybe it came down to simple differences in personal style. John O'Neill was no saint. A hard-drinking womanizer and adulterer in his personal life, he nonetheless insisted on strong professional ethics from the officers who worked for him, and it filtered down.

O'Neill's image might be summed up by his status as a regular at the famous Elaine's Bar on Manhattan's Upper East Side, described by *Vanity Fair* as a "hang-out for journalists and law-enforcement big shots." Scheuer demonstrated an almost pathological reaction to perceived "big shots" throughout his career. He valued acts of righteousness done outside the spotlight with no public credit taken.

Something deeper had to be at play, though. This was no mere rivalry. The animosity, at least from Scheuer's side, was so strong that years later he would drop jaws at a congressional hearing when he publicly confirmed a statement he was alleged to have made after 9/11. "I think I also said that the only good thing that happened to America on 9/11 was that the buildings fell on [O'Neill], sir,"[11] stated Scheuer in the hearing room filled with people, skipping a beat to look the congressman in the eyes and await his next question. He was conveying he stood by it.

"It wasn't pleasant," laughs Mark Rossini regarding the reception he received at Scheuer's office. Rossini moved to Washington, working at CIA headquarters Monday through Thursday and driving back to lower Manhattan on Fridays to be in his home office with O'Neill's team. He relished his opportunity to take in Washington politics more generally, and the culture of the CIA specifically. He was impressed by the speed at which they worked, the number of support staff available, how up-to-date their computer system was in contrast to the Bureau's, and the ease with which they responded to one another. He felt it made the FBI seem like a dinosaur by comparison. But another comparison also struck him.

"They have no concept of the law," Rossini came to believe. "They have no concept of the Constitution. They are only limited by their imagination because there's [sic] no rules, per se. If they wanted to do something crazy like put powder in Castro's shoes, they could do it. There's [sic] no rules to the game saying you can't. In the FBI, you can't even put a tape recorder on without someone's permission. Because everything you do is going to end up in a court of law some day. Different mentality."

Jen Matthews became Rossini's first friend at the agency. She had not been part of the original lineup at Alec Station, having left the agency to follow her husband on his job overseas and give birth to their first child.

Upon returning to the States, she had trained to be a spy on the Operations side. Bikowsky had apparently moved her friend into her office as one of its few DO people. Matthews held what analysts call "the ticket" on Southeast Asia, meaning she was in charge of anything Al Qaeda-related that came into the office from that region.

"Jen came up to me after my second week there," says Rossini. "We were in line at the cafeteria. She said, 'Okay, Rossini, what'd you do wrong?' See, everyone knows that people who get detailed to other agencies made a mistake. They fucked up. I said, 'I didn't do a goddamn thing wrong. I have an impeccable record. I'm O'Neill's hand-picked guy.'" Rossini says that Matthews laughed and told him, "Okay, great, we thought you were going to be deadweight." They ate lunch together and were pals from that day on.

Rossini also got to know another newly arrived staff operations officer, one with which he did not feel the same kind of instant connection. Michael Anne Casey was a twenty-seven-year-old woman who had joined Alec the year prior. "Well, I mean, she was pleasant enough," said Rossini, pausing to let out an anxious laugh. "Pleasant enough. But very agency-centric. Very forceful in her position. A real fighter, in many respects." Like Matthews, she came from "a legacy CIA family," says Rossini. "Many members of her family had been and perhaps still are in the agency. A true 'agency brat.'"[12]

Casey shared one of the most important tickets in all of Alec Station with deputy chief Tom Wilshere. "I know [Casey] and Wilshere had the proverbial ticket on Yemen. They were the ones most involved with Yemen and the Yemeni cell." This meant they were also the leads on info coming out of the Hada house.

In later explaining their failure to share critical information about the future hijackers with other government agencies, many Alec Station employees would emphasize the presence of four FBI agents detailed to their office for the express purpose of facilitating better information sharing.[13] Rossini was one of the four, as was manager Ed Goetz, who would leave in early 2000 due to health concerns. Doug Miller was another.

\* \* \*

Back in 2010, we rang up Doug Miller, who now works out of the Buffalo field office. Sounding unnerved by our call, he asked to call us back from another line. Minutes later, he instructed us to go through the FBI media office, though he pointed out they had turned down the past four or five media requests for him. He would say, "I wish I could speak. It's something I feel pretty strongly about. But unless you are in a position to pay my mortgage, send my child to college, then fund my retirement, I just can't talk without permission."

In his absence, his friend Rossini fills in the details. Miller was sent to Alec a few months after Rossini, and the two bonded within the alienating anti-FBI environment. "Very bright," was the description that first struck Rossini about his new friend. "An accountant by training. Great analytical brain. Asks very, very relevant questions. And very dedicated. And an emotional guy. A family man, very close to his parents and sisters and brothers."

Rossini says that while Miller and he were treated like outsiders at Alec Station, the same was not true of the fourth FBI employee there. "We were the only two FBI *agents* at Alec Station. There was an FBI *analyst* from the Washington field office there."

Young FBI analyst Maggie Gillespie, roughly Casey's age, had arrived at the CIA months before Rossini. "And the agency people loved her," he quickly recognized. "Maggie was treated from the beginning like a real CIA employee. I mean, she wrote [Central Intelligence Reports] (CIRs). She wrote [Telegraphic Disseminations] (TDs). She actually got the ticket, if you will, on a case, or a subject, and followed it. She was treated like a full member, whereas Doug and I were not. We were outsiders, and we were always going to be treated as outsiders." Rossini paused, considering, before laughing. "Well of course, it was all women too. Doug and I were like the only two guys there. Really. Besides Scheuer and Wilshere. We were the only two men."[14]

* * *

Richard Clarke had begun pushing George Tenet for change ever since the Intelligence Community's clear failure to prevent the embassy bombings.[15] It had actually been several months before that attack when President Clinton had the foresight to elevate Clarke to the first person to hold a newly created cabinet position in charge of US counterterror. Clarke's preferences now carried weight.

"The people who were running the [CIA's counterterror division] prior to the change-up were very ineffective," explains Clarke. "I was complaining about them." Striking deep into the heart of Alec Station, Clarke pushed for Mike Scheuer's departure, a move perhaps interpreted by his staff to be a proxy for the FBI's John O'Neill. The opportunity to remove him came, as Mark Rossini tells it, after Scheuer had an explosive fight with FBI detailee Ed Goetz.

Goetz was angry when Scheuer refused to grant him release authority for Alec Station cables. Their argument was loud enough to be heard by everyone in the office, including Rossini, who remembers Scheuer essentially screaming that "This is a CIA station, the FBI are guests."[16] Goetz, the highest-ranking FBI agent stationed at CIA counterterror, stormed out of his office and took the issue over Scheuer's head to the director of the CounterTerrorist Center, who then took the issue to the head of the spies division. "Man, the tension in the air was so thick. I mean, every one of Scheuer's Manson Family hated Ed Goetz now, and by extension, me," says Rossini of the period.

Upon being relieved of leadership of the office he had founded, the rumor was that due to Scheuer's reputation no other office in the CIA agreed to take him. Thus, for months he had arrived each morning and worked from the agency library until the end of the workday, then heading home. Eventually Scheuer had been accepted by the Crime and Narcotics Center. Fulton Armstrong, then CNC's chief of staff, says, "He was an extremely unhappy member of our office."[17] He is reported to have done fieldwork in narcotics in Afghanistan. A number of his former staffers kept a photo of Scheuer above their desks in his absence, "like a shrine."

One day, Rossini was called into the office of Scheuer's replacement, Rich Blee. "He and I sat down and—very pleasant. He always treated me very fairly, very nice. And he told me, I want you to be more operational, travel more, do more stuff in the field. I had no problem with that. But O'Neill did not want that. He wanted me to stay there. Because he said if you're not there, then I don't know what's going on. And that led to a confrontation between O'Neill and Blee." The CIA/FBI relationship would apparently not improve with Scheuer gone.

"[Blee] came from a legacy family in the agency, and clearly he carried that gravitas or that weight with that," says Rossini. "And having come from the seventh floor, this was a guy who clearly had direct communication to George. And that says a lot about a person who could get things done."

It appears that Rich Blee was born on a CIA assignment in 1957, in Pretoria, South Africa, while his father David Blee was there undercover. By that time, his forty-one-year-old dad had already spent a decade at the agency, having first served in the World War II intel service, the OSS, spying on the Japanese and then at the launch of the CIA after the war.[18]

In 1968, Rich's father was given the entire Middle East to run from Langley HQ. The family moved back to the United States to a house in a Bethesda, Maryland, neighborhood across the Chesapeake from CIA headquarters.[19] Rich continued at the DC-area branch of the American Embassy School, while his father was handed the Soviet Division during the heart of the Cold War. He was a major player.[20]

Blee graduated high school in 1973. His next decade is a mystery, but Rich reappears in 1984 at twenty-six years old, the same age his father joined the agency, working for the consulate in Central Africa.[21] There, one of two known photos of him was taken, printed in a State Department booklet called *Guide for Business Representatives*.

A couple of years later, Rich was in Niger.[22] After that, he was in Algeria—when he was thirty-five—during the bloody civil war between the government and Islamic guerrillas.[23] Around the time George Tenet became deputy director at CIA, Rich was appointed to an Iraqi task force to destabilize Saddam Hussein's government.[24] When Bill Clinton made Tenet his new CIA Director, Tenet brought Rich up to the seventh floor with him to work as one of his executive assistants, just in time for Rich's fortieth birthday. Later that year, Rich watched Tenet award his father a medal at a ceremony to honor the agency's fifty most important trailblazers.[25] The day Rich Blee walked in to take the helm at Alec Station, he was forty-one, five years younger than his dad had been when he took his first chief of station position.

A new leader for the larger CIA CounterTerrorist Center also arrived with Blee. Cofer Black had earned an unparalleled reputation within the counterterror profession as the captor of Carlos the Jackal and as the target of an assassination attempt ordered by Bin Laden himself while Black was serving as the station chief in Sudan. Some believed Black actively promoted his own legend, but Tenet was understood to have brought him in from the field to bring a more "covert action" flavor to counterterror.

"Cofer Black had a reputation for being hard-charging," reports Richard Clarke, who approved of Tenet's choice. "He had done a good job in Sudan.

THE WATCHDOGS DIDN'T BARK

You know, most CIA agents in those days didn't like to get their fingers dirty. They liked to work under diplomatic cover in embassies and go to cocktail parties and recruit Soviet spies. Cofer Black had been in the back alleys of Khartoum."

Cofer Black and Rich Blee had been put in place to bring a more spy-centric approach into action against Al Qaeda. With leadership in place at the NSA and inside the CIA's CounterTerrorist Center, "[Tenet and I] then together developed 'The Plan' [against Al Qaeda]," states Richard Clarke. One aspect of this plan has been detailed—the greater effort to capture or kill leader Usama Bin Laden. What were the other components of this plan?

"When Cofer Black became head of the CounterTerrorist Center at CIA," explains Clarke, "he was aghast that they didn't have sources inside Al Qaeda. And moreover, they had never tried to have sources inside Al Qaeda, because they thought it was too hard. So he told me, right after he became director of the CTC, 'I'm gonna try to get sources in Al Qaeda.'"

# 4

# SPY CRAFT

*"Falsehood flies, and truth comes limping after it;*

*So that when men come to be undeceiv'd, it is too late, the jest is over, and the tale has had its effect . . ."*

Jonathan Swift, *The Examiner*

By all accounts, the period leading up to the millennium was the most intense time for counterterror departments across the US government experienced up to that point.[1] It began with the NSA's Al Qaeda analysts apparently monitoring a call by Abu Zubaydah to Jordan in late November. Zubaydah told the man on the other end of the line, "The time for training is over." Presuming this meant a terror attack was imminent, Jordanian police were asked to arrest Abu Hoshar, the man Zubaydah had called, as well as fifteen others connected to him.[2]

Hoshar was a longtime Zubaydah associate, and at least one of the men arrested in the roundup had sworn the "bayat" to Bin Laden, essentially pledging an oath to do as Bin Laden wished. George Tenet contacted twenty foreign counterparts in order to spur on disruption against Al Qaeda plotters. "The threat could not be more real," he wrote to all overseas CIA personnel. "Do whatever is necessary to disrupt [Bin Laden]'s plans."

On December 14, 1999, a rather alert border guard caught a man named Ahmed Ressam smuggling explosives into the United States from Canada. At Port Angeles in Washington State, when pressed with questions, Ressam's demeanor aroused suspicion. Customs agents searched the trunk of his car. At first, they thought the one hundred pounds of explosives they found were drugs. After his arrest, Ressam would admit that Los Angeles International Airport was his intended target. Word also came that another planned target was Times Square on New Year's Eve.[3]

Given a clear sign of a domestic aspect to the attacks that Bin Laden associates were planning, President Clinton was said to have taken a personal interest. Efforts to disrupt Al Qaeda were coordinated by national security adviser Sandy Berger and by Richard Clarke.[4] FBI agents from John O'Neill's office began interrogations of suspects and overseas investigations. "Well, that was a very intense, intense period," remembers Rossini of the atmosphere inside CIA's Alec Station. "Working all the time. Never going home."

* * *

One week at the start of January 2000 has become the heart of an emotional he-said/she-said between the CIA and the FBI that has continued to the present day. That story began inside one of Fort Meade's jet-black buildings, where an NSA analyst we call "Betsy" held the ticket on the Yemen hub. In late December, she had received the translation of recent calls that had been made via Hada's house. The caller was a man named Walid bin Attash, nicknamed "Khallad," phoning from inside Afghanistan. The recipient was a resident in the house, Hada's son-in-law, Khalid al Mihdhar. Betsy learned that Mihdhar's and his friend Nawaf's presence were being requested at a meeting in Malaysia.[5]

Nawaf also called the house not long after to discuss the meeting. Another NSA analyst had been closely following calls between Nawaf and his brother Salem during this period. Betsy sent a communication to the FBI and Alec Station about the pending meeting. At the CIA, Cofer Black's CounterTerrorist Center and Rich Blee's Alec Station were keeping their ears to the ground amid the millennium scare, looking for any small signs of a plot, putting pertinent info into terror threat updates included in Clinton's daily briefings.[6] George Tenet made regular trips to the White House himself, likely with Rich Blee giving the updates.

Blee's deputy chief Tom Wilshere and staffer Michael Anne Casey, the ticket holders for Yemen, were no doubt keeping their attentions on reports from Al Qaeda's primary telephone switchboard.[7] Two days before New Year's, they received Betsy's NSA report, titled "Activities of Bin Laden

Associates."[8] From the document, we know at minimum that they knew a man named Khalid who was living at the monitored house received a call from a man in Afghanistan summoning him and two other men, Nawaf, in Pakistan, and another, Salem, to a meeting in Malaysia's capital, a terrorist hot spot, in the first week of January.

Mark Rossini remembers, "We were all just very curious about this summit in Malaysia. Why were these people going there?"

For his part, Blee gave regular briefings on the progress of the Malaysia meeting to his CIA bosses and to Clinton national security staff, including Clarke.[9] Casey, in collaboration with Wilshere, Bikowsky, and Matthews, began connecting with a worldwide network of CIA stations and friendly foreign intelligence services to coordinate the tracking of these individuals on their way to the meeting, as well as surveillance once they arrived.[10]

\* \* \*

A few days before the summit was to begin, Mihdhar took a flight from Yemen with a long layover in Dubai, United Arab Emirates. When he stepped out of his room at the Nihal Hotel for a bit, agents who had been waiting, presumably following a request from Michael Anne Casey, broke into his room and searched his things. Among them, they found his passport and photocopied it.[11]

The CIA station in the United Arab Emirates sent a copy of Mihdhar's passport to Alec Station and Riyadh Station in Saudi Arabia. It was included in a cable with the dramatic title: "Activities of Bin Ladin Associate Khalid Revealed." They had discovered a bombshell. Mihdhar possessed a multiple-entry visa to the United States, due to expire that April.[12] This was an incredible "get" by Alec Station.

Mihdhar would have to enter the United States within the next three months or his effort to acquire the visa would be fruitless. Clearly, if the CIA was willing to break into a hotel room to acquire his passport documents, they must have considered Khalid al Mihdhar and the meeting he was about to attend incredibly important.

Rossini reinforces the point, stating, "[T]hat was *the thing* going on at the time," conceding, "Yeah, there was a lot going on, but this was it; that was *the thing* going on at the time that was making us all nervous."

Jack Cloonan adds further emphasis, "We understood [from many interviews with Al Qaeda prisoners] the value Al Qaeda placed on getting someone into the United States or somebody with a US passport or visa. This was critical."

The morning following the arrival of the passport information, at 6:00 a.m., a second cable came into the CTC and Alec Station from the CIA Riyadh Station. Tom Wilshere was among the first to read it.[13]

Doug Miller arrived at work early that day, finding one of the two cables waiting for him as he turned on his computer. Within fifteen minutes of the arrival of the second cable, Miller began writing a warning to the FBI. His message was addressed to Miller's boss back at headquarters in DC. It was also addressed to Rossini's own home FBI office in New York, the domain of John O'Neill. The message described:

- *Mihdhar's travel to Malaysia*
- *Links between his home in Yemen and the US embassy bombings*
- *That photos of the Malaysia meeting had been taken and will be sent to FBI later*
- *Mihdhar held a multiple-entry visa for the US, where he planned to stay in New York for three months*

Miller requested that Alec Station receive feedback on any intelligence uncovered in the FBI's investigation. He attached the two CIA cables.[14]

"So the way it works over there," says Rossini, "is you write a communication, and then it goes into an electronic queue to be approved along the line to be released."

Normally the drafter, Doug Miller, would himself coordinate the communication in the computer system so that designated persons in charge of approving its release are notified. But in this case, without Miller notifying anyone, a person we now know to be Michael Anne Casey accessed his draft report—within less than an hour of his writing it,[15] as if she were on the lookout for it. Wilshere later acknowledged to investigators that this was not standard operating procedure.

About forty-five minutes after Casey read Miller's draft warning to the FBI, the manager from FBI headquarters, Ed Goetz, *also* accessed Miller's draft warning. The funny thing about this is that, at that time, Goetz had not yet opened the two CIA cables about Mihdhar's US visa. Two inspector general reports later mentioned that Goetz, as a deputy chief, had the authority himself to immediately release Miller's message for electronic dissemination.[16] However, as Rossini recounted—at least under Scheuer—Goetz *did not* have this authority, hence the screaming match that resulted in Scheuer's removal as chief of Alec Station. Whether he was ever given this authority is unclear, but the result is the same; he did not release Miller's warning.

Another four and a half hours passed. At 4:00 p.m., Casey reopened the draft message to add a now-infamous note for Miller: "Pls hold off for now per Wilshere."[17]

According to the Justice Department's investigation, which had the ability after the fact to see the precise moment each item was accessed by whom in the computer system, Tom Wilshere never opened Doug Miller's draft cable.[18] So how did he know to tell Casey to order the draft to be held off? It appears that she had been keeping her eyes open for any messages coming from the FBI detailees that morning. Once she saw Miller's cable, seemingly she went straight to Tom Wilshere to discuss it.

The FBI's Ed Goetz should also have been let in on the conversation, but "Eddie got colon cancer at the end of '99," explains Rossini. His medical condition caused his presence to be intermittent at Alec Station at the time, and perhaps for him to be distracted. He left his position there later that same week. "And who knows," continues Rossini, "what would have happened if Eddie had been in the office."

Two questions remain: What was the operational plan being executed by Alec Station managers in withholding Mihdhar's planned travel to the United States from FBI at that moment? On whose orders was this being done? "I'm cautious about saying it," John O'Neill's then-deputy Pat D'Amuro shared with us years later, "because you have to deal with the facts, but I had heard that Blee stopped it from coming over, that Blee and Wilshere had had the conversation and stopped it." D'Amuro wouldn't reveal his source on the Blee information.

On the same day that Doug Miller tried to warn the FBI about Mihdhar's visa, two more cables came into the CounterTerror Center and Alec Station, both discussing the Al Qaeda operator's passport, for a total of four. At 6:30 p.m., Tom Wilshere reread the first cable from Dubai and then read the second cable from Riyadh. A half hour later, Casey sent a lengthy message to several CIA stations around the world. It stated: "We need to continue efforts to identify these travelers and their activities . . . to determine if there is any true threat posed."

Casey then devoted an entire paragraph to Mihdhar, and that paragraph included a statement that, whether intentionally or not, investigators later determined had the effect of misleading the rest of her colleagues in the CIA. Critically, Casey's message asserted that a physical copy of Mihdhar's travel documents, including a US visa, *had* been copied and passed to the FBI for further investigation. When later asked by government investigators to name who had told her that a physical copy of Mihdhar's visa was passed, "[Casey] told the Team that she does not recall who in the FBI received the information or how it was passed."

At the same time, the CIA had an officer detailed to FBI headquarters in Washington. This officer, working for Cofer Black's CounterTerrorist Center, is known only as "Rob." What highlights this particular piece of the story as suspicious is that on the same evening that Casey was telling the CIA internally that the FBI had been made aware of Mihdhar's visa, Rob was at the FBI muddying the waters himself. That night, Rob updated an FBI supervisor about the ongoing Al Qaeda meeting in Malaysia. The supervisor did not know why Rob briefed him, since he was not Rob's designated point of contact. Further, this supervisor would later adamantly tell the Justice Department investigation that the Mihdhar visa was not mentioned in their conversation.

The next morning, Rob briefed a different FBI agent with details on Mihdhar's travel and the ongoing Malaysia summit. Again, the agent he briefed was not Rob's designated point of contact. Later, Rob was emailed by a CIA employee on behalf of an FBI colleague seeking an update on Mihdhar. Rob then began writing a series of emails explaining that he had already updated the FBI. The last email, which he conspicuously titled "Malaysia—For the Record," was cc'd to Tom Wilshere, Maggie Gillespie, and other unknowns at Alec Station. Rob wrote: "In case FBI starts to complain later . . . below is exactly what I briefed them on." The email mentions Mihdhar's transit through Dubai, his arrival in Kuala Lumpur, his activities in Malaysia—everything except his US visa.

The updates that Rob provided to FBI employees on Wednesday night and Thursday morning were then passed by those men upstairs to the seventh floor, called "Mahogany Row" by agents working there, where they were included in two briefings to the FBI director and top FBI officials. These are apparently the only two mentions of Malaysia and Mihdhar's travel ever found in FBI records. There are *no* mentions of his visa, which is the one fact that would have gotten the FBI involved in looking for and stopping him. An effective ruse had seemingly been run in which anyone at Alec Station or FBI counterterror who did not "need to know" was pushed out of the loop, while the appearance of propriety was generated in person and on paper.

\* \* \*

It had been two days since Miller drafted his message to FBI, and the information still had not moved. Without Ed Goetz there to help him resolve the problem, Mark Rossini says Miller turned to him. "Obviously me being the more senior agent, Doug comes to me," remembers Rossini. "'Hey, can you help me out here. I don't know why this thing isn't moving.'"

Rossini walked up to Michael Anne Casey's cubicle. "Hey, Doug's cable, what's going on? It's not going out the door? You gotta send it to the Bureau. It's not moving. What's happening?"

He recalls Casey's unhappy reaction to his approach, putting her hand on her hip and telling him, "Listen, it's not an FBI case. It's not an FBI matter. When we want the FBI to know, we'll let them know. And you're not going to say anything."[19] That heated conversation, if true, seems to connect the lie to her message sent throughout CIA only two days before, in which she wrote that the crucial info about the US visa *had* been shared with the FBI.

Despite the multiple-entry visa in Mihdhar's passport, despite the entire threat period they just went through the previous week, despite clear protocols sent to the staff the month prior reiterating policies for this exact type of matter, and despite the apprehension over Ahmad Ressam and his trunk load of explosives that had been heading for the Los Angeles airport, Casey insisted to Rossini that the next Al Qaeda attack would be in Malaysia.

Rossini did not believe Casey's assessment was reasonable at the time. "No, I didn't think it was a fair assessment, but that was her assessment. And it was like, 'Okay, if that's your posture, if that's your position—well, I don't agree with it, because the guy's got a visa to come to the US.' But that was the end of it."

The CIA's inspector general report was later tough on Rossini, writing, "He failed, however, to pick up on the New York angle, the US visas, or the potential travel to the United States."[20]

"I assumed at the time that [CIA] had a very good reason," explains Rossini. "I thought, 'you're a good American, you obviously have a handle on this, so I'll go along for the moment.' I figured they would do the right thing because it needed to be done. But never in my wildest dreams did I think they would keep it away forever. I never suspected they had an agenda."

* * *

In Kuala Lumpur, the CIA's local station had apparently asked their spy counterparts in the Malaysian government to surveil outside the condominium complex where the Al Qaeda meeting was taking place over several days. They reportedly recorded video of the terrorists the first day and secretly captured an unknown number of up-close photos of the men outside the building.[21] The day after Rossini was told that two of the attendees, Mihdhar and Hazmi, were not a matter for the FBI, the rare summit came to a close. Mihdhar, Hazmi, and the apparent leader, Khallad bin Attash, left others in Malaysia and flew to Bangkok.

When these three arrived, the CIA has maintained that their agents working from the Bangkok Station did not make it to the airport in time to track them as requested. The agents in the field apparently checked the hotels registered on the travelers' landing cards, but the men had not gone to those hotels. In the words of the Kean Commission, "The travelers disappeared into the streets of Bangkok."[22]

During their time in Thailand, Mihdhar and Hazmi stayed at the Washington Hotel.[23] The CIA officers might have run a standard check of the calls the men had been surveilled making from the pay phone outside the Kuala Lumpur condo building they had only just left. One source who saw some of the photos sent to Alec Station describes them as showing one or another of the then-missing terrorists at that pay phone. Those phone records would have revealed they had called the Washington Hotel. Man calls hotel in Bangkok. Man travels to Bangkok. Where is Man staying?

One contractor at the National Security Agency during that time, Tom Drake, reveals an allegation he claims to have learned years later. He says his NSA colleagues knew Mihdhar and Hazmi were staying in Bangkok "for the week before they arrived in the US."[24] He would not explain further. His statement implies that the terrorists were, in fact, lost for a short time, but the NSA's analysts who held this "ticket" were soon able to reestablish their whereabouts through electronic surveillance, perhaps simply checking the calls as described above. Drake calls it the "Rudyard Kipling elephant in the room."

Shortly thereafter, a foreign CIA station asked Rich Blee's team to pass a lead to the FBI's people overseas about "a possible family tie of al Mihdhar to an extremist in Yemen," likely Mihdhar's father-in-law Ahmed al Hada, owner of the surveilled Al Qaeda telephone hub. In response, an employee who appears to be Michael Anne Casey emailed her boss Tom Wilshere that the requesting station was "jumping the gun" on alerting the FBI's legal attaché. "FBI has been kept abreast of the situation," she asserted.[25]

That Thursday, after losing the terrorists, Bangkok Station sent a cable to Alec Station, "Efforts to Locate al Mihdhar." With Mihdhar and Hazmi officially lost anywhere in the world and the only lead being his US visa, FBI agent Doug Miller went over the head of his boss Casey, sending an email directly to Tom Wilshere. Attaching his earlier draft warning that had been blocked, Miller asked pointedly, "Is this a no-go, or should I remake it in some way?" There is no record of Wilshere having responded.[26]

The following day, Friday, Rich Blee gave George Tenet and Cofer Black a slide presentation.[27] This was his second briefing on the Malaysia surveillance operation since losing the two hijackers in Bangkok. Blee told his supervisors that officials were continuing to track the suspicious individuals who had now dispersed to various countries, directly contradicting the cable from Bangkok Station sent the previous day that stated that they could not find the terrorists.

On Saturday, Mihdhar and Hazmi, the first of what would become nineteen hijackers, arrived in the United States.[28] Once the two would-be hijackers were in the US, Rich Blee gave no further updates about the surveillance operation, as far as records indicate. The CIA's story to this day appears to be that from this point onward, George Tenet and Cofer Black never again remembered to follow up on any of this.

Jack Cloonan later called the Malaysia summit surveillance opportunity "as good as it gets . . . This is what you dream about." Standard procedure at the time would have been to put the known names of the summit attendees on a US terrorist watch list, so they could be discovered and tracked if any of them entered the country. This was also not done for over a year.

\* \* \*

The next month, the Malaysian Special Branch sent the CIA a videotape that they had made of Al Qaeda terrorists arriving at the summit in Kuala Lumpur.[29] It seemingly generated little interest. Also that February, a foreign government—most likely Thailand—offered to help the CIA search for missing Mihdhar in that country, but the agency turned the offer down, despite claiming they were in the middle of an investigation to "determine what the subject is up to."[30] The subject, Mihdhar, was living in San Diego, California.

Finally, on March 5, 2000, a Sunday, the CIA's Bangkok Station cabled Alec Station that travel records had been found indicating that Nawaf al Hazmi, suspected Al Qaeda operator, had flown with another person to Los Angeles seven weeks prior. The cable also noted that it was unknown if and when Mihdhar might have departed. This cable, which would cause the CIA so much scrutiny when discovered later by congressional investigators, was sent in response to a request from the Kuala Lumpur CIA station as to the whereabouts of Mihdhar,[31] so it should have been easy to assume that he was Hazmi's companion. They were, after all, sitting next to each other on the plane, and had purchased their plane tickets using their real names.

The CIA's Inspector General later clarified that "eight [Alec] Station officers opened" one of the March cables within a week of their arrival, while "another six officers" opened it at some point after. "Several of these fourteen officers were managers in [Alec Station]," meaning Blee, Wilshere, Bikowsky, or Matthews. The next day, March 6, another CIA station sent a cable that also went to Alec Station. The staff of this station noted that they had read about the travel of Mihdhar and Hazmi to the United States "with interest."[32]

"I can't explain why there was a 'hold off' to tell the Bureau," Rossini says, having given the matter a great deal of thought in the intervening years. "I can't explain that. And in particular when it was determined that they did go on to the US, that they did go on to America."

Asked if he remembered reading the messages reporting that Hazmi had arrived in America, the one the IG Report stated definitively that he had read, Rossini says his memory is "a little fuzzy." Regarding whether the CIA managers and staff read them, he felt more certain. "Well, I can't prove that they did or didn't, but my gut—and remember, you're talking about the people who have the ticket on the Yemen cell—of course they would have to know," he exclaimed. "It's their ticket. It's their case."

And the station chief, Rich Blee? Might he have been in a "management bubble," steering clear of the details? "No, it's impossible," stated Rossini emphatically. "No, no, no, absolutely not. Everything there is computer driven. Everything is there, seen by everybody. Everything comes in. That computer system is unique to anything I've ever seen in my life. As far as speed, ability, access."

Rossini explained that the way the CIA's proprietary Hercules cable system was then set up, incoming cables would have been difficult for Cofer Black or Rich Blee to miss. "It [was] right there in your face. You [could not] miss it. Right there in your face. That's the whole thing. And particularly something of such importance. George [Tenet], different story. George encouraged people to work beneath him and do what ya gotta do. But it would be impossible for Blee to say he didn't know about this. It would be impossible for Cofer to say he didn't know about it."

\* \* \*

Not long after the terrorists' arrival in the United States, Cofer Black moved Alec Station out of the OHB, placing them in a new office down the hall from his own, three floors belowground inside the sleeker New Headquarters Building. There, the entirety of the floor was home to Black's CounterTerrorist Center. The Al Qaeda fighters, now numbering around fifty, worked in open cubicles inside the agency's former computer strong room, no windows, only rows of fluorescents. Their door was marked by a small sign reading 1W01, though most simply called it what it was, "the Vault."[33]

With the move came promotions for nearly everyone. New management titles were created for Alfreda Bikowsky and Jen Matthews, which came with new responsibilities, staff, and almost certainly bumps in their paychecks. Sources claim Bikowsky was made chief of operations. Some in the DO grew angry, asking of Bikowsky, "How can you make an analyst [from the DI] a chief within Operations division?"[34]

Matthews, who did have some brief field spy training in the DO, was made chief for targeting.[35] "Jennifer Matthews didn't do recruiting," explains career field spy Bob Baer about the skepticism over her position. "She didn't go track people down and recruit them. She's an analyst. She looks at flat-screen TVs, and she processes information and does PowerPoints and reports. [These top analysts] get in [their] chauffeur-driven vehicle and are taken from one Washington meeting to another. I don't think [some of these analysts] would have a clue how to recruit somebody."[36]

"Jen was out of her element in CTC," agrees John Kiriakou begrudgingly. "She just wasn't cut out for that job. But it was [Bikowsky] who brought her in because they were friends. It was to the detriment of the organization."

Rich Blee moved down the hall into one of the CTC's inner offices, taking a door not far from Cofer Black's.[37] He would run a larger department, overseeing not only Alec Station but all offices countering Sunni extremists. Tom Wilshere may have noticed when he was passed over for Alec's open chief position, just as he had been when Blee took the job.

"I feel kind of bad saying this," says CIA officer John Kiriakou, "but Wilshere was one of those guys who you could tell had kind of topped out at GS-15." He remained deputy in the office, while Black and Blee brought in an outsider, Hendrik Van Der Meulen, as the station's third chief.[38]

Why he was chosen and many of his biographical details remain a mystery, though the decision may have signaled an intention to expand the use of Alec's renditions program. Van Der Meulen had been station chief in Jordan, and the Jordanian government were among the very few in the world that had agreed to accept the CIA's kidnappees.[39]

* * *

After their arrival in Los Angeles, Mihdhar and Hazmi would seem to have struck up an immediate friendship with a fellow Saudi living on the West Coast. They soon moved to San Diego to live near him, renting an apartment in his building.[40]

For the first half of the year, until Mihdhar again left the country, he repeatedly called his wife and father-in-law Ahmed al Hada in Yemen at the monitored house. Analyst "Betsy" received a notification on her computer at Fort Meade, a "ping," each time the domestic terrorist called the communications hub she was charged with monitoring.[41] It would later be reported that "NSA intercepted and transcribed seven calls from al Mihdhar to the Al Qaeda switchboard."[42]

"The technology itself will tell you what number is coming into a switch-board," says Tom Drake. He claims Betsy understood that US-based persons were calling the Yemen house. "NSA knew it was happening and actually had the [US] number," he continued. "Obviously any and all numbers that were connected to the Yemeni safe house would be *known*. You're an analyst in the CounterTerror Shop. A house you are monitoring calls the US. As an analyst, you can see the domestic phone number. But you cannot 'put it on copy' because it relates to a US person. Time to get a FISA warrant."

Another NSA analyst, who we call "Bob," later told Drake that he had made a request to the Chop Chain for a FISA warrant into this matter.[43] The "Chop Chain" was made up of director Michael Hayden's deputies and top executives at this point. Bob provided the probable-cause information; however, getting that warrant to listen in on the US-based portion of the calls—the Mihdhar part—would require the involvement of the FBI.

Drake explains, "NSA doesn't go to the secret court. [The] FBI has to go to the secret court because [the] FBI is [in charge of] domestic. They go to the court and make the case. NSA's entire role is summarized as follows: 'Here's the number. Put it on copy.'"

Kirk Wiebe, who was serving as a business manager and analyst inside the NSA's SIGINT Automation Research Center (SARC), later pointed out, "No warrant would have been required had Director [Michael] Hayden simply made use of the authorities available to him via Executive Order 12333, Part II, Section 2.3C, by which he could have obtained approval [directly] from the attorney general to target all communications with the safe house in Yemen, regardless of origination or destination. It remains unclear as to why this was not done."[44]

Drake cannot say for certain that a FISA warrant to listen in on Mihdhar and Hazmi in San Diego was not obtained, nor that Hayden did not get authority to do so from Clinton's attorney general. He only knows that the analysts in the counterterror and Al Qaeda "shops" were never allowed to listen to the calls. They believed their request had been denied. They were aware, however, each time Mihdhar placed a call to Yemen—and by extension so were the NSA managers who made up the Chop Chain—recognizing that people inside America were placing calls to the same Al Qaeda house involved in orchestrating the embassy bombings.

On June 10, 2000, Khalid Mihdhar left his friend Hazmi behind in San Diego, flying first to Germany and then back to his wife at the Hada house in Yemen.[45] From then onward, the NSA—and the CIA's Alec Station via their bugs and satellite station—should have been able to follow his conversations from the other angle, making calls *out*.

\* \* \*

On October 12, 2000, at 11:22 a.m. local time, a small boat with two men floated up to the Navy guided-missile destroyer warship named the USS *Cole*, which was refueling in the harbor in the city of Aden. Within moments, the small skiff exploded, blasting a hole in the side of the vessel.

John O'Neill was charged with running the investigation for the FBI, but due to disputes with the US ambassador to Yemen, he was soon barred reentry into the country. His protégé, Ali Soufan, became the de facto on-the-ground lead investigator.

Soufan was a Lebanese-born American citizen recruited into the FBI only three years prior by John O'Neill, who recognized the need for investigators fluent in Arabic. Once in Yemen, Soufan pounded the pavement, knocking on doors, stopping pedestrians, and checking rental offices before finding an apartment overlooking the harbor that had been used for the attack. Neighbors identified a man who had frequented the apartment, Fahad Al Quso, a known local member of Al Qaeda. Soufan visited Quso's family to question them. Quso soon turned himself in to local authorities.

Quso told Soufan a story. In December 1999, he had been asked by a peg-legged man named Khallad to bring $36,000 to Singapore during the first week of 2000. Soufan had already been told by Yemeni authorities that someone named Khallad was believed to be "the main guy" behind the *Cole* attack. Quso told Soufan that Khallad had flown from Kuala Lumpur to collect the money from Quso after he had been waylaid in Bangkok, Thailand.

Wondering what Khallad had been up to in Malaysia in January 2000, Soufan's team sent an official, high-level request to the CIA to see if they knew anything about this. Soufan sent this request for information from the FBI director's office to the CIA director's office. The message included phone numbers connected to Quso and Khallad, and no doubt, this request was passed to Alec Station.[46]

Soon after, the CIA responded officially from George Tenet's office to the FBI director's office stating they did not know anything about Al Qaeda gatherings in Malaysia. They suggested that the FBI ask the NSA, but that agency had no answer for Soufan.[47] This is a strange reply, as the FBI had been made aware of the Malaysia summit as it occurred, via "Rob's" awkward and misplaced briefings. Stranger still, FBI headquarters themselves should have been able to inform Soufan of this, as they too had been made aware of the Malaysia meeting.

Soufan's official request for information put Rich Blee, Tom Wilshere, Alfreda Bikowsky, and Jen Matthews in a very objectionable position. If they responded honestly, questions would soon arise as to when they had learned about Mihdhar and Hazmi and why they had not passed the information to FBI about two men who could now be connected to the USS *Cole* bombing plot via their connection to Attash. Their withholding—a mere breach of protocol in early 2000—might, by late 2000, have been used to argue that they held culpability in the death of seventeen US servicemen. The actions by managers of Alec Station from here onward appear to indicate they decided to double down, willfully withholding information from FBI analysts and outright lying to FBI investigators.

\* \* \*

"Omar" thought he wanted to be a jihadi, but after actually spending time with Al Qaeda, he decided he did not much care for them. He instead chose to help the Americans. The DEA had discovered him and tried to turn him over to the CIA, but the agency showed little interest. Instead, it was arranged that Omar would meet with FBI agents in Pakistan; however, none of the agents spoke any of the languages Omar was fluent in. The FBI contacted the CIA for help, and it was determined that Omar could be a joint source, and that the information he divulged would be shared between both agencies.[48]

Once the interviews of Omar began in mid-2000, he told FBI personnel that there was a man named Khallad who was a high-ranking member of Al Qaeda. He said that Khallad had been involved in the embassy bombings in Africa. Roughly a year later, the New York field office of the FBI was investigating the *Cole* bombing and received from the Yemeni government photographs of several of the attack's plotters, including a picture of a man named Khallad. According to the Yemenis, Khallad was the mastermind of the *Cole* attack. Wondering if the Khallad spoken of by Omar was the same man that the Yemenis were now claiming was involved in the *Cole* bombing, the FBI decided to present the photo to Omar for identification.

"Chris," from the CIA's Pakistan station, entered the secure room in Islamabad where Omar waited as an FBI agent named Michael Dorris was already seated inside. Chris pulled out the photo. Omar looked it over. Yes, the image was of Khallad, the high-level Al Qaeda member he knew.

Chris sent a debriefing report to Alec and other CIA stations stating that Omar had identified Khallad three times during their meeting. Ali Soufan, who was in Yemen with the FBI team investigating the *Cole* attack, also received the info. Inside Alec Station, speculation began. They quickly developed a working theory that this Khallad, the front-running suspect for having been mastermind of the *Cole* bombing, was actually Khalid al Mihdhar. Instead of discussing the matter with the FBI and military investigators working the *Cole* case, Alec Station sent a reply to Chris with a surveillance photograph that had been taken at the Malaysia summit, where they knew Mihdhar had been present. He was instructed to show Omar that photo as well.

In January of 2001, Chris again entered the secure room in Pakistan. As before, the FBI agent Michael Dorris was seated inside. Things transpired as usual until Dorris left the room for reasons unknown. Once gone, Chris pulled out some photographs. The first photo Chris handed to Omar showed two men, one of whom Omar identified as *his* Khallad, the one he had previously briefed them about.

"How certain are you?" Chris asked.

"Ninety percent," Omar replied. Chris sent the identification back to Alec Station. Unfortunately, Omar was mistaken. No one knew it, but he had misidentified Nawaf al Hazmi in the photo as *his* Khallad. The second photo presented to Omar featured a third, solitary man. This was a photograph of Khalid al Mihdhar, but Omar didn't recognize him.[49]

Omar's inability to identify Mihdhar was a bit of a distraction. At best, the gist of this episode, as neatly summarized by a later report, was that the "CIA recognized this was significant because it meant that the other attendees, including Mihdhar and Hazmi, had been in contact with key planners of the *Cole* attack for Bin Laden's network."[50]

However, it does not stop there. To be sure, the whole situation is a bit confusing. The CIA already had Mihdhar's photograph from his passport, which they obtained as he traveled through Dubai. The CIA also had photographs taken of the terrorists gathered in Malaysia, including a photograph of Mihdhar. They also possessed the videotape of the summit attendees. Could they not themselves match the face in the passport photo to the face in the surveillance photo? Further, the CIA had the photo of Khallad provided by the Yemenis, as the FBI had dutifully given it to them. Could they not see that the Khallad the Yemenis said was behind the *Cole* attack was not the same man as Mihdhar, and that these two clearly different men had met at the terror summit?

Why show pictures of Khallad and Khalid al Mihdhar to Omar, and why do it with FBI agent Michael Dorris absent? Was the CIA's greater concern that this joint source might mention Khalid al Mihdhar to the FBI when their agents, who could speak his language, came to interview him? Ali Soufan would later tell us he felt this incident was one of the most overlooked, damning tales of the pre–war on terror story.

Later that month, Michael Dorris wrote a lengthy debriefing report on the interviews of Omar, based solely on the CIA cables provided to him by CIA's Chris. Again, Dorris did not speak Omar's language, and relied on the information and translations he received from Chris. Dorris's report included no mention of the Malaysia photographs, and no mention of the name Khalid al Mihdhar. By contrast, Chris's internal cables to Alec Station, the "ops traffic," expressly stated that Khalid al Mihdhar had been identified by Omar as present in the photos, and therefore present at the Kuala Lumpur meeting. This meeting was beginning to be recognized as *Cole* planner Khallad bin Attash's operational kickoff for that attack.[51]

That February, Soufan made a special trip out of Yemen to Pakistan for the sole purpose of interviewing Omar. Showing him the photo of the *Cole* mastermind as provided by the Yemenis, Omar identified him as the peg-legged Khallad he had spoken about. Not knowing what more to ask, Soufan was not able to gain the depth of insight the CIA had into who Khallad was and how he was connected to the greater Al Qaeda network. He certainly did not know that Khallad, a prime suspect in his ongoing investigation, was hanging out with operatives with US visas.

\* \* \*

After the *Cole* attack, the NSA's technical leader for intelligence, Bill Binney, felt an urgency to take on the issue of terrorism with ThinThread, an innovative program he had designed. He walked up to the employees of the NSA CounterTerror Shop and asked, "What sites do you have that produce any meaningful information for you to analyze the terrorism targets around the world?" In NSA speak, "sites" are locations where the NSA has infrastructure to collect for signals espionage. The team of analysts provided a list of their key eighteen sites.[52]

Binney looked like a junior high math teacher, a kind of wry wisdom in his eyes, balding, with short black-gray hair and a smile that seemed to convey trustworthiness. Since beginning as a Russia specialist in 1970, he had become a technical director, then one of *the* technical directors.[53] These titles told only part of the story of Bill Binney. He was known by some to be the most accurate, astute, and capable analyst the NSA had, "the best traffic analyst, bar none," in the words of one colleague.[54] He had the mind of a classic code cracker.[55]

After predicting three startling events: the Tet Offensive in Vietnam in 1968, the Yom Kippur invasion in 1973, and the Soviet invasion of Afghanistan in 1989—the ultimate origin story of the problem now before him—his specialty had become determining reliable warning indicators of impending actions by foreign adversaries. He had boiled this down to a science, relying on only five intelligence indicators he found to be reliable again and again.

Collection in the digital age had greatly increased the information that analysts had at their disposal. Areas for foreign targeting now included people's downloads, what websites they visited, and what emails they sent, but many other outside-the-box sources of information were emerging: GPS, cell phones, EZ passes at toll booths, credit cards at stores, and on and on. It was a wealth of data, if it could be properly utilized. "Much like you use a Google query," Binney explained, "you get back thousands and thousands of returns. There's a high probability you are not going to get through it all in a given day." He realized the analysts were drowning in meaningless data. They had a volume problem to solve, and Bill Binney felt he was the man to do it.

Binney's trick was to use mathematics to approach human behavior, which he found to be "extremely patterned," and treat what he was looking at as "systems" that could be analyzed. Often, the breaks in the pattern were the most telling. Using this approach, Binney's ThinThread had solved the data deluge problem that was concerning Congress. "An analyst was able to do one simple query on participants on a targeted activity," Wiebe later wrote, "unit[ing] data associated with terrorists/criminals from all databases . . . and get access to all related content, be it from computer, phone, or pager."

Beyond saving hours of analysts' time each day, Binney also believed he had a better way to find terrorists. His epiphany had come when he recognized that the terrorists' activities existed, like everyone else's, inside the "ballooning communications network worldwide." He had been wrestling with how best to extract the terrorists' activities from within the larger stream.

One day, it occurred to him that for many years the NSA's work had largely focused on finding ways to monitor foreign telephones of interest. He realized they were looking in the wrong place. The best answers were not in the particulars of any conversation. They were in the relationships between people speaking. Seven years before Facebook and nine before Twitter, he recognized everything was about social networks.

Throughout the year 2000, Binney had pulled together analysts and techies from NSA headquarters and sites around the world for a daunting, visionary task, telling them, "We're going to graph the relationships [between two and a half billion phones] of everyone in the world." He also realized that much of the telephone data would need to be collected at "tap points" that included both foreign and American traffic. Binney devised a way to include privacy protections in ThinThread for the American public, calling it "the FISA filtering tool," removing any citizen or party inside the United States.

"Data on US citizens could be decrypted only if a judge approved it after a finding that there was probable cause to believe that the target was connected with terrorism or other crimes," later wrote Wiebe, adding that "stor[ing] such data in encrypted format rather than allow[ing] that raw information to remain vulnerable to unauthorized parties in unencrypted form . . . was also considerably cheaper, easier, and more secure. . . ."

Now armed with the list of the top eighteen counterterror sites, Binney sought permission from the NSA executives to finally deploy his ThinThread the first of the New Year, 2001. He went to the office of Maureen Baginski. Inexplicably, the answer passed back by Baginski was "No."

A thin, forty-six-year-old brunette in a suit, her medium-length hair kept in a perm, Baginski's intelligence, professionalism, and friendly smile had helped her a great deal. As a civilian, she had steadily climbed the chain in a little over twenty years, from an "entry level" Russian language instructor all the way to the new position as head of SIGINT. She would essentially become the NSA's number three, such was the growing importance of that division, reporting to Michael Hayden's new deputy Bill Black.[56] Black and Baginski, along with her analysis and reports division manager, Chris Inglis, were all also on the Chop Chain.[57]

Binney was an old hat at the politics of his agency, and he thought he knew what was going on. The SARC team had once struggled to figure out why their project could never seem to get any traction when it solved so many problems. They had eventually come to believe they were pissing off the NSA director. Binney turned to his greatest advocate in Congress, a staffer on the House intelligence committee.

Diane Roark had become terribly worried in 1997 when she had gotten "the NSA account" as a congressional staffer and discovered the agency, in her opinion, woefully unprepared for the needs of the digital age. She had secured a two-million-dollar budget for something she felt had promise, Bill Binney's NSA start-up, the Signals Intelligence Automation Research Center, SARC.[58]

Seeing that the NSA was drowning in information, Binney designed ThinThread to address the problem, but after first arriving, Michael Hayden sought to be the one to provide solutions to Congress's concerns. He had created the NSA Transformation Office. During the previous spring, Binney and his colleagues had taken note when "Hayden had announced 'TrailBlazer' to great fanfare . . . opening the door wider to the private sector [that would bid to develop it]."[59]

Binney's operational ThinThread, they understood in that moment, was in direct competition with Hayden's theoretical TrailBlazer concept. Binney crunched the numbers for Congress and found they could upgrade ThinThread to cover the entire world, and it would require only 300 million dollars. Diane Roark noticed that Hayden's program promised to do similar things, eventually, but would require multiple billions of dollars, and the use of outside contractors to make it happen. The rumor on the intelligence committees became that Binney had "a cheap TrailBlazer."[60]

"People thought Hayden was going to bring in a lot of outsiders, but he wasn't actually an outsider," says Tom Drake, who believes Hayden's time as head of the Air Force's intelligence had left him a well-connected inside player. "So they were shocked when he brought in Bill Black [as his number two]." Baginski's boss Bill Black had been there, with a few gaps, going back to 1959.[61]

Bill Binney felt his suspicions confirmed after walking through the door of his new direct report, a man brought in by Bill Black. "I do not want you briefing ThinThread to anybody again," Sam Vizner told him. Vizner had been stolen from his position as vice president of a private consortium, the Science Applications International Corporation, called SAIC, made up mostly of retired NSA managers. Binney also knew that in Bill Black's short absence from the NSA, he too had worked as an executive at SAIC. Further, he suspected the consortium was a contender to develop TrailBlazer.[62]

After Binney explained the situation, Diane Roark saw the SARC team called before the House committee for what was meant to be a private briefing. Uninvited, Hayden's entire NSA TrailBlazer team showed up. Binney and key members of his SARC team were called into Hayden's office immediately after. Without giving them a chance to speak, he berated them, then fired off a message throughout the NSA, writing that "individuals, in a session with our congressional overseers, took a position in direct opposition to one that we had corporately decided to follow . . . Actions contrary to our decisions will have a serious adverse effect on our efforts to transform NSA, and I cannot tolerate them."[63]

The SARC staff was being reprimanded for giving the best information to the people's representatives, at the best price. A group called the Red Team, "bringing the best of corporate America to bear at the NSA" as part of Al Gore's Reinventing Government program, conducted their own study of TrailBlazer. "That fall," later wrote SARC leader Kirk Wiebe, "an NSA Red Team predicted that TrailBlazer would fail unless major changes were made to the program. Hayden, however, ignored the Red Team report, and none of the Red Team recommendations saw the light of day."[64]

The SARC team describes it as "a case study in how the drive for big money and the power can squander big taxpayer bucks, chip away at our constitutional protections and, more importantly . . . play a crucial role in the worst intelligence failure since Pearl Harbor."

It was about this time that an ad went out for a new position being created at the NSA, a "senior change leader" who would report to Maureen Baginski. One hundred and thirty-five applicants responded. A contractor who had worked on the Red Team, Tom Drake, got the position. He was to report for work the second week of September.[65]

* * *

Tom Wilshere had reason to be optimistic about his new position. In the spring of 2001 he was sent to FBI headquarters to serve as the Bureau's new chief liaison to the intelligence community, working directly for Michael Rolince, the head of the terrorism section. Just as Mark Rossini and Doug Miller had been tasked to work at the CIA, Wilshere was now tasked to work at the FBI.[66]

To Doug Miller, Wilshere may have seemed an ironic choice for that particular position, given his history of *blocking* information from the CIA to the FBI. Miller's own warning to the FBI about Mihdhar was still waiting in the CIA queue for Wilshere's reply. Among the message's recipients was the same FBI headquarters where Wilshere would now be working. On the other hand, Wilshere had gained a good reputation as a team player with law enforcement in the 1990s, during Hezbollah investigations.[67] Headquarters leadership embraced him. Wilshere and his FBI direct report Michael Rolince would grow close.[68]

On May 15, working from the FBI, Wilshere sent a message to Clark Shannon, the CTC employee tasked with writing the CIA's internal report on what was known about the USS *Cole* attack. Wilshere asked to be sent the photos of the Malaysia meeting.[69] The same day, Wilshere and an unknown Alec Station branch chief, likely Matthews or Bikowsky, retrieved two cables from early 2000.[70] They were staring straight at communications explaining that Mihdhar held a visa to travel to the United States. To be sure, Mihdhar was the same man who was known to them to be an associate of the mastermind behind the *Cole* bombing and a player in the embassy bombings; known as the son-in-law of the Bin Laden comrade-in-arms operating the Al Qaeda switchboard; and known to have attended a summit of terrorist plotters. To boot, the cables stated his one-time travel partner Nawaf al Hazmi had flown to Los Angeles, and there was no reason to believe he ever left. Despite what they knew, and then refreshing their memories, they reported nothing to anyone outside of the CIA.

Back and forth came the messages between Wilshere and Shannon. Described as a "lengthy exchange to find out what the Mihdhar cables meant," Wilshere noted to Shannon that Mihdhar traveled to Malaysia and was connected to Hazmi. He also pointed out that Fahad al Quso, the man in Yemeni custody who was being regularly interrogated by FBI investigators Ali Soufan and Bob McFadden, had traveled to Bangkok, and that Mihdhar had traveled there shortly after.

"Something bad is definitely up," he wrote.

Shannon replied, "My head is spinning over this East Asia travel. Do you know if anyone in Alec or FBI mapped this?"

"Key travel still needs to be mapped," replied Wilshere.[71]

Wilshere headed down the hall to the office of Dina Corsi. He informed her that his office at the CIA was aware of travel by *Cole* conspirators to Malaysia and that they had photos of them. Either on her own or with help from Wilshere, Corsi found herself strongly under the impression that this information was solely to be shared with the *intelligence* side of the FBI, not the criminal investigative agents like Soufan working the prosecutable *Cole* case.[72]

Wilshere sent another email to Shannon, writing, "The reason (aside from trying to find a photo of the second *Cole* bomber) I'm interested is because Khalid al Mihdhar's two companions also were couriers of a sort, who traveled between Bangkok and Los Angeles at the same time (Hazmi and Salah)."[73] Salah was the name under which the peg-legged Attash traveled during the Malaysian meeting.

Wilshere continued, "Dina sounds really interested in comparing notes in a small forum expert to expert so both sides can shake this thing and see what gaps are common."

\* \* \*

The *Cole* investigators in Yemen caught word of "a meeting of great mystery" that occurred between FBI investigators and CIA reps from CTC.[74] When he arrived back at the New York office, Ali Soufan was filled in on the events concerning the strange and heated meeting that had occurred with CIA counterterror. Steve Bongardt, Soufan's top assistant in investigating the *Cole* bombing, told him his instinct was that the CIA was "withholding some information that would be of great value to the case."

The meeting in question occurred on June 11, 2001. It had been arranged by Dina Corsi at FBI headquarters with the intention of bringing together counterterror officers from the CIA and FBI agents who were currently investigating the *Cole* case. Held at the FBI office in lower Manhattan, the meeting was, according to Corsi, supposed to "address unresolved issues and produce additional leads or other activities."[75] Mark Rossini heard word about it within Alec Station not long before, and he offered to join. After all, New York was his home office, and he *was* a go-between for relations between Alec and the New York FBI. He was told his presence would not be necessary.[76]

Strangely, Tom Wilshere was not present, despite calling for the get-together. It appears that his in-person discussions with Corsi as well as his email correspondence with Shannon were an impetus for the dialogue. Despite the stated goal of sharing information, what unfolded was an apparent "fishing expedition" by the CIA to find out just what the *Cole* investigators knew.

The Department of Justice OIG report describes the scene: "Toward the end of the meeting, [Corsi] produced the three Kuala Lumpur surveillance photographs and asked the agents if they recognized [Fahad al Quso] in any of [them]."

Steve Bongardt studied the photos and said he did not see Quso in any of them. He followed with a series of questions that would seem reasonable. Bongardt asked, "Who are these guys? Why are you showing these pictures to us? Where were they taken? Are there other pictures? What is their connection to the *Cole*?" The majority of his questions were rebuffed. Bongardt was told that due to restrictions concerning the passing of information between intelligence and law enforcement, he could be told nothing.[77]

Corsi trotted out the infamous "wall" that had caused so many agents frustration since Clinton's attorney general Janet Reno had instituted the policy, creating a divided FBI by claiming intelligence-related agents and prosecution-building agents could not share info. The idea was that this "wall" would allow greater sharing from agencies like CIA, who would not have to worry about their sources being exposed in court. There are several reasons why this line of reasoning was not applicable in this June meeting, the least of which was that Bongardt *was* a designated intelligence agent. When he was stonewalled by Corsi and the CIA staff, the tone turned angry.

The New York FBI team knew that there must have been some reason they, the *Cole* investigators, had been called to this meeting and presented these photographs. It must have implied that somehow the people in the photographs were connected to their investigation. They were, of course, right.

Oddly enough, the CIA, at least theoretically, believed one of the men pictured may have been Khallad, as Omar had identified Nawaf Hazmi as such. Khallad *was* in fact an attendee of the Malaysia summit, regardless of Omar's misidentification of him. As Khallad was believed to have been the mastermind of the *Cole* attack, the agents from Alec Station would have had every reason to answer all of Bongardt's questions. The men from the Malaysia meeting were no longer only relevant to intelligence gathering, but were suspected of involvement in a crime.

The meeting devolved into a shouting match, and with that, Corsi finally revealed the name of the man in the solo photograph, Khalid al Mihdhar. Shannon also offered that Mihdhar was traveling on a Saudi passport, but Bongardt was given nothing else. He was given no birth date, definitely not the US visa, nothing. The entire exchange would later lead Bongardt to conclude that the whole point of the meeting was to determine if he and his FBI team knew who Khalid al Mihdhar was.[78] This echoes the earlier scenario in which these same photos were presented to Omar when an FBI agent was not present. Was the CIA running spy games on FBI investigators with the unwitting help of a confused analyst from FBI headquarters, Dina Corsi?

Bongardt would continue to press Corsi for weeks—and months—to try to convince her to get him information about Mihdhar and the men in the photographs. For months upon months, she would deny him.

Two days after this contentious meeting, Khalid al Mihdhar successfully renewed his US visa.

# 5

# IT ALL FALLS APART

*"The belief in a supernatural source of evil is not necessary;*
*Men alone are quite capable of every wickedness."*

Joseph Conrad

Inside the CIA, starting in early summer of 2001, CounterTerror staff, managers, and even the director were worried that something terrible was coming. They were even more concerned than they had been during the millennium period.[1] Apparently, unbeknownst to them, Al Qaeda had pushed back the date of their impending attack from July 4 to September 11. However, warning signs abounded that convinced the counterterror operators that something big was imminent.

Though Mihdhar had lived at the primary Al Qaeda hub, had been monitored traveling to a terrorist summit, and was actively being discussed with concern inside Alec Station, he had been issued a visa and landed at JFK Airport aboard Saudi Airlines Flight 53 on July 4. The address listed on his visa was, in what he must have thought a cute touch, the Marriott Hotel inside the World Trade Center.[2] Mihdhar reunited with his friend Nawaf al Hazmi, who had by then moved from California to New Jersey, living with would-be hijacker Hani Hanjour.[3]

On July 5, Wilshere fired off an email to "managers at Alec Station," likely both Alfreda Bikowsky and Jen Matthews, regarding "how bad things look in Malaysia." He was suggesting that the Malaysia summit of early 2000 was seemingly connected to the recent threat spike. "A massively bad infrastructure [is] being readily completed with just one purpose in mind," and he recommended that they reexamine all of their information about the summit in Kuala Lumpur.[4]

Five days later, the president's national security adviser Condoleezza Rice received a frantic phone call from George Tenet. He was en route with Cofer Black and Rich Blee to her office. It was claimed to be the first and only time he would come by unannounced. The whole thing had an air of theatrics, but perhaps well-intentioned theatrics. Tenet later wrote that his surprise visit was meant to get Rice—and, by extension, the Bush White House—stirred up enough to take serious defensive action against a coming terror event by Al Qaeda. If Tenet's claim is true, that was the day he and his counterterror team delivered to Rice their "starkest warning," yet they would leave feeling that she simply did not get it.

Richard Clarke was present at this meeting. A lot of information was presented, including information apparently gleaned from intercepts of the Yemen Hub. Rich Blee stated that multiple, simultaneous attacks within the United States were possible, and that they would be designed to inflict mass casualties. Clarke insists that during this spontaneous meeting there was no mention of Mihdhar and his US visa, and no mention of Hazmi and his travel to the United States.[5]

Boiling it down, Clarke would later tell us, "Here they are, in the NSC adviser's office, trying to make their best case possible for action. But, in trying to make this persuasive case, they never once mentioned that already two Al Qaeda terrorists, known to be involved in the Kuala Lumpur planning session, had entered the United States. Why don't you trot out what is the most persuasive piece of evidence you've got? *These guys are already in the country.* They are not here to look at the Grand Canyon. The people who were doing that briefing knew that fact, and didn't trot it out. So you ask yourself, why not?"

Three days later, Wilshere wrote to a Targeting Branch Chief, probably Jen Matthews, copying someone else in CTC management on the message. "Okay, this is important," he started. Wilshere had gone back through old cables and found Omar's identification of *Cole* attack mastermind Khallad bin Attash as being present at the Malaysia meeting. He again pushed Alec Station to examine the matter more closely. In the email, he called Khallad "a major league killer" and pointed out that he was "in Malaysia meeting with Khalid al Mihdhar."[6] Notice, in saying this he makes clear that there was no more speculation that Khallad and Khalid were the same man.

That day, the Targeting Branch Chief noted that she had already assigned one of the FBI detailees, likely Maggie Gillespie, to the task of looking through the Malaysia cable traffic, and Wilshere was sent a response to that effect. For the first time since he himself blocked passage of info about Mihdhar's US visa, Wilshere made a request: "Can this info be sent via official cable to the FBI?"

Such a question leads one to understand that Wilshere, at this point, understood that the information about Mihdhar's visa had never been passed to the FBI. Further, though Wilshere's name had been invoked in preventing Doug Miller's warning from being passed to the FBI, Wilshere was seemingly acting on orders from a higher-up, as he is here requesting permission to pass the information.

Ten more days passed. Reminiscent of the treatment Doug Miller and Mark Rossini had once received, Wilshere waited and waited at FBI headquarters for a serious response from Alec Station to his inquiry. He again emailed the person we believe to be Jen Matthews, also likely including Alfreda Bikowsky and Hendrik Van Der Meulen, "When the next big op is carried out by [Bin Laden's] hardcore cadre, Khallad will be at or near the top of the command food chain—and probably nowhere near either the attack site or Afghanistan."

Wilshere gives the appearance of begging the recipient at Alec Station to recognize that matters have reached an alarming point at which passage to the FBI has become a necessity. He continued, "That makes people who are available and who have direct access to [Khallad] of very high interest. Khalid Mihdhar should be very high interest anyway, given his connection to [redacted]." (The redaction is a likely reference to the Yemen hub, or perhaps the *Cole* or embassy attacks.)

The response to Wilshere is telling. According to the Inspector General, in a note presumably written by Matthews to her station chief Van Der Meulen, she "vent[s] about the request," complaining that, "We are well aware that Khallad is an important lead. But he is no more important than any of the other Yemen targets who we know were part of the *Cole* bombing." She stated she respected Wilshere "as much as anyone but this is ridiculous. I'm sick of getting second-guessed by him and having him send you notes about his pet theories."[7]

\* \* \*

Like dominoes falling, events started cascading on top of each other throughout the month of August 2001. In hindsight, it was a poorly chosen time for the president and the CIA director to each disappear on vacations. George W. Bush took a monthlong break starting on August 3, traveling to his property in Texas.

At the president's ranch in Crawford, his CIA briefer Mike Morrell presented him the soon-to-be-infamous August 6 presidential daily briefing entitled "Bin Laden Determined to Strike in US." The briefing did not mention Mihdhar or Hazmi or any connected intelligence.

Bush's response to Morrell was, "Okay, you've covered your ass."[8] Was Bush just being Bush? Was he on to something? Or did he feel that he was constantly being given confusing or non-actionable intelligence? After all, his national security adviser would later give the Bush administration position that the August 6 briefing was primarily composed of historical information and did not provide warning of any new threat. While there were items included in the briefing that could certainly have caused Bush to tell his attorney general or FBI director to step up looking into certain strange instances, there was nothing in it with an obvious target.

Nine days later, on August 15, Cofer Black gave a speech to the Defense Department's annual Convention on Counterterrorism. He did not mince words. "We are going to be struck soon. Many Americans are going to die. And it could be in the US."[9]

The day after Black's speech, on August 16, the Minnesota FBI office arrested a man that local flight-school trainers had become suspicious about. Zacarious Moussaoui had moved to the area only a week prior after having his home in Oklahoma broken into and vandalized. He had done a number of strange things while taking lessons at the Pan Am International Flight School, strange enough to cause two staff members to contact the FBI. For reasons unknown, Tenet flew the next day, August 17, to Texas to interrupt the president's vacation for a one-on-one meeting.[10]

Based on the timing, the obvious reason for the visit would seem to be the news of Moussaoui's arrest, but Tenet's counterterror team would not be officially informed of this until the next day, and Tenet claims he would not learn of Moussaoui for another week when he received a briefing entitled "Islamic Extremist Learns to Fly."[11] It is entirely possible the conversation with the president was about something unrelated. Few details are known about the meeting because Tenet later forgot about the visit when questioned by investigators.

In an account later written by Tenet, it was on August 18 that a Minnesota FBI agent first alerted the CIA's Alec Station regarding Moussaoui. A team that included Bikowsky and Matthews looked into prior knowledge of Moussaoui.[12] Had they not called off the surveillance of the condo in Malaysia where the Al Qaeda terrorists had met in early 2000, a move that befuddled the Malaysian intelligence, they would have known that Moussaoui stayed in that condo in September of 2000, which would connect him to Mihdhar, Hazmi, and Attash.[13]

The information the FBI drummed up led them to believe Moussaoui was a "suicide hijacker" involved in "suspicious 747 flight training."[14] After news of Moussaoui was passed from Alec Station to George Tenet, the Kean Commission later determined that, in a bureaucratic slip, the same news never made it from the Minnesota FBI to the FBI's own acting director.[15] Tenet became the only cabinet official with knowledge of Moussaoui who was capable of briefing the president about him.

\* \* \*

On the afternoon of August 20, 2001, Maureen Baginski asked Bill Binney and Kirk Wiebe to her office. She explained that she was officially terminating their program ThinThread.

"My decision is based on whether I need to make six people unhappy [who back ThinThread] or five hundred unhappy [who back TrailBlazer]," Baginski explained. She was the ultimate bureaucrat. The decision was simple, and had nothing to do with the best outcome for the American people.

The shutdown of ThinThread, as Binney saw it, was entirely due to the politics of bureaucrats who saw low-budget, in-house projects as undesirable. Lacking the glamour and grandeur of big budgets and outside contracts, ThinThread had been discarded at the behest of the NSA director, Michael Hayden, in favor of a multibillion-dollar boondoggle that would never go fully operational after years of development.

Bill Binney also later came to believe that if ThinThread had ever been implemented on the eighteen key sites around the world that had been recommended by the CT Shop, the travel of hijackers into the United States would have been automatically recognized and then the proper intelligence analysts working NSA counterterror would have been alerted. He believes certain bureaucrats' allegiances toward budgets, status, and friendly relations with corporations who might reward them post-government trumped the interests of the American people.[16]

* * *

John O'Neill became livid when he read the *New York Times* headline: "FBI is Investigating a Senior Counterterror Agent."[17] Someone had leaked news of the Bureau's investigation into his lost briefcase in Tampa early in the year. The briefcase had contained classified documents and had been stolen from a hotel conference room; it was quickly recovered.[18] "This is despicable," he told his friend Mark Rossini, traveling with him on an assignment. O'Neill sensed that the leak was intended to destroy him.

Friends pointed the finger at acting FBI director Tom Pickard for the targeted leak, but that has always remained a rumor.[19] With Pickard set to retire in the fall, it would have been a purely malicious move on his part. O'Neill had once been considered a rising star, perhaps destined for J. Edgar Hoover's old job; now he felt his advancement would stall. He knew Washington well, and he decided to retire.

Days later, on August 22, O'Neill took Ali Soufan across the street from their offices to Joe's Diner, as they had done many times. Soufan confided that he was planning to propose to his girlfriend, and was surprised when his boss avoided his usual critique of married life and instead encouraged him to go forward.

O'Neill then pulled out an email he had written to a parent of one of the sailors killed in the USS *Cole* attack, and read it to Soufan. "Today is my last day. In my thirty-one years of government service, my proudest moment was when I was selected to lead the investigation of the attack on the USS *Cole*. I have put my all into the investigation and believe significant progress has been made . . . God bless you, your loved ones, the families, and God bless America."[20]

After exchanging hugs, Soufan watched O'Neill walk north, on his way to Mark Rossini's fortieth birthday party on the Lower East Side. When O'Neill arrived, Rossini saw him from across the room and walked over to embrace him. His now former boss explained that he could not stay long, so the two snuck off to a quiet corner to share a quick drink. It went by fast, and O'Neill told his friend that he was tired and had to go.[21]

"Alright, boss," Rossini replied, giving him a kiss good-bye, "I'll see ya."

"Yeah," O'Neill responded. "You know where to find me."

Rossini laughed. "Okay, you know where to find me too."

* * *

The next day began with a phone call into the New York FBI office, now absent O'Neill. Jack Cloonan answered and heard headquarters' Dina Corsi greet him on the other end. She was calling to inform them that the CIA had discovered that two men connected to Al Qaeda, Khalid al Mihdhar and Nawaf al Hazmi, were likely inside the United States. A search had to begin immediately. Cloonan assigned a rookie agent.[22]

Learning the news, Steve Bongardt flipped out. After having been stone-walled on the details regarding Mihdhar at the strange meeting with the CIA back in June, Bongardt had been haranguing Corsi for more information ever since. He called Corsi to give her a piece of his mind. "If this guy is in the country, it's not because he's going to fucking Disneyland!"[23] Corsi explained that inside Alec Station the day prior, Maggie Gillespie had finally noticed the March 2000 cable that in plain language declared that Hazmi had flown to Los Angeles.

Richard Clarke would note years later with a touch of bitterness, "It's not clear why for eighteen months [some in the CIA] do not tell us about these two in the country, and then one day, suddenly, they tell the FBI."

The prevailing story that emerged was that CIA management had pushed Maggie Gillespie to look at cable traffic surrounding the Malaysian terror summit in her spare time, and that she had simply taken three months to do so, finally stumbling upon the March cable that explained Nawaf al Hazmi had flown to Los Angeles. Years later, the CIA Inspector General's team would audit the computer usage from the time. As explained in footnote 23 of his report, they made a disturbing discovery: Gillespie had never herself actually accessed the March cable in the database at any point. What was the explanation?

The report also speculated that she might have been provided a hard copy. It further noted that Tom Wilshere was the only individual to have printed the cable. The inference seemed to be that he might have simply handed it to Gillespie. Had he reached his breaking point with Alec Station? Had he gone "rogue"? Perhaps a rebellion against a CTC that had stopped promoting him and was not taking him seriously in his new position at FBI headquarters? Or was he simply trying to do his job by putting the brakes on something dangerous by making sure the FBI saw what the CIA had been hiding from them?

The major reason Maggie Gillespie had been tasked to peruse the Malaysia cable traffic in the first place had been because Wilshere, in May, had himself reread those cables. So had Clark Shannon and an unknown female at Alec, likely in management. Being very clear: Wilshere read the cables explaining that Mihdhar and Hazmi, respectively, had a US visa and had traveled to the United States. This supposedly stirred him so much that he did nothing more than request that Alec Station task someone to review those same cables. The story that has been told is that Gillespie was given that assignment. When, months later, she stumbled onto the exact cables that stirred Wilshere in the first place, she immediately recognized, as anyone would, that it was imperative to warn the New York FBI office.

Why was tasking Gillespie to read this traffic even necessary? All she found was the very same information that Wilshere himself read. Indeed, she found something that dozens of employees within the CIA had already read. Wilshere could have handed her the relevant cables or pointed them out directly when he read them in May. Why run in a giant circle, spurring someone to discover what was already known? And if Wilshere did present a printed copy of the cable in question to Gillespie the day of John O'Neill's retirement, are we to accept that as a coincidence? Were members of Alec Station staff concerned that O'Neill would alert his friend Richard Clarke at the White House?

Whatever the reason and process behind her discovery, Gillespie turned to Immigration, who informed her that Mihdhar had arrived in the United States on January 15, 2000, that he had left months later, and that he had returned again in 2001, on July 4. On August 23, Mihdhar and Hazmi were belatedly added to the terrorist watch list, a system that checked for listees on international but unfortunately not domestic flights.[24] Meanwhile the FBI's hunt was on for the men, but only as an intelligence investigation, not a criminal investigation, due to Corsi's insistence that this was required because of the "wall." Had Alec Station come clean about Mihdhar's and Hazmi's contact with the *Cole* bombing plotters, the "wall" would have been irrelevant, and the FBI could have used far more tools to find the wanted men.

* * *

After Maggie Gillespie's "discovery," as the FBI searched for Mihdhar and Hazmi in the United States, Alec Station leadership must have moved to do their own search into the whereabouts of the Al Qaeda operatives. If they had somehow missed the significance of those two dots up to that point, they should have been starkly aware of the importance of connecting them now. Little is known from the record.

What is known is that on the same day Jack Cloonan received his phone call, August 22, Alec Station and FBI headquarters received word back from the French spy agency that the man detained in Minnesota, the one they had previously assessed as training to be a suicide hijacker, was also Al Qaeda connected through a Chechen rebel group.[25] Over at FBI headquarters, a supervisory special agent also wrote an email to Tom Wilshere briefing him on the Moussaoui case.[26]

On August 25, Mihdhar bought a plane ticket departing the morning of September 11 with a credit card in his name. On the 27th, Hazmi bought his and his brother Salem's tickets for the same morning. It might be worth noting that had anyone at the NSA been assigned to follow Hazmi's transactions—and we do not know if anyone had—they might have noticed that after a year and a half inside the United States, he had recently booked a flight dated for the morning of September 11. Eighteen other men with mostly Saudi names and various terrorist connections also booked for flights the same morning.[27] According to Bill Binney, ThinThread, if operational, would have highlighted this as notable.

Another seemingly unrelated event took place on the final day of the month, August 31. Prince Turki Al Faisal resigned with little warning as head of Saudi Arabia's spy agency, the General Intelligence Directorate (GID). It was a position he had held with the kingdom since 1979.[28] Again, the timing was strange.

Tenet placed a call to George W. Bush that day, interrupting his vacation for a second time. Again, nothing is known of the subject they discussed. It has never been claimed that he mentioned Mihdhar, Hazmi, or Moussaoui, despite his later claim that he "held nothing back from the president."[29]

\* \* \*

George W. Bush finally returned to the White House at the end of Labor Day weekend. That Tuesday, it was back to work. A meeting of the national security "principals" of Bush's National Security Council was called, one for which counterterror adviser Richard Clarke had been eagerly pushing over the entirety of Bush's seven months in office. This was their first meeting specifically to discuss terrorism. It would be led by the national security adviser, Condoleezza Rice, though for this meeting, the president would be absent.[30]

Inside the NSC adviser's office on September 4, Tenet carried a great deal of useful information inside his head. He had been briefed repeatedly on Moussaoui. More importantly, unless CIA counterterror staff and management had begun withholding details from him, the notification to the FBI should have left Tenet crystal clear on the fact that Mihdhar and Hazmi were believed to be inside the United States. If his counterterror team had once missed the significance, they had ample time to go back and put together the story of Mihdhar's and Hazmi's long and deep connections to Al Qaeda, their relationship to the owner of Bin Laden's telephone hub, their connection to the African embassy bombings, and their involvement in a meeting that apparently birthed the recent *Cole* bombing, as well as some of their activities since entering the United States.

In this first principals meeting on terrorism, with an invisible clock ticking down seven days left, Tenet mentioned none of this. Asked later during a public hearing about his silence that day, Tenet would provide a barely comprehensible answer. He said, "Well, it just wasn't—for whatever reason, all I can tell you is, it wasn't the appropriate place. I just can't take you any farther than that."[31]

"If he had told us," retorted Richard Clarke with apparent fury, "even as late as September fourth, we would have found [Mihdhar and Hazmi]. There's no doubt in my mind." He took a breath, then continued, "They were listed in the Yellow Pages under their own names. They were staying at the Charles Hotel in Harvard Square, for heaven's sake. If we had put out a request on the AP wire, they would have been arrested within twenty-four hours." He paused, then stated with utter conviction, "We would have found those assholes."

\* \* \*

One week after the NSC principals meeting, a government employee walked assertively through the busy restaurant at the upscale St. Regis hotel and up to the table of the CIA director. George Tenet accepted the secure phone from his aide's hand and placed it against his ear. After a moment, he asked a question into the receiver. "So they put the plane into the building itself?"

Earlier during the meal that day, Tenet's breakfast companion and one-time mentor, the former Oklahoma senator David Boren, asked the spy chief, "What are you worried about these days?"

"Bin Laden," had been his prompt, two-word response. The name would have been unknown to most Americans at that moment in time, but he knew Boren would recognize it. "You don't understand the capabilities and the reach of what they're putting together."

That conversation immediately took on the appearance of eerie prescience as Tenet finished his call, apologized for abruptly departing their reunion, and walked off. Boren pondered something his friend had said before he left, almost as if to himself. "I wonder if this has something to do with the guy who trained for a pilot's license?"[32]

\* \* \*

In Fort Meade, Maryland, Tom Drake was not yet fully moved into his new office inside the headquarters of the National Security Agency. On this late summer morning, Tuesday, Drake's second day as a manager within the electronic data collection division, the forty-four year-old decorated Air Force and Navy veteran was surrounded by twenty senior colleagues inside the conference room of the Legislative Affairs Office. Someone turned on a television.

Drake and the group had barely registered one burning tower when they collectively reacted to witnessing an airplane smashing through the second. "Initially it was an 'oh shit' moment, like a deer in the headlights," Drake recalls. "It was crystal clear this was a crisis."[33]

A mood of collective anxiety filled the room. In that moment, Drake had a sudden flashback to the bombing of the World Trade Center nearly nine years before, when he had been working the Pentagon's alert center. Around him now he noticed the room of executives having a different reaction, seemingly filled with repressed panic and what he sensed was self-concern. "We're the pointy end of the sensing spear," he immediately understood. "Our whole system was set up to alert the authorities, including the president, about things like this."

Drake, tall, balding, and thin, with a serious disposition, saw his newest job working for Maureen Baginski, also present in the room, as the culmination of a long career serving his country with distinction in several military and intelligence roles, punctuated by stints in the private sector. Signals Intelligence, or SIGINT, the division they were running, was emerging as the agency's most important. It seemed to him in this moment that concerns about public perception were primary among the senior staff, perhaps trickling down from Michael Hayden. He was disturbed by the immediate tone around the conference table full of the NSA's executives. No one was asking "who" or "how" yet. Instead, he paraphrases, the question was, "What is this going to mean for us?"

* * *

Across the Potomac, at CIA headquarters, Cofer Black stepped out of his office expecting to find John Kiriakou. The two were scheduled to head to the White House for a meeting with the president's national security adviser. Instead, he found Kiriakou running through the halls like Paul Revere to announce the crisis after the second plane hit. All of Black's headquarters employees had followed Kiriakou back to the CTC director's outer office. Black looked in stunned silence at his roughly two-hundred-person staff, all standing around TVs that hung from the ceiling. No one uttered a word. Another moment passed before an unknown staffer yelled, "Will somebody please lead?"[34]

This snapped Black into action, and he began barking orders. He happened to be short two of his most trusted deputies that day. Hank Crumpton, Black's operations head, had recently retired, while Rich Blee had already fortuitously arrived in Afghanistan earlier that week, following the assassination of the head of the Northern Alliance, and was there finalizing a plan reportedly approved by President Bush for the CIA to provide greater covert aid to the Northern Alliance against the Taliban government there. Given emerging events, that US aid might not need to be covert much longer. Absent his best men, Cofer Black arrived solo upstairs to the seventh floor to join George Tenet's executives.[35] In the scramble to begin responding to the attacks in real time, Bikowsky and Matthews were pushing their teams hard to receive the flight manifests of the two doomed planes.[36]

A vehicle containing George Tenet made its way along an entrance road through the edge of the rich surrounding forests. As Tenet pulled up, most of the staff was now a few hours into the workday. In a hurry, he entered an elevator from the main entrance to his office floor.

He found his men waiting for him in the executive conference room outside his office, a table of trusted and loyal managers. Seeking the latest, they reportedly had few details, only the broad understanding of who their adversary was. "The anxiety level . . . in that first hour was extraordinary," Tenet later described. "I don't think there was a person in the room who had the least doubt that we were in the middle of a full-scale assault orchestrated by Al Qaeda." The men in the room also informed their boss that both flights had originated from Boston's Logan International Airport.

On the television behind them, their president, George W. Bush, gave a press conference from a school in Florida, announcing a "national tragedy." Tenet had still not managed to speak with him. Then, live footage of two smoking towers in New York City switched to video from a much closer location. A Boeing 757 had crashed into the Pentagon.

Someone—likely Cofer Black—piped up to remind Tenet that the bombers of the World Trade Center in 1993 had drafted a plan to crash a plane into CIA headquarters—and that they themselves were now sitting on the top floor. Then someone apparently arrived from CTC downstairs to communicate something to Black, which he seems to have announced to the room, the first truly helpful piece of information Tenet had received: a fourth plane was indeed off its flight plan and heading toward DC.[37]

Tenet turned to his chief of security for advice on the safety of his own building.[38] His deputy John McLaughlin and Cofer Black, meanwhile, belatedly joined an emergency teleconference from the White House. There, they were greeted by the face of Richard Clarke from the Situation Room, a 5,000-plus-square-foot conference area in the basement of the West Wing. He had been leading the conference for ten minutes before the CIA joined.[39]

Clarke saw his friend George Tenet reenter the room on the other end of the teleconference and state definitively, "We have to save our people. We have to evacuate the building."[40]

"Sir," Black responded, "we're going to have to exempt CTC from this because we need to have our people working the computers."

Tenet realized the CounterTerrorist Center, "with its vast data banks and sophisticated communications systems," would need to remain in operation. Downstairs, inside Alec Station, Mark Rossini was wishing to himself that they were still working in their previous office. Inside the Old Headquarters Building, they had the privilege of windows facing west across the 250-acre compound's rolling fields. They could always spot incoming thunderstorms. Now, with a flight approaching, he and his colleagues were blind below the New Headquarters Building.

The counterterror staff discussed the likelihood that they were under threat. Rossini argued to the group, "We're four floors belowground anyway. Even if the plane goes into the first floor, it won't affect us." The group agreed, deciding to remain. Rossini assured them, "We'll be okay."[41]

A security staffer ran through the floor of CTC announcing a mandatory evacuation, then ran back out. John Kiriakou had seen one CTC staffer hide under her desk in a moment of "irrational blind panic" after the Pentagon crash before running out of the office. She would be fired soon after. Among those still in the room now, no one budged from their chairs.[42]

Cofer Black had just returned from Tenet's seventh floor. He stood up on a desk to give an impromptu speech. "As of now, we are at war. And this is a war that all of us are going to have to fight. Not all of us are going to make it home." To hammer home the point, Black insinuated that those not willing to possibly see this new challenge through, even to their own deaths, should pack up their things and quit. "If you do not want to fight, leave now, and no one will think less of you."

The same man from security again entered the room and said, "The evacuation is mandatory. If you do not leave now, you will be placed under arrest."

* * *

Two hundred and fifty miles northeast, inside a forty-one-story office tower in lower Manhattan, the FBI's Steve Bongardt was pulled into a conference call by his boss. He was a mix of emotions—angry, tired, consumed by grief, but feeling fortunate. Covered in white dust as he spoke into the phone, he had just escaped the collapse of the South Tower. Everyone who witnessed it would be forever emotionally scarred. As he tells it, the former Navy pilot and his colleagues in the Joint Terrorism Task Force had headed straight to the action as the attacks unfolded. Approaching the World Trade Center, they ran into a senior fireman who was heading toward the South Tower. They asked the fireman what they could do.

"By the grace of God," Bongardt later recounted, "he turned to us and replied that he did not know what we could do, but that we were not going anywhere close to the buildings without a respirator." Bongardt did not know who the man was, but after watching the towers come down from several blocks away, he knew the firefighter had saved his life. "I also truly believe, based on the direction [at which] he was looking, toward the southern Tower, that moments later he entered that tower and perished in the attacks."[43]

The attacks in lower Manhattan this morning represented everything that Bongardt and his colleagues had fought to prevent. Like John O'Neill, who was now among the missing and presumed dead, Bongardt had been a Cassandra warning in vain of a growing threat within US borders. His warnings received little attention or respect, he felt, especially from his CIA counterparts.

Sitting in an office, lucky to be alive, Bongardt listened as his supervisor Ken Maxwell asked the Washington, DC–based headquarters agents on the other end of the line if they had yet received the manifests for the doomed flights. Could they determine the names of any of the hijackers yet?

"We have some," replied Dina Corsi casually. Agents of the Washington field office had arrived at Dulles Airport where they confiscated security tapes from the checkpoint the hijackers passed through before boarding Flight 77. Some of the men on the tape were recognized. As Corsi read through the names, one sparked a violent reaction from Bongardt, as she must have expected.

"Khalid al Mihdhar?" he interrupted. "Did you say Khalid al Mihdhar?" Not waiting for an answer, he began shouting. "The same one you told us about? He's on the list? The same al Mihdhar we've been talking about for three months?" On the other end of the line, Corsi's supervisor piped up in her defense. "Steve, we did everything by the book."

"I hope that makes you feel better," Bongardt continued, unable to control himself. "Tens of thousands are dead—" Bongardt's supervisor stopped the tirade by hitting the mute button. "Now is not the time for this," he instructed his colleague sympathetically. "There will be a time, but not now."[44]

\* \* \*

The hijackers' names were also causing a stir back at Alec Station. Cofer Black had gotten his way. Along with the emergency operations center on the sixth floor, the counterterror staff were the only CIA employees to remain in the buildings, empty for the first time since they were opened. The plane they had braced for earlier, Flight 93, had not reached its target. The tattered shards of the aircraft as well as the bodies of passengers and their belongings were being reported to have been scattered across a several-mile-wide debris field in rural Pennsylvania. CIA employees later learned of evidence that their headquarters had not, in fact, been the plane's intended target, but rather the White House.[45]

As the passenger lists finally came in from the Customs Office of Intelligence, one employee printed them out and hightailed it out of the building. The counterterror staffer ran across the yard and entered the printing plant. It was a place rarely seen by most CIA employees, now home to an ad hoc workspace filled with key evacuated workers. Scanning the room, the CTC employee laid eyes on George Tenet, and barreled up to him with the printout.

Pointing to "Khalid al Mihdhar" and "Nawaf al Hazmi" on the document, the staffer stated that "Two names, these two we know."[46]

America's top spy leader processed this for a moment. Col. Larry Wilkerson, former chief of staff to Colin Powell, claims he later heard that Tenet's reaction to the passenger manifest was to say, "Oh, God, it's all of them."[47]

\* \* \*

As darkness fell over Washington, DC, fierce beacons emanating from the searchlights and rescue vehicles outside of the Pentagon drew all eyes to the thick plume of smoke still rising over Arlington, Virginia. Four miles northeast, inside the White House, the recently arrived president finished his seven-minute televised address to reassure the nation, and he then headed to the safety below the building, where his cabinet was waiting for him inside a little-used room called the Presidential Emergency Operations Center. It would be his first meeting with his National Security Council since the events of that morning.

George Tenet's eyes met George W. Bush's. They had spoken by secure teleconference that afternoon, where Bush had been delivered for security reasons at a military base in Nebraska. During that virtual meeting, Bush had begun by declaring, "We're at war," before asking his DCI who, exactly, they were at war with. Tenet had asserted, based on the information of his best advisers, it was Al Qaeda. He explained their evidence, that the flight manifests for the Pentagon plane had included three men his counterterror department knew to be members of the jihadist group.[48]

Tenet had further told Bush his assessment that Al Qaeda and the Taliban-controlled government in Afghanistan were one and the same. Bush instructed the room, "Tell the Taliban we're finished with them," before continuing, "I want you all to understand that we are at war and we will stay at war until this is done. Nothing else matters. Everything is available for the pursuit of this war. Any barriers in your way, they're gone. Any money you need, you have it. This is our only agenda."

Now inside the impenetrable emergency bunker below the White House, in a rather crowded space, the civilian head of the military, Donald Rumsfeld, informed his commander in chief that international law only allowed military force to prevent future attacks, not for retribution.[49] Earlier in the day, inside the famed War Room of the Pentagon just down the hall from the smoking burial grounds of hijackers Khalid al Mihdhar and Nawaf al Hazmi, Rumsfeld had speculated among his team whether the information they were getting about the attacks was good enough for the United States to retaliate against not only these men's sworn leader, Usama Bin Laden in Afghanistan, but also Saddam Hussein in Iraq. Bush's defense secretary was thinking big, a reaction that would include "things related and not."[50]

"No. I don't care what the international lawyers say," Bush yelled back to Rumsfeld. "We are going to kick some ass."[51]

One of Rumsfeld's deputies, Stephen Cambone, jotted handwritten notes of the conversations, summarizing the incoming news. Near the end of their hour-long meeting, at around 9:53 p.m., an unknown person delivered some news to those in the room, which Cambone quickly noted in shorthand:[52]

AA77 – 3 indiv have been followed
since millennium + Cole
1 guy is assoc of Cole bomber
2 entered US in early July
(2 or 3 pulled aside and interrogated?)

Who was it that brought this bit of information that Cambone jotted down? Which agency followed the three hijackers "since millennium + Cole?" Which agency had possibly "pulled aside and interrogated" some or all of them?

Richard Clarke was inside the room, and he does not remember this moment. He speculates that "By 9:53, it's not hard to imagine Cambone was talking to people in CIA who were dumping everything that they had. Cambone was the senior guy in the Pentagon with oversight of the Pentagon's intelligence operations, so he knew everybody in CIA. I'm sure on that day he called out to his contacts in CIA and told them, 'Tell me everything you can tell me.'"[53]

\* \* \*

It was the middle of the night in America as two federal criminal investigators, Ali Soufan of the FBI and Bob McFadden of the NCIS, sat inside the VIP lounge of the Sana'a International Airport in Yemen, accompanied by two supervisors and the CIA's local station chief. The sun had just appeared over the horizon.

"What's John's status?" one asked.

It was a question that had come up every few minutes since watching the collapse of the Trade Towers live on CNN International. Soufan had spent most of the last year there in Yemen investigating the murder of seventeen US sailors in the *Cole* attack. He knew that switching gears to investigate in New York and DC would be incredibly personal. For one, he would rejoin his co-case agent Steve Bongardt. Bongardt and Soufan had been partners on the ground in Yemen early on, but Bongardt had returned to work the investigation from their home office due to back problems.

At the airport, the FBI managers sat on a gaudy, overstuffed couch, talking with the CIA's man in the country. The bureau group had come to know and trust him. The shabby venue that surrounded them suffered from the general neglect that characterized most public spaces in the country, which is one of the poorest on the Arabian Peninsula.

Minutes from boarding their flight, one of their cell phones rang. It was Dina Corsi with a change of plans. "Listen, tell Soufan and McFadden they need to grab their bags and head back to the embassy immediately and stand by for a secure fax." All the FBI staff was also told to head back to the embassy with a couple of their SWAT shooters in tow.

"What the fuck?" they said to themselves. "Mentally, physically, spiritually, we're ready to get on the plane with the rest of the team, get to UAE and then take the transport home."

"I can't tell you anything else over the open line," Corsi concluded with characteristic terseness. "You need to get back to the embassy."

Once there, their local CIA rep glanced at the contents of a secure fax from Washington. He brought McFadden and Soufan into his office and closed the door, unable to look them in the eyes. Silently, he handed them the fax.

"This is un-be-lievable," McFadden said, followed by a repetition of the words "What the fuck. . . ."

"Hey," the CIA station chief later tried to explain, "there were marching orders not to share that information."

Soufan was silent. He and McFadden stared at the contents, including three photos and a report. The pictures had been taken in January 2000, in Kuala Lumpur, by covert photographers working for the Malaysian intelligence service at the request of the CIA's Alec Station. They showed two operatives known at the time to be connected to Bin Laden, Khalid al Mihdhar and Nawaf al Hazmi, meeting outside a condominium with other men that Soufan's and McFadden's detective work had discovered many months prior to be the plotters of the *Cole* bombing.

Could this have led their investigation to the hijackers? How many of the CIA agents that Soufan and McFadden had been briefing in good faith had all along been aware that Hazmi and Mihdhar were connected to *Cole* attack plotters?

Soufan suddenly got up and darted out the room, past the SWAT members outside and down the hall to the bathroom. There, he fell to his knees and vomited.

One of the SWAT team entered the bathroom after Soufan, finding him on the floor. "What's wrong, bud?"

Soufan could only utter, "They knew. They fucking knew."[54]

# 6

# THE BIG SELL

*"If you see the lion's canines, do not ever think that the lion smiles."*

Al Mutanabbi

The orange glow of halogen lamps hung heavy over the silent Baltimore-Washington Parkway. Bill Binney turned off onto Canine Road. In the darkness he noticed the color of the surrounding light change to fluorescent-green as his vehicle approached the NSA buildings peeking above a line of American basswood trees. Driving past the crisscrossing maze of yellow lines, he found his parking spot, as he had for more than thirty years, and turned off his engine.

Stepping outside, Binney was dressed for janitorial work, a bold ruse. He knew there had been a failure somewhere inside the NSA to heed warnings he was sure existed, evidence of which probably lived inside the agency's mainframe. He believed a day of harsh accountability was upon him and his coworkers. "We got rid of generals throughout World War II for all kinds of negligence," he thought as he walked toward his building.

Once his janitor disguise allowed him past the gate guards and inside the officially closed building, Binney quietly headed to the SIGINT Automation Research Center he had founded. While looking at material on his computer, "to see what I could do to maybe help in getting information on who did this," he was met by the lead contractor for his office, who in contrast to Binney had actually been called into work that day.

For the first time since being built, the NSA's headquarters were closed for business on Wednesday, September 12, 2001. Only essential personnel were now inside, including Binney's friendly associate Tom Drake, who had received a call very early in the morning from Maureen Baginski. Everyone remembered how traumatically the day before had ended, with Drake, Binney, and the rest of the agency's employees waiting in hours-long car lines trying to evacuate the parking lot after the Pentagon had been hit.

Drake felt like a ghost haunting the building, as the emptiness swelled and swallowed the corridors. Only he and the CounterTerror Shop, a group of just over a dozen analysts backed by many more foreign translators, milled about with a few agency executives. The NSA director Michael Hayden was there too, observing the work of the rest. It was eerily quiet.

Binney's lead contractor told him he was worried after leaving a meeting with Sam Visner, Bill Black's hire, who had just instructed him, "Do not embarrass large companies [that NSA is involved with regarding this failure]. You do your part, you'll get your share. There's plenty for everybody. We could milk this cow for fifteen years."[1]

* * *

By the time John O'Neill's deputy for several years, Pat D'Amuro, left the parking garage across the street from the FBI's office in lower Manhattan that Wednesday to return home to his wife in New Jersey, he had opened the US government's criminal investigation into the events of the previous morning. He code-named it TWINBOM. The central hub of the investigation would be his team, the New York counterterror specialists of the Joint Terrorism Task Force, and squads dubbed I-44 and I-49, among others. In total, though, D'Amuro had the resources of six thousand special agents in FBI field offices across the country and, indeed, the world. Before their investigation was concluded, they would claim to follow 500,000 investigative leads, resulting in the collection of 137,000 pieces of evidence and the conducting of 167,000 interviews. It was immediately the largest effort in the Bureau's history.[2]

The flight manifests were the Rosetta Stone from which the detective work into the plot had already begun. It was initially determined that eighteen men had been part of the hijacking teams on the four airliners, soon amended to nineteen. Field agents in Boston, Newark, and DC, where the flights originated, had searched the men's rental vehicles left in parking garages, as well as nearby trash cans and any luggage that had survived. They sought the radio transmissions and "black box" recordings from the doomed planes and that morning's airport surveillance camera videos. They also collected video from cameras around Pentagon City that had been in a position to capture the crash of Flight 77. They worked to create a chronology of the morning's attacks, how they had unfolded, and what it told them.

D'Amuro's team turned to US embassies and consulates to get these men's visas and learn their travel histories and dates of entry to the United States. They subpoenaed their bank accounts and financial records and looked at where their money came from and where they spent and sent it, using these leads to develop early timelines of their lives. They wanted to know everything: addresses, jobs held, schools attended, known associates.

Special Agents in charge of field offices in California, Arizona, and Florida, where the bulk of the hijackers' activities were determined to have been concentrated while living in the United States, were tasked with interviewing the staff of their flight schools, their employers, their landlords, and their neighbors. As they learned of Internet cafes frequented by the men, their hard drives would allow them to read some of their email communications. They were also working with intelligence being provided by the CIA and NSA. Everything was being reported back to the TWINBOM investigators in the office just down the street from what was being called Ground Zero.[3]

The past thirty-six hours had been pure hell for D'Amuro. On September 10, while trying to return from a conference to his home in New York City, he had been waylaid in DC by weather. He was back at Dulles Airport in the morning where, unbeknownst to him, Khalid al Mihdhar and Nawaf al Hazmi were boarding a plane with their allies. Before he could get on his own plane, he had gotten a call from a colleague informing him of the first plane crash. Flights shut down, so he tried to take the metro to Central Station to catch a train back to New York. While he was at the Pentagon City stop, Mihdhar's and Hazmi's hijacking team flew their captured American Airlines jet over his head and into the Pentagon. D'Amuro's subway then closed as well, and he walked to Crystal City where he commandeered a rental car and began the longest drive of his life. The sun had just set as he laid eyes on his beloved city.[4]

He pulled up to the FBI field office in lower Manhattan, where he had begun and spent most of his career. Four of those years he had been deputy to John O'Neill, whose position he had taken over in late August when O'Neill retired. When he arrived, he found his entire operation had been moved. Flooding, which occurred after the collapse of the towers, had created telecommunications issues at 27 Federal Plaza, causing his counterterror team to create a makeshift office in their Twenty-Sixth Street parking garage. Rows of computers and telephone lines were set up around one major indoor floor. There, Pat D'Amuro had officially opened the daunting criminal case before them.

At the courthouse on Pearl Street in lower Manhattan, all who enter pass the quote across the front of the building that reads, "THE TRUE ADMINISTRATION OF JUSTICE IS THE FIRMEST PILLAR OF GOOD GOVERNMENT." There, the New York FBI and their parent organization, the Justice Department, had successfully arrested and convicted the plotters behind the '93 WTC bombing, the foiled '95 "Day of Terror," and "Bojinka," and the foiled "Millennium" attacks. Presently, they were still readying the cases for the '98 East Africa embassy and 2000 USS *Cole* bombings. D'Amuro added one more to the docket: the September 11 attack.

* * *

The next day, Thursday, September 13, the NSA's parking lot was again filled to the brim with cars. The place was open for business. Gone for mere hours, again Tom Drake parked for only the fourth time and passed through the front doors. There, the agency's communications director felt himself engulfed by an unmistakable air of emotional burden.[5]

The trauma and pain that draped over the nation like a blanket hammered down upon the rank-and-file workers who populated the NSA's CounterTerror Shop. In the usually quiet and compartmentalized halls, moments were playing out that defied the standard culture of a place where the running joke had always claimed, "You can tell the extroverts because they stare at *your* shoes."

A forty-something man was witnessed openly crying, breathlessly, while speaking with three women in a hallway, in open view of anyone who passed. "All those people did not have to die. We could have saved them," he explained between heaving sobs. "We knew this was being planned months ago, but they would not let us issue the reports we wrote."[6]

Maureen Baginski brought Tom Drake along for visits to the counterter- ror analysts, the meetings in their cubicles feeling to him like a strange mix of information gathering and therapy sessions. Baginski and Drake wanted to learn where the core mission had failed while at the same time offering a sympathetic ear. "I was effectively the head of communications," remembers Drake. "So I'm going out to help console the workforce but also to listen to them. I recognized they needed to get some stuff off their chest. I spent a lot of time going to their offices and they would come to my office."[7]

Drake found the frontline workers were far more realistic about the events of that week than the executives. "The people that do the real work at NSA knew that NSA and the intelligence community—the whole national defense effort—had failed the nation," he quickly concluded. "Because our primary responsibility as an intelligence agency was to provide indications of warning, and we had obviously failed at that."

As a military man, Drake recognized signs of post-traumatic stress. These employees were punishing themselves over the responsibility they felt, some going to their cars to sleep, splashing water on their faces inside NSA's restrooms, then starting the next day's work. Management pushed them to keep at it during a time of crisis. "Psychologically," he says, "it was extraor- dinarily difficult. What do you tell your neighbors, what do you tell your friends, what do you say?"

That first day back, the global employees of the agency stopped to tune in for a videoconference with the director. Michael Hayden instructed his people "to keep America free by making Americans feel safe again."[8]

The desk visits with the counterterror foot soldiers caused Drake to feel he had established a sincere rapport with them. As a longtime contractor, he was relatable, not a true outsider, yet as a newcomer to the cadre of agency management, he also had not been there in the run-up of the attacks, excluding him from the sense of denial many perceived was emanating from those at higher levels. Something about his manner also contrasted with the style of the more aloof and less personable Baginski. These differences mattered.[9]

"I decided I would join the military for the experience," Drake explains. "I wanted to see what it was like." During two enlistments amid the Cold War under Ronald Reagan, he received a commendation, a Military Meritorious Service Medal, and an Air Medal. He developed an expertise in electronic and signals intelligence working on spy missions against the notorious East German "Stasi," where a distaste was cemented within him against authoritarian governments and the way they keep tabs on their populations.

Twelve years before, Drake had left the military to begin work as an NSA contractor. He became an expert in the quality testing of software and working on a system for measuring the quality of computer codes at the agency.

Drake points to the most tangible expression of how personally the staff took the week's events: the physical and psychological implosion being suffered by several at the heart of the Al Qaeda electronic surveillance team. The toll was striking to him. Two staffers soon suffered heart attacks, one dying. Within the first week, word reached Drake that a female analyst, "Becky," had left in an ambulance. Most called it a nervous breakdown. She never returned. "[Becky] was the person most responsible for [monitoring the Al Qaeda communications hub at Ahmed al Hada's house in Yemen]," Drake noted.

Some quality about Drake made him seem approachable to a man we will call "Bob." When Bob came to Drake's office, he seemed to be "almost looking over his shoulder." He nervously requested that they set up a time to meet, explaining nothing more about why. Drake agreed.

* * *

Around the same time, a meeting between NSA director Mike Hayden and his boss, George Tenet, was taking place. Few details have been forthcoming. Hayden's memoir provides a tantalizing clue as to the setting and a third participant: the Oval Office and George W. Bush.[10]

Tenet had been spending a lot of his time with the president since the traumatizing events, beginning the evening of September 11 and regularly thereafter, where he was taking in cues about the president's evolving instincts on the response. Tenet likely had been passing what he learned to his counterterror director Cofer Black, who was spending his days and nights inside his Langley basement office preparing a plan of action they would soon present to the White House.[11]

"I had not met President George W. Bush prior to 9/11," later wrote Michael Hayden. "My first encounter with the president was that September 2001 morning when George Tenet ushered me into the Oval to discuss what more NSA could do."[12]

Tenet, Hayden's boss since he had taken over leadership of the NSA two years earlier, asked him pointedly, "Could you do more?"

"Not within current law," Hayden replied coyly.

Tenet was unfazed. "Well, what could you do more?"

Hayden explained to his Director of Central Intelligence what was "technologically possible" and what was "operationally relevant." He was known to be a fast talker who liked to use similes and analogies, a lot of tech talk, often leaving those he spoke with wondering what exactly he had just said. Finally, Hayden turned to what he understood to be the main problem: "the question of lawfulness."[13]

The US Constitution's Fourth Amendment had, after all, clearly limited the government's abilities in this regard, reading:

> The right of the people to be secure in their persons, houses, papers, and effects, against unreasonable searches and seizures, shall not be violated, and no warrants shall issue, but upon probable cause, supported by oath or affirmation, and particularly describing the place to be searched, and the persons or things to be seized.

The unusually clear language had kept these rights mostly untouched and unassailable in the intervening 210 years. A blanket collection of the digital "effects" of "the people" without their knowledge appeared out of bounds.

"After the 9/11 attacks," Tenet later wrote of this moment, "using his existing authorities, Hayden implemented a program to monitor communications to and from Afghanistan, where the 9/11 attacks were planned. With regard to NSA's policy of minimization, balancing US privacy and inherent intelligence value, Mike moved from a peacetime to a wartime standard. He briefed me on this, and I approved."[14]

Hayden later stated in a PR piece for the CIA, "I know George Tenet well. I have said publicly that I thank God that George made some incredibly difficult decisions. I don't know how I would have decided them, but I thank God George made them, because, since George did, I didn't have to."[15]

The programs Tenet and Hayden commissioned that week in September were partially revealed to the public years later. Hayden would hold a press conference explaining what George Tenet—and he alone—had chosen to ask NSA staff to do in those first days after the attacks. "Let me be clear on this point," he stressed, "except that they involved NSA, these programs were not related," he repeated, "these programs were not related to the authorization that the president [provided two weeks later]."

"These decisions were easily within my authorities as the director of NSA under an executive order known as Executive Order 12333 that was signed in 1981, an executive order that has governed NSA for nearly a quarter century. Now, let me summarize. In the days after 9/11, NSA was using its authorities and its judgment to appropriately respond to the most catastrophic attack on the homeland in the history of the nation. That shouldn't be a headline."

"Are these individuals? Are these phone numbers? Are these email accounts and so on?" Hayden asked in response to a reporter's question. "Hard for me to get into the specifics. I would just say that what it is we do is that we use our art form, we use our science and our art to, as best as we can, okay, specifically target communications we have reason to believe are associated with Al Qaeda, and we use all of the tools."[16]

Hayden would give another speech before a university audience many years later in which he returned to those critical times. He described how September 11 drastically shifted his notions on what is and is not constitutional, telling the room, "[T]he death of three thousand countrymen kind of took me in a direction over here, perfectly within my authority, but a [to] different place than the one in which I was located before the attacks took place."

"Privacy is the line we continuously negotiate," he continued, "between ourselves as unique creatures of God and ourselves as social animals. In the first category, we have a right to keep things to ourselves. And in the second category we have a responsibility to reveal things about ourselves to the community for the greater good."[17] Of course, "reveal" implies choice.

* * *

George Tenet arrived at the expansive presidential retreat of Camp David on Saturday morning ready to give the presentation of his career. Cofer Black had been working around the clock, punctuated by a few moments of sleep in his office, preparing a document entitled "Destroying International Terrorism." It was a thing of art, a wish list accumulated from decades of CIA directors' and employees' wildest dreams, spun to fit the clear inclinations of George W. Bush at that moment. Before Tenet and Black was a truly rare opportunity. The politically astute CIA director had an opening to take the lead in a new "war on terror" that would dominate Washington thinking for the foreseeable future.

Designed as a day to discuss ideas and ask questions, the president had assembled his cabinet and advisers to formalize the national response to the attacks earlier that week. He spoke briefly beforehand to the media, telling reporters that his administration was not going to go into tactical specifics, but that one thing was certain: "We are at war."

Richard Clarke was apparently absent. The already small group of invitees became smaller as the NSC session began. After an opening prayer, the State Department's head Colin Powell was the first to present. He focused on the way in which the recent events had sparked global solidarity, which could be exploited. "Not in a bad way," added Powell's then chief of staff, Col. Larry Wilkerson, arguing that they could look to get a lot done with so many other nations around the world, big and small, willing to extend a hand to the United States.[18]

Unbeknownst to the secretary of state, Bush had already signaled his feelings on the matter to Black, after Wilkerson had mentioned during breakfast his belief that it was critical to "reason with the Taliban and ask them to turn over Bin Laden and his senior Al Qaeda leadership." After he had walked away, Bush looked to Black and Bush's CIA intelligence briefer Mike Morell and declared, "Fuck diplomacy. We are going to war."[19]

A sitting president for less than a year, Bush knew he had surrounded himself with people who were entirely unstirred by the issue of terrorism. Wilkerson thinks that Bush's failure to prioritize terrorism made him fearful. "I think for about the first seventy-two hours, Bush and Cheney were scared shitless."

Both Clarke and Tenet had aired concern to the president at various times regarding the threat Al Qaeda posed. On paper, President Bush received a daily briefing on August 6 entitled "Bin Laden Determined to Strike Within the United States." In person, the president was warned again, as Tenet traveled to Bush's ranch in Crawford, Texas, in the month prior to 9/11.

"They were scared that they would be impeached successfully and removed from government," Wilkerson added. "They had just presided over the largest death toll of Americans in peacetime on US territory since Pearl Harbor. Wouldn't you be frightened? You were elected, and you know damn well you have not been 'seized' by [the Al Qaeda] issue, and all of a sudden it bites you in the ass big time."

At Camp David, Tenet sat directly across the conference table from Bush. When his turn came, he made a striking proposal that was a substantive departure from all prior US policy. If approved, it would give the CIA by far the greatest authority it ever held across its history. As the only representative of an agency in the room that had been fully invested in the Al Qaeda threat, and as the only person there who was on record as having brought aspects of this threat to the president before it was on everyone's TV screens, Tenet had Bush's full attention.

Tenet opened his presentation by describing how the CIA could run the invasion of Afghanistan using assets they already had on the ground. They would "close the safe haven" with a multipronged strategy that would include working with various anti-Taliban elements within Afghanistan, linking up CIA paramilitary forces with military special forces, and leaning on neighboring states to close their borders. Tenet presented the CIA as a force that was capable, present, and ready to start kicking ass and taking names immediately. On a roll, Tenet pushed his agenda further.

The heart of his proposal "was a recommendation that the president give the CIA what Tenet labeled 'exceptional authorities.'" As revealed by Bob Woodward, "Tenet wanted a broad, general intelligence order that would allow the CIA to conduct the necessary covert operations without having to come back for formal approval for each specific operation." It was too much trouble to have to bother the president each time. "Tenet said he needed the new authority to allow the agency to operate without restraint—and he wanted encouragement from the president to take risks."[20]

Tenet must have recognized that what he proposed during his thirty-minute speech would have seemed absurd less than two weeks prior, when the previous cabinet meeting on terrorism had taken place on September 4. At that time, others had noticed that the CIA director was strangely silent. Now, he presented with bravado. He made a case for the significant expansion of his agency's budget, staff, and powers.

Though no one in the room would say it, some of what Tenet proposed represented a clean break by the United States from legality. The CIA had already conducted what might be called "extraordinary renditions" for six years, beginning under President Clinton, with the number of people kidnapped and dropped off in the secret prisons of nations with "spotty" human rights records coming in at just under seventy.[21] Congress had passed the Foreign Affairs Reform & Restructuring Act in 1998. The law prohibited anyone from engaging in actions to "expel, extradite, or otherwise effect the involuntary return of any person to a country in which there are substantial grounds for believing the person would be in danger of being subjected to torture, regardless of whether the person is physically present in the United States." Violating both international and local laws against kidnapping and US laws regarding knowingly delivering someone to torture, it had been employed minimally. Tenet was saying that needed to change, and in the process, illegality would become official American policy.

Moving on to a top-secret document entitled "Worldwide Attack Matrix," Tenet explained to the president that in dozens of countries around the globe, there was a need for a host of covert activities, from propaganda to killings. Further, the drone technology that had been a rising star for covert surveillance had also recently been weaponized, and Tenet asserted that a terrorist assassination list should be developed and updated by his counter-terror staff. Drone operators half a world away could do it with the pull of the trigger.

The *Washington Post* would report, "On the financial front, Tenet called for clandestine computer surveillance and electronic eavesdropping to locate the assets of Al Qaeda. . . ." The NSA would be well suited to this. Michael Hayden was not present, but Tenet was there that day as Director of Central Intelligence, representing Hayden's agency. He likely knew of the early "turning inward" of data collection from foreign to domestic.

The FBI, being a law enforcement agency, had long held the nation's interrogation powers and believed themselves to be quite good at it. During the prior decade, their interrogations of terrorists had yielded one successful prosecution after another. Tenet's proposals to the president and his staff ultimately suggested that terrorists no longer be considered criminals protected by law, but war actors. He showed an astute understanding of the ideology and desires of Bush and his vice president. This change in classification would shift interrogation duty from the FBI to the CIA. Such a bold transfer of responsibility and domain would likely have ruffled the feathers of a seasoned FBI director.

Robert Mueller, however, was not a seasoned FBI director. He had been appointed to his position only weeks before 9/11. He was likely aware that a major domestic terror incident on his Bureau's watch had not strengthened the FBI's position. Mueller, clean-shaven with a defined jaw, no sideburns, and short cleanly combed dark gray hair above the prominent worry lines on his forehead—he looked like a police commissioner—was a fish out of water in this cabinet-level meeting. In fact, he had not even anticipated being asked to attend. For the duration of the conference, he remained mostly silent, and what few remarks he made revolved around the ongoing investigations into the attacks themselves. After he cut himself short, murmurs in the room suggested that, unlike the CIA, the FBI was too focused on prosecuting successful terrorists instead of thwarting attacks.

The defense secretary, by contrast, should have been more argumentative when Tenet stepped into his territory. Donald Rumsfeld was close with Bush, yet he knew his attention had been far from Al Qaeda in the months prior. He was playing catch-up. Like the FBI director, the perception of the defense secretary's presentation was that it fell well short of Tenet's. Others in the room commented that Rumsfeld seemed unprepared.[22]

Tenet later pointed out, "Nobody knew this target like we knew it. Others hadn't been paying attention to this for years as we had been doing. And nobody else had a coordinated plan for expanding out of Afghanistan to combat terrorism across the globe . . . This was the right way to go, and we were the right people to do it."[23]

Thus, when the subject turned to the immediate invasion of Afghanistan, home to Usama Bin Laden and his key leadership, Rumsfeld kept his mouth shut as Tenet proposed for the first time in American history that a war be run principally by his civilian intelligence agency, rather than the generals and their Defense Department. Again, the CIA had already been working with resistance elements in Afghanistan. They already had people and resources in place. The president was impressed.

If anyone in the room held a disagreement with Tenet's plan, they knew to keep it to themselves following Bush's excited response to his presentation. "Great job!" the president praised. The meeting ended with Bush addressing the room: "Thank you all very much. This has been a very good discussion. I'm going to think about all of this on Sunday, and I'll call you together Monday and tell you what I've concluded."

After Colin Powell and Donald Rumsfeld left the facility, as the attorney general and national security adviser played piano and sang songs, Tenet sat with Bush at a table. While Bush assembled an elaborate jigsaw puzzle,[24] what did the two men talk about? What did they have in common to connect over at that moment? Any hunt for accountability inside Tenet's agencies would no doubt also have political repercussions for the president too. Did the men ever discuss this? Or were they on the same page, no words necessary? Did Bush have any anxiety about the leverage Tenet had over him, having laid out a series of warnings about Al Qaeda in the previous months, resulting in little offensive action from the leadership that received it? Bush didn't need enemies. He needed friends.

On Monday, September 17, 2001, George W. Bush signed an order granting the CIA what Tenet had asked for. This directive gave the CIA the authority to kill, capture, and assassinate Al Qaeda operatives, as well as the authority to establish a network of secret prisons. Bush also signed off on secret legal justifications that rested on the argument that the need to acquire information quickly, essentially to prevent an incoming terrorist attack, nullified the Geneva Convention restrictions on the questioning of prisoners.[25]

\* \* \*

On the last Saturday in September, John O'Neill's funeral was held at St. Nicholas of Tolentine Roman Catholic Church in Atlantic City, New Jersey, O'Neill's birthplace. Inside the spired stone church, the sound of voices resonated against the vaulted ceiling, and the solemn autumn light was painted blue and red as it fell through the stained glass windows. Police outside formed a barricade that extended two blocks in all directions, and an army helicopter circled overhead.

He had been in his office on the thirty-fourth floor of the North Tower when the first plane struck and was last seen heading in the general direction of Tower Two before it collapsed. At this service, his loved ones, his former counterterror team, former FBI directors Louis Freeh and Tom Pickard, and federal prosecutor Mary Jo White celebrated his life and work. His boss, assistant FBI director Barry Mawn, gave a eulogy, pointing out that the very information O'Neill had collected while investigating the USS *Cole* attack "could well help us solve this case."

Surely the ironic coincidences surrounding O'Neill's death were lost on no one. There was the obvious fact that Usama Bin Laden had been his great white whale, and that O'Neill had died in a plot ordered by the man. Deeper still, though, had been the seeming randomness of events that had added up to his death. First was the incident of his stolen briefcase containing classified documents that placed O'Neill as the subject of an investigation. Then there was the matter of who had decided to leak that story to the *New York Times* that summer, causing O'Neill to decide the public exposure left him with little hope of future advancement in his beloved FBI. Finally, there was his choice of a second-act career, running security for the very buildings that Bin Laden had chosen as his target. It was heavy stuff.

After the service, most headed to dinner at a country club in New Jersey. "These are all suits," Rossini thought about the people attending the after-event. They did not seem like they fit the spirit of the man himself. John O'Neill had changed Rossini's life, inspiring him in his attitude and style to fight for the good guys without living like a monk. You didn't have to forsake audacity just because you had an ethos. Without the sound guidance of his boss, he would be increasingly adrift.[26]

* * *

The morning after O'Neill's funeral, Bush made an appearance at CIA headquarters to reassure the workforce, an appearance broadcast by the major media. The press had been told Bush was there to thank the employees for their work. Looking on presumably was the entire Langley staff, including Cofer Black, Rich Blee, Mike Scheuer, Alfreda Bikowsky, and Jen Matthews,[27] all of whom should have recognized the unique responsibility they held for the circumstances that now faced the nation.

"There is no question," the president began, at one point putting his arm around George Tenet, "that I am in the hall of patriots, and I've come to say a couple of things to you. First, thanks for your hard work. You know, George and I have been spending a lot of quality time together." The speech was interrupted by candid laughter from the assembled. "There's a reason," Bush continued. "I've got a lot of confidence in him, and I've got a lot of confidence in the CIA. And so should America."

"And in order to make sure that we're able to conduct a winning victory, we've got to have the best intelligence we can possibly have," the president declared. "And my report to the nation is, we've got the best intelligence we can possibly have thanks to the men and women of the CIA." Applause broke out, leaving Bush to take a moment.

"So, anyway," he concluded amid occasional roars of like-minded laughter, "I was sitting around having coffee with George and I said, 'I think I'd like to come out to thank people once again; I'd like to come out to the CIA, the center of great Americans, to thank you for your work. And I hope all the Americans who are listening to this TV broadcast understand how hard you're working, too.'" He concluded with an instruction: "Go back to work."[28]

Work that day included the invasion of Afghanistan. A team had been sent in with some of their best covert operatives, code-named "Jawbreaker." They were to liaise with the anti-Taliban Northern Alliance and be the front lines, in first, before the military. The invasion would be fought mostly by the Northern Alliance and three hundred military Special Forces, all relying on a core of more than one hundred CIA officers, reporting back to the CIA's CTC. For years, the agency and the military would disagree on who really led that war. It was an ego trip for the spies.[29]

Inside the safety of Langley headquarters, the executives were also figuring out how to execute the larger worldwide "war on terror," a malleable political concept being promoted to the public by their president, one that had been introduced to him by Tenet and Black at Camp David the weekend after the attacks. In the basement of NHB, Black noticed quickly that the one thousand extra bodies they had received on September 12 were the least qualified in the agency.[30] "I'm not taking all these bums," he asserted to George Tenet. "We need the best people."

Weeks later, they had gotten the best people the agency had to offer. "The number of officers working on terrorism—including contractors— nearly tripled, and the dollars flowing to the terrorism problem jumped even more," writes Tenet's briefer to the president, Mike Morrell. "Terrorism became the focus of nearly every overseas station and operational division in the agency . . . For the first time, terrorism analysts became the fighter pilots of the analytic ranks . . . now [attracting] some of the best and brightest of the agency's analysts. . . ."[31]

Their world had become a mix of old guard and new. The former were those at the CIA who had worked for several years on stopping Al Qaeda and felt they had been ignored. The latter were a growing number of would-be ladder climbers, now reporting to the former. The center of gravity for future advancement in the agency shifted quickly to counterterror.

Symbolic of this turnabout was the return of the man who had designed the blueprint for combating Al Qaeda and signed off on the hiring of most of the original CIA warriors for that cause: Mike Scheuer. If a failure had occurred, he certainly would bear some degree of blame for it, even if he had been out of the game; 9/11 saw him invited to return after his two years of banishment from Alec Station.

Scheuer certainly could have carried a big fat I-told-you-so in his swagger as he marched back into Alec Station as its "special adviser" days after the attacks, reporting to the new station chief, Hendrik Van Der Meulen. Scheuer was again working with his closest colleague, Alfreda Bikowsky.

"It was actually very sad," John Kiriakou tells it. "The title 'special adviser' really meant nothing. He had been shunted off to the side." Kiriakou points to the seating as evidence. "Everybody's at the front of the vault, all the leadership, [Bikowsky], Blee. I'm at the back of the vault and am heading what is arguably the least important branch of CTC, and I'm sitting next to Scheuer. No one cared what he had to say at that point."[32]

The same was not true for the rest of the longtime employees, those hired by Scheuer's former protégé, Bikowsky. She was running operations now significantly beefed up by the president's eager political backing, the prior restraints removed.[33] Her old friend Jen Matthews, one of few on the original Alec team with any training in clandestine operations, was put in charge of looking at Al Qaeda activity in the domestic United States, where one of her colleagues believes it is likely she was "read into" Michael Hayden's new NSA surveillance program.

Tenet's presentation had led to the targeting of terror operatives as a pivotal part of the CIA's mission, including creating and implementing kill and kidnapping lists. A High Value Target Unit (HVTU) had been created within the larger CounterTerrorist Center, staffed mostly with former Alec Station employees along with bright young people flooding into the agency in much the same way others had once enlisted to fight the enemy after Pearl Harbor. Matthews, who had previously overseen a handful of people in the targeting area, would within months join the HVTU as one of its key leaders.[34]

Overnight, people who had previously scoffed at the "Manson Family's" obsession with Al Qaeda were now reporting to them, even the highly critical operations officers out in the field. "I worked on Latin America," explains Fulton Armstrong. "Our issues were no longer Mexico, Central America, the Andean region, and problems in Columbia. That was taken away from us, and priorities were given to terrorism or transnational crimes. That left us subordinated to the so-called 'substantive experts' who knew nothing about the context we were working in."

"CTC, in the years immediately after September 11, was like this isolated stand-alone organization within the CIA where all the info was compartmentalized," says John Kiriakou. "No one else in the agency knew what was going on in CTC, and I think they all reinforced each other in there." Bikowsky and her close team members began to stick out to him more beginning then. He frequently found them holding court at a local restaurant on afternoons for long lunches, carrying on.

"I remember there was no crying in Alec Station [after September 11]," says Kiriakou. "There was crying all over the building, but there was never any crying there." His explanation is that "they really believed in their hearts that they had done everything they could to get the White House engaged, and the White House wouldn't engage. And so these three thousand deaths were the responsibility of the Bush administration and not of the CTC. They really believed that."

Having given themselves a psychological "out," if Kiriakou's opinion is correct, rather than being crushed by guilt or responsibility like some of the analysts over at the NSA, for the Alec staff, he says, "it was energizing."

\* \* \*

Inside the New York office, on October 3, a classified FBI report arrived. It was apparently either sent from Pat D'Amuro's team to the San Diego office or, more likely, vice versa. The US government had found their first living suspected facilitators for the September 11 criminal case—one, Omar al Bayoumi, who was now in Saudi Arabia, and another, Osama Basnan, still at large in southern California. Their report, presumably briefed by D'Amuro to the FBI director and the attorney general, also stated something troubling: "The possibility of [Basnan] being affiliated with the Saudi Arabian government or the Saudi Arabian Intelligence Service is supported by [Basnan] listing his employment in 1992 as the—." Unfortunately, the rest of that sentence remains redacted.

The report also explained that one of Bayoumi's school applications listed that he worked for a company called "Dallah/Avco." They had found that Avco Dallah was reported to hold the contracts for cleaning and maintenance at the three major Saudi airports. Having spoken with someone at the company, they learned Bayoumi's pay had started at $465 per month. Then, beginning about a month after Hazmi and Mihdhar had arrived in San Diego, Bayoumi's pay jumped to over $3,700 a month and stayed constant until the end of the year, when Hazmi left San Diego. It then dropped by $500 per month and remained there until Bayoumi left the country in August 2001.

The report further noted that Basnan moved into the same San Diego apartment building where hijackers Nawaf al Hazmi, Khalid al Mihdhar, and their associate Omar al Bayoumi had lived. Right after Bayoumi had moved away, Basnan moved in, which FBI investigators felt "could indicate [Basnan] succeeded Omar al Bayoumi and may be undertaking activities on behalf of the Government of Saudi Arabia."[35]

Around the time of that report, Pat D'Amuro was attending a national security conference at headquarters in DC when he ran into Robert Mueller, who asked him to come to his office. Mueller had been briefing George W. Bush and his staff about threats on a daily basis, and he wanted the man who would be giving him his own briefings on the investigation, D'Amuro, close. "I'll give you whatever you need to run [the 9/11 investigation] down here."

"I believed at the time," says D'Amuro, "that if I agreed to the director's request, I would be successful at bringing the case back to the New York office quickly. The reason being that the investigative body of knowledge regarding Al Qaeda resided in [that office]."[36]

Soon after arriving at headquarters, D'Amuro learned that executives at the Justice Department wanted the case investigated from the FBI's Washington field office and had already been making plans for the Eastern District of Virginia to prosecute any viable criminal case into 9/11. That was when he first met James Comey, a prosecutor for the district. For the first time since 1993, the prosecutors of New York's Southern District would not be handling a major Al Qaeda case. Comey would.

\* \* \*

"We are going to get all the money we want," she said. You could have heard a pin drop. Maureen Baginski did not realize it, but this was the second worst thing she could have uttered to the forty to fifty NSA analysts, many counterterror, and tech employees jammed inside a small conference room in

Fort Meade. The worst thing she could have said had been the sentence that preceded it. "You have to understand, 9/11 is a gift to NSA."[37]

It was early October, and Baginski had called the session, ironically, to try to address the crisis of grief and exhaustion felt by her staff. It was meant to be a kind of pep rally, yet this moment of candor, providing little consolation and drawing no sympathy, backfired. It deepened the ambivalence felt by the agency front line. "The staff took it as a betrayal," Tom Drake recalled. "They interpreted that management was in denial about the failure, denial that we did not keep America out of harm's way. A couple weeks after our inexcusable failure, you're saying this is a gift to NSA?"

One man in the room, "Nicholas," had been concerned about undue influence inside his CounterTerror Shop being exerted by the CIA, specifically from Rich Blee and "the CTC folks." Nicholas had heard that at one time the NSA's liaison to Alec Station had even been rumored to have dated Blee. There was always a lot of gossip within the insular world of any office, and more so for those doing spy work.

Still, Nicholas had seen firsthand Blee asking that NSA information not be provided to the Federal Bureau of Investigation. It had caused him to turn to Congress at one point over the summer, where he had been told to speak with superiors back at NSA first. Now, he was feeling that only weeks after the attacks, Blee still pushed too hard to contain information flow to the FBI. Knowing full well it would result in being moved to another department, Nicholas sent a message up the chain complaining about this. That chain included Baginski. He predictably was informed to pack up his desk, spending the remainder of his career working another subject.[38]

At least one other person in the room as Baginski spoke, "Bob," another employee of the CounterTerror Shop, felt deeply about the line of thinking Baginski was conveying. He became convinced that upper management was not going to take responsibility for their failure. "In the navy, the commander is supposed to take the hit," Tom Drake later remarked. "It happened on your watch. You're supposed to take responsibility for it." Bob had resolved to take matters into his own hands. The time came for the meeting he had nervously scheduled with Drake. It involved a crucial exchange.

Breaking protocol, Bob delivered to Drake a report both in hard copy and electronic form. The report, completed at the beginning of the year, was nothing less than devastating to his agency. Drake immediately viewed it as a "smoking gun." It detailed how the NSA had culled immense material from an NSA-monitored Al Qaeda telephone hub in Yemen, the one worked by departed analyst "Becky." Further, the report showed that the NSA had accurately mapped, in rich and extensive detail, Bin Laden's networks, cells, and associated movements.[39]

It was, in Drake's words, "an extraordinarily detailed long-term study of Al Qaeda's activities" that identified "the planning cells [for 9/11]," including "a number of the hijackers based on actual copy: Atta, Hazmi, Mihdhar." The three men were coming to be suspected as key players in the plot, having entered into the United States well in advance of most of the rest. The majority of the hijackers were now being called the "muscle men," coming to America somewhat last minute to play that role on the flights. A handful, though, seemed to be the leaders, having spent months or years in the United States. Drake could see that, by the start of 2001, those men had become known to the NSA.

That was just one part of the document, which Drake took to calling "The Finest of the NSA." He attributed to it and its creators "extremely thorough and sophisticated analysis." Perhaps most devastatingly, from the viewpoint of agency executives, the report contained specific warnings about September 11. "It lays out the history, it lays out the network, [and] it lays out the threat. It goes back and analyzes the *Cole* bombing, embassy, Khobar Towers," he said, referring to past Al Qaeda attacks against US interests.

It even warned of the use of planes.

"It was well known, I will flat out tell you, that using airplanes as weapons was a real threat," Drake told us, a statement that would contradict the later protestations of government officials such as Condoleezza Rice, who did not "think that anybody could have predicted that these people would take an airplane and slam it into the World Trade Center."

Drake added that the document also included "the pattern, the techniques [of Al Qaeda's terror operations], and more importantly the network." In terms of the terrorist cell structures, in other words "where they are putting their teams," Drake says it was "remarkably prescient." And the takeaway of the document was also clear: "These guys are serious, and they are coming back."

Regarding the report, Drake tells us, "I read it. I'm horrified. Horrified because it is operational intelligence," meaning it was written to be followed by specific military action against Al Qaeda using the information. "It is rarely [*sic*] that there are 100 percent indications of warnings that you were in advance planning stages in the network. You had certain names, some of the key names that were part of that. We had the network. But remember the 'Chop Chain'?"

For reasons unknown, and to the extreme frustration of the likes of Bob, the document representing the NSA's finest work was never approved by these individuals for passage to the White House, the military, the CIA, or the FBI. Despite repeated attempts by Bob and others, that group had apparently never approved the report to be shared outside of the CT Shop, where it might have been put into action. If true, that document might have been presumed only weeks after the attacks to be career-ending for the parties involved, if it were now to be shared outside of the NSA.

"So you can imagine Bob's extraordinary frustration and grave concern," Drake reflected. "He was feeling incredibly guilty. Culturally, the workforce knew we utterly failed the nation. It's one thing when people die overseas. It's another when it's your own nation that's been attacked and it's happening on your watch. You try to get someone to take action, that we have to share this with others, and you're told 'No'?"

We asked Drake what could have been done with this information even late in the plot. He responded, "You would have activated the system and gone directly after the players in those cells. Military through JSOC [Joint Special Operations Command]. Law enforcement in certain countries. People forget FBI has an international presence, both international and domestic. There could have been arrests."

Drake was determined to find out why this had not happened. After Bob gave Drake the "finest of NSA" document, Drake brazenly walked across the hall to Maureen Baginski's office and set it on her desk. Drake watched her body language change.

"Tom," she told him, "I wish you had not brought this to my attention."

At least she was being forthright.

* * *

It is likely that Tom Drake also told his ally Kirk Wiebe what he had learned. Drake knew Wiebe from a previous contract he had worked on at the agency, and they shared information. Wiebe, as noted earlier, was now serving as a business manager and analyst inside the SIGINT Automation Research Center (SARC) after a thirty-year career in US intelligence, most of it at the NSA.

Wiebe's SARC was a very small and intimate team of about a dozen, including another of Drake's allies, Bill Binney, the Center's cofounder, and Ed Loomis, a computer scientist serving as its "integrator." They were rounded out by a few other creative and flexible employees and contractors. The term used for their kind of activity was "skunkworks," meaning "an experimental laboratory or department of a company or institution, typically smaller than, and independent of, its main research division."

Binney had accumulated enough credibility within the agency to ask for what was essentially his own "start-up" inside the NSA, like a bunch of guys working on a project from their garages, except their garages were inside a steel and glass high-rise and were funded by the US government to the tune of just over a million dollars. When Wiebe met Binney a year after he started the SARC, his eyes were opened. He later told Austrian documentary filmmaker Friedrich Moser, "I saw the answer right before me. This little research organization had the keys to NSA's future."[40]

Weeks earlier, shortly after the attacks, Binney had stepped outside his door and literally stumbled over "big boxes of servers coming in from Dell, lining the hallways." His team wondered what was happening.

Soon after, "I was in my organization [the SARC]," says Wiebe, "and we had a little conference room for meetings and stuff, [but when I] walked in there, the door was shut for some reason. Somebody got very angry when I entered, an analyst that we knew. He became very irate and asked me to leave."

Wiebe asked his boss, "Bill, what's going on here?"

Bill Binney was a take-charge kind of guy. He suspected the worst, and he was determined to find an answer. Then, in early October, Binney again stepped into the hallway outside SARC to find the equipment outside gone. Binney believed the hardware's disappearance meant it was being assembled in offices nearby. He turned to a contractor who had helped him develop his prized software, what he called ThinThread.

The contractor said to Binney, "You know what they are doing down the hall? They're taking in data on every US citizen in the country."[41]

Tom Drake may have been tipped off about this by his friends in the SARC, or it may have been other unspecified analysts, as he describes vaguely, who quietly approached him complaining that they were being asked to spy on Americans without a warrant. However it happened, Drake says he became aware of the same information that his friend Wiebe inside the SARC had learned. Again, he approached Maureen Baginski with both questions and protests concerning what he was hearing.

He was more hesitant this time around, as senior officials recently made him aware of a growing concern among the executive leadership that he might be a "problem person." Drake had been there only weeks, so this, he understood, was not boding well for his career. His decision to bring Baginski the "finest of NSA" document had obviously cost him.

This time, Baginski conceded that Drake had a right—working at a high level inside SIGINT—to understand what was going on. She suggested he reach out to the NSA's attorney for the rest of the story.[42]

* * *

Pat D'Amuro moved to Washington, DC, on October 7, where headquarters executives immediately renamed his investigation "PENTTBOM." As big moves were taking place at the NSA that would soon be feeding information to the FBI, the director had personally asked the favor that D'Amuro run his work from the nation's capital.

D'Amuro brought in agents he liked from across the country to be his deputies. He also had thirty to forty agents back in the New York office working the investigation for him at any given time. Some of them moved back and forth between New York and DC for periods of time, working the case from both offices. Others from New York City shifted in and out of the investigation, including Ali Soufan. D'Amuro's team also began receiving assistance from another man in the building who had been detailed to the counterterror office, the CIA's Tom Wilshere.

"I didn't know at the time," says D'Amuro, "that the CIA had blocked notification about two of the hijackers from my team, and that the agency actually sent one of the people who made that decision to work for me at FBI headquarters," referring to Wilshere. He would learn that years later.[43]

By the end of D'Amuro's first week in Washington, the New York Times was reporting that "while law enforcement officials say the investigation of 9/11 is continuing aggressively, 'At the same time . . . efforts to thwart attacks have been given a much higher priority.' Attorney general John

Ashcroft and FBI director Robert Mueller 'have ordered agents to drop their investigation of the [9/11] attacks or any other assignment any time they learn of a threat or lead that might suggest a future attack.' Mueller believes his agents have 'a broad understanding of the events of September 11,' and now need 'to concentrate on intelligence suggesting that other terrorist attacks [are] likely.'" The *Times* quoted an unnamed law enforcement official as stating, "The investigative staff has to be made to understand that we're not trying to solve a crime now. Our number one goal is prevention."[44]

* * *

"You don't understand, Mr. Drake. The White House has approved the program," the NSA's lawyer told him by phone that October. Feeling the hairs stand up on the back of his neck, Drake was shocked by Vito Potenza's casual dismissal. In Drake's mind, this response from NSA counsel was reminiscent of Richard Nixon's notorious rejoinder in his interview with David Frost, that "If the president does it, it's *not* illegal."[45]

The program George Tenet and Michael Hayden apparently started under their own discretion immediately after the attacks had been given further legal protection when, right after his photo op at CIA headquarters, President Bush secretly expanded the decades-old executive order under which the NSA had been operating since Reagan had initially issued it.

The last week of September, "StellarWind" is said to have gone live. It was "a number of new, highly classified intelligence activities" devoted to "the interception without a court order of certain international communications where there was 'a reasonable basis to conclude that one party to the communication is a member of Al Qaeda, affiliated with Al Qaeda, or a member of an organization affiliated with Al Qaeda.'"[46]

Bill Binney claims he learned that the early StellarWind "included not just eavesdropping on domestic calls but the inspection of domestic email," the obtaining of "billing records on US citizens," and was "keeping [call logs called] 'pen registers' on everyone in the country." Binney was told by insiders, "At the outset, the program recorded 320 million calls per day . . . which represented about seventy-three to eighty percent of the total value of the agency's worldwide intercepts." The American public had no idea.

Binney suspected ThinThread, the revolutionary targeted surveillance tool code he had created with his team inside the SARC—a program that had been rejected by NSA managers less than two months prior—had been reverse engineered by other parties working for the NSA to create StellarWind. "They had to use the only software that managed large-scale information," he thought. He had some educated guesses as to which people would have been hired for that task and learned from a source that one of the first things they had done was to remove all the encryption algorithms he had placed in ThinThread to protect the privacy rights and identities of US citizens inside the database.

As Binney knew, his software would be capable of graphing the relationships of US citizens using their various means of communications. "You don't really care about what's in the conversation [by phone or email]," says the SARC's Ed Loomis, a statement that seems absurd at first hearing. The program did not include recording phone calls, unless a warrant was obtained for a particular caller, something Bush believed kept them on the right side of the ethical question. But the SARC team had recognized in designing ThinThread that people "said" far more with their metadata. "The better information," says Loomis, "is in knowing who's talking to who, when, how often. Are there patterns? What is the organization of the relationships?"[47]

This was no small operation. On October 1, at Hayden's stated insistence, he had briefed the members of the House of Representatives who made up the intelligence committee, headed by Rep. Porter Goss, about the existence of the program. After watching Hayden test the waters with Congress and receive little pushback, Vice President Dick Cheney began communicating with Hayden through messages passed by George Tenet. The White House wanted to take what had been started to the next level.[48]

Two days later, the vice president's lawyer David Addington had written an order, signed by George W. Bush, officially creating an expansion of Tenet's and Hayden's StellarWind.[49] It was described in a later government report as a combination of a telephone surveillance initiative, that part dubbed the "Terrorist Surveillance Program," as well as "Other Intelligence Activities."

"The NSA was also able to access, for the first time, massive volumes of personal financial records," the report explained, "such as credit-card transactions, wire transfers, and bank withdrawals—that were being reported to the Treasury Department by financial institutions. These included millions of 'suspicious-activity reports,' or SARS, according to two former Treasury officials who declined to be identified talking about sensitive programs."

"The NSA identified domestic targets based on leads that were often derived from the seizure of Qaeda computers and cell phones overseas. If, for example, a Qaeda cell phone seized in Pakistan had dialed a phone number in the United States, the NSA would target the US phone number—which would then lead agents to look at other numbers in the United States and abroad called by the targeted phone."[50]

Bush made the decision, reportedly, to keep the program a "close hold." The order was so closely guarded Drake was told it was being kept by Addington in his safe. The attorney general, John Ashcroft, and the White House's attorney for intelligence policy, James Baker, were made aware and gave verbal approval as to "form and legality" of the program. It was considered so sensitive, so important, that this combination of programs remains unknown to the public, that it was not even given a code name by which to be referred. It was most often called the President's Surveillance Program, or simply the Program.

Bush's authorization for the Program had a sunset clause, expiring within a mere forty-five days. It was being used in the short-term, it was said, during a time of emergency and meant to detect and prevent another attack. Bush, however, was free to reauthorize it for another forty-five days when the time came, if he felt it was still necessary, and yet again after that.

It immediately became a trans-government project. The NSA "was responsible for conducting the actual collection of information," government investigators later confirmed, but the information collected through domestic electronic surveillance was then "disseminat[ed by] intelligence reports to other agencies such as the Federal Bureau of Investigation [and] the Central Intelligence Agency . . ." Bush required that he personally sign off on anyone "read in" on the Program, unless they were involved by operational necessity at one of the agencies involved.

The FBI director, Robert Mueller, was therefore read into the Program, along with some of his managers and agents, and so were some working inside the CIA. In fact, every forty-five days, as the Program was set to expire, analysts inside the CIA's CounterTerrorist Center, possibly at Alec Station, were asked to prepare a terrorism assessment "focusing primarily on threat to the US homeland." They were not initially aware of the purpose behind it.

George Tenet's chief of staff John Moseman was described as the "focal point" for the preparing of the memoranda. CIA attorneys then reviewed the memo and weighed whether it made for "a compelling case for reauthorization." If so, it would be signed by Tenet and sent to the president, who would reauthorize the domestic spying program for another forty-five days.

A couple dozen people in Washington were the only Americans aware of a monumental change in how their government had historically operated. Among them were now Tom Drake, Bill Binney, Kirk Wiebe, and Ed Loomis, who had sleuthed it themselves.

When Drake spoke with the NSA attorney, the attorney had confirmed it like it was nothing. Drake sat silently on the other end of the line, in his office, breathing into the phone. He claims a warning instantly entered his mind, once made by Senator Frank Church, investigator of the intelligence community in the 1970s.

> I know the capacity that is there to make tyranny total in America, and we must see to it that this agency and all agencies that possess this technology operate within the law and under proper supervision, so that we never cross over that abyss. That is the abyss from which there is no return.

This decision was sure to have enormous downstream consequences. This Drake knew. The effect of StellarWind and the Program was to treat the domestic population as an enemy, not as citizens with rights, but as targets of suspicion. "The US was being turned into [the] equivalent of a foreign nation for blanket dragnet mass surveillance on a scale that we had never seen before, the world had never seen before," Drake said, reflecting on the magnitude of the moment.

He thought a bit about the man running his agency and why he was choosing to take this path. He came to an epiphany. "Michael Hayden is pathologically refusing to accept any responsibility or accountability for 9/11," he thought. "He is choosing, in his mind, that he will instead put his secret stamp on history. And his secret stamp on history will be [these domestic spying programs]." He understood in that moment: "We were going to use the attacks as the excuse, protected as an extraordinary state secret; the United States government would willfully, as an act of commission—not omission—violate the Fourth Amendment and subvert the Constitution on an extraordinarily mass scale."

"What do I do?" Drake tells us how he thought of his predicament. "If I remain silent, I will be an accessory to a crime." He determined he was not going to break the oath he had taken four times to support and defend the Constitution. "Now I was having to defend the Constitution against my own government."

Drake went to see the guys in the SARC. He had decided he was going to stay and do what he could to fight the good fight from the inside. For Wiebe and Binney, they simply could not go along with it. An official legal opinion was in the works over in the Office of Legal Counsel to justify the Program, by John Yoo, the lawyer in charge of national security matters within the OLC. Congress would pass the USA PATRIOT Act at month's end, a law including language that would later be argued to bolster the legal status of the NSA program. It passed the Senate 98 to 1 and the House 356 to 66.

Yoo's memo would not be completed until the second day of November. In the meantime, as a later government report noted, "the first [legal] opinion explicitly addressing the legality of the [President's Surveillance Program] was not drafted until after the program had been formally authorized by President Bush in October 2001." It was illegal until someone could make an argument why it was not.

Yoo's primary initial arguments in his later legal opinion would lean heavily on precedent that had allowed for searches of persons crossing the border. Therefore, electronic data crossing the border in or out of the United States had a similar "border crossing exception." A second argument he would mount was that the Fourth Amendment had been created primarily to curb abuses by law enforcement people, so electronic surveillance justified to be in "direct support of military operations" was not a violation. His arguments had the appearance of trying to loophole the Constitution.

It was not enough for Binney and Wiebe, who were convinced a crime was being committed. With more than three-quarters of a century of combined experience at the NSA, they walked out of the building for the last time on Halloween 2001. And they had a plan.[51]

* * *

When journalist Lawrence Wright wrote a piece about John O'Neill for *The New Yorker,* he contacted Pat D'Amuro, who then instructed his team of agents to skip the normal chain of protocol and "leak" their stories directly to Wright—en masse.

To Mark Rossini's surprise, Wright, the Austin, Texas-based writer, made a transatlantic trip to Spain to speak with him. Rossini was there investigating a Madrid-based terror cell. He had only begun a long process inside himself, questioning what responsibility he held for his mentor's death.

Wright wrote longhand on a large yellow legal pad as Rossini told him a story he had yet to explain to his fellow agents, compelled by the credibility of his trusted boss. "None of us who were interviewed in that book ever got permission from FBI headquarters," says Rossini. "D'Amuro essentially told us, 'You talk, I'll handle it. Tell him what he needs to know.'"[52]

The story Rossini imparted to Wright in Spain would not emerge publicly for nearly another five years, when it was included on page 311 of Wright's book *The Looming Tower*.

> There was a cable that same day [January 5, 2000] from Riyadh Station to Alec Station concerning Mihdhar's American visa. One of the FBI agents assigned to Alec, Doug Miller, read the cable and drafted a memo requesting permission to advise the FBI of the Malaysia [Al Qaeda] meeting and the likelihood that one or more of the terrorists would be traveling [from that meeting] soon to the United States. Such permission was required before transmitting intelligence from one organization to another. Miller was told, "This is not a matter for the FBI." Miller followed up a week later by querying Tom Wilshere, a CIA deputy chief . . . Miller sent him the memo he had drafted and asked, "Is this a no-go or should I remake it in some way?" Wilshere never responded. After that, Miller forgot about the matter.

We asked Rossini why he imparted this startling story to a journalist while keeping it from official channels. "*I'm* going up against George Tenet?" Rossini asked rhetorically in response. "*I'm* going to go up against the CIA? Who the fuck am *I*? Who's going to believe me? What, am I going to call [FBI director] Robert Mueller on the phone? You know what can happen [as a result of such an action]?" At the end of the day, Rossini simply did not trust that what he told government investigators would not be used to destroy him.

\* \* \*

Around November, a CIA historian, Rudy Rousseau, was poring through counterterror documents to prepare the Director of Central Intelligence to deal with the coming government investigations. His work had been given an official name, the DCI 9/11 Review Group. Most of Rousseau's early findings had been fairly positive in defending the agency's performance. Then, while searching through the incoming and outgoing cables of Alec Station from January of 2000, he discovered the names of two hijackers: Nawaf al Hazmi and Khalid al Mihdhar.[53]

A cable from March 2000 had been sent from a CIA station overseas to the employees of Alec Station informing them that a known Bin Laden operative, Nawaf al Hazmi, had flown to Los Angeles. Several cables also found from January of 2000 detailed the travel of that same man to a meeting of suspected and known terrorists in Malaysia, where he was met by another Bin Laden operative known to Alec Station, Khalid al Mihdhar. Several of the cables made clear that Mihdhar possessed an American visa allowing him multiple entry into the United States. Rousseau no doubt found this somewhat alarming to read.

What is less clear is whether Rousseau also provided Tenet with the electronic message written at the time by FBI agent Doug Miller to alert John O'Neill. The warning, never sent, was the one recently described to Lawrence Wright by Mark Rossini, which included an attachment: Mihdhar's visa. The Miller email should still have remained in CIA's computer system for Rousseau to find. As a later investigation determined, "[Miller] accessed the draft again [five weeks later] on 11 and 16 February 2000. In a series of mid-February notes, the [FBI] detailee instructed a [CIA] computer systems contractor to delete numerous 'dead' cables in [the system] but specifically asked this contractor to retain the draft CIR."[54] On that Central Intelligence Report was another message, digitally placed there by a staff operations officer, Michael Anne Casey: "pls hold off [on sending] for now per [deputy chief] Wilshere."[55]

If Tenet had any question as to whether Alec Station's information about the future hijackers' American travel had or had not been passed to the FBI, that message would seem to point to the negative. Rousseau seemed to agree, telling Tenet that he had "determined that CIA might have failed for more than a year to notify the FBI of the pair's presence in the United States."

Tenet was arguably flying higher at that time than any previous CIA director ever had. He was enjoying enormously expanded powers and budget provided to the agency by a grateful White House. Now his archivist was handing him documents that could unravel it all.

"The FBI failed, the CIA failed, the State Department bureau of consular affairs failed, the FAA failed. We all failed [before 9/11]," John Kiriakou admits to us, but expanding on the significance of what Rousseau had told his DCI that day, he says, "But it wasn't the FAA that could have prevented the attack in the planning stages, right? It was the CIA, who had the information and just never shared it with anybody."

Tenet's chief of staff immediately believed that what Rousseau had found could undo everything, "the 'smoking gun' anecdote that the investigators would seize on to blame the CIA for 9/11." Rousseau tried to convince Tenet it was not as bad as it seemed, but the director knew better.

"No," Tenet said. "This is bad news."

# 7

# ABYSS

*"Men of God and men of war have strange affinities."*

Cormac McCarthy, *Blood Meridian: Or the Evening Redness in the West*

The Rousseau briefing represents the moment the Director of Central Intelligence could no longer allege ignorance about pre 9/11 failures inside his counterterror department. Whatever George Tenet may or may not have known prior, the documents he was shown should have left him with little deniability that managers including Cofer Black, Rich Blee, Tom Wilshere, Alfreda Bikowsky, and Jen Matthews owed, at minimum, an explanation.

This was an unwelcome development. Tenet's big sell at Camp David only weeks prior had already brought an early Christmas to those same individuals. Many might assume that under a well-functioning and accountable American government, a briefing like the one George Tenet received from his employee Rudy Rousseau that November would have immediately resulted in a "come to Jesus" meeting with his key managers. Black, Blee, Wilshere, Bikowsky, Matthews, and desk officer Michael Anne Casey might have been relieved of their duties pending the outcome of a thorough investigation by the agency's inspector general, with the full cooperation and active encouragement of the agency's leadership.

"It was never spoken about. Not at all," Mark Rossini makes clear. He retained his position at Alec Station as a detailee from the FBI during this period. From what he saw and heard, he does not believe such a meeting ever occurred between Tenet or CIA lawyers and those working at Alec Station. "It wasn't raised, suggested, not even an idea."

John Kiriakou, working across the hallway at the time, confirms Rossini's memory. "Nobody ever talked about it," he said, adding after a pause. "Interesting."

"A self-protective bureaucracy" is what career CIA officer Bob Baer calls it, highlighting the contrast to the way a similar incident was handled in a different time. "I mean, after Pearl Harbor, you had the commanders there, whether they were responsible or not, they were simply removed. All sorts of people lost their jobs. That's not how we do things in the United States anymore. You know, we came clean after Pearl Harbor. Why can't you do it now?"

"It's the senior managers, they call them, and mid-level managers who are supposed to set the value system," says Fulton Armstrong. "If the value system atrophies, and no one is held accountable, then you have a downward spiral. The downward spiral driven by the incompetence and errors, as well as by the politicization during the Bush-Cheney period, I think have completely redefined, certainly the image, but also much of what the definition of 'intelligence' is today, to the detriment of our national security."

\* \* \*

"It was a month or two until I learned about [the CIA's pre 9/11 withholding from the FBI about] Mihdhar and Hazmi," says Pat D'Amuro. "At the time, we were too busy trying to stop another attack rather than worrying about the mistakes of the past."

D'Amuro was working at FBI headquarters from 5 a.m. to midnight, then back the next day at five again to do the morning briefing. "I didn't get out a lot then to talk socially with my team," he remembers. "And you know, information doesn't always filter up, unless it's in writing. And I do not recall seeing that in written communications."

One day in November, Ali Soufan walked into D'Amuro's DC office. His first time back from Yemen since the attacks, Soufan explained to his boss that the CIA's CounterTerrorist Center had apparently known Mihdhar and Hazmi had been inside the United States for eighteen months but had deliberately lied to the FBI.

"We sent a number of leads from our official FBI investigation into the USS *Cole* bombing to the CIA," Soufan informed his boss. "They never responded to certain of the requests." One of the requests to the spy agency had wanted more information about a phone number across the street from the Washington Hotel in Bangkok in early 2000. Then he unloaded the twist. "Mihdhar was a son-in-law of Ahmed al Hada."

D'Amuro's eyebrows went up. He recognized that Hada had been a person of interest to the New York office since they had discovered in 1998 that his home in Yemen served as one of, if not *the*, key telephone communications centers for the plotters of Al Qaeda's attacks. Hada's house was very important to them. They had used calls in and out to create a chart of Bin Laden's network in their JTTF bull pen back in New York. The switchboard had been used by plotters of the '98 embassy bombings, and it was suspected to have been used for the 2000 USS *Cole* bombing.

Had they known of a connection between the USS *Cole* bombing in Yemen's capital and Mihdhar himself, they would have been all over him. After all, Soufan pointed out to D'Amuro, two of Hada's other sons-in-law had already martyred themselves. All this he had apparently put together from the folder handed to him by the CIA's Sana'a station chief after the attacks. For the first time, it occurred to D'Amuro that the attacks could have been stopped, and stopped by his FBI team.

"If that information had come to me," D'Amuro thought, "please, you don't have to be a rocket scientist to know that you have to pull out all the stops to find out what the hell is going on, as soon as you can. We would have requested an emergency FISA to conduct electronic surveillance, we would have put them under physical surveillance and, if we still couldn't figure out what they were doing here, we would have pulled them in for questioning."[1] That would indeed have seemed a sensible reaction to learning about the connection between the Yemen phone hub and Mihdhar.

* * *

Outside the sparse mountains of Tora Bora along Afghanistan's border with Pakistan, veteran CIA operative Gary Berntsen knew the primary target of the war, Usama Bin Laden, was close at hand. A maze of intense cliffs and winding caves set beneath snow-covered caps, Tora Bora had long been Bin Laden's fallback stronghold.

Only days before, about three dozen US special forces had positioned themselves in strategic locations throughout the mountains. These special forces were armed with handheld laser target designators that could "paint" a target, which would then be obliterated by ordnance dropped by US warplanes. Holed up in a nearby schoolhouse, Berntsen fed intelligence to his men while reporting back to Washington. His covert team known as Jawbreaker had Bin Laden and his closest Al Qaeda fighters cornered. By the end of November, the battle for Tora Bora had begun.[2]

Berntsen and his Jawbreakers had tracked Bin Laden's convoy of several hundred cars as it fled from the town of Jalalabad weeks prior. Though Al Qaeda's leader, in an attempt at a ruse, had given his satellite phone to another man who deliberately took a different route,[3] Berntsen's team heard Bin Laden's voice on shortwave radio coming from inside Tora Bora. Human sources also confirmed to Berntsen that Bin Laden was, in fact, positioned in the mountain complex.

For days and days, US warplanes absolutely pummeled the region from above.[4] Meanwhile, Berntsen had been warning his boss back at Langley, Cofer Black's director of operations Hank Crumpton—a man Black had pulled out of his short retirement specifically to run the Afghan invasion—that the "back door" of the mountain cave system was open.[5] If Bin Laden wanted it, he had a clear route into Pakistan. This fact was reported to the president in his daily briefings, but Bush was reportedly assured by Pakistan's president that their army would cover the southern pass.[6] Crumpton was wary, so he went in person and explained to Bush and Cheney with the aid of satellite imagery that, Pakistani assurances aside, the border was wide open.[7]

Berntsen was concerned that their opportunity to make good on all of the rhetoric about taking Bin Laden alive might slip away. Berntsen's CIA colleague Gary Shroen, who had been one of the first officers dispatched to Afghanistan, was given clear instruction by Cofer Black before departing: "You have one mission. Go find the Al Qaeda and kill them. We're going to eliminate them. Get bin Laden, find him. I want his head in a box . . . I want to take it down and show the president."[8] Berntsen received a similarly blunt order. An unguarded exit for the most wanted man in the world was unacceptable, and so Berntsen made a request for eight hundred Army Rangers to assist his Jawbreaker team and Afghan allies in closing the trap. To his absolute dismay, his request was denied.[9]

Though the CIA was running the show on the ground, the military might still had to come at the approval of the Department of Defense. Back in DC, General Tommy Franks, Commander of US Central Command, was reluctant to commit troops, suggesting that it would take too long to get them in place, despite the fact that hundreds of soldiers were stationed at Bagram Air Force Base and twelve hundred Marines were waiting near Kandahar.

At this stressful time, a message came to Berntsen that upped the tension. His team could see the concern on his face as he read it. "I'm being replaced by Rich Blee," he stated plainly. Those around him let out an audible sound of unhappiness. Berntsen felt as if a bucket of cold water had been thrown in his face. "I couldn't believe," he later wrote, "they were doing this in the middle of the most important battle of the war."[10]

His men were familiar with Blee, and they were resolute in their response. "No disrespect to Rich, but when you leave, we leave." Berntsen came to believe the move to name Blee as Afghanistan's station chief at that time was political, attributing it to Blee's closeness to George Tenet and his spies division director James Pavitt.[11] Some have more deeply questioned the motivations behind this ill-timed rotation. The Intelligence Committees of Congress were gearing up to begin their official investigation into 9/11 matters the following month. As Blee arrived in Afghanistan to take over for Berntsen, he also brought with him the young staff operations officer from Alec Station, Michael Anne Casey.

Mark Rossini asserts his belief that Blee took Casey along to "hide her" from the coming congressional investigation. "They obstructed justice by pushing her away," he says. The public affairs officer at CIA later issued an email in 2011 calling this claim "absurd."

Rossini counters, "How could you hide government employees? It seems absurd. But the fact is she was placed physically far away, and it made it very inconvenient [for investigators] to talk to her." Was Rossini's speculation right, and if so, had Blee been sent to Kabul for the same reason?

Seven years after Berntsen raised the question in his book, Hank Crumpton came forward to take credit for the decision to transfer Blee. "Berntsen and his team had done a great job. As we turned to the occupation, Rich was the right person to hold the first station chief position in Afghanistan." Crumpton places the timing of the transition as completed "before Christmas."[12] Berntsen is more precise. He learned he was being replaced on December 9.

Berntsen's place on the ground at Tora Bora was taken up by a major in Delta Force, Thomas Greer, who assembled a small cadre of elite American and British commandos as well as a ragtag group of Afghanis. Later, Greer would write, "our nation was relying on a fractious bunch of AK-47–toting lawless bandits and tribal thugs. . . ."[13]

Kiriakou once heard a story. "There had been a communication from a middleman on the mountain, asking CENTCOM to not bomb during that night so that women and children could be evacuated. Then, Bin Laden, his lieutenants, and his fighters would give themselves up in the morning. Tommy Franks agreed to that. We were on the Al Qaeda comms, but they knew that we were on their comms. So they went silent for a period. And as it turned out, they all evacuated down the back side of the mountain."

One report had Bin Laden's voice last heard on his shortwave radio, praising his most loyal fighters and asking their forgiveness for his having drawn them into defeat. There are varying accounts of his escape, but he is believed to have made it out of the mountains and into Pakistan shortly thereafter. It was a walk Bin Laden had made numerous times, and it usually only took him about twelve hours.

This epic failure on the part of the CIA and the Defense Department roughly coincided with the transition from Berntsen and his Jawbreakers to Blee and his staff. Did the transition from Berntsen to Blee have an effect? Would things have been different had the Jawbreaker lead remained until the Battle of Tora Bora completed? Why was anyone in Washington reluctant to commit the necessary forces to finish the job of capturing or killing Bin Laden? It is almost unthinkable, as the nation had a president talking like a cowboy about smoking Bin Laden out, a counterterror director of CIA demanding his head in a box, and an apparent public frothing at the mouth for vengeance.

"They later got an intelligence report claiming that Bin Laden had escaped in the back of a pickup truck dressed as a woman, never to be seen again," says Kiriakou. "Everybody in the CTC blamed CENTCOM for Bin Laden's escape. Everybody."

The war would begin to lose its singular focus after this, as tangential pet projects were given undue priority, and the quick march across Afghanistan metastasized into the war that will "not end in our lifetimes."

\* \* \*

As soon as Pat D'Amuro learned that bombs had started falling in Afghanistan, he had gone into a briefing with the FBI director and told him, "There's going to be tremendous amounts of intelligence coming through the military. Soldiers on the ground don't know anything about Al Qaeda. We need to have agents attached to the military in combat areas, after it has been deemed safe, and look for pocket litter, computers, and other physical and electronic intelligence."[14]

He knew it would be helpful in investigating who else was involved in the attacks, not to mention his second role in spotting current threats. D'Amuro assigned two of his team, George Crouch and Russell Fincher, to the Bagram area of Afghanistan to do that job. By the time Ibn Al Libi was captured by the Pakistani army and handed over to US forces at Bagram in mid-December, one general was so impressed by what he saw of the FBI that he asked D'Amuro to send more of his New York agents to be assigned to their team at Bagram.

"You guys are outstanding at these interrogations and debriefings. We want more of it," said the general.

"We had five-plus people sitting in jail in the US serving anywhere from twenty-five years to life who had been put there by us using our interrogation techniques," D'Amuro responded proudly. "That's how you get people to talk. Ali Muhammad, Joe the Moroccan, they all folded under our techniques without any use of enhanced interrogation techniques or torture."

Over the successive weeks, including the Christmas and New Year's holidays, D'Amuro's interrogators, Crouch and Fincher, spent more than eighty hours with Ibn Al Libi, who seemed genuinely friendly. They attempted to form the kind of bond that had yielded results for them in the past. Fincher, being a devout Christian, prayed with Libi and talked religion. Their tactics paid dividends, as Libi told his interrogators about a man named Richard Reid, a British citizen and Al Qaeda member who planned to carry out a suicide bombing on an airplane. Libi expressed an interest in further cooperation should the United States strike a deal with him whereby his wife and family could emigrate, and he would be prosecuted within the framework of the American legal system. They were getting somewhere.[15]

Only weeks into his new tenure as CIA's station chief in Afghanistan, Rich Blee got word of the FBI's successes on his new turf. Blee complained directly to George Tenet.[16] Tenet, in turn, made his case to the decider himself, George W. Bush. Fincher and Crouch could not believe what happened next. It was all the more startling because of how valuable the target was considered. There, at the US military's new Bagram Air Base in the

Parwan Province of Afghanistan, the FBI agents first learned their inter-rogatee would be theirs no longer, after a man named Albert (last name unknown), a member of Cofer Black's CTC, burst into Libi's prison cell and screamed at him, "You're going to Egypt."

Sometime not long after, the FBI men again watched Albert enter the cell, this time accompanied by his darkly dressed muscle team. They strapped Libi to a stretcher and wrapped his feet, hands, and mouth with duct tape. It was as if the FBI investigators were not even there. Albert leaned over the stretcher and, quieting to a whisper, spoke into Libi's ear. Like a schoolboy challenging somebody weaker on the playground, Albert was heard to utter that while Libi was in Egypt with their secret police, Albert would be "going to find your mother and fuck her."[17]

Fincher was disgusted by what he overheard, knowing the words meant that trust would forever be broken with the suspect. A hood was placed over Libi's head before the stretcher was wheeled out to a waiting pickup truck that drove directly onto a cargo plane. The FBI men remained behind in what had been Libi's cell, quietly steaming and wondering what this turn of events meant for them and the Bureau.

* * *

The final battles of many years of a cold war between the CIA and FBI were playing out at the start of 2002, with the ultimate victor to be chosen by the White House. Throughout the Clinton era, the CIA had been forced to play second fiddle to the Bureau as the White House had largely favored a law enforcement approach to the problem of terrorism. Attorneys who would become famous, like Patrick Fitzgerald and David Kelley and Mary Jo White, had successfully convicted those who had threatened the country, backed up in their investigations by law enforcement officers of the FBI's New York office, eventually led by John O'Neill.

Now, four months after the attacks, the CIA knew its actions in the lead up could possibly do them in, but they also knew that no one else knew that yet. No smoking gun had yet emerged publicly to lay blame directly at the door of CIA for their failure to prevent the attacks, while, by contrast, stories were already circulating that FBI headquarters in Washington had blown it regarding Zacarious Moussaoui, a suspected terrorist arrested in Minnesota the previous August. Another story would emerge late that spring that would also capture the popular imagination, regarding a memo from the FBI's Phoenix office pointing to Arab men attending flight schools.

There were other factors weighing against the FBI in early 2002. They did not have a direct seat at President Bush's table in the way their counterpart the CIA did, led by a cabinet-level director. As part of the Department of Justice, the FBI's director reported to the cabinet-level attorney general, one extra layer between their own advocate and the White House. While George Tenet had been bold in advocating for the power of his agency, his counterpart Robert Mueller, appointed FBI director only at the start of September, was playing defense.

"I can't prove this," says FBI agent Mark Rossini, "but a blind person could probably see it too. I think Mueller was told early on, 'Just keep your mouth shut, and we won't take away your agency.'"

Word spread that the Bureau's continued existence was at stake after September 11. There was a perception of "arrogance and malfunction" at head-quarters, which the *Washington Post* noted upon Mueller's nomination, stating that, "the bureau is facing political pressure unlike any in its history."[18]

Rossini adds, "Right or wrong, Mueller did everything in his power to keep the FBI as an institution alive. And he did." Mueller's number one concern, Rossini believes, was to not further perpetuate the rift between the CIA and FBI, especially as the agency's star appeared on the rise. "The FBI is a law enforcement agency," reminds Rossini. "At the end of the day, all those cocksuckers in Congress are lawyers, and they know the law must survive and persevere."

On an ideological level, the CIA's approach also gelled better with the objectives of America's most powerful vice president in history, Dick Cheney, who famously entered office with a goal of restoring the power of the presidency to its pre-Watergate glory, a matter being worked on by White House lawyers under a theory known as the "unitary executive." If terrorism could be redefined as "acts of war," something the post–9/11 public seemed more than willing to accept, and if war could be redefined not as something waged against a single nation or their government but against networks of individuals with shared goals, then the entire world could become a theoretical battlefield, with wartime decisions made without the interference of the judicial branch, but solely by the commander in chief.

Tenet's Camp David speech had not only been a power grab for his agency, but was perhaps recognized by Bush and Cheney as an opportunity for them as well. With legislation passed by Congress on September 14, 2001, the Authorization for Use of Military Force, the third branch of government had also essentially ceded its case-by-case war-making authority to the White House, granting all presidents going forward the right to use all "necessary and appropriate force" against those he or she determined "planned, authorized, committed, or aided" the attacks, including those who harbored them. Given the inclinations of this particular White House, and its civilian head of the military, Donald Rumsfeld, that blank check was increasingly looking to be cashed inside the nation of Iraq.

Many across the government were getting the impression from White House meetings that the decision had already been made to take out Saddam Hussein after Afghanistan. If that goal was to be accomplished, however, the White House would need the help of its bureaucracy. Would the FBI or CIA be more helpful to that goal and others?

Even within the conservative halls of Langley, few were enthusiastic about helping the president tie the recent attacks to Saddam Hussein. Rossini had spent much of the time since the attacks in Spain working to take down a Madrid Al Qaeda cell and continuing to prepare for the federal embassy bombings trial. He remembers that at the beginning of this time, a lot of energy inside Alec Station was exerted toward Iraq, something he says was widely understood among his CIA colleagues to be a White House–created "fraud."[19]

"We knew he had no weapons of mass destruction. We knew there was no link between Al Qaeda and Saddam Hussein. But we kept feeling pressure from the White House to push it," asserts Rossini, who does not believe anybody at CIA, "even [Alfreda Bikowsky]," believed it was a good idea to turn American attentions to Iraq. Rossini was unaware, however, that Bikowsky was married to David Silverstein, a vice president of the Foundation for Defense of Democracies, described as an "aggressive neoconservative think tank" founded two days after September 11, 2001. FDD would soon take to the media to help promote the case for invading Iraq. Was Bikowsky finding her loyalties split between her Bush-aligned husband, Silverstein, and her one-time mentor, the expressly anti-interventionist (and anti-Zionist) Mike Scheuer?

Inside FBI headquarters, Pat D'Amuro also began feeling pressure to produce connections between terrorists and Saddam Hussein. One day, he had to go brief the defense leader Donald Rumsfeld and his deputy Paul Wolfowitz. They explained that they were trying to find evidence and intelligence that Saddam Hussein was in cahoots with Usama Bin Laden. "There is nothing in FBI files to support that connection," D'Amuro calmly told them. "In fact, Bin Laden tried to put out a fatwa to have Hussein killed. There was no relationship." They dismissed him.

D'Amuro then went with one of his deputies to Robert Mueller's office and explained, "At the FBI, we report facts. We don't provide justifications for White House wars." Mueller apparently agreed, and word passed to Bush. The FBI was not going to be helpful to the president's goals.[20]

*  *  *

No one from the CIA was physically present as the notorious chief of Egyptian General Intelligence Service, Omar Suleiman, went to work on Ibn Al Libi, as he had on many of his citizens.[21] Blee's deputy in Afghanistan, Michael Anne Casey, led the operation and continued to hold the "ticket" on the handling of Libi thereafter.[22] Back at headquarters, Hendrik Van Der Meulen, Alfreda Bikowsky, and Jen Matthews, newly moved to the HVTU, remained closely involved.[23] Libi soon divulged big information: Bin Laden had sent two Al Qaeda members to Iraq for training with weapons of mass destruction.[24]

The Defense Intelligence Agency (DIA), the military's other major intel unit outside the NSA, was privy to the intelligence gleaned from Libi's interrogations, and they sent George Tenet's office a strong "dissent" the following month. The DIA members noted that Libi could not name any Iraqis involved, could not name any chemical or biological material used, and could not name where the alleged training took place. "[Libi] has been undergoing debriefs for several weeks and may be describing scenarios to the debriefers that he knows will retain their interest. It is possible he does not know any further details; it is more likely this individual is intentionally misleading the debriefers." In short, the Defense Intelligence Agency was calling "bullshit."[25] Libi's testimony nonetheless made it from the DCI to the president.

A little over a year after his initial statement connecting Al Qaeda and Iraq, Ibn Al Libi would recant it. Having been subjected to waterboarding and other forms of torture, he claimed he only told interrogators what he thought they wanted to hear.[26] It was a bad sign regarding the effectiveness of torture if anyone at the CIA wanted to see it.

Had the useful information from Libi regarding the case against Saddam Hussein affected White House thinking? Small signs of presidential decisions began to show themselves during the month of Libi's rendition, when twenty alleged Al Qaeda members were transferred to the military-controlled prison in Guantanamo Bay, Cuba, by the CIA, not by the FBI.[27] Bob McFadden and Ali Soufan took notice in February on a visit to interrogate prisoners at Guantanamo Bay when they were instructed for the first time in their careers not to read prisoners their Miranda rights before questioning them.

"By choosing the CIA over the FBI," *New York Times* journalist James Risen later noted, "[President] Bush was rejecting the law enforcement approach to fighting terrorism that had been favored during the Clinton era. Bush had decided that Al Qaeda was a national security threat, not a law enforcement problem, and he did not want Al Qaeda operatives brought back to face trial in the United States, where they would come under the strict rules of the American legal system."[28]

Shortly after the CIA received Libi's statement tying Al Qaeda to Iraq, Bush issued an executive order, again secret, building upon his prior CIA-empowering secret order in September, authorizing the agency to build a network of clandestine prisons for interrogations and detention. Maybe, after the Libi operation, it had been recognized that renditioning people to other nations left the CIA less in control of their own information, with the possibility of leaks from foreign interrogators or interlopers like the DIA. The time for renditioning captures into the hands of interrogators of a foreign nation was coming to a close.[29]

John Kiriakou had been moved to Pakistan.[30] Most of Al Qaeda's top people who had escaped Afghanistan had done so by crossing into Pakistan, making the country central to the counterterror mission.

During his first fourteen years with the CIA, Kiriakou had been absolutely in love with it. "I've compared every subsequent job I've ever had to that one, and nothing has ever come close," he says. He was the one who had always felt completely comfortable operating in the legal and ethical "gray areas" associated with the agency's work. Somewhere along the way, he began to feel a line was being crossed.

"We started talking about things that I just disagreed with in my gut," he says, pausing to consider what details he can provide that are not still classified top secret. "I gotta be really careful what I say here," he told himself before finding his words. "For example, endless incarceration. That's not the kind of country we have. Everybody gets their day in court. That's part of the Constitution. That's what makes us great."

Kiriakou noted that what had been at first theoretical became reality in the spring of 2002. "We've started capturing some of these guys, important guys," he says. "Well, what do we do with them? One, we started using Guantanamo as a temporary way station until they could be put on—that was the original idea, that they would go on trial.

"And two," he continued, "we started establishing these secret sites to take the 'real heavy hitters' to 'squeeze' them."

The contest between the CIA and the FBI over control of the nation's approach to terrorism and the rule of law was heading toward a last stand. Cofer Black flew to Pakistan one day. As Black's control officer for the region, Kiriakou met him on arrival. Black had some important news. He was leaving the CIA by year's end to head to Colin Powell's State Department, where he was to become ambassador at large for counterterror.

It was an impressive promotion; Black was technically going to be an American diplomat. He would be among the first from the small, insulated world of CIA counterterror to expand outward to populate other agencies of government, but he would be far from the last.

Why had Black chosen this moment, after a twenty-eight-year career, to call it quits at the CIA? Had he wished to avoid the potential legal fallout coming from what they were about to do? More likely, Black was heading to State to play a role in the instrumental negotiating of "status of force" agreements necessary to implement the new powers provided to the CIA by Bush's executive order. They were ultimately worked out with fifty-four nations who participated in one form or another in the agency's new program, mostly to allow agency-contracted flights through their airspace. Only seven to ten of them would ever agree to allow one of these "black site" prisons to be housed inside their territory.[31]

The first site was created in Afghanistan under the leadership of Rich Blee. Inside a drab complex of buildings set against bare desert mountains, detainees were kept naked and cold in constant darkness while loud music was always blaring. This dungeon was referred to by its residents as "Dark Prison," but to the Americans, it went by the code name "Cobalt," or more colloquially as "The Salt Pit." As if to underline the irony of the United

States heading down this path, the location chosen had been notorious under the Taliban as a place of torture.[32] Nonjudicial prisoners, now dubbed with the dehumanizing term "High Value Individuals," would be interrogated "with unprecedented harshness" outside the view of the prying eyes of international human rights groups.

Kiriakou remembers a number of moments when State Department officers overseas were proclaiming the United States as a shining beacon of human rights. "I knew it wasn't true. We were kidnapping them. We were sending them to secret sites to be further tortured or held incommunicado. What is that?" he asked rhetorically. "We are still a country of laws. We still have a Constitution. If you don't like the Constitution, fine, amend it. But you can't just decide to ignore it. And you can't—or shouldn't be able to—decide to find some sweetheart lawyers in the Justice Department to twist the law and bastardize it so you can do whatever you want, and there's no fallout from it." He concluded his point simply. "I didn't like that at all."

"They were going to 'out-Cheney' Cheney," says Fulton Armstrong, "and they were going to be heroes and stars. It was a wink and nod culture. We know what you want us to do, and we'll do it. And then the CIA did it with greater alacrity than even the [Justice Department] people who wrote those horrible memos thought they were going to do. The CIA lied internally. What those guys in [Justice] were doing was evil, but I don't think even they knew how all this crap was being done [by the CIA]."

"How the torture program came about? I don't know, but the obvious suspects would be the ones who advocated this," says Mark Rossini, who was still on the inside of Alec Station at that time. More than a decade later, NBC News would report that their sources had identified one name as being listed more than three dozen times in the classified version of the Senate's Torture Report, and Glenn Greenwald reported the name: Alfreda Bikowsky.

"The report singles out the female expert as a key apologist for the program," wrote NBC, "stating that she repeatedly told her superiors and others—including members of Congress—that the 'torture' was working and producing useful intelligence, when it was not. She wrote the 'template on which future justifications for the CIA program and the CIA's enhanced interrogation techniques were based,' [the report] said."[33]

Rossini speaks with certainty on the issue, saying, "And to do something like that had to come from the top, from George's office to allow it. There was this belief that these people needed to be tortured to get information out of them. Because none of these fucks had ever been in the field and interviewed anybody. They were living in a delusional James Bond movie. They had a visceral hatred of the FBI, *still*, and Ali Soufan, who was trying to interview people, and Russ Fincher, who was trying to interview people—and they were getting information."

"One would think that an issue like this would have several layers of oversight," insists Armstrong. "The more sensitive the operation—with torture, how much more sensitive can you get? You're bringing people's bodies and minds to [the brink of] collapse and then you bring them back so that they don't die; hopefully [they] don't freak out on you too much and become useless."

CIA executives began working with the Justice Department and the White House's National Security Council to create a list of interrogatory "enhanced techniques," consulting with Egypt and Saudi Arabia.[34] The CIA Office of Technical Services gathered data from a number of psychologists and knowledgeable academics in the area of psychopathology, and the military's Joint Personnel Recovery Agency, hastily putting together a rough program, studied methods used by communist Chinese interrogators.[35]

At headquarters, inside Cofer Black's CounterTerrorist Center, Bruce Jessen and James Mitchell, former military psychologists, were contracted to consult on the agency's first major foray into interrogations, despite the two holding no prior experience in the area. They were recommending a program of psychological and physical torture to get captives to break and submit to their captors, a reverse engineering of the military's Survival Evasion Resistance and Escape (SERE) program.

Against this backdrop, John Kiriakou was talking with Cofer Black in Pakistan about his impending departure when Black shocked him with the name of his replacement as head of the counterterror division: Jose Rodriguez. Kiriakou understood the choice was significant. "Jose was generally an unknown, because he had spent almost his entire career in Latin America, and the rest of us hadn't." says Kiriakou. "But those of us who did know him were aware of this history of impropriety."[36]

Rodriguez arrived at CTC just prior to the attacks already twice officially reprimanded. Kiriakou explains, "Once, because he unethically used his influence to help out a high school friend with the government of the

Dominican Republic, and once for sexually harassing a young female case officer who was working for him. This guy has been dogged for the entirety of his career by multiple accusations of sexual misconduct."

Kiriakou was bothered by Rodriguez in a way he was not by most others he worked near, and he does not mince words. "You work with so many sociopaths in the agency and recognize them as potentially dangerous, but he's a psychopath. I really believe that."

Rodriguez was making an astounding leap up the hierarchy, to lead, among other things, the powerful new program, which they were calling "Renditions, Detentions, and Interrogations," or RDI. When George Tenet personally made the call to promote Jose Rodriguez to head the counterterror division, Kiriakou believes it was the DCI acknowledging he understood the nature of his RDI program. "I think Tenet was being advised by [his spies director] James Pavitt. Pavitt knew Rodriguez very well. The message from the seventh floor was," Kiriakou believes, "'If we're really taking the gloves off, then we're going to put this psychopath in charge.'"

\* \* \*

On the night of February 20, retired NSA technical director Bill Binney drove to the home of a congressional intelligence committee staffer in Hyattsville, Maryland.[37] Diane Roark was a whip-smart veteran of congressional oversight. Jane Mayer described her as having "flowing gray hair and large, wide-set eyes, looks like a waifish poet."[38] She had been on the intelligence committee for seventeen years, a career staffer and a registered Republican. (So was Binney. And Wiebe. And Drake.) She had monitored the budget and effectiveness of the national intelligence effort for seven years, with the last five of them dedicated to keeping tabs on the NSA.

Roark would later explain her style to *PBS Frontline*, saying, "NSA regarded my oversight as far more intrusive than anything they were used to, and far more critical also than anything they were used to."[39] She had been shocked by how far behind the curve of the digital age the NSA was when she arrived, and how delusional its leadership seemed about it. When Binney and his SARC team had briefed her about their developing ThinThread project four years ago, she had been enthused, getting them funding from the intelligence committees.[40]

She also began to use them as her "sources." Roark treated her job as a congressional staffer like that of a journalist, or a spy. She knew she would not get the real story of the agency she was responsible for overseeing if she did not find "leakers" giving her unvarnished info from the inside. Then she could help Congress do its job of ensuring well-functioning bureaucracies. Binney, Wiebe, and Loomis had become guys she could count on for good information.

Before meeting Roark at her home, Binney had explained forcefully to her that they would not be entirely in a secure meeting at her place of work, at the Capitol Building. To avoid prying ears and eyes, Binney met her at her suburban house, where he unloaded everything he knew. Roark understood this was going to be unlike any conversation they had before.[41]

The NSA was spying on the people of the United States, and in Binney's mind, doing so unconstitutionally. This was not just a matter of illegality but fundamentally *un-American* behavior, as he saw it. Roark believed him. The issue was how to elicit some admission from the agency about what they were doing.

She knew the budget for the NSA's next year was up for review. It would give her the opportunity to grill management on their activities. Roark asserted herself, telling her NSA contacts, "The members [of Congress] are going to ask us what you are doing to prevent another 9/11, and we have received nothing."[42]

NSA managers realized they would have to answer this with some measure of access to Fort Meade, so they tried to appease her with a walking tour of their expanding counterterror section, a boring labyrinth of cubicles. Roark knew a dog and pony show when she saw one. After doing a perfunctory meet and greet, she began asking difficult questions. The response to her shift in approach was typified by a particular meeting with officials, where upon arrival she discovered a long conference table with no chairs. They had all been taken away, she believes, so that no one could sit down. "I have never seen anything like it, and so I knew they were covering up stuff," she recalls, laughing.

She politely asked them to go get the chairs. During the meeting she was able to draw an admission on email collections. It was taking place, they confessed. ThinThread was the operative program behind this. Roark had championed the early ThinThread. She now felt a personal guilt over its repurposing to surveil the American public's digital information. She felt her committee existed only because of its post-Watergate creation as a means to stop just such a thing. It was why she was there doing her job.

\* \* \*

After spending ten million dollars for intelligence and Pakistani government assistance, John Kiriakou, working for the CIA alongside FBI agents in Faisalabad, conducted raids on several safe houses with a pretty good idea that Abu Zubaydah was inside one of them. At the location where Zubaydah was hiding, a firefight with the American and Pakistani authorities ensued.[43]

Bleeding from several bullet wounds and piled in the back of a truck with other injured men, Zubaydah was transferred to a hospital. Kiriakou kept watch at Zubaydah's bedside as a surgeon was flown in from John Hopkins to make sure that the "high value" prisoner did not die. Once medically stable, the CIA had Zubaydah promptly delivered, "renditioned," to one of their new secret "black site" prisons.[44]

Kiriakou's team discovered among Zubaydah's possessions a phone book that included at least two US telephone numbers. An FBI team, seemingly reporting back to Pat D'Amuro's PENTTBOM investigators, ran the numbers and found that one belonged to a man working as a bodyguard at the Saudi embassy in Washington, DC. The other belonged to an obscure corporation called ASPCOL located in Colorado.[45]

The FBI's Aspen field office began investigating ASPCOL. Meanwhile, in an account given to only one journalist, Gerald Posner, its place in the chronology of Zubaydah's imprisonment uncertain, "the CIA had set up a room . . . that was meant to appear as though it was a medical room in a Saudi jail. Considerable effort went into duplicating every possible detail about what Zubaydah might expect if he had been handed over to the Saudis. Two Arab Americans, now with Special Forces, would play the role of his new inquisitors."[46]

The CIA's goal was supposedly to scare Zubaydah into believing he was in a country, Saudi Arabia, where he might be brutalized, thus more open to sharing information without having to actually use those tactics. Two Arab Americans connected to the US government played his Saudi interrogators, while CIA personnel in another room viewed the questioning via video relay and suggested questions to the men through tiny earpieces.

"What transpired in the next hour took the American investigators completely by surprise," Posner wrote; again, the only journalist to receive this information. Zubaydah, drugged with "truth serum," seemed relieved to discover it was the Saudis who had him. He told his captors to call Prince Ahmed, a nephew of the Saudi King. Zubaydah reportedly provided the men a cell phone number from memory and instructed, "He will tell you what to do."

The Americans left, pretending to follow his lead. The prince in question was known to them as highly "westernized," a raiser of thoroughbred horses that had repeatedly done well at the American Triple Crown, a Louisville player with no known connections to terrorism. The unknown CIA people, perhaps including Rich Blee, claimed to believe Zubaydah must have been trained to provide such misinformation as a distraction effort. In the early hours, they reentered his cell and angrily explained that the prince had denied it. He needed to come clean to them.

Without any use of torture, relying simply on trickery, Zubaydah gave the Americans their first direct account of how he believed 9/11 had come about. He claimed to have been told personally by Usama Bin Laden of a quid pro quo relationship between Al Qaeda and the Saudi Kingdom going back to 1991, arranged through in-person meetings between Bin Laden and the Saudis' intelligence chief Prince Turki. As a result of the agreement, money and other assistance had been passing from the Royal Family's government to terrorist operatives using intermediaries like Prince Ahmed.[47]

Again from memory, he provided more names and numbers of Saudis with which he, and by extension Al Qaeda, held a relationship, including another of the King's nephews, Prince Sultan, and a more distant relative, Prince Fahd. He also detailed a relationship "blessed by the Saudis" between "pro-Islamist elements" of Pakistan's intelligence agency, the ISI, and Al Qaeda, a deal made by Pakistani military officer Mushaf Ali Mir in 1996. Another deal had existed between the former Taliban government and the Saudi royals as well since 1998, one Zubaydah claimed he had been present to help facilitate. He asserted both Mir in Pakistan and Prince Ahmed of Saudi Arabia were told beforehand that an attack would happen inside the United States on September 11, though "they just didn't know what it would be, nor did they want to know more than that."

If Posner's sources are accurate, the information tricked from Zubaydah would likely have been briefed to George Tenet, who would have briefed it to President Bush. According to Posner, America's allies in Saudi Arabia and Pakistan were asked to respond to the intelligence. Not surprisingly, they sent back blanket denials.

\* \* \*

Jen Matthews had been focused on domestic matters until her recent promotion to the stand-alone High Value Target Unit, from the first floor of the Old Headquarters Building.[48] "It was kept physically independent of Alec Station, but her team was staffed almost entirely with former members of that office," says Kiriakou. He continues: "She was not senior enough to be in the top leadership [of the HVTU], but she was certainly one of the top people." She also happened to have held the "ticket" on Abu Zubaydah for many years.[49] Consequently, she and some of her HVTU members would be heading the CIA's first interrogations inside a black site.[50] Matthews would seem to have been pregnant with her third child at the time.[51] Alfreda Bikowsky would allegedly be made the godmother.[52]

By chance, Matthews and her team missed their initial flight out, so D'Amuro's FBI agents, Ali Soufan and Stephen Gaudin, beat them to Thailand. This, despite catching a ride on a CIA plane.[53]

Ali Soufan claims that when he arrived he found Zubaydah strapped to a gurney with a bag over his head. He was still in bad shape, but he was able to speak. In a matter of hours, using classic interrogation techniques hinging on rapport-building, Soufan and Gaudin got a useful piece of intelligence out of Zubaydah regarding a potential dirty bomb attack in Chicago. The agents sent the information to CIA headquarters via their secure cable system.[54]

George Tenet was impressed by the progress, until he learned the information was coming from FBI interrogators. Reportedly slamming his hand down on a table, he forcefully instructed, "Get [Matthews and her team] there now and have them take over."

As they were en route, Zubaydah provided Soufan something US intelligence and law enforcement agencies had been eagerly seeking for six months—the name of the 9/11 plot's mastermind. Zubaydah explained the planner was "Mokhtar,"[55] an alias used by a man so well-known in counterterror circles that they called him simply by his initials, "KSM." Khalid Sheikh Mohammed was known to be the uncle of the 1993 WTC bombing mastermind, who also had ties to a multi-airplane explosion plot called "Bojinka." Zubaydah's information made sense within the larger picture. He did not appear to be misleading. The pieces were coming together.

Kiriakou says that Ali Soufan "was doing it the way that [the US] had been doing it since the end of the Second World War, where you establish a rapport with a person." He points to the precedent set by westerners who questioned Nazi officials to build the war crimes case against them. "Famously, the Nuremberg interrogators would play chess with the people they were supposed to be interrogating," he says, "and got volumes of incriminating information by treating them like human beings, right? Rather than put them in a box with a bug or poke their eyes out or whatever one might do in these secret locations."

"[Soufan] was succeeding," Kiriakou believes, based on his reading of the accounts. "But this rapport-building takes time. The CIA [leadership] didn't want to spend that time." He believes their priority was less driven by getting good information and more by "breaking some faces and showing they were the tough guys on the block."

While Zubaydah continued to recuperate, a CIA employee identified by one source as Jen Matthews arrived at the new "black site," bringing with her the agency's contract psychologist James Mitchell and a number of young women from her "High Value Target" unit.[56] Alfreda Bikowsky, in charge of al Qaeda-related operations, and a woman named Gina Haspel, a new associate of the incoming CTC chief Jose Rodriguez, may have also been intimately keeping tabs from headquarters.

Haspel, a forty-five-year-old brunette with glasses who was raised in Kentucky, had joined the agency three years earlier than Bikowsky and Matthews and, unlike those two, had held a number of undercover assignments overseas, including in Ethiopia and Turkey, before Rodriguez had made her a "deputy group chief" inside CTC. Within a few months she would be sent to Thailand to take over running this new secret prison, one that would remain home to Zubaydah and soon to other "disappeared" individuals.[57] Code-named "Cat's Eye,"[58] Haspel's future jail would begin that month as a hastily thrown together fenced pen within a brick room, equipped with audio and video recording.[59] According to John Kiriakou, Jen Matthews also would be given a direct role in operating Cat's Eye.

CIA employees would try a method the psychologists had developed, intended to slowly increase Zubaydah's discomfort until he submitted to what Mitchell described as "his god." He believed Zubaydah would come to recognize his CIA interrogator as his sole source of pain or pleasure. This was explained to agents Soufan and Gaudin as they sat together at a hotel by James Mitchell, who told them, "Washington wants to do something new with the interrogation."

Soufan, disgusted, pointedly asked, "Why is this necessary given that Abu Zubaydah is cooperating?" He received no answer.

"Ali called me," says Pat D'Amuro, "and told me, 'They are going to start the enhanced interrogations.'" When he learned what was happening inside the black site, he told Soufan and Gaudin, "Guys, make sure every word you put in that communication to FBI headquarters is accurate, because we are going to go to war [with the CIA] over this."

D'Amuro had just moved upstairs to "Mahogany Row," the executive seventh floor down the hall from the FBI director. He was freshly promoted, the new assistant director of the FBI's CounterTerror Section. "I can tell you there were numerous conversations I had with people," D'Amuro recalls, "asking why can't we just get first crack at these people before they go into any 'enhanced interrogation techniques.'" He pointed to one of his agents, Frank Pellegrino, who had spent his life pursuing Khalid Sheikh Mohammed. When KSM was captured, why wouldn't Pellegrino do the first interrogation? On one occasion, he was brought by Mueller to the White House for a briefing related to the matter. Afterwards, he would try to convince the CIA director to allow the Bureau access before any enhanced techniques were utilized. It never happened.[60]

For several weeks in Thailand, Soufan and the CIA interrogator took turns, with the CIA using increasingly depraved methods from their new list of Enhanced Interrogation Techniques, and Soufan each time giving Zubaydah back his clothes and attempting to reestablish a rapport with him. This went on, back and forth for at least a week, Soufan's work yielding diminishing returns as his connection with the terrorist was understandably hurt by the man's bouts with torture.

Mitchell's work repeatedly yielded nothing, yet Soufan felt that Matthews and her team remained strangely confident the approach would work. He also thought they seemed rather flippant about it all, beginning to see them as "a contingent of wisecracking cheerleaders."

Finally, the day came when Soufan's line in the sand was crossed. As CIA interrogators placed Zubaydah in a box resembling a wooden tomb—a technique that had finally yielded results when the Egyptians applied it to Libi—Soufan stepped outside to call his boss in DC.[61]

D'Amuro told him, "Ali, it's time to come home. You and Steve come home now."

When Soufan landed, he informed D'Amuro of two pieces of information his boss had never had before. "He and Steve Gaudin had for the first time obtained direct evidence that Khalid Sheikh Mohammed was the mastermind of 9/11 and that Jose Padilla was looking to attack soft targets in the United States," says D'Amuro. "That was the information they obtained without the utilization of the enhanced techniques."

D'Amuro went to the Justice Department and stated his opinion. "We can't. We can't do this. We [the FBI] are both intelligence officers and criminal investigators, and we can't separate those two. We can't participate in torture." It would be the final time a significant outsider would be present at one of the CIA's black sites.

"The torture started before the administration authorized it," points out Fulton Armstrong—as had happened at the NSA with domestic surveillance. "You have people in the agency who realized that they blew it big time. They blew it. They completely mis-analyzed the 9/11 threat beforehand. [Then they went on to] completely blow the WMD stuff [before Iraq].

"What do you do when you completely blow something?" he continued. "You try harder to compensate because you want to become the hero that finds the solution to the problem you created, right? So they were extremely aggressive. Also, they knew what the political bosses wanted, and they knew it was very difficult for the political bosses to give them the green light, so they went ahead and just did it."[62]

* * *

An entourage of eight planes containing the de facto ruler of Saudi Arabia, Crown Prince Abdullah, and his entourage cruised above the Atlantic en route to the George Bush Intercontinental Airport in Texas. This was a rarity. It was the first such visit since George W. Bush had taken office, the first since the attacks, and only weeks since all had presumably been informed about Abu Zubaydah's alleged fingering of prominent Saudi royals in helping facilitate the plot.

The US president was at his Crawford ranch when he received an unwelcome update from Robert Mueller. It was perhaps beginning to seem to Bush that news he did not want to hear always came from the FBI. This time, it was so serious that it could prompt an international incident: One of the men in the Crown Prince's entourage was wanted by the FBI; another two were on a terrorist watch list. The Houston FBI office had agents ready to "storm the plane and pull those guys off."

Bush found himself in an awkward position. The possibility of the press getting hold of this was a serious concern, as was anything that highlighted the questionable dichotomy between the cordial state of US/Saudi relations—and the fact that the latter pumped vast amounts of money toward terrorist activity.

The issue would be resolved, quietly. There were no arrests. The men in question were simply to be kept away from the president's ranch, while the issue of royal associates and their possible ties to 9/11 would be brushed under the carpet for the moment. A frustrated FBI could do nothing about it.

Over the next two days, Abdullah, Prince Saud Al Faisal, and the Saudi ambassador to the United States, Prince Bandar, met first in Houston with Vice President Cheney, Donald Rumsfeld, and the head of the military's Joint Chiefs of Staff, then moved to Crawford where they were provided the hospitality of the Bush ranch, meeting privately with Bush, Cheney, Colin Powell, and Condoleezza Rice.[63]

Back in Houston, CIA operatives were keeping close tabs on one of the men in the entourage who had arrived on Abdullah's flight, a member of the royal family with "responsibilities for intelligence matters." Technically, the CIA was barred by law from running such surveillance operations on domestic US soil, but nonetheless, they reportedly watched with intense interest as the Saudi royal spy met with a US-based man who suddenly arrived in town and was given "a significant amount of cash."

They recognized the man who received the money as Osama Basnan of San Diego. Pat D'Amuro's criminal investigation had been investigating Basnan since the week after the attacks as a person of interest in helping hijackers Mihdhar and Hazmi during their first year inside the United States. There were already strong suspicions that Basnan was a Saudi intelligence asset. Now, receiving money directly from the Saudi ruler's entourage, it was hard to ignore the connections between Saudi royalty and the hijackers.[64]

\* \* \*

John Kiriakou returned to Langley that May. Word flew like a speeding bullet through the halls that the Zubaydah operation was a stunning success. "Enhanced interrogation techniques" had worked, it was said. Kiriakou was told that the terrorist had "broken" after a single application of waterboarding, spilling to his interrogators a jackpot of actionable intelligence that had saved American lives. "He gave us everything," Kiriakou heard, "cracked after one time."[65]

How could this be doubted? After all, the agency now knew the name of the 9/11 mastermind and could put the FBI to work arresting Jose Padilla before he could attack Chicago. Questions might rightly remain about whether such techniques were legal or ethical, but no one could question that they certainly were effective. Despite his personal qualms about torture, Kiriakou told a like-minded colleague, "Hey, wow, maybe I was wrong."

He would maintain that belief for another seven years.

George Tenet appeared to believe the same. Inside an off-record National Security Council meeting that was "without the formality of statutory attendance," before the president, vice president, secretary of state, national security adviser, and one other unidentified person, Tenet made the case that he could not continue to use these rather effective techniques without further legal cover. Colin Powell's chief of staff Larry Wilkerson later heard tapes of the meeting when they were acquired by an ABC News investigative team. Wilkerson remembers, "They were talking about torture. And they were talking about ongoing torture. And they were talking about what they are getting out of the particular individual they were torturing. They don't use that word, but it's clear that's what they were talking about."[66]

Based on the power of the intelligence gleaned from Zubaydah, the room agreed that lawyers in the Office of Special Counsel at the Justice Department would immediately be directed to begin work on a secret legal finding that would allow Tenet's counterterror team to continue their efforts with some amount of legal assurance. "This is your baby," Rice said to Tenet. "Go do it."[67]

Back at FBI headquarters, Pat D'Amuro walked down the hall and into Robert Mueller's office. "You know I have no love lost for the terrorists," he declared. He knew he had to put it in terms Mueller could understand. He appealed to him as an attorney.

"Number one, there's [sic] 'Giglio' issues," he said, a reference to the court requirement that prosecutors provide the defense any information that might reasonably be used to impeach them, for instance if their client only confessed after a mock burial. "You are going to put an agent in a position where they are going to get involved in these 'techniques.' If it goes into their personnel file, they will never be able to testify in a court of law again. Never."

D'Amuro went on. "Number two, do I think it's going to produce information that we really want? No. They are going to tell you things that aren't true just to get you to stop. That will cause us to spend a tremendous amount of man-hours trying to determine if the information is accurate."

He saved the ethical issue for third. "Number three, am I opposed to it? Yeah."

Finally he turned to the personal. "Number four, this is Washington, DC. Do you really believe this will be kept a secret? Someday, a lot of people are going to be seated at a 'green felt table.' If I'm sitting there and have to testify, I want to be able to stand up and say, 'The Bureau did not participate.'

"We are being shortsighted," he concluded. "None of these people will ever be prosecuted in a court of law in the United States once they have undergone these interrogation techniques. You gotta be kidding me. It's never gonna happen. What are we going to do with these people after this is all done? Are they going to walk the plank of a ship? Are they all going to disappear?"

Mueller was persuaded. The FBI would not be a part of the torture program. The CIA was doing it, though, and that meant the US government was doing it. That meant the use of the judicial system in the war on terror would be significantly impaired. That meant the agency would have the lead henceforth. It was in that moment D'Amuro realized that his PENTTBOM investigation would never result in any 9/11 trials.[68]

By the time a fifty-page legal memo was completed late that summer by deputy assistant attorney general John Yoo, Jen Matthews's team in Thailand had already waterboarded Abu Zubaydah eighty-three times,[69] as captured on ninety hours of self-recorded video footage. The memo forbade only one of the eleven techniques for which Tenet had asked: burial while alive. What many may not know is that this legal opinion contained a big caveat:

> *Our recommendation is based on the facts that you have provided us. We also understand that you do not have any facts in your possession contrary to the facts outlined here, and this opinion is limited to these facts. If these facts were to change, this advice would not necessarily apply.*

The facts as reported were, in fact, incorrect. The viable intelligence gained from Zubaydah was the product of Soufan's classic techniques, not the torture experiments being run by the CIA and their contractors.

"It was all a lie from the very beginning," John Kiriakou tells us, ready to jump out of his chair. He had learned this much later. "They were lying even internally!"

Taking a more thoughtful tone, he continued, "I would like to see the raw cable traffic that was coming back from the 'Abu Zubaydah compartment' [in Thailand run by Jen Matthews], and then I would like to see the analytic products prepared for the White House [by Alec Station and Alfreda Bikowsky]. Because that's where the lie would take place."

"If the raw traffic were telling us one thing and the analytic products going to the White House were telling something different, the responsibility for that would fall to Alec Station and CTC leadership," he continues. "Whispers in the hall [at CIA] are one thing, but it's another thing to report to the president that he cracked after one time. I would like to know from those blue-border analytic products what they were telling the White House?"

The *Washington Post* ran an article in 1968 with a photo on the front page.[70] It showed an American soldier waterboarding a North Vietnamese soldier. The story caused the Defense Department to conduct an investigation. The soldier was arrested, court-martialed, and tried for torture, resulting in a guilty verdict and the man's incarceration. "Why was waterboarding illegal—and torture—in 1968, but it's not illegal—and torture—in 2002?" asks John Kiriakou. "The law hasn't changed. The law is still on the books. Somehow," he concluded, "September 11th seems to have changed our government's notion of what ought to be prosecuted."

\* \* \*

Inside the J. Edgar Hoover Building on July 2, it is likely that Pat D'Amuro briefed Robert Mueller and Bush's attorney general on his FBI teams' determination of "incontrovertible evidence that there is support for these terrorists within the Saudi Government." After the CIA had monitored Osama Basnan receiving a large sum of money from one of the Saudi ruler's entourage in Houston that spring, it appears San Diego FBI agents searched Basnan's home. There, they had found copies of thirty-one cashier's checks from the period February 22, 1999–May 30, 2002, the time when the hijackers' plot had determined to be in motion, totaling $74,000. They were all from a Riggs Bank account of the wife of none other than the Saudi ambassador to the United

States, Prince Bandar. As a personal friend of the American president's family, it was no doubt recognized that this was extremely sensitive territory.

The checks had been written to Basnan's wife, and the FBI had determined that a standing order once existed on Princess Bandar's account that began in January 1999 to send $2,000 a month to Mrs. Basnan. It was further discovered that the wife of Basnan's San Diego associate Omar al Bayoumi had also attempted to deposit in her own account three checks written to Mrs. Basnan. On one occasion Mrs. Bayoumi had received a check directly from Bandar's account. On another occasion, Basnan himself had received a check for $15,000 directly from Prince Bandar himself. The obvious question remained: Why?

Further Saudi connections to Mihdhar and Hazmi in southern California were also being investigated. Agents of the FBI's Los Angeles field office had learned that the future hijackers had been in contact with Shaikh Al Thumairy, described to headquarters as "an accredited diplomat at the Saudi Consulate in Los Angeles and one of the 'imams' at the King Fahad mosque in Culver City, California . . . reportedly attended by members of the Saudi Consulate in Los Angeles and . . . widely recognized for its anti-Western views." The mosque, it had been reported, was provided funding by Crown Prince Abdulaziz. D'Amuro's briefing may also have detailed connections between Omar al Bayoumi's San Diego employer and the Saudi government.

Lastly, Abu Zubaydah's address book found in Pakistan had led FBI agents in the Washington field office to interview the Saudi embassy bodyguard whose phone number had been found inside. The man, living in Virginia, claimed to have no idea why a terrorist leader would have his number. During the conversation, however, he had mentioned regularly providing services to one of Prince Bandar's personal assistants. Looking into the assistant led the FBI agents to the assistant's driver, who also happened to work as a bodyguard at the Saudi embassy in DC. The kicker? The driver's phone number was also identified inside alleged Al Qaeda leader Abu Zubaydah's phone book.

Nearly two weeks later, in mid-July, D'Amuro's team likely received an update from the Denver field office regarding their investigation into another US number in the phone book, that of the ASPCOL Corporation. Agents had discovered the company turned out to be responsible for managing the affairs of the Colorado residence of Prince Bandar. ASPCOL's phone number had been unlisted and not registered, as most other businesses were, with the

Colorado Secretary of State.[71] How and why it had been included among Zubaydah's contacts remained a disturbing question.

No known actions were taken by President Bush or his administration against the Saudi government upon learning this news, not even sanctions. This, despite the FBI having accumulated a mounting case for their direct support of the attacks that had created the "war on terror." Instead, that same month, Tommy Franks, with Bush's approval, went to Congress to secretly request $700 million to fund preparations for a war against Iraq. Vice President Dick Cheney and his lawyer Scooter Libby began visiting the CIA to work directly with analysts on building the case for the invasion. British officials met with George Tenet at month's end and came away feeling "there was a perceptible shift in attitude," describing in a memo of the meeting how "military action was now seen as inevitable."[72]

Some people inside the CIA took notice late that July after the man Zubaydah had named as his main Saudi contact, Prince Ahmed, was reported dead of heart failure in Riyadh at age forty-three. It was the talk of Langley in some circles.[73] His thoroughbred, War Emblem, had just won the Kentucky Derby in May, making him the first Arab owner to achieve that feat. CIA analysts became further suspicious the following day, July 23, when his forty-one-year-old cousin was killed in a single-car accident en route to the funeral. The man, Prince Sultan, had been another reportedly named by Zubaydah. Credulity began to be strained when, one week later, the Royal Family announced Prince Fahd, the third man he had been alleged to have named, age twenty-five, while traveling fifty miles outside Riyadh during the height of a hot summer, had died of thirst.

In August, General Tommy Franks provided President Bush a war plan for Iraq.[74] A "White House Iraq Group" was formed to essentially "market" the invasion to the public. Members of the administration began months of outreach to the news media to make the case for the removal of Saddam Hussein. Documents declassified years later indicate to the authors that D'Amuro's team heard from Washington field office agents that September. Those agents had looked into the Saudi embassy bodyguard's contacts with a residence in McLean, Virginia. Looking up the address, they found it belonged to Prince Bandar. Two days later, the field office in Colorado reported that another number found in Abu Zubaydah's possessions was the unlisted home number of, unsurprisingly, Prince Bandar.[75]

The American public would remain in the dark for many more years regarding evidence the FBI had found and reported to the president in 2002 connecting Saudi Arabia to the attacks that had killed so many of their countrymen and women, and specifically to hijackers Mihdhar and Hazmi. By the following spring, opinion polls would demonstrate that 72 percent of Americans were in favor of military action against Iraq.[76] Four out of five of those strongly supported it.

\* \* \*

On the strength of the resumé bumping Zubaydah capture and rendition, John Kiriakou had originally been named head of the Arab Nationalist Terrorist Branch, in charge of all Sunni Arab terrorist groups that were not Al Qaeda.[77] One of the incoming CTC chief Jose Rodriguez's chosen deputies was Mike D'Andrea, later described by the *New York Times* as "a gaunt, chain-smoking convert to Islam who was chief of operations during the birth of the agency's [secret prisons and torture] program." D'Andrea had worked with Kiriakou previously and knew him as a good officer, so he insisted, "No, no, [John's] going to Alec Station."[78]

In that office for the first time, Kiriakou became its chief of counterintelligence.[79] He reported directly to Alfreda Bikowsky. The offices had been moved up to the first floor, main entrance. Rossini says he watched as Bikowsky grew close with Rodriguez, as she had with previous bosses Scheuer and Blee. One of her critics would later describe her as "a person who inspires little confidence, and who is highly adept at working her way through the bureaucracy, but has no leadership ability."

A CIA spokesman would make the counterclaim, "Her work, and the work she has led, has stopped terrorist attacks and saved innocent lives."[80]

While working for Bikowsky, a senior officer approached Kiriakou and asked if he wanted to be what the person called "certified" in enhanced interrogation techniques. He estimates around a dozen people were asked. Weighing the decision, he turned to a senior officer friend who told him, "First of all, let's call it what it is. This is torture. Secondly, torture is a slippery slope."

The man spoke prophetically. "What's going to happen is that someone is going to go overboard and kill a prisoner. Then there's going to be a congressional investigation, then a Justice Department investigation, and somebody's going to go to prison. Do you want to be involved in that?"[81]

Kiriakou became one of only two people he is aware of at his agency to be offered the torture training and turn it down. Sometime after, he happened to be sitting in the office in Langley on a Saturday morning when he saw a man walk in, Marty Martin. Martin was a Louisiana native with a Cajun accent that he had worked with a decade earlier in the Middle East.

"Hey, what are you doing here?" Kiriakou asked.

Martin answered, "I'm the new chief [of Alec Station]."

"Get out of here," was Kiriakou's response. "I thought they were bringing in some big muckety-muck from the Middle East?"

"Yeah, dude, that's me."

The two laughed. Kiriakou took the moment to bring his attention to a problem on his mind, pulling Martin in close.

"Dude, you have to get rid of the redhead [Bikowsky]," he told him. "She's a malignant force. You have to get rid of her."

Martin was not surprised to hear it. "You're the twentieth person to tell me that," he responded. "I'm going to get rid of her."

Kiriakou was shocked shortly thereafter when Martin not only kept Alfreda Bikowsky, but promoted her. She was to be, at long last, the deputy chief of Alec Station.[82]

Tom Wilshere was pushed out that June, retiring to the private sector.[83] "Wilshere just wasn't going to get promoted again," asserts one colleague, who thought of Wilshere as "a gentle guy" who "didn't have that taste for blood that Marty Martin had." That, it was believed, was why Martin was named head of Alec Station, not Wilshere, who was being passed over for the last time.

Wilshere's replacement as the CIA liaison to FBI was Rich Blee, freshly returned from overseas. "After Wilshere left, then the CIA sent me *the other guy* who had hidden information from my team before the attacks," fumed Pat D'Amuro, "but again I didn't know it at the time, not until Blee was gone."

\* \* \*

In January 2003, while preparing to deliver a speech before the United Nations, Secretary of State Colin Powell pulled his chief of staff, Army Colonel Larry Wilkerson, into a private meeting. Literally, he dragged him by his coat into the empty offices of the National Intelligence Center at Langley. "We didn't think we were bugged there. We didn't know for sure, but we didn't think we were," Wilkerson remembers. Slamming the door,

Powell vented to Wilkerson regarding the content of the speech he was supposed to give. "I am so sick and tired of this goddamn bullshit about Mohab begat Ahab begat Abdullah. There's nothing to this. There is no meaningful connection between Saddam Hussein, Mukhabarat, the Iraqi secret police, and Al Qaeda. So why am I saying all this bullshit?"

His boss's frustration was clear. Sensing that Powell was telling him this because he expected him to object, Wilkerson set him straight. "Boss, I agree with you one hundred percent. It stinks. Let's throw it all out."

"Good," was Powell's one-word response. Wilkerson then headed to Powell's speechwriter. "Lynn," he said, "I got a monumental task for you." Wilkerson instructed her to take anything out of Powell's speech that contained any references connecting Iraq to terrorism. She proceeded to do just that, removing all such instances in the sixty-seven-page text.

Wilkerson returned to the conference room where Powell was running an early rehearsal of the speech. It was rough, interrupted several times by Powell expressing his disgust. "Jesus, this stinks." George Tenet, who was watching Powell rehearse, was called out of the room.

Moments later, the CIA director returned and interrupted. It was a bombshell. "We have just learned from high-level sources that there was substantial contact between Al Qaeda and the Mukhabarat in Iraq, including"—Tenet paused for emphasis—"training them in how to use biological and chemical weapons."

Powell leaned over to Wilkerson and whispered, "Put it all back."[84]

Powell would infamously go on to damage his international credibility when he spoke before the UN, making the case for war against Iraq with the CIA director seated symbolically behind him. He never knew that an official DIA dissent had been offered concerning Ibn al Libi and his statements while made under torture. When Colin Powell's team learned later that this dissent existed, they went ballistic. They had explicitly asked that any intelligence included in their speech to the international community be drawn from two separate sources—and all dissents provided. When Powell's chief of staff confronted Tenet on the fact that the DIA dissent never made it to his team, Tenet claimed the absence was a mistake due to a computer error.

That March, US bombs fell on Baghdad. The American people would deal with the consequences of that decision for the next two decades.

# 8

# GETTING AWAY WITH IT

*"The glory which is built upon a lie soon becomes a most unpleasant incumbrance."*

Mark Twain

Everyone in Washington knew the investigations were coming. After an event of the political magnitude of 9/11, it was simply inevitable. No fewer than ten inquiries followed Pearl Harbor, nine of them within the first five years after the attack. Such investigations were an American tradition, with a record of repeatedly falling short of their stated goals, but continuing to be held after each such incident.

The first major investigation, excluding the FBI's PENTTBOM, would be run by the intelligence committees of Congress. Officially named the Joint Inquiry into Intelligence Community Activities before and after the Terrorist Attacks of September 11, 2001, it was more casually referred to as the Joint Inquiry. Launched in February of 2002, the Joint Inquiry was chaired by Senator Bob Graham and House Representative Porter Goss, both of Florida. Their final report would be completed in December of 2002.

The Kean Commission, officially called the National Commission on Terrorist Attacks Upon the United States and better known as simply "the 9/11 Commission," was an independent "blue ribbon" panel created by Congress, signed into existence by the president and chaired by a former New Jersey governor named Tom Kean. It began its work just as the Graham-Goss inquiry was concluding.

Simultaneous to the work of the Kean Commission were two additional investigations led by US inspectors general. The Department of Justice tasked its inspector general, Glenn Fine, with investigating the FBI's handling of intelligence information related to the attacks beginning in 2002. The Fine Investigation's final report was issued in classified form in 2004, with a public version released in 2006. John Helgerson, CIA IG, conducted his own look into questions of his agency's accountability, his team investigating from late 2002 until delivering the first draft of a classified version in 2004. The public would not be able to see it in unclassified form until 2015.

"The people who investigated these things after the fact admit they were bothered by what they found," Richard Clarke told us, ". . . admit they never felt they got to the bottom of it." This slew of investigations were run by different divisions of government employees with different levels of access to insiders, as well as levels of funding and amounts of time. Each accomplished something to further develop the known facts regarding the intelligence and law enforcement communities' stories regarding Khalid al Mihdhar and Nawaf al Hazmi. Graham's and Goss's inquiry unearthed the CIA story from scratch. They were forced, upon review of evidence, to determine what to make of it, and determined that despite CIA statements to the contrary, the FBI had not been informed about Mihdhar's and Hazmi's entry into the United States.

"Clearly the people in the agency who were dealing with this issue on a daily basis knew about it," says Graham-Goss inquiry staff director Eleanor Hill. Lacking a smoking gun, however, her final report fell short of concluding anything more than a simple mix-up. "We never had anybody say to us it was intentional," Hill explained. "I'm not saying it didn't happen. I'm saying we couldn't conclude something like that happened unless we had pretty solid proof. And we didn't have the proof that that happened."[1]

The Kean Commission built on the Graham-Goss inquiry's work. Underbudgeted, lacking time, and subscribing to a philosophy that a stern approach toward agency cooperation would backfire, their investigation would add little knowledge about the Mihdhar and Hazmi story, apart from footnotes drawn largely from the work of ongoing inspector general investigations.

We asked Tom Kean about the seemingly intentional withholding of information by Alec Station staff regarding Mihdhar's US visa. He responded rhetorically, "Does it surprise you the CIA was brought up to lie?" Taking on a more serious tone, he continued, "It wasn't careless oversight [in not passing that information]. No question about that in my mind. It was purposeful. But it was purposeful, we believe, because the agency was so obsessed with keeping secrets that it was actually hurting national security."[2]

One of the bombshell pieces of information to come out of the Kean Commission was buried in an endnote at the bottom of chapter six in the Commission's final report. Known as "footnote 44," the text reads:

"Activities of Bin Laden Associate Khalid Revealed." January 4th, 2000. His Saudi passport—which contained a visa for travel to the United States—was photocopied and forwarded to CIA headquarters. This information was not shared with FBI headquarters until August 2001.

An FBI agent detailed to the Bin Laden Unit at CIA attempted to share this information with colleagues at FBI headquarters. A CIA desk officer instructed him not to send the cable with this information.

Several hours later, this same desk officer drafted a cable distributed solely within CIA alleging that the visa documents had been shared with the FBI. She admitted she did not personally share the information and cannot identify who told her they had been shared.

We were unable to locate anyone who claimed to have shared the information. Contemporaneous documents contradict the claim that they were shared.[3]

Footnote 44 added three startling new facts to the public record. One, an FBI agent (Doug Miller) had been positioned at the CIA at the time who took an interest in this matter in real time. Two, he was instructed by a superior (Michael Anne Casey) who worked for CIA not to inform the FBI. Three, the same person who instructed him not to inform the FBI promptly turned around and told the rest of her counterterror colleagues that the CIA had just informed the FBI, potentially preventing them from doing so.

Kean told us that he considered footnote 44 to be "one of the most troubling aspects of our entire report."

Like Hill before him, Kean's doubts about the CIA were tempered by a high bar in Washington for findings of deliberate withholding in an official report. However, he would casually say to us, "The CIA got in a lot trouble years back for operating domestically. And whether they are off doing it again, I don't know. We never found anybody who told us [the] CIA was up to anything, other than obviously not sharing information. And why you don't tell your fellow law enforcement agency [the FBI] about a terrorist coming to this country, or who has a visa to come to this country, it's almost inexplicable to me."

* * *

The NSA knew what was coming, and they were prepared. A special office, known as Corporate Solutions, had already begun the internal process of collecting pertinent information. The six- to eight-person CS team, personally chosen and given special instructions by Mike Hayden's deputy, had spent several months searching keywords to collect what the agency had known, or should have known, prior to the attacks. It was an effort Tom Drake believes was intended to "find the skeletons, so we knew how to respond, and, if possible, bury them."[4]

Whatever they were finding, it was "air gapped" from the mainframe, walled off from the rest of the bureaucracy. Drake had still not been able to get a glimpse of their findings. He had been working to resurrect Bill Binney's ThinThread, along with a number of other programs that could be of use in the war on terror.

At one of their daily staff meetings, Maureen Baginski surprised Drake by asking that he serve as the "enterprise level lead," the designated "senior" in drafting the NSA's Statement for the Record. This statement would be given to the Graham-Goss inquiry. Another employee was already doing this, but it was agreed that the person was failing the initial assignment. Drake, running a "virtual team" of nine employees, pulled one, an analyst named "Fred," from his continuing duties to work with him. They were given just two weeks to complete their monumental task.

If the effort was an exercise in burying skeletons, as Drake suspected, he was signing up to become the man who knew too much about the number and location of those bones. "We went to the ends of NSA to find out what NSA could have known, should have known, and did know before 9/11," he recalled.

Drake and Fred first went back to the analysts who had been so troubled in the weeks after the attacks, including "Bob," the man who once slipped him the "finest of NSA" document that had mapped the Al Qaeda network. This time, his visits would be in an official investigative capacity. Taking a proactive approach, they often skipped the chain of protocol by reaching out directly to the analytics shops, the data flow people, and those in the field operationally. The effort often involved the pair enduring eighteen-hour days.

While the workload was almost unbearable, the timing turned out to be fortuitous. Months prior, Drake had also been given the lead on following an all-points-bulletin directive by George Tenet, overseeing the NSA in his role as Director of Central Intelligence, to go back through every area of the agency to find anything they had ever tried to develop in the lab or among their research that could be "put into the fight" against Al Qaeda. Drake's recommendation, delivered via a classified implementation plan, was to resurrect ThinThread, running it on the eighteen most critical counterterror collection locations around the world as recommended by the members of the CounterTerror Shop, just as Bill Binney had once tried to do. The software, after all, had been ready to go operational since late 2000.

When his recommendation was rejected by senior colleagues, just as Binney's had been in August 2001, Drake refused to give up. He approached Baginski with another option.

"Mo, this doesn't have to be operational," he told her. "Why don't we point ThinThread at our *internal* databases and see what it will find?"

She approved the initiative, providing "a couple million dollars" in budget. The work to implement the plan had taken a couple months in order to build an operational ThinThread that could analyze the existing primary databases. Though Binney was gone, his core ThinThread team at SARC was still in place. Drake pushed them to do rapid application development on the fly. The SARC team pulled it off, informing Drake that ThinThread's trigger was ready to be pulled.

* * *

Tom Drake and his analyst "Fred" moved through the home of American intelligence's main computer facility like mice in a labyrinth, dwarfed by endless rows of supercomputers. After some initial test runs, on a February afternoon, in 2002, they unleashed their ThinThread bot on the system, scanning "umpteen" terabytes of data. Their bot was trawling stored raw data from the preceding years.

For the next eighteen hours, it would comb metadata from the information collected and "unwrap associations" to see connections possibly never before recognized. From these connections, Drake lays out two categories of

9/11 failure at the NSA. One was the information that was known and not acted upon. The second was information collected but not known. The ThinThread bot was finding everything in one place—phone numbers, emails, location info, routing info, equipment identifiers (like those possessed by routers or cell phones).

As the bot worked, the men wondered, "What if we find something significant? What if we find indications of a warning, or something that is still useful intelligence today?" Drake wondered aloud if some of this might be useful in the current fight against Al Qaeda. The group headed home to sleep and wait.

The next morning, the look on Fred's face said it all. He was holding an initial report spit out by ThinThread's engine of preliminary associations. Drake finally broke the silence with two words: "Holy shit."[5]

Among the most powerful discoveries in this deep trawl of the NSA's communications dragnet was information concerning the travel plans of the eventual hijackers. To Drake's and his deputy's horror, the printout from ThinThread was able to identify the suspect fact that the 9/11 hijackers had booked airline tickets *all flying on the same day*. Having been previously identified as members of Al Qaeda cells in the "finest of NSA" report, this stunned Drake.

The program that Bill Binney had fought so hard to see implemented, the one canceled permanently one month before the attacks, if cross-referenced with one of the NSA's internal reports, would have recognized something significant was in the works for those men on the morning of September 11, 2001. It was difficult to get around the idea that, by fixing the data collection stream inside NSA's AQ Shop, the plot certainly could have been stopped.

A sudden overseas assignment pulled Drake from his important work on the 9/11 memo for the record. In retrospect, he believes this was done on purpose. Soon enough, his colleague Fred called to deliver some news. "Tom, we're getting taken off the project."

Drake stormed into a formal NSA leadership meeting, fresh off a plane, knowing full well he was playing with fire.

"Why have I been taken off the effort?" he rudely interrupted.

A startled Baginski eventually found her reply. "I'll have to tell you later."

Inside her office, Baginski explained as best she could that the NSA's deputy chief of staff would be taking over the effort due to an undefined "data integrity problem" related to Drake. He understood that what he had found inside the databases had resulted in the internal investigation being politicized, with efforts to control it at Michael Hayden's level. The Legislative Affairs Office, working with Hayden's office, would end up rewriting the Memo for the Record in full.

When House investigators made arrangements to meet a number of NSA employees, they did so in a small briefing room. Before they arrived, the NSA staff had been given talking points by the Legislative Affairs Office. "This is an opportunity to help you prepare," the LAO rep explained while handing them out. In a moment of apparent concern, Baginski had pulled Drake aside to tell him, "Careful, Tom, they're looking for leakers."

"[The investigators] were asking the right questions," Drake says. As he began to give real answers, with a "minder" from the agency seated beside him, the investigators let them know of their concern the room might also be bugged. They cut the conversation short. Soon after, through private channels, the intelligence committee investigators made arrangements to meet Drake at a nondescript government office in downtown DC.

Drake opened the next conversation by passing the investigators a series of documents. "What could you have done with this information as late as September 2001?" he asked. Drake told the investigators his story and gave them every document he had unearthed. Included were Bob's report and all that he had collected through ThinThread. There on the table lay a "smoking gun," in Drake's opinion.[6]

* * *

Joint Inquiry staffer Diane Roark remembers trying to grill the NSA director, Michael Hayden, during his two days of little-publicized, closed-session hearings before the Graham-Goss committees. She had recently learned from Bill Binney of the background behind the shutdown of ThinThread, and her other sources inside the agency, including Tom Drake, had begun filling her in about the NSA's failure regarding the hijackers. She knew Hayden had no idea of her knowledge, and she was on a fishing expedition for a "gotcha" moment. She got one.[7]

"NSA had no [indications] that Al Qaeda was specifically targeting New York and Washington," explained Hayden, "or even that it was planning an attack on US soil." Roark and Hayden went back and forth for a while before he continued one step further. "NSA had no knowledge . . . that any of the attackers were in the United States," the NSA director asserted.[8]

Hayden's bold claims ruffled Tom Drake when he heard about them. "I've yet to say this because I've never been asked since the [Graham-Goss inquiry]," says Drake. "[Hayden] flat-out lied about this. NSA knew what the numbers were. The numbers point back to where they come from. It's the way the system works. You cannot be monitoring the Yemen hub without knowing what the [number calling into it is] because that's what you're monitoring. And when the number comes in, you know the ID for the number that comes in. I'll say it that way." So when Khalid al Mihdhar called the Yemen hub from the phone Nawaf al Hazmi had in his own name at their San Diego apartment, the NSA knew the origin of the calls.

Hayden's session before Congress instead mainly focused on the wrong "gotcha," as the NSA director must have known. The NSA had intercepted two messages on September 10, 2001, but had failed to translate them prior to the attacks. It was a minor mistake compared to all that lay collected inside the agency. Hayden, acting defensively, explained the messages had included the phrases "The match is about to begin" and "Tomorrow is zero hour."[9]

Hayden's admission may have been strategic, acting as what a former deputy director of the CIA once called a "limited hangout," which is "spy jargon for a favorite and frequently used gimmick of the clandestine professionals. When their veil of secrecy is shredded and they can no longer rely on a phony cover story to misinform the public, they resort to admitting—sometimes even volunteering—some of the truth while still managing to withhold the key and damaging facts in the case. The public, however, is usually so intrigued by the new information that it never thinks to pursue the matter further." If this was the strategy, it seemed to have worked.

Hayden's admission to Congress about the September 10 intercepts, among the least damning of many damning items already uncovered and turned over to Hayden's staff by his the NSA communications director Tom Drake, had been channeled into a way to defang the intelligence committees. Issues regarding the NSA's monitoring of the Yemen hub, which should have led them to Mihdhar's and Hazmi's presence in the United States, never came up.

* * *

On August 12, 2002, with the first anniversary of the attacks fast approaching, and as the CIA's counterterror team were torturing Abu Zubaydah with new legal cover from the Justice Department, Congress turned to conducting interviews with Alec Station. Interviewees included Michael Scheuer, Tom Wilshere, Alfreda Bikowsky, and the FBI employees who had been working at Alec Station before the attacks. At the Robert F. Kennedy Department of Justice Building in downtown DC, staffers for the IG Glenn Fine conducted the interviews on behalf of their own ongoing investigation, as well as for the congressional committees, a means of using limited resources to kill two birds with one stone.

Mark Rossini remembers his interview session lasting no more than a half hour, with a CIA "minder" across the table from him staring in his direction. "Every word I said, this girl just kept taking notes. I'm saying to myself, 'This is ridiculous. I'm not going to be part of this.'" Rossini remembers remaining tight-lipped. He was asked about the cable that came in during January 2000 stating that Khalid al Mihdhar held a US visa. "I told them, 'I read the cable. I thought it was important. I don't know what happened.'"

Rossini believes the rest of Alec Station responded similarly on that matter, an assumption backed up by a reading of the final DOJ IG report. He told us, "The air in Washington at the time, the feeling was that somebody's gonna be made to pay for this. We were told, 'You have to go speak to DOJ OIG or Congressional Inquiry.' And you're offered no protection. You could not have a lawyer present. At all. No right to counsel, with no guarantee that what you said would not be used against you. We were cautious in what we said."

Bikowsky was less cautious, and less ambiguous. Not long after his own interview, Rossini had a conversation in a hallway with a colleague from the FBI's CounterTerror Section who was angry after learning that Bikowsky had told her interviewers that the information about Mihdhar's visa had, no question, been delivered to the FBI. It was therefore the Bureau's failure for not pursuing it, not Alec Station's in keeping it from them. How did Bikowsky know with certainty that this information had been shared? She claimed to investigators that she had herself walked the information to FBI headquarters on Pennsylvania Avenue. What Bikowsky had not realized, Rossini's colleague informed him with a laugh, was that all visitors to the J. Edgar Hoover building are made to sign a guest log.

Eleanor Hill's team, doing their basic due diligence to run down her story, checked the log and discovered that she had not visited the building on the date in question—nor on any other. Rossini was told that when Bikowsky was pressed to explain her statement in light of the fact that she had never signed into the FBI headquarters building, she waved off the contradiction claiming, "I must have faxed it over. I don't remember." Rossini was incensed by what he saw as a bold effort by Bikowsky to muddy the waters of doubt before Congress.[10]

We sat with Graham-Goss inquiry staff director Eleanor Hill trying to puzzle through claims made by Alec staff. She said, "We asked the same question you're asking, the same question anyone who looks at this asks. How could the same people make the same mistake so many times?" But with so little known at the time, it was easy to accept CIA officers' claims that this failure was a mistake. She appears to have considered Bikowsky's lie as well-intentioned. "There were people who really believed it had been passed," Hill stated, "whether they forgot or really thought they had done it, truly believed it had been passed."

The investigators began to determine that "no one could provide any evidence that the information was passed to FBI."[11] It would remain a he-said/she-said, largely due to Bikowsky's efforts. Still, there were many who could have cleared up the matter who chose otherwise. Mark Rossini and Doug Miller could both have mentioned Miller's cable that was blocked. Rossini could have relayed to investigators the story about Michael Anne Casey telling him that "This is not a matter for the FBI," but he didn't. With CIA minders chaperoning his interview with investigators and no legal protection, he kept it all a secret, afraid that he would be the one hung out to dry.

\* \* \*

Even obscured by an opaque screen that had been placed before him, Tom Wilshere looked uncomfortable to the seated audience. Perhaps it was because he was seated in front of the members of the Senate and House Intelligence Committees. Or perhaps it was because he was seated next to FBI agent Steve Bongardt, a man with reason to believe Wilshere had double-crossed him and his colleagues.

The public hearing had been called essentially to get to the bottom of a single subject: Why had the CIA learned of two future hijackers entering the United States and apparently failed to notify any other government bodies?

"Today," Senator Graham began, "the Joint Inquiry will receive testimony regarding three of the nineteen hijackers. These three are notable because they had came to the attention of the Intelligence Community at least twenty months before the September 11 attacks. We will review what actions the Intelligence Community and law enforcement agencies took or failed to take with respect to these individuals." It was a subject on which Wilshere happened to be one of the country's foremost experts.

The reason for the hearing that day was a question that Tom Wilshere was in a unique position to answer. Miller's draft message had attached to it a second message directed back to the sender, a note placed there before delivery that read, "Pls hold off for now per Wilshere." But Wilshere knew that the congressional investigators assembled before him did not know of this message. Wilshere likely knew the draft had been long since scrubbed from CIA databases. And so, in his prepared statement, he continued to muddy the waters in the same fashion as his colleague Alfreda Bikowsky.

"How could these misses have occurred?" Wilshere asked rhetorically, reading his prepared statement. "I do not want to speculate at any length about this, because I do not have the definitive answer. . . . Of the many people involved, no one detected that the data generated by this operation crossed a reporting threshold, or, if they did, they assumed that the reporting requirement had been met elsewhere. . . . What I will say here is that, new procedures and training aside, they are also the kinds of misses that happen when people, even very competent, dedicated people such as the CIA officers and the FBI agents and analysts involved in all aspects of this story, are simply overwhelmed."[12]

His argument seemed reasonable. His office has to get it right 100 percent of the time. The terrorists only have to get lucky once. Mistakes were made. The sentiment was, "Let's look forward." While the congresspeople in front of him did not know everything Wilshere knew, Senator Levin and Representative Burr seemed to know enough at that point to smell that something was rotten.

At one point, Levin stopped to recap. "This is sixteen months after the CIA knew that these men had visas to come to the United States, had entered the United States. Still, according to our staff report, there is this refusal on the part of the CIA to share this information. And this is critically important information."

When Burr got his turn, one by one he hit Wilshere with simple and direct questions. And one by one Wilshere responded with a kind of mild confusion.

"Let me ask our CIA officer," began Burr casually, "were officials notified of al Mihdhar's and al Hazmi's plans to enter the United States?"

"As I noted in my statement," Wilshere replied, "the answer to that is no. It's very difficult to understand what happened with that cable when it came in. I don't know exactly why it was missed. It would appear that it was missed."

Burr asked respectfully, "What transpired between January and the transmission of that cable in March, that sixty-day period?"

"Maybe I misunderstood your question," replied the seemingly dimwitted CIA analyst. "I'm sorry."

"You answered the question, this is a follow-up," clarified the congressman. "To the best of your knowledge, was the FBI ever notified?"

"To the best of my knowledge, the intent was to notify the FBI, and I believe the people involved in the operation thought the FBI had been notified. Something apparently was dropped somewhere, and we don't know where that was."[13]

Wilshere played as if it all seemed so *confusing*. Again, had the congresspeople been supplied the missing Doug Miller message, everyone in the room would have known precisely "where that was" that something was dropped—the where was Wilshere. And they would have known the intent was just the opposite of what he had stated, not to notify the FBI but to hold off notifying the FBI, for reasons that might have been explored before the committees.

Throughout the day, Wilshere tried to make the case that the names Mihdhar and Hazmi were not 100 percent recognized to be Al Qaeda-connected at the time they flew to the United States—despite their having in the same time frame been surveilled at meeting of known Al Qaeda operatives. Burr wasn't going for it.

"Was there an active investigation still underway into the East Africa bombing [of two US embassies by Al Qaeda]?" he asked.

"Yes."

"So the fact that these individuals were connected [to the embassy bombings] could have been and probably was pertinent to the current investigation."

"Certainly,"[14] was Wilshere's reply.

The FBI's Steve Bongardt seemed strangely neutered that day. As Ali Soufan's co-case agent on the investigation that had begun almost exactly two years prior into the bombing of the USS *Cole*, he had seen firsthand the devastation brought to dozens of very vocal military families who had either mourned sailors lost that day or would spend their lives nursing others who had been seriously injured by the blast. And he had lived with the reality for over a year that CIA's Alec Station had not been forthcoming with multiple requests for information related to those attacks—information, it had turned out, that Bongardt now believed would have led them to future hijackers Mihdhar and Hazmi inside the United States. If anyone in that room had an axe to grind, it was Bongardt.

Bongardt's prior knowledge of hijacker Khalid al Mihdhar had eaten away at him in the year since the attacks. This was the man who, two weeks before 9/11, had responded to the news that the FBI was now searching for Mihdhar inside the country by emailing FBI analyst Dina Corsi that he was not here to go "to fucking Disneyland!"

This was also the man who had argued strenuously that his office's criminal investigators should conduct the search for Mihdhar, not a rookie intelligence agent, adding prophetically, "Whatever has happened, someday someone will die and, Wall or not, the public will not understand why we were not more effective in throwing every resource we had at certain 'problems.' Let's hope [your department] will stand behind their decisions then, especially since the biggest threat to us now, [Bin Laden] is getting the most 'protection.'"[15] These were fighting words from a Navy man.

Now, seated next to Wilshere in front of Congress, Bongardt took on a more deliberately neutral tone. "I do not hold any US government affiliated individual or group of individuals responsible for the attacks on September 11, 2001. I truly believe that, given a chance, any one of them would give or sacrifice anything to have prevented what occurred. Then and now I hold the system responsible. Information is power in the system of intelligence and law enforcement. This will never change, nor could or should it."

Coyly, Bongardt next seemed to slip in a shot at Wilshere, and perhaps Dina Corsi as well. "The system as it currently exists, however, seduces some managers, agents, analysts, and officers into protecting turf and being the first to know and brief those above. Often these sadly mistaken individuals use the Wall described herein"—a reference to that legal separation of law enforcement and intelligence information—"and others, real and imagined, to control that information."

Then Bongardt used the opportunity to offer his opinion on two areas that day's hearing should get to the bottom of, if nothing else. "I, myself, still have two key questions today that I believe are important for this committee to answer. The detailed answers to them will deserve, and be afforded, the scrutiny of a nation and must stand the test of time and exhaustive investigation.

"First, if the CIA passed information regarding al Mihdhar and al Hazmi to the FBI prior to that June 11, 2001, meeting—in either January 2000 or January 2001—then why was that information not passed, either by CIA or FBI headquarters personnel, immediately to the New York case agents, criminal or intel, investigating the murder of seventeen sailors in Yemen when more information was requested?"

The question was a good one, and should have lit a fire under the inquiry. If the CIA officers were so convinced that they had shared information about Mihdhar and Hazmi right after the Malaysia summit, why were they hell-bent on *not* sharing that same information over a year later?

"Second, how and when did we, the CIA and the FBI, learn that al Mihdhar came into the country on either or both occasions in January 2000 and/or in July 2001, and what did we do with that information?" Bongardt was asking that investigators do their best to home in on this issue and to lay out a detailed chronology surrounding it, seemingly hoping that such an effort could tease out culpability.

However, what began as a hearing that seemed designed to get to the bottom of matters quickly became a "love-in," in the words of the Jersey Widows, a group of mothers who lost their husbands on 9/11 and who famously hounded politicians and media alike seeking answers as to why the attacks succeeded. They were seated in the audience that day, staring at a screen that blocked their view of Bongardt and Wilshere. Only three hearings in, they were already becoming disgusted with the realities of Washington "investigations."

Wilshere began running the show early on, registering extreme discomfort when Representative Burr turned to the matter of photographs of Mihdhar and Hazmi taken by Malaysian intelligence and provided to the CIA. At least one photo showed the future hijackers standing with the mastermind of the USS *Cole* bombing, recognized as such by the CIA ten months before September 11. These were the same photos that, when provided to Ali Soufan within twenty-four hours after the attacks, had caused him to vomit.

"I don't believe this has been declassified, sir," Wilshere lectured the congressman. "And I have a hard time talking about this in public. I'd be happy to talk about it in closed session in detail."

Burr turned to Bongardt for answers. "Did any of these three go on the watch list at that time? Connections to the East Africa bombing by two of them and connections to the *Cole* bombing by a third, did any of the three go on the watch list?"

"From what occurred," responded the FBI agent, "there were actually, it turns out—and I know my CIA colleague doesn't want to get into it too much—there's a little bit of confusion. There were four photographs that were taken out of a certain operation."

Wilshere interrupted to again instruct the congressman, theoretically his overseer, "Sir, this shouldn't be talked about in public. I'm sorry, it should not be. We can't go there."

"I will move on," Burr passively replied.

Senator Kyl took his turn to summarize the lessons that appeared to be emerging from this session. "Obviously everybody can make mistakes. I make about four hundred a day myself, and we will never change human nature . . . a couple things that we've heard from these witnesses here today point us in the right direction. One, a lack of resources . . . and two, risk aversion due to the creation of Walls and misunderstandings about authorities." If this was a glimpse into the emerging "lessons learned" by the committees, Wilshere must have felt pretty good.

Wilshere piped up with his final comments. "In general, speaking as somebody who has been doing this kind of work for a long time, working with the FBI on terrorism cases, I arguably should probably know better, but in general, what happens is that when a CIA CTC person deals with the FBI on a terrorism issue, they don't distinguish between criminal and non. They just say, 'You're my FBI counterpart, here's the information.' Or they pass it formally."

It was a final attempt by Wilshere to put it out there that it was still unclear whether the info had been shared with FBI or not, as it tended to be shared not "formally" but verbally by good CIA folks treating FBI agents as part of their team. Whether that happened or not, he seemed to be saying that the issue would remain a mystery, but good intentions were there.

"Well," replied chairman Porter Goss, "I think that's a very good observation."[16]

* * *

Like Wilshere, the CIA director also had some information that Congress did not, giving him the upper hand in the final hearing that took place a month later. George Tenet walked in that day alongside Michael Hayden. At that moment, the two were arguably the most powerful men to ever hold their positions. Each shared a secret with the Bush administration that could put themselves, their staffs, and the White House in legal jeopardy. In Tenet's case, that secret was the systematic torture-as-interrogation effort, along with the emerging assassinations program. In Hayden's case, that secret was the turning inward of the NSA's massive electronic spying apparatus on the American people. Joined by the FBI director, Robert Mueller, the three looked confident.

Tenet spoke first. "We need to be honest about our shortcomings, and tell you what we have done to improve our performance in the future. There have been thousands of actions in this war—an intensely human endeavor—not all of which were executed flawlessly. We made mistakes.

"One of the most critical alliances in the war against terrorism is that between CIA and FBI," Tenet asserted, listing some achievements in that alliance, before admitting "the relationship is not perfect."[17]

Tenet was asked about a message that arrived at Alec Station in March 2000 stating plainly that Nawaf al Hazmi had arrived in Los Angeles. "The cable that came in from the field at that time," Tenet responded, "was labeled 'information only,' and I know that nobody read that cable."

One senator, Carl Levin, appeared incredulous and pushed further. "But my question is do you know why the FBI was not notified of the fact that an Al Qaeda operative now was known in March of the year 2000 to have entered the United States? Why did the CIA not specifically notify the FBI?"

"Sir," Tenet replied. "We weren't aware of it when it came into headquarters. We couldn't have notified them. Nobody read that cable in the March time frame."[18]

When Richard Clarke would learn years later that, in fact, fifty to sixty employees had read one of the pertinent cables on the hijackers within the time frame in question, he would flash to the CIA director's testimony. It was his realization of Tenet's obfuscation that had, more than anything, caused him to doubt his friend.

When the congresspeople pushed Tenet later in the hearing to tell them the name of an analyst who had been involved in the failure, Michael Hayden watched as Tenet "feigned leaning over to reach into his briefcase" and used the moment to whisper in the NSA director's ear, "I'm not giving her up." He repeated quietly, "I'm not giving her up."[19]

* * *

It had been a year since the attacks, though it felt like much longer, and it was about ten months since Bill Binney and Kirk Wiebe had taken a conscientious stand and resigned their positions at the NSA. Their concern for what went on behind the black, copper-laced glass at Fort Meade, however, had not rested in their retirement.

They founded, with Ed Loomis, a consulting company, Entity Mapping LLC. Their goal remained to bring ThinThread to the US government. Maybe they could even make a few bucks doing it. Over the ensuing months, they had shopped it to the National Reconnaissance Office, to Customs and Border Protection, to the CIA, and to the Pentagon. At one point, they analyzed material already analyzed by the NSA and, using ThinThread, they found useful information that had been missed. It was understood they were going to embarrass Michael Hayden.[20]

Each time they felt they were about to land a contract, it suddenly disappeared, and friends inside the NSA let them know that Hayden and his executives had interfered behind the scenes to squash their potential deals. With their plan B exhausted, they spoke with Diane Roark, still on the intelligence committee and beside herself over the breakdown in oversight and accountability she was witnessing. They agreed the time had come to file an official complaint.

All were continuing a relationship with Tom Drake, who was still working at the NSA. He had been fired by Maureen Baginski from his position reporting to her shortly after he had turned over the 9/11 documents to congressional investigators. He had eventually found another position within the agency, where he had been making formal complaints to his higher-ups about illegal domestic spying, hoping that someone at either the NSA's inspector general office or the Defense Department IG would take up his cause. Working in the thick of it, Drake was able to keep his former colleagues and Roark current on the alleged legal violations that had become business as usual at the NSA.[21] Another secret executive order had been issued by Bush earlier in the year, further empowering the domestic electronic collection activities, and deals had been worked out with the major telecommunications companies who would assist the NSA in this work. Secret NSA rooms were even built into some telecom facilities to tap the digital stream.[22]

Not wanting to violate the law themselves, Binney, Wiebe, Loomis, and Roark figured the best way to bring needed oversight to the NSA's bulk surveillance was to alert the Defense Department's IG, using a "hotline" channel that was designated for just this type of whistle-blowing. Wiebe drafted the statement and Roark, Binney, and Loomis signed on. Upon reception of the letter, the IG began an investigation into the circumstances around ThinThread's dismissal and TrailBlazer's embrace.[23]

Tom Drake willingly told the IG that he was in communication with the ex-employees turned whistle-blowers, and he enthusiastically told them everything he could about the failures of the bloated and overpriced TrailBlazer project. Even more enthusiastically, Drake detailed what he saw as spying on US citizens that the NSA had begun with a retooled version of ThinThread.

Drake felt he was finally getting the attention necessary directed at some of the biggest missteps his agency was making. His goal was a better agency. Managers were too interested in increasing their budgets and justifying their jobs, he felt. Internal investigators were a built-in safeguard against bureaucratic waste and overreach.

Drake was not feeling any sense of relief as he spilled everything to the IG staff. "How long could I last at NSA when I would now surely be directly targeted?"[24] he thought.

Diane Roark was feeling the same. Around this time, she retired from a career in Congress and moved to a small town in Oregon.[25]

* * *

One day, in the fall of 2002, Mark Rossini claims he simply could not hold back the truth any longer. He walked into the office of a superior in the FBI, James Bernazzani. "Mark walks into my office one day at Langley," confirmed Bernazzani, "and says, 'Something's really bothering me.'" Rossini unloaded his story about Doug Miller's attempt to alert the FBI when the CIA received cables regarding Mihdhar and Hazmi.

Bernazzani, well aware of how Washington works, told Rossini something he already knew: if it wasn't on paper, it never happened. Rossini headed to Alec Station and then returned to Bernazzani's office with Doug Miller by his side. Miller confirmed Rossini's account and, even better, said he had printed his blocked email to the FBI.

"Are you shittin' me?" responded Bernazzani. "Go get that email for me right now." Miller headed to his desk and pulled the printed copy of his never-sent message to John O'Neill. He had kept it carefully preserved for over two years, waiting for a moment like this.

When Miller returned with the email in hand, Bernazzani called Pat D'Amuro. "Pat, I need to see you now. I don't care what you're doing." D'Amuro was on his way to a meeting and asked that Bernazzani meet him in the basement of FBI headquarters. There, Bernazzani claims he handed O'Neill's former deputy the printout, solid proof that the CIA's assertions that they had warned the FBI about Mihdhar were an abject lie.[26]

It's not clear what happened after that. For what it's worth, D'Amuro says he has no memory of this taking place. At some point, though, it seems that FBI leadership took possession of it. There is no evidence they ever provided it to any government investigation.

* * *

John Helgerson had been the head of the analysts division of the CIA when Kiriakou arrived in 1989. "He still had twenty-five years left in his career at that point, and he was already at SES-4," Kiriakou raves. "That's unheard of. The guy was so smart and so good at what he did that they could not help but promote him.

"I always found John Helgerson to be one of, if not the, most honorable people in the agency," continued Kiriakou. "He was really someone who wanted the truth to be told no matter what the fallout was, and that was not normal at the agency. He was as honest and as ethical as the day is long. So if you wanted something done and you wanted the truth to be told, you turned it over to Helgerson."

At the end of 2002, James Pavitt walked down a fifth-floor hallway at Langley with a lot on his mind, entering the office of Helgerson, who was now the CIA Inspector General.[27] A CIA agent for nearly thirty years and Tenet's deputy director of the spies division for three,[28] Pavitt was the top spy in charge of all the rest, and he perhaps felt it was time to come clean to Helgerson, one career officer to another. Something had just taken place in Afghanistan that was certainly going to merit an investigation. Better it come from him, Pavitt may have figured, as he went on to explain to his IG that a man had died while in CIA custody. Helgerson listened.

For months the agency had undertaken a top-secret program to indefinitely hold and interrogate suspected terrorists at foreign locations they called "black sites." The CIA had started an interrogation program that included techniques previously widely held to be torture. Some involved in the program were becoming increasingly concerned that their activities might be illegal. Word was that one captive, a thirty-three-year-old Saudi man named Abd al Rahim al Nashiri, a man who had allegedly co-conspired to bomb the USS *Cole*, had felt a drill held to his head by CTC interrogator Albert—the same man who had threatened to go find Ibn al Libi's mother. The power drill incident had taken place inside the Thai-based black site then being run under the leadership of Jose Rodriguez's protegé Gina Haspel. It was a matter deemed so sensitive Pavitt had sent his own team to look into it.[29]

That brought him to the incident that forced his hand in coming to Helgerson's office that day. Gul Rahman, an Afghani man, had been found one morning in November chained semi-naked to the concrete floor of the CIA's "Salt Pit," frozen to death.[30] It is not clear what more Pavitt did or did not impart to the IG. After an agency medic determined hypothermia to be his cause of death, Rahman was buried in an unmarked grave, his family never notified, and his name never having been added to a list of captives. Officially, Rahman had simply disappeared.

The Salt Pit black site had apparently been set up under Rich Blee, before he left his position in Afghanistan to head to FBI headquarters for his stint as an agency liaison.[31] Under Kiriakou's replacement in Pakistan, Rahman had been captured after allegations linked him to militants in the area, and he was renditioned to the secret prison.[32] Rahman was an unruly prisoner, throwing a latrine bucket at guards and threatening them. The Afghan guards, working for the CIA under the supervision of Blee's replacement, doused Rahman with water and dragged him around the floor before chaining him down and leaving him for the night.[33]

The "enhanced interrogation program," still in its infancy, was already showing signs of getting out of control. These activities now met the threshold under which top management no longer believed they could be withheld from the inspector general. Pavitt was not a whistle-blower. He was there in an official capacity to ask for an investigation.

In truth, the conversation with Pavitt was not the first time Helgerson had heard of the torture program. He had reportedly been receiving visits from CIA agents concerned that the things they were participating in might qualify as human rights violations. They believed it was only a matter of time before someone—or all of them—would find themselves vulnerable to prosecution.[34]

With Congress's inquiry concluding, Helgerson had also been asked by its cochairs Bob Graham and Porter Goss to probe matters of accountability regarding the CIA's pre–9/11 performance. Over the next year, the CIA's IG would be spending a lot of time with employees of the CounterTerrorist Center and Alec Station, both looking back into their performance before the attacks and simultaneously their current performance as actors in the newly minted "war on terror."

\* \* \*

As both the Kean and Helgerson investigations were ramping up in early 2003, Alfreda Bikowsky landed at the Szczytno-Szymany International Airport in rural Poland, three hours north of Warsaw. This was not a trip she was taking as part of her official CIA duties. For Bikowsky, this seemingly was pleasure. She had flown to Poland to witness the torture of 9/11's mastermind.[35]

Champagne popped all over CTC when news arrived of the capture of Khalid Sheikh Mohammed in Pakistan. "This was the guy who came up with it, did the hiring, implemented it," explains Kiriakou. "It was a happy day [among CIA counterterror people]. The only thing that ever beat the mood of that day was later when we got Bin Laden."[36]

Bikowsky was perhaps the happiest of all. She had booked this half-day trip as a private person, not a government employee, paying for it herself. "I thought it would be fun," she is reported to have later told superiors.[37] She had sent a message to her team after Mohammed was captured, gloating that "Ole 'Muki' is going to have a bad day on this one."[38]

To play the devil's advocate, if any American was going to experience *schadenfreude* over the torture of another human being, it would probably have been Mohammed, the man who came up with and pitched to Bin Laden the plan that had resulted in the murder of almost three thousand people eighteen months prior. Perhaps Bikowsky thought about this as she made the thirteen-mile drive through Poland's forests before arriving at a high barbed-wire fence with dense rows of conifers just outside the little town of Stare Kiejkuty. Behind the fence was one of the Polish military's intelligence training centers.[39]

Moving to an area called Zone B, she came to two large two-story country homes that until recently had served as accommodations for high-ranking visitors. No longer. Now code-named "Quartz,"[40] it was reportedly the CIA's third black site, following those in Afghanistan and Thailand, designated Cosmic Top Secret, one of a host of new "war on terror" classifications.

A local contractor had been commissioned to build a cage, now inside the quaint country house in a small room, and within the cage sat the man Bikowsky had come to see. Short, chubby, mustached, and by now a nearly broken human being, Mohammed sat dressed in a tracksuit. Immediately after his capture only days prior, Mohammed had first been held at the notorious Salt Pit facility in Afghanistan before being flown to the same airport Bikowsky landed at, where he was then transported like a caged animal to his present destination.

As Bikowsky watched and a video surveillance unit recorded, three male CIA interrogators, all over the age of sixty-five, fit and strong, took turns at sessions lasting four to eight hours, usually with a doctor present. According to Mohammed's later account to the Red Cross, a female sometimes took part. "If I was perceived not to be cooperating I would be put against a wall and punched and slapped in the body, head, and face. A thick flexible plastic collar would also be placed around my neck so that it could then be held at the two ends by a guard who would use it to slam me repeatedly against the wall. The beatings were combined with the use of cold water, which was poured over me using a hosepipe. The beatings and use of cold water occurred on a daily basis during the first month."

He was beaten for half an hour on one day, he claimed, his head banged against a wall until it began to bleed, with cold water then poured over him before the beating continued until a doctor—who was violating his or her medical oath by merely being present—intervened.[41]

Alfreda Bikowsky, too, was playing with fire in her presence at the black site. Though the Golden Shield memo theoretically was providing a veneer of legal protection for those working in an official capacity during "enhanced interrogations," an unassigned trip just to voyeur might someday be argued to put her outside the boundaries of said legal protection, especially given that the sessions were videotaped. Upon her return to headquarters, higher-ups would "scold" her, explaining, "It's not supposed to be entertainment."[42] There is no information publicly available that any disciplinary action occurred.

\* \* \*

When boxes of videotapes labeled "Cosmic Top Secret" arrived at the office of John Helgerson, they were treated with due care. These tapes contained some of the most sensitive footage then in existence inside the US government, footage of some of the interrogations.

As Helgerson's staff reviewed countless hours, they began to discover sporadic issues with the tapes. One video appeared to be blank. Skipping it, they discovered another. Continuing along, a third was blank. By the time they were finished, they realized that the collection they had been provided included two broken cassettes, eleven blank ones, and two others that strangely included one or two minutes of footage with the rest blank.

Going back to meticulously compare time codes for the bad tapes with logs they had been provided and raw CIA cable traffic sent from the black sites, they came to a conclusion: a single twenty-one-hour period was missing. During that time, two waterboarding sessions appeared to have occurred. The remaining tapes allowed the team to make a count of Abu Zubaydah's known instances of waterboarding: eighty-three times in 2002, most lasting for less than ten seconds.[43]

The following month, the Kean Commission team sent a request to the CIA asking for all reports of intelligence information pertaining to the 9/11 plot gleaned from the interrogation of a list of 118 names. Abu Zubaydah was among the list. George Tenet's staff responded by providing commission executive director Philip Zelikow's office with piles of reports summarizing the interrogations. They did not volunteer to the commissioners that they also possessed videos of the interrogations of three people on the list.[44]

* * *

Mark Rossini was starting to wonder if the CIA's Inspector General had forgotten about him. One day in the spring of 2004, he was called upstairs to a room at NHB. Sitting down at one end of a table that fit four on each side, Rossini found John Helgerson himself waiting at the other end.[45]

CIA employees in the crosshairs, like Bikowsky, had been given the option of saying no to interviews by the other ongoing inspector general investigation, the one at the Justice Department.[46] This was because they were not employed under the DOJ banner. The same was not true of Helgerson's investigation. When it came to the matter of Mihdhar and Hazmi, the former members of Alec Station remained as forgetful as ever. They could recall few conversations about the US visa or the later cable saying Hazmi had arrived in Los Angeles. No one seemed to know what had happened, nor would they volunteer anything useful that might allow Helgerson to get to the bottom of it.[47]

In place of the CIA minder who had so disturbed Rossini at his previous interview inside the DOJ, he now found his interview would take place before an entire room of CIA employees, around ten to fifteen. "And, again, no legal representation," he says. His interview was short and sweet, no longer than fifteen minutes.

"Do you have anything to add or say?" he was asked.

"No," he replied. "I just do my job, read my cables, and whatever is important for the Bureau to know, I let them know." He had determined he was not going to volunteer a spare word. "I had no faith or confidence in the outcome of that process," he explains.

Rossini had already allegedly come clean to his FBI superior Bernazzani and had even given an interview on the matter to journalist Lawrence Wright, who had not yet released the material. Clearly, the style in which these interviews were conducted left those with the most valuable things to say terrified that their words would be their undoing. The effect of this fear was to create a perfect cover for those who did have something to hide.

\* \* \*

Every cable news channel played the footage of Senator Bob Graham on July 24, 2003, holding his newly declassified report with twenty-eight full pages blank. Congress had concluded its work into the subject of intelligence failures seven months earlier and moved on to other issues. Their 832-page report was sent to the White House for declassification review in December 2002 with the expectation that they would be releasing it the following month. Instead, Graham and Porter Goss spent seven months negotiating with the Bush administration over how much of their report the public would be allowed to see.

The executive branch took a hard line initially, suggesting two-thirds of the report should remain classified.[48] Was this a tactic, asking to classify a lot, so the amount that they eventually settled on would seem reasonable, and ultimately cover everything they wanted hidden in the first place? The report had been delivered to Bush only three months before the intended invasion of Iraq. It therefore may have seemed inconvenient to their goal that the report found little connection between 9/11 and Saddam Hussein but had found twenty-eight pages' worth of evidence of Saudi Arabian facilitation of the plot.

The invasion had been declared over by July, with George W. Bush infamously posing on an aircraft carrier under a banner reading MISSION ACCOMPLISHED, and the occupation was officially underway. The White House sent the final, publicly consumable version of the report back to Congress for release. The level of declassification was considered a "win" by most on the intelligence committees, given the president's original position.

Graham, by contrast, was livid at the removal of evidence pulled mostly from the FBI's own investigations on behalf of the United States, led by Pat D'Amuro, of direct involvement by Saudi royals and government officials in helping the plotters, particularly Mihdhar and Hazmi. Many small portions would be redacted throughout, but the area that would understandably yield the most attention was the twenty-eight blanked-out pages. What, the cable news channels asked, were Bush and company keeping hidden?

Graham had already strategically created a buzz around the issue at the end of his committee's work, going on news programs in December to speak about one of the most troubling findings to his mind. "I was surprised at the evidence that there were foreign governments involved in facilitating the activities of at least some of the terrorists in the United States," he said on PBS's *Newshour.* "I believe the American people should know the extent of the challenge that we face in terms of foreign government involvement. I think there is very compelling evidence that at least some of the terrorists were assisted not just in financing—although that was part of it—by a sovereign foreign government and that we have been derelict in our duty to track that down."[49]

\* \* \*

It may be fair to assume that John Helgerson flipped out when his team discovered Doug Miller's attempted warning to the FBI. In January 2004, already a year into his 9/11 investigation, the matter of whether Alec Station had informed the FBI had taken up serious attention among his team, with doubt cast on both sides. Not one of his interviewees had volunteered the existence of Miller's warning. Not its drafter, nor fellow FBI detailee Mark Rossini, nor the CIA officer who stopped it from being sent, Michael Anne Casey, nor any of her overseers at Alec Station, Alfreda Bikowsky, Jen Matthews, Tom Wilshere, or Rich Blee.

The bigger question might well have occurred to Helgerson: why had it not been found in the CIA's computer system from the beginning, back in early 2002 when congressional investigators had originally requested all relevant documents from George Tenet's Review Group? While Miller's original CIR had gone missing, fortunately for Helgerson, Miller had followed up with Tom Wilshere nearly two weeks after via a Lotus note. That note to Wilshere had read simply, "Is this a no-go, or should I remake it in some way?" Miller had attached his original CIR to that note. There, in the attachment to the January 13, 2000, message, the CIA inspector general discovered it.[50]

The following month, over at the Justice Department's IG office, Glenn Fine, whose team was closing out their own 9/11 investigation after conducting more than seventy interviews related to "the Mihdhar and Hazmi matter," wrote in his report that the CIA had made available for review relevant documents. "In February 2004, however, while we were reviewing a list of CIA documents that had been accessed by FBI employees assigned to the CIA, we noticed the title of a document that appeared to be relevant to this review and had not been previously disclosed to us."[51]

After nearly two years of the Doug Miller warning remaining missing, had both IGs truly discovered it by happenstance within one month of each other? Or had they been tipped off, as Bernazzani had in late 2002 when Miller and Rossini had walked the printout into his office? More importantly, why had Pat D'Amuro—presuming Bernazzani is accurate in his claim that he gave the Miller message to D'Amuro months earlier—not turned it over, at minimum, to his own Inspector General at the Justice Department? Had he turned it over to the FBI director Robert Mueller, and if so, why had Mueller not given it to Glenn Fine? Or had one of them, in fact, done just that at start of 2004?

The work of both IG investigations—feeding into the concurrent Kean Commission—caused delays in completing the final reports. Teams were sent back to reinterview employees at Alec Station and FBI detailees. Fine wrote in his report, "As a result of the discovery of this new document, a critical document . . . we had to reinterview several FBI and CIA employees and obtain additional documents from the CIA. The belated discovery of this CIA document delayed the completion of our review."

The interviews John Helgerson's team conducted following the revelation had the feeling of a stonewall. They wrote, "Four years after the fact, no one—including [Doug Miller]—recalled anything about the draft CIR."

All of the relevant participants involved in the attempt to pass Mihdhar's visa information to the FBI in early 2000 continued to feign amnesia, even those who should have been vindicated by the existence of this newly discovered draft warning. One would think FBI agents Miller and Rossini would have jumped at the chance to tell the inspector general how they made several efforts to warn the FBI about incoming Al Qaeda operatives. It is difficult to explain other than by assuming that those involved had an unspoken understanding that silence is survival in the presence of an investigation.

\* \* \*

If George Tenet had hoped his agency might continue to remain out of the spotlight, the sudden media interest his old friend Richard Clarke thrust upon the public hearings of the Kean Commission might have disavowed him of that notion.

Clarke took himself from obscurity to fame in the spring of 2004 as he became, in the later derisive words of Clinton's FBI director Louis Freeh, "the self-appointed Paul Revere of 9/11."[52] Clarke's new book, *Against all Enemies,* raised serious doubts about Bush White House motives and competency in pursuing regime change in Iraq and the war on terror in general. He was interviewed on *60 Minutes* and *Charlie Rose* a week ahead of taking the commission hot seat.

Up until that point, the investigation hearings had mostly been ignored by the media, to the great frustration of many of the victims' families. "I also welcome the hearings," stated Clarke before a packed room, "because it is finally a forum where I can apologize to the loved ones of the victims of 9/11. To them who are here in the room, to those who are watching on television, your government failed you, those entrusted with protecting you failed you, and I failed you. We tried hard, but that doesn't matter because we failed. And for that failure, I would ask—once all the facts are out—for your understanding and for your forgiveness."

One month after Clarke accepted responsibility, to great publicity, for the failure of the government to prevent the attacks, George Tenet found himself in the same meeting room, a crowd of victims' families behind him, and a line of commissioners in front.[53] After Tenet's first public grilling, the commissioners had privately formed an assessment of him as evasive. Even staff director Zelikow, much criticized as a Bush insider guarding the henhouse, would later state that "Tenet simply could not tell the truth to the Commission."[54] After reportedly spending all night before private sessions studying up on CIA documents, Tenet still experienced frequent memory problems in both the closed and public session.[55]

With Tenet returning to the Kean hearings that April, commissioner Tim Roemer of Indiana drilled down on Tenet's briefings to the president during August of 2001. With three suspected Al Qaeda terrorists inside the country, and having previously testified that there was a flood of threat intelligence throughout the summer, what had the CIA director told Bush?

"I didn't see the president. I was not in briefings with him during this time. He was on vacation. I was here," said Tenet under oath.

Roemer seemed taken aback. He must be misunderstanding. "You didn't see the president between August 6th, 2001, and September 10th?"

"Well, no, but before—I saw him after Labor Day, to be sure."

"Okay. I'm just confused. You see him on August 6th with the PDB."

"No, I do not, sir. I'm not there."

"Okay. You're not the—? When do you see him in August?"

"I don't believe I do."

"You don't see the president of the United States once in the month of August?"

"He's in Texas, and I'm either here or on leave for some of that time. So I'm not here."[56]

Roemer sat for a moment, just staring at Tenet, seemingly unsure what to make of the testimony. After the session closed, with the final public interview of the CIA director now in the rearview, Tenet's staff messaged the commission that he had misspoken. Tenet had in fact spoken with Bush at least twice, on August 17 and 31.

"It was a very suspicious moment," recalls Tom Kean. "How could you forget—does anybody ever forget a meeting with any president? I mean, even if you're working in the White House full time, your time with the president is limited, and when you have time with the president, that's seared into your memory. So it made no sense to me that he decided, for whatever reason, not to tell us about that meeting." Kean went on, "I don't think he misspoke. I think he misled."

* * *

Khalid el Masri emerged from the Albanian desert telling a pretty crazy story. A German citizen born in Lebanon, he claimed he had been kidnapped five months prior while heading to a vacation in Macedonia and had been held ever since in a secret jail by the American CIA. The border guards did not take him seriously but returned him to his rural hometown of Neu-Ulm, Germany. Back at his house, he discovered his wife had moved out, assuming her husband had abandoned their family. She had returned to their native Lebanon and taken their children with her. Masri contacted a local attorney.[57]

Alfreda Bikowsky may have seen Masri as just another unfortunate case of collateral damage in the just fight against terrorism. She had no way to suspect that his rendition would be the thing that would finally result in her public unmasking, though it would take a while. More immediate would be the damage to her CIA director, George Tenet, who had been forced to inform the White House that due to a bad decision by one of his counterterror managers, the United States now had to deal with what the Associated Press later described as "the biggest diplomatic embarrassment of the war on terror."[58] An international court would also later reach a rare verdict declaring the actions criminal human rights violations.[59]

The matter had begun at the start of 2004, New Year's, as fruit and vegetable grocer and sometimes salesman Masri boarded a bus from Serbia into Macedonia. He had left his wife and children back home to begin a weeklong vacation when border guards detained him due to his extreme misfortune in sharing the exact name of Al Qaeda's number three. For a time, he was held and interrogated in a hotel in Macedonia's capital, Skopje.[60]

Back in Langley, Alfreda Bikowsky had reportedly been promoted, at long last the fifth chief of Alec Station and, it would turn out, its final.[61] She had worked there for nine years. In charge, the impetus behind the Masri operation was hers. CIA agents argued with Bikowsky that the German government should double-check his passport. She was resolute that she didn't trust the Germans to do it and, based solely on her hunch that Masri was a terrorist, ordered him kidnapped to a black site.[62]

As was standard for most who experienced one of CIA's "extraordinary renditions," Masri was grabbed, handcuffed, and blindfolded. The grocery store worker was then driven to an airport where he was beaten from all sides and had his clothes cut off with scissors by eight CIA officers who videotaped the event. Once naked, they removed his blindfold so he could gaze upon his rendition team, masked and dressed all in black. They shot him full of drugs, forcibly sodomized him with an enema, and put him in a diaper, flying him to Afghanistan on the floor of a plane, then driving him in the trunk of a car to the Salt Pit just outside the US Bagram Air Base.[63]

Months of torment passed by, and eventually those in the CIA who believed that Masri wasn't a terrorist pressed for his release. One official says he came in every morning and asked, "Is that guy still locked up in the Salt Pit?"[64] Despite clear evidence to the contrary, Bikowsky continued to argue he was a terrorist. Her status had allegedly been greatly elevated within the agency due to the relationship she had developed with George W. Bush during her White House briefings, and it was considered politically unfeasible to try to override her decision.[65]

Only when Tenet finally learned the news—reportedly exclaiming, "Oh shit! Just tell me, please, we haven't used 'enhanced techniques' on him, have we?"—was the matter finally rectified. After months of hell, the innocent Masri was dumped without apology or explanation by the side of the road, wandering in fear and confusion until he was picked up by border guards near where his nightmare began.[66] When Tenet made the matter known to the Bush administration, the secretary of state had to personally smooth matters over with the German government.[67] Whoops.

Tenet again had a clean opening to remove Bikowsky from leadership, as he had once done to her mentor Mike Scheuer. Again, somehow, Bikowsky remained.

\* \* \*

At an executive meeting, Tom Drake looked across a sea of "SESers" inside a Fort Meade building. They watched the NSA director, Michael Hayden, chortle with laughter over how little attention his agency was receiving from the Kean Commission. "We get to sit back while CIA and FBI take all the heat," he laughed.[68]

Hayden was right. On the whole of the commission staff, only one person had taken an interest in the NSA. The previous year, Hayden had turned over a batch of documents to the staff. "Perversely," wrote journalist Phil Shenon, "the more eager General Hayden was to cooperate, the less interested Zelikow and others seemed to be in what was buried in the NSA files."[69]

In the final months before their report would be issued, staffer Col. Lorry Fenner, a former Air Force intelligence officer who had worked closely with NSA in the past, began sitting in the commission reading room going through the documents by herself. She found they did not include many of the smoking guns Drake had seen. There was nothing about intercepts of Mihdhar's or Hazmi's communications with the Hada house in Yemen in the documents volunteered by Hayden.

During the final month of their work, Fenner asked two commission colleagues to take a look. After one confirmed her feeling that the NSA materials offered a "gold mine" into the pre-9/11 world, they approached Zelikow, who managed to set up a single day to go through the NSA's archives. Fenner and two others arrived at the NSA, where they were given "huge piles of documents" to go through. With no time left, the report would remain largely clear of NSA information.

This is likely the greatest of the many failings of the Kean Commission. To be sure, many issues surrounding the plot were not explored to a satisfactory degree, but it is inexplicable that the agency responsible for monitoring the Yemen hub for the better part of five years before 9/11, the agency whose intelligence is responsible for the majority of every presidential daily briefing, would be overlooked.

The anonymity granted to the various agents and officers surrounding what Chairman Kean dubbed a "purposeful" withholding of vital information on the part of the staff of Alec Station made for a tangled and difficult effort to track responsibility across the reports released by the government investigations.

\* \* \*

John Helgerson might have felt nervous as he put the finishing touches on his official report. Having exhaustively examined the matter of Mihdhar's and Hazmi's seemingly ignored travel to the United States, among a number of other issues, he was ready to recommend seventeen specific agency employees for disciplinary procedures. These individuals ranged from the managers at Alec Station up through Cofer Black in the CounterTerrorist Center and even included George Tenet and his deputy James Pavitt. It was the biggest move toward accountability within the government since the attacks, not one person having lost their job as a result.[70]

Tenet, however, would beat Helgerson to the punch. On June 3, 2004, the second longest-serving CIA director in history announced his resignation. He claimed personal reasons. Tenet had taken a break over Memorial Day weekend with his son and wife, a bestselling author of women's do-it-yourself repair books. With his family, he had discussed his future and informed the president he would be leaving.[71]

Tenet had first tried to resign in the fall of 2003 but had been talked out of it by Bush.[72] The president again tried, but this time Tenet was resolute. The Senate Intelligence Committee was readying to release their report on

Iraqi weapons of mass destruction, one that would find widespread failures in intelligence gathering and analyses before the invasion. Only the previous month, Helgerson had completed yet a third report delivered to Congress pertaining to Tenet, the findings of his investigation into the CIA's Renditions, Detentions and Interrogations.[73] Although that investigation had been "stopped in its tracks" months earlier, in the later words of journalist Jane Mayer, by the vice president who had invited John Helgerson to his office to discuss the matter, the final report still had teeth. The IG had concluded that a number of instances of interrogation methods, even those theoretically protected by the Justice Department's "Golden Shield" legal memo, were applied in numbers and combinations that may have constituted breaches of the law.[74]

Was it Iraq, torture, Khalid el Masri, or 9/11 that had caused Tenet to resign? A perfect storm of all four? Or had the he truly had personal reasons? Whatever the case, the resignation the next day of Tenet's spy leader James Pavitt set off widespread speculation in Washington.

\* \* \*

Eleven days before Christmas, 2004, George Tenet along with two others were announced and entered the Blue Room of the White House to applause from a group clad in suits. The president and his wife entered next. Those gathered clapped again and took their seats.

"The Presidential Medal of Freedom is our nation's highest civil award, given to men and women of exceptional merit, integrity, and achievement," Bush explained. "Today, this honor goes to three men who have played pivotal roles in great events and whose efforts have made our country more secure and advanced the cause of human liberty."

Turning to his retired CIA director, gone for six months, Bush declared, "Applications to join the agency have now soared to more than 138,000 per year. Under George's leadership, the number of yearly graduates from the clandestine service training program [has] increased nearly sixfold."

"Early in his tenure as DCI," Bush continued, "George Tenet was one of the first to recognize and address the growing threat to America from radical terrorist networks. Immediately after the attacks . . . George was ready with a plan to strike back at Al Qaeda and to topple the Taliban. Since those weeks, CIA officers have remained on the hunt for Al Qaeda killers. More than three-quarters of Al Qaeda key members and associates had been killed or detained, and the majority were stopped as a result of CIA efforts. CIA officers were also among the first to enter the battle in Iraq, alongside their colleagues in uniform." As stated, it was an impressive record. "In these years of challenge for our country, the men and women of the CIA have been on the front lines of an urgent cause, and the whole nation owes them our gratitude."[75]

Tenet stepped from his chair and stood grinning, his arm brushing up against Bush's. His eyes seemed to well up as the president placed the gold star held by a blue ribbon around his neck, shaking Tenet's hand and holding it for an extra beat, straightening his former DCI's tie with his left hand like a doting wife.

Things had felt on the verge of going off the rails so many times since he had received that phone call inside the St. Regis Hotel, but Tenet would be leaving unscathed, with one of America's highest honors to boot. There was no question he had made his mark. As he departed, his nation was fundamentally different than when he had arrived.

# THE SWORD AND THE SCALE

*"Evil may so shape events that Caesar will occupy a palace, and Christ a cross."*

Dr. Martin Luther King Jr.

More than three years had passed since the attacks. Two national elections transpired in the interim, a congressional contest in 2002 and a presidential race in 2004. During these campaigns, the voting public were kept in the dark about a number of significant policy changes within the government. Still secret were the domestic electronic surveillance program, the international kidnappings, the secret prisons and torturous interrogations, and the assassinations program. Many significant details had also remained hidden about several agencies' staggering failures in safeguarding the country before September 11, despite the terror wars dominating the political discussions.

Eventually, a form of accountability began to take shape, though it was not quite what people like the vocal "Jersey Widows" had in mind. With many of the official avenues for righting the ship exhausted, concerned individuals in Washington began to leak like a sieve. The witch hunt that people like George Tenet had hoped to avoid did happen, but in an entirely cynical way. It would be those seeking to tell the truth who were brought to the stake.

During this period, those who had been in the orbit of Alec Station began to receive promotions into true power positions. The agency became "The Rodriguez & Haspel Show," with Jose making a quick leap from CTC director to take over the CIA's spies division, taking his chief of staff Gina Haspel with him, who would continue her climb from there.[1] This would not instill some people at the agency with much confidence.

Longtime CIA employee Fulton Armstrong explains, "The constant complaint from professionals that are still on the inside is that an entire generation who accepted positions for which they were very generously paid in Afghanistan and Iraq, including do-nothing positions, later inherited the agency and now run the agency. There are a surprising number of graduates of the so-called war on terror, and the Iraq operation, in positions of influence without any background in that region. Institutions always reward these things, and it weakens the institutions."

After Alec Station, John Kiriakou had moved on to an assignment that saw him giving a daily 7 a.m. briefing inside the CIA's seventh-floor executive conference room. One day he noticed Rodriguez's new chief of staff, Gina Haspel,[2] sitting at the side of the room as a note taker. Kiriakou knew of her. In the hallway, they called her "Bloody Gina."

During the briefing, he noticed something he felt was odd in her interchanges with her boss Rodriguez. "They had this almost unspoken understanding. She was his right hand. Nothing romantic, but this very strong mutual respect." He was struck by it because he "never saw Jose show respect to anybody like that."

She forcefully took on the role of chief of staff, demanding that people go through her to get to him. Rodriguez's other allies, including Alfreda Bikowsky, took top spots in the CounterTerrorist Center.[3]

Bikowsky's Alec Station was increasingly focused on the assassinations program and potential expanded use of drone technology. Her former boss, Rich Blee, took over Los Angeles station,[4] known as the agency's West Coast headquarters. Alec Station's founder, Mike Scheuer, had released a book criticizing American foreign policy. When it became a bestseller, he retired to become a regular pundit on cable news. He was now shaping public opinion from the outside, while many of his own loyalists, once referred to as "the Manson Family," were now running the larger CIA.

"They became, just over the span of a few years, the leadership of the CIA, at least in Operations," says Kiriakou. "They were all promoted rapidly, in many cases well into the Senior Executive Service (SES). I know of a few that I would consider monsters of human rights who spent virtually their entire careers in Alec Station."

"To be promoted from GS-14 to GS-15 is a big deal," continued Kiriakou. "Sometimes people go their entire careers without being promoted to

GS-15. But to go from 14 to 15 to Senior Intelligence Service-1, to SES-2, to SES-3, and then 4 over the course of a decade, it's like somebody going from major or lieutenant colonel to a four-star general in ten years. Unless you're Colin Powell, it just doesn't happen."

Kiriakou had two little boys in Pittsburgh, ages nine and six, who he felt "really needed their dad."[5] Working in a large CIA station inside the domestic United States, he asked his boss if instead of working nine to five, he could work eight to four, allowing him to make a weekly plane trip to Pittsburgh where he could see his sons. He had been denied.

He also learned he would soon be heading back overseas, farther from his kids. A colleague made him aware of an opportunity as a corporate spy for a Big Four accounting firm. He got the job, making double his agency paycheck, and he could visit his kids whenever he wanted.

The night before he was to submit his resignation, Kiriakou lay in bed next to his wife Heather and asked, "Am I doing the right thing? My entire adult life, twelve years, has been with the CIA. Am I making a mistake?"

"No," she responded, herself a CIA employee. "Your kids are more important. You should go for it."

His supervisor looked at him like he was crazy when he told her. "You made me choose between my job and my kids," he explained. "What did you think was going to happen? My kids are going to win every time."

One day soon after, Heather rang him up from CIA headquarters, where she was working within the analysts division on non-terrorism issues. She asked if her husband wanted to meet for lunch.

They walked into a popular Washington spot, where Bikowsky and several of her female colleagues frequently held court. As the Kiriakous walked in, they found an empty restaurant, with the exception of the "Manson Family."

"We were seated at the next table," he says. "They looked at me, and I looked at them, and not a word was spoken." It was the last time he saw them. It would not be the last time that they saw him.

* * *

Rossini had worked with George Tenet to help found the National CounterTerror Center (NCTC) at Langley.[6] This center was "owned" by the newly created bureaucracy of the Director of National Intelligence. It was a position the NSA's Michael Hayden had reportedly angled for but was not granted. He had settled into the office's number two slot.[7]

At the NCTC, counterterror leadership had come together in one place to work on the problem of preventing future attacks. Rossini sometimes saw Maureen Baginski there. She had left the NSA to help implement the FBI's intelligence program.[8] This may have included aspects of the NSA's domestic collection, which had expanded beyond telecom companies to use Internet companies as well, employing the same techniques they had with phone calls for email, Internet searches, instant messaging, and more.[9] Baginski soon after retired to the private sector.[10] Her deputy Chris Inglis would become number two at the NSA, helping run it and its surveillance programs until 2014.[11]

Mark Rossini's friend John Miller of ABC News flew into DC to interview for the position of lead media liaison to the FBI. Rossini picked Miller up at Dulles. When Miller was offered the job, he invited Rossini to be his special assistant. Rossini felt he had accomplished all he could at the NCTC. He was ready to return to his home Bureau, and to New York City.[12]

The FBI's New York office, long a politically powerful counterbalance to DC headquarters, had been steadily losing that power under Director Mueller. This had begun with the move of Pat D'Amuro to Washington to bring the 9/11 investigation closer to the top executives. There D'Amuro had remained, as executive assistant director for both counterintelligence and counterterror.

John O'Neill's former loyalists had been attending a succession of good-bye parties. Jack Cloonan made a true retirement to home life in New Jersey. Rossini's friend Doug Miller was moved to the Buffalo office. Steve Bongardt headed to Quantico to become a profiler and researcher of behavioral analysis, later an instructor, then moving into computer forensic examinations from a laboratory.[13]

Most of the old crew would have little involvement in the significant counterterror cases going forward. "Pushed out," was how several referred to it. The FBI's one-time best and brightest on the issue of Al Qaeda called it a day. By the time D'Amuro returned to the New York office to lead it in 2003, few of those who had worked counterterror under him remained.

In early 2005, D'Amuro saw an opportunity and jumped to the private sector, convincing Ali Soufan to leave as well. Soufan was still young and should have believed he had a bright future at the FBI. Maybe it was the moment he was nominated for an Intelligence Award that was denied by a rare CIA veto, or maybe his private questioning before the Kean Commission that began with investigators asking, "Why does the CIA hate you so much?" Whatever the case, D'Amuro would take Soufan to Giuliani Partners, where they would create the security arm. The former mayor's attempt at a presidential bid would later find D'Amuro and Soufan leaving to start their own firms.[14]

D'Amuro got a phone call from Robert Mueller a couple of months after he retired, asking him to return. "You were right about not participating in torture," Mueller told him. "I need that kind of thinking from a guy like you." It was not enough. John O'Neill's former right hand was done with government.[15]

One senior intelligence official told Seymour Hersh that inside the CIA at that time "the good guys are gone."[16] Perhaps the same could be said for the broader intelligence and law enforcement arenas. Hayden's people and the Alec Station offshoots, reporting to President Bush, were now in charge.

* * *

John Helgerson's report would hang over their heads like an anvil. In late 2004, seventeen agency employees, former and current, received letters informing each that the IG investigation concluded they had failed to "discharge their responsibilities in a satisfactory manner . . . in accordance with a reasonable level of professionalism, skill, and diligence."[17]

Each was invited to come to a room at headquarters where they could read the draft report and take handwritten notes. The former counterterror leadership expected to find their names inside. They were shocked, however, to see those of some of their employees.

Mark Rossini says he was unaware, never having heard anyone in counterterror mention it, despite rumors as to what was in the report and who was named for fault. He himself was never allowed to read it. "It was almost as if everyone [in counterterror] knew what was going to be in there, but no one wanted to talk about it," he speculates. "People probably felt that they knew that no one in that building would ever be held accountable for anything, particularly 9/11."

That proved to be a good read of the situation. While the American people may have had a strong interest in learning the truth of the matter, multiple leaders of the CIA under two different presidents would see little to be gained by releasing the IG report. That report had been sent back for revisions twice, first by Tenet's deputy in the period after Tenet resigned,[18] then by Tenet's successor, Porter Goss.[19] In a game of Washington musical chairs, though it was House Representative Goss's committee that had instructed Helgerson to begin his investigation in the first place, once he became CIA director, Goss chose to return the report, requesting that Helgerson soften direct findings of accountability.

Helgerson obliged his director, removing one of the seventeen names and recommending instead that an independent accountability board be convened to assess punishments.[20] Goss would not convene that board. Further, he would choose to keep the final report classified, a decision carried forward by the next four CIA directors.[21]

Apparently, it was public exposure the CIA officers feared, not accountability from leadership. An agency lawyer who had spoken with Jen Matthews about the matter summarized her thoughts. "The worst part was that her children would know [someday]. She would be indelibly tarnished, forever linked to the failures of September 11th."[22]

This, too, seemed to be the concern of Cofer Black and Rich Blee, who among others drafted a rebuttal letter to Helgerson. They sent it to the other thirteen employees originally singled out for blame, asking each to provide notes, before they then sent it forward to Helgerson in January 2005. Their central message was that it was inappropriate to include the names of people like Matthews.[23]

"Overall, we would characterize the draft IG conclusions as unreal," they began. "We were responsible for the activities of the [CTC] under our watch. To hold more junior officers responsible for the environment they found themselves in, and over which they had no control, would only encourage an environment of risk-aversion or discourage individuals from taking the hard missions."[24]

By way of defense for "junior officers" like Bikowsky, they blamed the workload and a stressful work environment resulting from a lack of resources, namely too little funding and staffing. Responding to the failure to watch-list Mihdhar and Hazmi, they pointed outward to foreign CIA stations within the spies division, arguing that "watch-listing was primarily a field function." They provided only one paragraph by way of attempting to defend their withholding about the hijackers from the FBI. For this they stuck with their old story. "The written record indicates the CIA passed, at least informally, the relevant information to the Bureau," they rebutted. "Travel information was disseminated by [redacted]," likely a reference to "Rob" stationed at FBI HQ.

They continue, claiming "[T]he Bureau was clearly briefed on the results of [redacted]," this redaction likely referring to the Malaysia summit in January 2000. "In addition, a number of FBI officers—in the Center and at the Bureau—were clearly aware of the information."

Their defense concluded, "At most, CTC can be faulted for not following through with a formal CIR on al Mihdhar's visa. This would have left an official record of the information passed to the FBI, although we believe copies were informally sent to the Bureau," an apparent reference to Bikowsky's story of having walked it into the J. Edgar Hoover Building. "But, again, CTC clearly intended to share the information with the Bureau, did in fact share information, and did not purposefully withhold anything."[25]

In a second letter drafted by the seventeen that June, upon reading the final version of the IG's report, they tipped their hats to their concern not that they would be held accountable, but that their names would be associated with the failure to prevent the attacks. "It is clear," they wrote, "that this OIG report may eventually—perhaps sooner than later—be released to the public." The American taxpayer might someday be allowed to assess the performance of government bureaucrats whose salaries they paid.[26]

\* \* \*

Among a long list of activities in which the public was being kept in the dark by the people in their government, perhaps the most sensitive secret of all was that Americans' electronic communications were being collected and stored, some of which was being analyzed. Because this secret directly affected every US citizen, it would have heavy political fallout when revealed. But that would have to wait.

With the 2004 election over, it began to sink in that the day would come when some of the secret powers they had accumulated might be undone. Cofer Black recognized this as he and his team created the torture program. "Ten years from now, we're going to be sorry we are doing this," Black had once stated. "But it has to be done."[27] By the start of 2005, signs were pointing to an earlier arrival, fueled by a surge of leaks to the press.

At the CIA, employees began to wonder what would happen if the general public became aware of their torture program. "Of particular concern," a senior intelligence official told Douglas Jehl of the *New York Times*, "is the possibility that CIA officers using interrogation techniques that the government ruled as permissible after the Sept. 11 terrorist attacks might now be punished, or even prosecuted, for their actions in the line of duty."[28] Some in the intelligence community rightly believed they were surrounded by secret enemies. Many who had come up inside non–Alec Station parts of the agency were quietly nursing animosity toward their colleagues in counterterror and their unprecedented rise. A growing number had moved to the private sector, where their communications with reporters were far easier and held less potential for repercussion.

A number of CIA officers held a particular grudge toward the quickly advancing Alfreda Bikowsky.[29] Her apologists wrote it off as sexism, while her detractors saw her only real strength as being her knack for creating close relationships with key supervisors, first Mike Scheuer, then Rich Blee, then Jose Rodriguez,[30] and finally Rodriguez's replacement as CTC director, Mike D'Andrea.[31] Alongside Bikowsky, Rodriguez's former deputy D'Andrea would remain in the role as head of the CIA's CounterTerrorist Center, helping run the "war on terror," for the next decade.[32] Among the odd nicknames he would be given by those at the agency were "The Wolf," "The Undertaker," and "The Dark Prince." He was reportedly Bikowsky's kind of leader. "Those two [Bikowsky and D'Andrea] were thick as thieves," says one agency source.[33]

While she had friends in high places, she also had a growing list of people upset over her prior decisions. The intelligence community as a whole was feeling vulnerable, and the sense of a growing number of enemies with the ability to speak to journalists was feeding their paranoia.

\* \* \*

At the end of 2005, a handful of government insiders and two journalists working for America's top newspapers would prove out the fears of intelligence management by exposing their biggest secrets and fundamentally turning the tables on their power going forward. The Bush administration's nightmare began the last week of October, as the *Washington Post* called to inform them they would be moving forward with a story revealing the existence of the CIA's black site prisons. The author, Dana Priest, arrived at the White House accompanied by her executive editor Len Downie. There, Vice President Dick Cheney and unnamed National Security Council members attempted to convince them that publishing the story would be dangerous to national security. Downie decided to proceed.

Priest began to unravel the CIA prisons story in late 2002, when a source had informed her about stress and duress techniques being used. Her inside source or sources had allowed her to build to the story throughout 2005, including information that exposed the torture-death of Gul Rahman.[34]

"I discovered that there was a secret prison run by the CIA in Guantanamo," explained Priest. "The *New York Times* reported that there is one in Thailand. Once you knew that the agency and not the military were handling these prisoners, we wanted to know where were they? Well, people were telling us right out that they weren't in Guantanamo, so where were they?"

On November 2, the *Washington Post's* front-page story was headlined "CIA Holds Terror Suspects in Secret Prisons." It caught the public attention. The next year, Priest would accept the Pulitzer Prize.

Behind the scenes, George W. Bush ordered the CIA to begin moving all prisoners held in black sites to Guantanamo Bay.[35] The agency's power to imprison and interrogate would suddenly be stripped and awarded to the US military. At the same time, Bush began supporting a proposed ban on torture making its way through the Congress. Calling its author, Senator John McCain, to the White House, Bush told McCain that he would agree to sign the bill if McCain would alter some of its language so that CIA officers, if ever charged with a war crime, could offer a defense of having followed a lawful order. McCain agreed, a press conference was held announcing Bush's support, and the Detainee Treatment Act was signed into law.[36]

The official use of torture techniques within the US government was over. The *Washington Post* had managed to do what none of the government's internal mechanisms had, inducing a swift reversal of the detention and torture programs.

* * *

The videotapes containing footage of waterboarding and other so-called "enhanced techniques" had been securely kept by Michael Winograd, the CIA station chief in Bangkok. When the *Washington Post* broke the torture story, Winograd sought permission from Jose Rodriguez to destroy the tapes. Rodriguez granted that permission, passed in a message sent by his second Gina Haspel.[37]

During the three years in which those torture tapes sat locked in a US embassy safe, there had been an internal discussion at the CIA, that even on occasion reached ears in the White House, as to whether or not the tapes could legally be destroyed. Ultimately, every time the question arose, the final call was that it was probably best to leave the tapes intact.[38] The CIA employees in that footage, possibly including certain Alec Station managers, had also lobbied for the destruction of the tapes. Answers from senior agency officials concerning the tapes advised against destroying them.[39] Interestingly, Rodriguez himself seemed aware that destroying the tapes would result in political and possibly legal fallout, so before he granted permission to Winograd to do so, he consulted with two agency lawyers. Rodriguez asked CIA lawyers if he had authority to destroy the tapes, and if doing so was legal. They responded in the affirmative. When sending the order to Bangkok through Gina Haspel to destroy the tapes, neither Rodriguez nor Haspel included these lawyers on the message, which is standard protocol.[40]

Internal emails appear to demonstrate that Rodriguez thought the footage on the tapes was so damning that if it were ever to be made public it would devastate the agency.[41] By not including CIA counsel or the director on the cable, Rodriguez and Haspel prevented them from being able to intervene. The attorneys were also spared any liability. With the footage destroyed, the CIA employees and contractors who took part in torturing suspects, allegedly including at times Bikowsky and Matthews, had also been further insulated from accountability.

On the issue, Mark Rossini, who mentioned he liked Rodriguez, said about him, "He's a fucking lawyer, for Christ's sake, he should have known better."

* * *

Another troubling call came into the White House from another major media outlet, this time the *New York Times*. They would soon be releasing a story exposing another big state secret, the NSA's domestic surveillance program. Another meeting followed, with a *Times* publisher and editor invited to the White House.[42] Bush personally explained that they would have "blood on their hands" if they published their story and another terrorist attack occurred. Nonetheless, after having already withheld this story for a year, they plunged forward.

On December 16, 2005, the *Times'* front-page story was headlined "Bush Let US Spy on Callers Without Court." Written by James Risen, it became a milestone in the exposure of the surveillance programs. In the days before the Snowden revelations, such news caused shock waves.

Perhaps the line most closely read by the leadership in Washington was the following: "Nearly a dozen current and former officials, who were granted anonymity because of the classified nature of the program, discussed it with reporters for the *New York Times* because of their concerns about the operation's legality and oversight."

* * *

On December 17, 2005, second-term president George W. Bush stepped into the Roosevelt Room of the White House to face the press. Officially, he had convoked the meeting to build consensus for the renewal of the USA PATRIOT Act. The timing of the event, however, only a day after the *Times'* big scoop, was suggestive of dual intentions. For the first time, the president would be telling the public the story of Khalid al Mihdhar and Nawaf al Hazmi.

"Two of the terrorist hijackers who flew a jet into the Pentagon, Nawaf al Hazmi and Khalid al Mihdhar, communicated while they were in the United States to other members of Al Qaeda who were overseas," Bush declared. "But we didn't know they were here, until it was too late."

The president added, "The activities I have authorized make it more likely that killers like these 9/11 hijackers will be identified and located in time."[43] It was the first time a representative of the US government had used the story of these two hijackers to illustrate the motivation behind broad domestic surveillance. He was no longer denying an intelligence failure had taken place—but, suddenly admitted, it became the reason to empower, not punish, the agency. Bush continued this talking point the next month, now joined by former NSA director Michael Hayden. They also provided what would prove to be highly misleading statements about the program itself.

"The program focuses on calls coming from outside of the United States, but not domestic calls," Bush claimed. The vice president stated, "Some of our critics call this a 'domestic surveillance program.' It is not domestic surveillance." Hayden appeared at the Press Club, stating, "The intrusion into privacy is also limited: only international calls."[44]

Hayden and Bush were inverting the apparent lessons of the September 11 tragedy, keeping details that would contradict their arguments classified secret. It was a nice power to have.

* * *

The search began immediately for the former and current government officials who had provided the CIA's and NSA's big secrets to the major newspapers. Inside the Justice Department, Steven Tyrrell, the incoming head of the Fraud Section, was given the "go" to open preliminary criminal investigations, leading a staff of sixty lawyers and thirty support employees.[45] The leadership at both agencies affected, the CIA and the NSA, were cooperating enthusiastically. They wanted the leakers found.

At Langley in early 2006, director Porter Goss made unauthorized disclosures to journalists—and the public—one of his top priorities.[46] Whether this was at the behest of the Bush administration or of his own accord is unknown. What would come to be a long-term trend, later referred to as a government "war on whistle-blowers," began quietly and without much debate.

A former officer told the *New York Times*, "This [is] a very aggressive internal investigation. Goss [is] determined to find the source of the secret jails story." Goss held no qualms in telling Congress of his desire "that we will witness a grand jury investigation with reporters present being asked to reveal who is leaking this information."

He assigned the job to a unit known as the Security Center. The obvious place to begin looking was inside John Helgerson's office. Multiple stories by Dana Priest included revelations that corresponded to information inside the various inspector general reports. Some stories in the *New York Times* over the same period also seemed to draw from information inside what were still-classified IG reports.

The reports themselves, it should be pointed out, had been read by a number of people at the CIA, as well as the congressional intelligence committees and people at the White House. The Justice Department was also aware of their contents. While it may have been reasonable to suspect Helgerson or his staff, they were certainly not the sole possible point of origin.

For reasons still unknown, the Security Center investigators took a strong interest in one of Helgerson's former deputies, Mary McCarthy. By then, she had left the CIA to return to a position on the National Security Council. In an unusual move, Goss ordered McCarthy to take a polygraph test.

One day that April, McCarthy was called into a meeting. In fact, it was an interrogation. McCarthy was questioned about apparent inconsistencies in her polygraph examination. Though she and her lawyers have continued to deny it to the present day, according to an account given to the *Times*, she "confessed." Due to retire in May after a long career in government, instead, she was stripped of her security clearance, watched as she packed up her office, and escorted out past her colleagues.[47]

That evening on NBC News, Andrea Mitchell explained, "Now they've found someone who was about to retire, and they're sending a very tough message. The bottom line is that no one is going to have the courage or the stupidity or the will to talk to reporters from now on. Very few people will, because they can see from this example what can happen to you."[48]

From the private sector, John Kiriakou remembers learning what had happened to her. He had a great deal of respect for Mary McCarthy and took notice when he read about it in the press. "I thought, 'Wow, that was gutsy. Good for her, if she did it. If she did, I thought that was really something. But it never occurred to me that I should do it.'"[49]

Mary McCarthy retired to her native Minnesota. Though her dismissal was referred to the Justice Department, no prosecution ever followed.[50] The case simply disappeared. A little over two weeks later, so would Porter Goss, who would be replaced as CIA director by the architect of the NSA's domestic spying program, Michael Hayden. Hayden would choose to continue Goss' decision to keep the CIA Inspector General's report about 9/11 classified out of public view, releasing a statement clarifying, "This is not about avoiding responsibility. In fact, the opposite is true. [emphasis his.]" He would be the first in the history of the United States to be director for both the NSA and CIA, holding the new position for the remainder of George W. Bush's presidency.

\* \* \*

Meanwhile, the leaks kept coming. Lawrence Wright published an article in the *New Yorker*, "The Agent," followed by his book *The Looming Tower*, naming the recently retired Tom Wilshere for the first time. Thanks to the attention brought by the bestseller list and a Pulitzer Prize, Wright helped set the record straight on those who had worked in the New York FBI as a more accurate version of events leading up to 9/11. This was a matter relished by many now in retirement, the private sector, and the few still at the Bureau.

The leak that stung Rich Blee and Alfreda Bikowsky came in the spring of 2007, as they were nominated for the station chief and deputy positions in Baghdad. In the midst of the Iraq occupation, this was one of the most politically important assignments for the CIA. The astute ladder-climber Bikowsky may have smelled the whiff of advancement surrounding this key Operations position. After Hayden's arrival as head of the agency, Alec Station had quietly been shuttered after ten years in operation, and Bikowsky had moved up to lead a larger office within CTC called the Global Jihad Unit.

A curmudgeonly antiauthoritarian reporter named Ken Silverstein, Washington editor and blogger for *Harper's Magazine*, was contacted by one or more of Blee's and Bikowsky's growing secret enemies inside the agency. He reported on this in March 2007, providing criticisms from insiders about her qualifications, resulting in a follow-up story in which a CIA representative claimed she "is neither considering, nor being considered for, service in Iraq." The story also criticized Blee, who remained anonymous in the article (and in all other press reports at that time).[51]

As a result of the attention, apparently Blee, too, was removed from consideration for the Baghdad post. Seeing his advancement stalled, Blee retired that year, maintaining a home in Los Angeles.[52] Bikowsky would remain, perhaps wondering if the many accusations against her would leave her in middle management for the remainder of her career.

In May, another leak and another story came out, this one in the *Baltimore Sun*, revealing the history of the NSA's TrailBlazer program. Hayden surely noticed, as the story contained an allegation of "mismanagement" under his tenure. It explained that this mismanagement drove "into the ground [the] six-year, multibillion-dollar . . . program to adapt the NSA's collection and analysis capability to the age of digital communications."[53]

* * *

Siobhan Gorman had been publishing a series of reports focused on the NSA since arriving at the *Baltimore Sun*. Each report revealed details considered sensitive by NSA leadership. Tom Drake, still working inside Fort Meade, had liked the direction of Gorman's articles. For those working at the NSA, the *Baltimore Sun* was the paper of record. Drake was also aware of "an even more secret program within StellarWind" designed to monitor members of the news media, and he was aware that Gorman was on that list.[54]

Diane Roark cautioned Drake to tread carefully as he began using encrypted email to send Gorman information beginning in February 2006. In an account reported by Jane Mayer, Drake established "three ground rules":

- Neither he nor she would reveal his identity.
- He wouldn't be the sole source for any story.
- He would not supply her with classified information.[55]

In early 2007, Drake decided to go to the *Baltimore Sun*'s building in person, beginning a series of meetings with Siobhan Gorman. He did this openly because he believed he was doing nothing wrong, and he felt certain that he provided nothing classified. He also knew, though, "it didn't matter that it was all unclassified. I knew it wouldn't matter to the government. They would find a way to say it was classified."[56] Nonetheless, he proceeded.

When the investigation to find the whistle-blowers who exposed the domestic surveillance program began, Roark had been contacted by the FBI to actually aid in that investigation.[57] She agreed, but found in her first meeting with investigators that they were entirely hostile to her. It was then that it occurred to her that they considered her a suspect. As the three-hour meeting progressed and the tone became more friendly, Roark assumed she had eased investigators' suspicions of her. She heard nothing from them again until the morning of July 26, 2007, when the FBI raided her Oregon home, guns drawn.

Roark knew the law and knew her rights, but she was told the affidavit that justified the raid was classified secret. She suspected the agents had entered her home previously because they knew precisely where to look to gather all the data she had collected about NSA on behalf of her previous employers in Congress. They confiscated many of her personal papers and electronics.

Bill Binney was in his home near Fort Meade when his son answered the door to the sight of twelve gun-toting FBI agents. Heading upstairs, they next pointed their guns at Binney's wife. Finally they entered his bathroom, pointing a gun between his eyes as he stood in the shower.[58]

Kirk Wiebe and Ed Loomis were also raided that morning. Four simultaneous raids on four specific homes belonging to four people united by one thing: the two-page letter they had all sent to the Defense Department's inspector general five years earlier complaining about the waste and malfunction of the NSA's TrailBlazer program. In their hunt to find the sources behind the leaks to the *New York Times*, investigators had pressured managers at Defense's IG to give up names of whistle-blowers. Not only is even trawling for leads in an inspector general's office considered highly unethical, it is potentially criminal for someone at DoD IG to divulge any names. The office was created by Congress to be a safe place for reporting abuse.

John Crane, who had been an assistant to the IG until 2006, explains that the Inspector General's act—which he carried a copy of in his pocket—clearly laid out the only circumstances in which a whistle-blower's identity is to be revealed without their consent. "Only under exigent circumstances . . . where you needed to act so quickly for safety." Essentially, a ticking-bomb scenario, which, of course, finding media leakers is not. Crane explains, "For a whistle-blower system to work, whistle-blowers need to have the confidence that they will not have their identities revealed, and they will not be subject to reprisal. Period."[59]

Not only were Roark, Binney, Wiebe, and Loomis exposed and now subject to reprisal, they had absolutely nothing to do with the leaks to the *New York Times*. That source would later turn out to be a person working, ironically enough, at the Justice Department. Either investigators were shooting in the dark and decided to take a swing at whistle-blowers who had successfully challenged NSA hierarchy in the past, or perhaps they knew these four were not the likely culprits, but that with enough pressure and intimidation they could be pressed into divulging who was. Crane suspects this was the case, and that investigators incorrectly believed Tom Drake was the *Times* leaker all along.

After talking with Binney and Wiebe about the raids, Drake was certain a knock would come at his door any time. Drake, of course, knew he was not the source of the leak in question. He also knew, however, that he *had* given a lot of nonclassified information to the *Baltimore Sun*. It was likely the political powers behind this FBI investigation would not be happy with him about the waste, fraud, and abuse he had exposed. "The big fish is the last one they go after," says Drake, "because they want to find out as much as possible before they move in."[60]

That fall, it was Drake's turn to have his home raided by armed FBI agents. On more than one occasion, he sat down to cooperate with them. Their interest, however, was in the *Times* leak, not in any of the illegal behavior the NSA was engaging in that he wanted to talk about. Drake, so sure that he was guilty of nothing, admitted right from the outset that he had given unclassified information to Siobhan Gorman.

He was not charged with any crime initially. His legal status did not change, though he would eventually fear that the NSA would strip him of his security clearance. Drake went on administrative leave, finally clearing out his desk in February of 2008, ending his six-year stint there. Finally, Drake was called into a meeting with the FBI at a facility in Washington, DC, where a prosecutor was waiting for him.

The prosecutor tried to apply heat, telling Drake that they had enough information on him to put him away for life if he did not take a plea. He refused. Over the course of years, changing prosecutors, and changing White House administrations, Drake found himself charged with ten felony counts. Five fell under a bastardized interpretation of the Espionage Act, four were for making false statements, and one was for obstruction of justice.

\* \* \*

Almost two years to the day after informing the White House of their plans to run the exposé of domestic surveillance, the *New York Times* again called the Bush administration. This time, reporter Mark Mazzetti had learned of Jose Rodriguez's and Gina Haspel's destruction of the CIA's collection of tapes, documenting torture of prisoners inside their black sites. He called up the agency to let them know he was publishing about this, though without their names. "Are you really going to do this story?" they asked him dumbfounded. He was a journalist, so his answer, of course, was, "Yes." In an apparent move to punish him, CIA director Michael Hayden reportedly had the forthcoming story leaked to the Associated Press. Nonetheless, on December 6, 2007, a front-page *New York Times* headline read, "CIA Destroyed Tapes of Interrogations."

Another public furor was ignited, and this one would not go away for some time. Scandals in Washington surrounding potentially illegal actions of officials doing their jobs tended to be a more difficult matter to see prosecuted. The common wisdom since Watergate had been that the cover-up, not the crime, was what would get you. The destruction of tapes, with clear echoes back to Nixon, seemed to fall into the area of cover-up.

In 2008, the Justice Department began investigating the decision by CIA manager Jose Rodriguez to order the destruction of the videotapes. After an almost three-year investigation, it would be announced that no charges would be brought against anyone involved.

\* \* \*

One night, John Kiriakou turned on the TV to watch President Bush responding to a report from a human rights group, stating to the American public, "This government does not torture people."[61] Kiriakou sat up.

"I knew that was a lie," he said emphatically. "Not only were we torturing, but the president authorized it as an official US policy."

Kiriakou became angrier as he watched what he perceived as Bush inferring that if any torture had occurred it must have been the result of a rogue agency employee. "I knew *that* was a lie too," he says. "This was an official program."

Days later, he got a phone call from ABC News. Reporter Brian Ross was on the other end of the line, informing him that he had a source who claimed that Kiriakou had tortured Abu Zubaydah.[62]

"That is absolutely untrue," Kiriakou responded. "Not only have I never laid a hand on Abu Zubaydah, I've never laid a hand on anybody. This source is either wrong, mistaken, or a liar."

Ross made an offer. "You're welcome to come on the show and defend yourself."

Kiriakou has come to believe he fell for "an old journalists' technique." Now working in the private sector, he agreed to come on the show to defend himself against allegations that were likely invented by the journalist.

"I suppose I can say," Kiriakou told Brian Ross before his cameras, "that my understanding is that what's been reported in the press has been correct in that these enhanced techniques included everything from what was called an 'attention shake,' where you grab the person by their lapels and shake them, all the way up to the other end, which was waterboarding."

"And that was one of the techniques?" asked Ross.

"Waterboarding was one of the techniques, yes," responded Kiriakou. He continued, "This had the signature of the president on it. And not just the president but Condi Rice as national security adviser, John Ashcroft as the attorney general, George Tenet as director of the CIA, and about a dozen lawyers from the National Security Council."[63]

Jaws must have been dropping in Washington and Langley. Kiriakou was spilling many of the beans. "And it wasn't just that one day that Tenet signed this paper and then they started torturing people," Kiriakou made a point of clarifying to Ross, as he tried to defend the CIA. "It was every single time they wanted to torture someone, they had to get the [Director of Central Intelligence's] signature."

At the time of the interview, Kiriakou still believed the lie that had floated around Langley in 2002. He told Ross that Zubaydah had "broken" after one application of waterboarding, spilling Al Qaeda's secrets—the ones Ali Soufan would later make clear he had received using classic interrogation methods. Kiriakou, though morally perturbed by the CIA's use of torture, still had continued to believe for five years it was effective and necessary. He tried to frame the whole interview from that perspective.

"I felt good coming out of ABC News studio," Kiriakou reflects. He had asked his CIA employee wife to join him during the taping. As they walked out, he asked her, "How did I do?"

"Great," she replied enthusiastically.

"I didn't say anything classified, did I?"

"No, nothing classified." she confirmed.

He laughs about it now. "Well, little did I know the CIA was going to file a crimes report against me the next morning." CIA staff did not share Kiriakou's perspective that he was defending the agency.

"They were furious at the CIA this morning," a senior DOJ official told ABC News a week later, "but cooler heads have apparently prevailed for the time being." Prosecutors decided Kiriakou had not shared classified information during his interview, as everything he confirmed had already been reported in one form or another. Nonetheless, CIA director Michael Hayden passed around a classified memo to remind employees "of the importance of protecting classified information." Several days later, the CIA made a criminal referral in the matter, and the FBI launched an investigation.[64]

"The CIA never forgave me for going on TV, saying we were torturing prisoners, and airing their dirty laundry," Kiriakou claims. "And so [some at] the CIA insisted, they demanded, that the FBI and the Justice Department continue to investigate me."

Speaking to us about the FBI's long investigation into his activities, Kiriakou points to a study that alleges "the average American on the average day going about his normal business commits three felonies.[65] The bottom line being that if 'they' want to get you, 'they' are going to get you. They waited until I made a mistake."

\* \* \*

It would be easy for an outsider to think that Tom Drake was a man possessed by some quaint notions. After multiple attempts at blowing the whistle via the proper channels at the NSA on issues of waste and constitutionality, he found himself the target of an FBI investigation. He was cooperating with the FBI. "I wanted them to know who I was," says Drake. "I'm talking to criminal investigators and sharing prima facie evidence of crimes being committed by people in the government, and they did not want to hear about it."

"I felt for the guy," remembers Kiriakou, who read about the case in the newspapers. He could not figure out why they were going after Drake, seeing no proof of wrongdoing.

The prosecutor in his case retired. Drake hoped the appointee of the incoming president would be far more lenient, until he heard that William Welch would be stepping in. The previous prosecutor had been trying to create a phantom conspiracy between Drake and the other NSA whistleblowers, Binney, Loomis, Roark, and Wiebe. At least Welch dropped that angle, but still indicted Drake for violating the Espionage Act, primarily based upon the notion that the copies of nonsensitive documents Drake kept after reporting to the inspector general was, in fact, a flagrant act of retaining sensitive material.

Absurdly enough, despite the pretense that their case against Drake was an attempt to ferret out the person who leaked information to the *New York Times*, after one of the actual leakers, Thomas Tamm, came forward, the Justice Department kept up their case against Drake. Further, they chose never to prosecute Tamm.

Drake's almost retro sense of truth and justice paid off in the end. By holding strong through five years of investigation and a year of indictment, and refusing to bend to the threat of massive prison time, right before his trial was to begin the prosecution cracked.

"By the end, I felt I was in the driver's seat and worked out a deal on my terms," he says. The government, ever concerned with saving face by obtaining some form of guilty plea, regardless of how watered down, conceded that if Drake would accept a lesser charge of retention of classified information with intention to disclose, the ten greater charges would be dropped, and he would serve no jail time.

Of course, for all of his efforts and attempts at honesty, transparency, and legality, his life was largely ruined. Financially decimated and with most of his social networks in tatters, Drake currently works at an Apple Store fixing computers. He has turned down several higher-paying gigs as a media personality—he says out of principle.

* * *

John Kiriakou felt optimistic that a new era had begun as Barack Obama arrived in the White House.[66] "I believed in the whole Hope and Change thing. I believed it was a new chapter in America," says Kiriakou, who took his children to the inauguration so they could be part of the moment.

President Obama had been clear during the campaign that the Bush administration's approach toward the fight against terrorist attacks, and toward the government generally, would be fully rebuked.[67] Accountability and transparency, he declared, would be the hallmarks of his policy. With the presidency and the Congress now controlled by the *other* party, investigations into torture were underway in both the House Judiciary and Intelligence committees.

When Senator John Kerry was elevated to chairman of the Senate's foreign relations committee, he had an idea about how best to exercise oversight of the State Department and the foreign policy community. He wanted to reestablish an investigative unit that had been disbanded back in the 1970s. Via connections that Kerry's chief of staff had in the media, Kiriakou's name came up as a potential hire.[68]

Kiriakou remembers arriving at his fourth-floor office in the Senate's Dirksen building in early 2009, which he describes as "your typical slap-dash government office with completely mismatched furniture." It came without a chair, so he had to find one down the hall, broken, which he sat in for another six months before he got a replacement. The highlight was the view of DC's Union Station, where he often watched the commuters.

With Obama as the president, "everybody thought that this was a new day [for the Intelligence Community], turning a new page," says Kiriakou. "I didn't think so. I told [Senator] Kerry, 'If there's one thing the CIA is good at, it's co-opting new presidents and new CIA directors. People think the president or the director are [sic] going to come in and reform every-thing. They are not. The civil servants at the CIA know they can wait out this director, and they can wait out this president. The civil servants don't want anything to change. They like things just the way they are.' And that's precisely what happened."

"I have always believed," says Kiriakou, "that whenever a new president is elected, the CIA works very hard to 'recruit' that president. And by that, I mean 'bring him into the fold,' make him feel like he's one of the guys. We whisper the top secrets from around the world to him. We show him those blue-border reports. We brief him on the most sensitive human intelligence assets that we have in the world. Okay, so now you're one of the guys. You're not going to come down hard on your friends at the CIA, right, because you're one of the gang."

He says that, in contrast to Bill Clinton, Bush and Obama were "sucked right into the CIA and, for lack of a better term, were 'fellow travelers.'"

Kiriakou began investigating a potential violation of the cover agreement between the CIA and the State Department. Word had reached him that summer that his one-time boss, Alfreda Bikowsky, had been placed under "cover status" for the first time in her long career. Up until then, there had been less legal peril for insiders to provide her name and information about her to reporters. Many had, over the years, but no outlets had yet printed her name. Now she would be officially protected. Kiriakou wrote a letter to Langley asking why a woman included on the list of newly hired State Department officers was going undercover for the first time when she had been with the CIA for twenty-five years.[69]

"Some time passed," Kiriakou says, "and then a colleague comes into my office and he [said], 'You got a letter of response from the agency.'"

Kiriakou replied, "I haven't seen any letter."

His colleague told him, "They classified it 'top secret.'"

Kiriakou, as the CIA knew, was not cleared for top secret. He asked, "What's it say?"

His colleague responded, "It says, 'Go fuck yourself.'"

That August, Obama allowed the public to see as-yet-unreleased portions of one of John Helgerson's reports into the CIA's torture program. Kiriakou read the release and was beside himself. Abu Zubaydah had been water-boarded eighty-three times; not a single time had "broke" him, as he had been told—and as he had himself repeated to ABC News and the American public two years prior. He also learned that Khalid Sheikh Mohammed had been waterboarded 147 times.[70]

"When John [Kiriakou] and I first talked about this in 2009, John was pissed," confirms Fulton Armstrong, who had also taken a position working for Kerry. "He was pissed because it was an embarrassment to him but also because he realized that even internally [people he worked with at the CIA had] lied to each other." The release of the redacted Senate "Torture Report" five years later would make clear another falsehood passed widely inside Langley. Using primary source documents, the Senate investigation confirmed that "enhanced techniques" simply did not work.

Kiriakou was very unimpressed by the power of the nation's representatives. He says he was close three times to exposing a CIA scandal when Kerry visited him and ordered him to drop it. After complaining, a Kerry staffer gave Kiriakou some useful advice. "Before you determine the subject of each investigation, you need to ask yourself, 'How does what I am investigating help John Kerry to become Secretary of State?'"

Kiriakou had promised Kerry two years. After two and a half, he decided "there was no point in even remaining in that job." Kerry closed the investigative unit immediately after Kiriakou's departure. Obama would nominate Kerry to be Secretary of State a year later. It was a position he held for the remainder of the administration.

\* \* \*

Alfreda Bikowsky had been placed in "cover status" because she was heading to the London station, perhaps as chief, though it is not known. It was her first field position, and she would be reuniting with an old friend, Jen Matthews, who had been serving there as counterterror liaison for nearly five years, having left the United States for the spot in 2004.[71]

Once dreaming of becoming the first female CIA director, Matthews knew her time in Europe had not gotten her much closer to the goal. She was growing impatient. During visits to headquarters, she sought the advice of upper management, who confirmed her suspicions. Matthews had never had an overseas tour. She had made it all the way up to GS-15 as a career analyst, a rare matter. The jump into the SES, the Senior Executive Service, would be harder, though. She would need two things to continue up the ladder: a spies division assignment plus either a State Department or Defense Department assignment. An ally offered to help her solve the spies division job problem by making her chief of the base in Khost, Afghanistan.

"She didn't have the foggiest idea what she was doing in that position. It wasn't Jen's fault," Kiriakou insists. "It was headquarters' fault. They didn't send her to 'The Farm'"—where the CIA trains officers—"Literally nothing. They put her on a plane and sent her to Afghanistan."

Around the time of Obama's inauguration, and against the advice of her career CIA officer uncle, Matthews accepted the new position. She did not know it, but her career decision was about to set off a chain of events that would have far-reaching consequences.

It was around 4:30 in the afternoon on December 30, 2009 when the car carrying Abu Mulal al Balawi was waved through three security checkpoints at Forward Operating Base Chapman on the outskirts of Khost. As the car came to a stop near the building where Balawi was to be debriefed, Jen Matthews stood nearby, along with others on her team.[72] Balawi stepped out of the vehicle and detonated the explosives that were sewn into his vest. The resulting blast killed Balawi, Matthews, and eight other people.

Balawi had already provided intelligence to the CIA on low-level operatives. Originally a Jordanian asset, the CIA had come to trust that Balawi was indeed working for them. In this meeting, they believed, he was going to provide intelligence on a high-level Al Qaeda operative. The awaiting CIA agents were so eager, they planned to call President Obama right after the meeting. A decision was made not to search Balawi upon his entry to the base.

The decision not to search him was made, it is claimed, as a show of respect. An internal review concluded that the assailant had not been fully vetted, and it cited failures of "management oversight." But no senior managers were mentioned by name.[73]

A source put the accusation more bluntly, and laid it at the feet of Alfreda Bikowsky, claiming, "She interfered from headquarters with how Jennifer ran her own operation on the ground in Afghanistan." The source explained with anger, "She instructed her not to search him because it would offend him as a Muslim. She got Jennifer killed."[74] This claim comes from an excerpt of an internal CIA report on the matter that was never released. Such direct guilt is hard to confirm without acquiring the report in question.

Matthews's body was returned to the United States, met by her grieving husband and three children. A memorial service was held in Langley amid a snowstorm,[75] where someone matching the description of Alfreda Bikowsky gave a kind of eulogy. Some might argue that Matthews's and Bikowsky's efforts to lower the bar for accountability at their agency had paved the way for the tragedy. One source tells us that Bikowsky took away a different lesson from her friend's death, believing that she herself had been spared by God, so she could kill Usama Bin Laden.[76] Over a year later when the Al Qaeda top leader was killed by US forces in Abbottabad, Pakistan, becoming the greatest public relations coup of the Obama White House, sources claim Bikowsky would be the CIA employee given the most credit, potentially opening the door for her future rise to the very top of her agency.[77]

\* \* \*

John Kiriakou's interview on ABC had staff at the CIA livid. To many at the agency, he had broken a sacred code of silence. Reporters had been calling Kiriakou frequently ever since the interview, and he spoke with them.[78]

A colleague who "had never been undercover in his entire life" retired. When former alleged torturer Deuce Martinez left the agency, he went to work for the firm owned by the two psychologists who had developed the CIA's interrogation program. Meeting Kiriakou, Martinez handed him a few of his business cards. Later, when Scott Shane of the *New York Times* contacted Kiriakou about a story on the torture of Abu Zubaydah, Kiriakou provided him the business card of a former CIA employee, who was now in the private sector. He did so again when a different journalist, Matthew Cole, approached him concerning a story regarding another agent. Unfortunately for Kiriakou, Cole passed the agent's name on to defense attorneys for people being held in Guantanamo Bay. When the CIA got wind of the names of current and former agents that these defense attorneys had, they were incensed, and made sure to ferret out their sources.

Kiriakou was invited to an FBI field office in 2011, he believed, to discuss work as a consultant. As the discussion centered entirely on whether or not he had passed the names of agents to Scott Shane or others, he quickly realized he was the target of an investigation. Months later, he was approached by FBI agents and arrested. He was charged with five felonies, including three counts of espionage.

The CIA made a point on that same day of announcing that the information he had provided to the *New York Times*, resulting in one of the espionage charges, was being declassified solely for the purpose of prosecuting him.[79] That top secret information was revealed: the CIA had run a program to capture or kill Al Qaeda members. This was hardly a secret. "That's not espionage," Kiriakou insists to this day. "Having a conversation with the *New York Times* about torture is not espionage."

Kiriakou hired an attorney. "I gave them everything I had, $150,000 to start."[80]

One day, his lawyer sat him down early on to beat an idea into his head. "Look," he said, "there's actually a legal definition for 'whistle-blower,' and it's 'any person who brings to light evidence of waste, fraud, abuse, or illegality.'"

"I'm not a whistle-blower," Kiriakou responded to him strongly.

The lawyer corrected him. "You're the definition of a whistle-blower."

Kiriakou came to believe that the FBI and the Justice Department have a strategy. He suggests, "They heap on charges. Charges that are specious, but they are going to make you defend yourself, knowing that most juries in this country would convict a bologna sandwich."

After spending hundreds of thousands of dollars on legal fees, and being told by his lawyers that going to trial would cost another million, Kiriakou spoke to his wife. He asked her how long she and the kids could get on without him financially. After running the numbers, they decided it was two years. "I was facing forty-five years, and they offered me a deal for two-and-a-half years," he says, asking rhetorically, "So do I roll the dice?"

Reflecting on the situation, Kiriakou opines, "They want you worn down. They break you financially, they isolate you socially. You're likely fired from your job, so professionally you're ruined. And you've got multiple felony accounts hanging over your head."

Kiriakou got the full story of the government's long investigation into him, and what was driving it, during the "discovery" phase. Because it's sealed, he cannot detail it. He will only say, "It was very clear that [the impetus for] this was coming not from the Justice Department or the FBI. It was coming from elsewhere." Asked if there was a particular group at the CIA that he had heard was pushing this, Kiriakou answers, "Yes. It was CTC. And it was two individuals in particular in CTC who were driving it.

One of whom I had never met and never heard of." At the time, Alfreda Bikowsky was still a key leader in the CTC.

Kiriakou was tried in the eastern district of Virginia, as would be other future government worker defendants like Jeffrey Sterling and Edward Snowden. "No national security defendant has ever won his case in the eastern district of Virginia," points out Kiriakou.

In discovery, Kiriakou's attorneys had identified seventy classified documents that were needed for his defense. They submitted seventy separate motions for declassification and blocked off two days to present the cases for each. At the start of the first day, the judge spoke up, "I can take care of this in two minutes. All seventy of these motions are denied."

As Kiriakou walked out the front steps, he asked, "What just happened?"

"We just lost this case," answered his attorney.

Staring down the barrel of a one-million-dollar trial and a potential sentence of twelve to eighteen years if convicted, Kiriakou took the plea. He was sentenced to thirty months in prison. As this happened, he thought back to the advice he had followed, given by his CIA colleague back in 2002. That colleague had predicted he should steer clear of participating in torture because those involved would later be prosecuted. "Well," he says, "it turned out I was the only one who went to prison anyway, out of the entire program."

One of the only two men to have turned down involvement in the "enhanced interrogations" found himself spending the next two years in the Federal Correctional Institution in Loretto, Pennsylvania. Kiriakou had once hated what he believed George W. Bush had done to his country. Yet he came to feel a personal loathing for the man who had gained office running as Bush's antithesis, Barack Obama.

"There was a double standard in that administration," he says. "If you were a friend of the president, or if you had four shiny stars on your shoulder, you could essentially say whatever you wanted to whomever you wanted; but if you were blowing the whistle on waste, fraud, abuse, or illegality, you were going to go to prison." Kiriakou believes he learned a lesson about the system that is hard for him to swallow. "If I had tortured, I never would have gone to prison."

* * *

FBI agent Mark Rossini had filed for divorce from his wife at the end of 2006. Many of the people he once worked beside at Alec Station had also seen their marriages end in recent years, including Mike Scheuer, Alfreda Bikowsky, and Tom Wilshere. Rossini believes the guilt over 9/11 was a factor. "It destroyed my life, it destroyed me, as it destroys me every day," he stated with passion. "It didn't have to happen. The guilt I have over not being more forceful. The guilt I have for not saying, 'Fuck you, I'm taking the memo to the Bureau.'"[81]

One night, over drinks, he remembers former New York supervisor Ken Maxwell stewing to him, "How could they [in the CIA] not fuckin' tell us about these guys havin' a visa? How could they not have told us?"

"And when Kenny said that," recounts Rossini, "my heart just sank . . . I followed the rules. And look what happens when you follow the rules. And from then on, I didn't give a shit about the rules anymore."

One night at Elaine's Bar in Manhattan, the place where his friend John O'Neill spent his last night, Rossini was nursing his troubles when his own undoing began innocently, as he was introduced to an up-and-coming Hollywood actress. The two became an item.

In January 2007, almost seven years to the day after his heated argument over the passage of Doug Miller's cable, Rossini began conducting what the Justice Department would later calculate to be forty illegal searches of the FBI's ACS computer system. He downloaded and printed a number of reports, which he turned over to his new girlfriend. She had asked for his help on behalf of her friend, a "private detective to the stars" who was on trial in Los Angeles. Rossini claims that those forty searches were actually only a handful, but that each term used in a search was counted individually to inflate the charges against him, such as multiple spelling attempts of the same name. Regardless, the documents he sought ended up in the hands of his acquaintance's defense team. This was noticed, and followed by a government search for the source.

Rossini received a letter from the inspector general at the Justice Department, calling him into the FBI New York office. There, he was informed he was being investigated for his ACS searches. Rossini admitted nothing and called his attorney. He was told they would be continuing their investigation. He was not terribly worried at the moment.[82]

Months later, emboldened by years of guilt, Mark Rossini and his friend Doug Miller decided they wished to tell their story to journalist James

Bamford, known for his work on the NSA. They were denied permission by the head of FBI Public Affairs, Rossini's boss and friend John Miller.

Though for Doug Miller the denial would be final, Rossini was an old hand in playing Washington politics, and his years at the CIA had certainly taught him a trick or two. To force the FBI's hand, he turned to a journalist friend working for the *Congressional Quarterly*. The bureau's quiet decision to deny an interview hit the Internet, where it looked a lot like they were covering up. Not to be meddled with, the Justice Department then reopened their investigation into Rossini's accessing of FBI files.

Rossini asked a friend to intervene on his behalf. His friend checked and came back, explaining, "You pissed too many people off. No one can save you now."[83]

Rossini thought, "Other people would have been slapped on the wrist or demoted. But you had to get me for something. I'm not saying I didn't do wrong. But give me a break. Seventeen years of service, an incredible record, commendations, letters recommending my work, sources around the globe developed over my career that would be useful to counterterror, [including] terrorists, criminals, politicians, sources in the Muslim community in New York that no one else had in the FBI—and you kick me out the door?"

Rossini resigned in November 2008, walking out of the FBI's New York office a civilian. He felt a great weight as he made his way to his car, which he discovered was leaking coolant. A bad omen, he thought. His life was forever going to be fundamentally different, but on the upside, he realized, he was no longer beholden to the Bureau. He could travel as he wished, live as he wished, and he could even unburden his soul by sitting down for an interview with Bamford, which he did the very next day.

Three months later, Mark Rossini watched his appearance in Bamford's *NOVA* special on PBS with a group of buddies at a friend's apartment in New York. For the first time, the public learned in some detail how the blocking of Doug Miller's warning to John O'Neill had taken place. Viewers watched as Rossini recounted his argument with Michael Anne Casey, now nine years in the past.[84]

He began receiving calls from his many friends, who told him what he had done had taken real courage. Some questioned if there was a connection between the words he had stated on TV and the legal trouble he was presently in. "Don't ask me," he responded.

Bamford's *NOVA*, which was viewed by millions and later won an Emmy Award, added still further detail to previous accounts of the withholding of Doug Miller's 2000 warning to the FBI. By 2009, however, the public had moved on. The CIA had managed to contain the revelations for long enough, with the details bubbling out in multiyear gaps. The impact was minimal.

Still, for those watching TV, it was the first time they could look someone in the eyes—Mark Rossini—and consider the truthfulness as he explained his own first-person account. Had this very same story come out in late 2001, as citizens were still sifting through the rubble of the World Trade Center, the public might have tarred and feathered the CIA employee in question. At minimum, the pressure would have been there for a congressional investigation into this matter, if not a case opened by the Justice Department.

That May, Rossini pleaded guilty to five misdemeanor counts that had been brought against him for illegally accessing FBI records. He laments, "There were a lot of things I could have brought up that were explosive. I didn't have the fight in me anymore. I was defeated."[85]

Rossini was sentenced to a year's probation and a $5,000 fine, leaving him feeling, as he later told the judge, "so profoundly and deeply ashamed and remorseful." He eventually would take a new job as a management consultant, spending most of his time in Europe. "I still try to help my country however I can," he says. He has worked over the past two years to see a book published of his experiences. Even with a famous coauthor, he is mystified that "no one wants to touch it."

"The question of why Doug Miller's cable didn't go remains key," he says all these years later. "I'm appalled at the lack of ability [by the CIA] to answer something so simple. All the rest of this is superfluous. It all means a hill of shit until you get to the reason why that one person sent a message back to Doug saying, 'Please hold off.' You spent seven committees going after Benghazi, and you don't go after this? They're not stupid people. There's something there. There's something there that is being hidden."

He concludes, "If they had a rogue operation to recruit somebody, or they had the delusion they could work with Saudi intel in America, tell us. You're talking about 9/11, man. You're talking about something that changed the world. It's like why they can't let JP Morgan go down [during the financial crisis]. Too big to fail. That's what they fear coming out, because it would be the end of the CIA. They would be dismantled, if that were to come out."

# 10

# IDENTIFICATION

*"The truth! But it is just the truth that cannot be known of the multitude,*
*for truth is revolutionary."*

Charlotte Despard, 1912

On September 8, 2011, a representative of the Central Intelligence Agency sent a message to our joint work email account.[1] We had prepared a podcast that was an investigation into pre–9/11 failures at CIA's Alec Station. Our basic thesis was that the office was the Al Qaeda unit at the CIA, and since Al Qaeda had successfully attacked the United States, there should have been some level of accountability brought to the members of that CIA office. There had been none, as far as we could tell, for approaching ten years, and most of Alec's staff and their actions were still being obstructed from public view by a protective government.

We did not expect the CIA to be thrilled that we wanted to tell their story, revealing names of employees in the process, but we certainly did not expect to be threatened. Their email read:

> First and most importantly, we strongly believe it is irresponsible and a potential violation of federal criminal law to print the names of two reported undercover CIA officers whom you claim have been involved in the hunt against al Qa'ida.

We responded:[2]

> Can you please make me aware what federal criminal law the CIA believes we ourselves—the journalists—would be violating by releasing these two names?

The answer came back:[3]

The Intelligence Identities Protection Act.

*   *   *

We, the authors, were twenty years old on the day of 9/11, an age that tends to define. After the major investigations had completed without leading to accountability, we found our way to New York City and Washington, DC, in 2004. Having graduated from film school in Chicago the previous year, we set out to make our first movie on a shoestring budget of a few thousand dollars.

People who lost loved ones in the attacks welcomed us into their homes, sharing their stories and their pain. We were touched as we attended the third anniversary ceremonies in the footprint of the old World Trade Towers, having been entrusted with a "death code" by a victim's family member. Our intent was to produce a documentary that would explore why so many deeply disturbing truths seemed too often buried in the reporting of the major news media, if printed at all.

With too little money to take cabs, we carried all of our gear on our backs and took subways, buses, and trains when not walking long distances across Manhattan and the boroughs and suburbs. We hoofed to the *Columbia Journalism Review*. A retired Walter Cronkite made our week when he told us "that was a pretty good interview," something we realized in retrospect he no doubt told every young journalist. In DC, we walked into the offices of the *Washington Post*, the shrine of Woodward and Bernstein, to interview executive editor Len Downie.

The concern we heard again and again from the news community was that the government had grown exponentially more secretive under Bush and Cheney, and it was making it more difficult to do their jobs. More documents were being classified out of public hands. In their absence, news outlets were being forced to rely on the truthfulness of officials. The default policy prior had been for government employees to speak with journalists if there was no compelling reason not to, but now that was being inverted. This was layered on top of budget constraints and an editorial attitude that insisted journalists restrain their investigative "passion projects" until after hours.

Meanwhile, the New York press was also in the midst of a gut check over their reporting in the lead-up to the Iraq invasion. They were acknowledging that cozy relationships with inside sources and narrative biases coming from the top down of news outlets were not resulting in the kind of feet-to-the-fire reporting that could unearth corruption or incompetence *before* it did its damage.

After a friend brought us into contact with the so-called "Jersey Widows," we found that their story of lobbying for the Kean Commission was the perfect backbone for our documentary. The final result, *Press For Truth*, was released in a limited theatrical run in select cities across the United States in 2006. We had never wanted to be "9/11 guys." We saw a story that needed to be told that had been ignored, so we told it, through the voices of six widows and the parents of victims. We were turning to other projects and passions when one of those widows released a memoir.

Kristen Breitweiser's book *Wake Up Call*[4] left us asking one more question: What exactly was the deal with the CIA's pre–9/11 performance? There had been similar questions about many other agencies, but the story that had been slowly emerging about the top spy group seemed unexplainable by anything other than some kind of scandal. We were not huge fans of either George W. Bush or Bill Clinton, so we eager to know how high up that scandal had gone. We would set about planning just one more "war on terror"–related project that would get to the bottom of everything, we told ourselves.

By the end of 2008, we had begun conducting interviews. With no eager financiers to back our planned film, we eventually decided the best way to make our content public was to use the audio from the interviews and tie it together inside a kind of true-crime narrative. Since *Serial*, these types of programs have been all the rage, but when John Cook at *Gawker* reported on it back then, he had to put quotes around "investigative podcast."[5]

Ringing up and asking our questions directly to people involved, most of them now retired from government employment, we were immediately struck by how willing many were to discuss matters they believed had received too little sunlight from the "important press." A lesson from film school documentary classes rang too true. People *want* to tell their stories; you just have to let them.

Most of our interviewees expressed strong concern over the policy changes of the recent years and the direction the country seemed headed in, just as we were. Rather than make us feel silly for asking the questions, as we had expected, they left us believing the track we were on was correct, and that we actually had no idea how bad it all was.

Another revelation for us was the realization that many players in this story, despite having been on the inside, were aware only of their small piece of the total picture. Veteran agents and officers would seem skeptical when the documentary crew that showed up at their home or office turned out to be two guys in their mid-twenties. We laughed later when, by the end of the conversation, these same bureaucrats were asking us what we thought had happened. We were not yet ready to provide an answer.

* * *

We have often been asked how we got our interview with Richard Clarke. The truth is simple: we contacted him and told him what we wanted to talk about. Like Mark Rossini, Clarke seemingly agreed that we were cutting to the heart of the national matter by investigating why it was that Alec Station staff not only refused to pass information about Mihdhar and Hazmi to the FBI and himself, but also why they then went on to run several games with FBI investigators, giving them limited briefings and coyly trying to determine exactly what the bureau knew.

In our interview with him, Clarke was careful to explain how inexplicable it was that he was never informed about Al Qaeda operatives traveling to the United States. "You have to understand, the way CIA updates us at the White House," explains Clarke. "Every morning I come in, I turn on my computer, and I get a hundred, a hundred fifty CIA reports. I'm not relying on somebody calling me and telling me things. I get a flood of CIA reports." According to Clarke, for the CIA cables about Mihdhar and Hazmi to not have come across his computer screen, someone would have had to "intervene." Someone would have had to intentionally pulled him out of the loop.

Clarke explained that the reason, he believes, that he was prevented from knowing about Mihdhar and Hazmi traveling to the United States was because the CIA was running an operation to attempt to flip these men, in an effort to get sources within the terrorist organization. This operation, if it occurred, would have been illegal, as the CIA is not to operate domestically. Again, Clarke admits that this is "conjecture and hypothesis." Years after the Graham-Goss inquiry and the Kean Commission, as the facts in this case became public in small pieces, more and more counterterror agents have come to believe that this theory is accurate.

\* \* \*

A few months after interviewing Richard Clarke, we called up Mark Rossini for the first time. He responded to our mention of the Mihdhar/Hazmi topic by exclaiming, "That's *the* 9/11 story. That's the story that hasn't been told."

Among FBI counterterror agents from the time, opinions on the theory that the CIA was trying to "flip" Mihdhar and Hazmi seemed to differ slightly, we noticed, depending on whether the individual in question had worked out of John O'Neill's New York office or out of DC.

Dale Watson, John O'Neill's boss at FBI headquarters, said to us, "If you're trying to say that Cofer and Tenet got together to keep us out of it, I don't necessarily agree with that. Ya know, I know Cofer. I know Tenet. I know those guys very well, and, if that occurred, that had to be down lower in the organization than those guys. And for somebody to say that there was a conscious effort by those folks to do that, I just don't believe that. I think if there was some conscious effort, it was probably at the GS-14 level, as we call it in the Bureau, or the GS-13 level, not to tell people what was going on."[6] Watson was suggesting that any conscious decision not to share information with the FBI would have been made at the level of people like Alfreda Bikowsky, Jen Matthews, or perhaps Michael Anne Casey.

Mike Rolince, the number two counterterror man at the FBI and Tom Wilshere's boss when he was detailed to the Bureau, chose not to interview with us after over a year of occasional back and forth emails, voice mails, and brief conversations. In response to what Clarke had told us, he wrote us, "I know many buy into the 'conspiracy.' Based on where I was, who I knew, and what I knew, both then and now, I choose not to. I'm not saying I'm right and I'm not saying they are wrong. We may never know. I'll leave it at that."[7] We found this vague, and unsatisfying.

Less vague was Pat D'Amuro, who revealed to us, "I had heard that Blee and Wilshere had the conversation in January 2000 and stopped it from coming over." He did not stop there. "There's no doubt in my mind that that went up further in the agency than just those two guys. And why they didn't send it over. To this day, I don't know why."

"What was so sensitive about Mihdhar, Hazmi, and the meeting?" asks Jack Cloonan. "It's just never been explained adequately to me why we don't have answers. For whatever reason or reasons, the agency makes the decision—it's not an oversight, it's a conscious decision—not to share the information. If you look at this, it's really just a handful of people. I don't know how they sleep at night, I really don't."

Over the course of years of conversations, we watched Mark Rossini's beliefs evolve, especially after he learned of Richard Clarke's statements to us. Finally, he sent us an email explaining, "I believe it can be proven circumstantially the CIA was engaged in a recruitment operation within the United States (in direct violation of every rule, regulation, and law), and that they (the management of the CIA, Alec Station, and the CTC) did not want the FBI, in the persona of John P. O'Neill Jr., to interfere in their effort."

Larry Wilkerson made no bones about telling us what he thought on the issue when we asked. He claims that in early 2003, just before the invasion of Iraq, a bunch of "the boys" were hanging out in the basement of CIA headquarters, down the hall from the CTC and Alec Station, gossiping while they waited for the latest satellite photos of Iraq to update. During this time period, Wilkerson says he spent a week essentially living at CIA headquarters, working around the clock with George Tenet's executive employees.

"We didn't sleep for five days and five nights . . . I mean, I slept on the DCI's couch a couple of times for an hour or so," he says. To pass the time, these high-level national employees engaged in off-the-cuff conversation. "During the interludes sometimes," Wilkerson explained, "we had these yack-yack sessions, and the guys would tell me all sorts of shit. They're telling me different things that happened with regard to 9/11. And I'm hearing this shit about Tenet trying to 'turn' somebody and getting caught, and not wanting to share the information with FBI because he was afraid of really being caught badly and maybe losing his job."

Wilkerson now claims he learned from no less than three different executive-level CIA officers variations on the same story, that a domestic operation regarding Khalid al Mihdhar did take place. "People who were in a position to be in the room and hear it directly or to be outside the room and hear [Bush's CIA briefer] Mike Morrell or somebody else tell them. These are very, very reliable people." We asked if these people were higher up than the head of the CTC. He replied, "Oh yes, higher than Cofer. Serious people."

Wilkerson expounds, "The people that the CIA were trying to turn—one of them was inside the United States, which is against the law. And that's the reason they didn't reveal that that person was here to the FBI, because then the FBI being bureaucratically competitive and stupid would have said, 'God damn we're coming after you, you're breakin' the law again.'"

"The CIA was trying desperately to 'turn' them, and they shouldn't have been operating domestically," says Wilkerson. "I got many things I blame George [Tenet] for, including that he lied to me and he lied to [my boss] the secretary [of state]—*lied*, not fudged things, *lied*. But I do understand his motivation here. The only way he was ever going to get real evidence on Al Qaeda was to turn somebody and get inside."

In a Maryland suburb of DC in the fall of 2016, we sat down for a long interview with Tom Drake. Confirming the veracity of Wilkerson's story and Clarke's charge, Drake said that he had been told directly from senior sources in the intelligence community that the attempt had taken place to turn members of Al Qaeda. He specified his sources were close to a network that had developed around Vice President Dick Cheney, long-standing intelligence professionals.

"I had someone who spoke to me—and I believe it was a moment of conscience," recounted Drake. "There were several people, but there was this one particular person who was directly involved. This person told me they tried to 'flip' someone in Malaysia, an Iraqi. And then Hazmi and Mihdhar in San Diego."

After reflecting for a moment, Drake added, "I understand the fullness of this coming out. It's like 'Oh my God, we would actually risk the security of the United States just to attempt to flip somebody?'" He searched for how he wanted to explain it, continuing, "Remember, there was this obsession for years—again, I have someone very familiar with this who I can't talk about, a very senior official, very peer level. He told me [at the time], 'We've gotta get someone inside of Al Qaeda.' They knew this plot against the West was coming. They were desperate."

Drake says the operation had been set up in January 2000, when Mihdhar and Hazmi flew into the country. According to his sources, the CIA counterterror staff was fully aware of their terrorist links and their identities. It was then, he claims, that George Tenet green-lit an illegal, off-the-books operation to try and turn them while they were in the United States.

The operation ran for some time, through both the Clinton and Bush presidencies, and right up to 9/11 itself.

* * *

Perhaps it is easy to level accusations after the fact, but what specifically would such an operation even look like?

When Khalid al Mihdhar landed at the Kuala Lumpur airport on January 5, 2000, after leaving the Hada house in Yemen where he had been surveilled in his conversations by both the NSA and the CIA, he was picked up by an Iraqi named Ahmed Shakir. The conservative *Weekly Standard* reported on the story,[8] in an apparent effort to tie the attacks to the Iraqi government as justification for Bush's invasion:

> In August 1999, Shakir began working as a VIP greeter for Malaysian Airlines. He told associates he had gotten the job through a contact at the Iraqi embassy. In fact, Shakir's embassy contact controlled his schedule—told him when to report to work and when to take a day off. The contact apparently told Shakir to report to work on January 5, 2000, the same day September 11 hijacker Khalid al Mihdhar arrived in Kuala Lumpur. Shakir escorted al Mihdhar to a waiting car and then, rather than bid his guest farewell, jumped in the car with him. The meeting lasted from January 5 to January 8. Shakir reported to work twice after the meeting broke up and then disappeared.

Shakir drove Mihdhar to a posh suburb where, overlooking a golf course, he met with other Al Qaeda operatives in a condominium owned by a man friendly to the terror group, Yazid Sufat. Rossini says that he was aware at the time of a recruitment effort to flip Shakir, though he is vague on details. He had always believed Shakir, not Mihdhar or Hazmi, was chosen to be the entry point to Al Qaeda. In early 2010, journalist Aram Roston reported on information he learned from intelligence sources regarding the topic.[9]

"Intelligence officials tell *The Observer*," Roston reported, "that the character at the center of the intrigue was an enigmatic but jovial man named Ahmad Hikmat Shakir, or 'Shakir el Iraqi.' 'He was tall as a mushroom, fat and gay,' one source familiar with the case told *The Observer*, 'and the idea was to exploit him as an agent against Al Qaeda. . . .' And as the terror summit went on, the CIA became convinced that it had found the perfect mole to help the agency crack the jihadi circle."

Another source described Shakir to *The Observer* "as a potential 'access agent,' espionage jargon for an informant whose function is to spot other potential spies and turncoats." Roston wrote, "Though he may not know secrets or terrorist plots himself, the access agent is likely to know people who do, and is expected to facilitate meetings. As this officer explained, the agency 'looked to him as a social broker.' Mr. Shakir was no James Bond. In fact, he was short and fat and sociable, and was surmised to be gay, which would have opened him up to being flipped."

"Unfortunately," the report continued, "the CIA's ambitions to employ Mr. Shakir as its terror mole didn't pan out. Agents reached out to him and one day even reportedly rifled through his house for anything that they thought might be of use; Mr. Shakir rebuffed them . . . Shortly after the Malaysian summit disbanded, he fled the country, which further raised the CIA's suspicions about him."

Mark Rossini has come to believe that when that recruitment effort failed, simultaneous to the discovery that Mihdhar held a US visa, a new plan was hatched. He wrote to us, "That effort failed, so the CIA had to turn their focus on another member of the group who had, or would come to, the USA. By all indications, it seems that Khalid al Mihdhar was targeted for one very simple reason, [because he was coming here]."

As the summit in Malaysia was ongoing, regular updates on surveillance efforts were being passed up to the White House. When the meeting disbanded and the reports stopped coming, why did Richard Clarke not ask what happened to the men involved? He says, "I assumed these guys got on planes and went back to Saudi Arabia or Yemen."

At meeting's end, Mihdhar and Hazmi, along with Khallad bin Attash, were again driven to the Kuala Lumpur airport, where they boarded a flight to Bangkok, Thailand. This is where the official CIA story claims that they lost the men. Even if true, it leaves a bigger question. Why does everything that emerged from the record to date suggest that they were only interested in following those three individuals, out of perhaps up to a dozen terrorists who met at the condominium complex? "How do you know they didn't follow them?" retorts Jack Cloonan, suggesting the agency may still not have come clean about their activities all those years ago. "I mean, the stated line would be, 'Ya know, we didn't.' I just don't buy it."

"I don't think we can say what they *didn't do*," says Richard Clarke, affirming Cloonan's point. In fact, Cloonan told us his private sources specifically informed him that others besides just Mihdhar, Hazmi, and Attash were monitored following the meeting. "And then when the meeting splits up, the groups go in two different directions. And I know there was surveillance put on the groups when they leave. I heard that they followed two groups. I thought one group went to Bangkok and I thought another group went some other place, that they followed them. That's what I was told."

Tom Drake says the NSA knew where Mihdhar and Hazmi were staying in Thailand. He adds he saw no indication they told the CIA. "[They were] just going to keep monitoring. As long as nothing has happened, we'll just keep monitoring them for more info." Drake made a point of stating, however, that "cutouts" could have been used for plausible deniability. "There's [sic] other ways to inform the CIA without a piece of paper. Just because there are no documents doesn't mean it didn't happen or that certain people weren't told." Drake refused to provide further clarity on this point.

If there was an operation, it would have moved into motion here. "What they normally would do," says Clarke, "they contact the Thai service and ask the Thai government to keep an eye on them. And the Thai government does. And the Thai government belatedly informs them [in March 2000 that] they have come to the United States."

"They may very well have come to the conclusion that, rather than have the CIA station in Los Angeles show up with some blonde-haired guy with blue eyes trying to flip them," Clarke surmised, "it would be better to use a Saudi intelligence agent. These guys were Saudis after all. We do know that [Mihdhar and Hazmi] show up in Southern California, and pretty soon thereafter they are approached by a Saudi [Omar al Bayoumi]. And that Saudi has connections to the Saudi government. And some people believe that Saudi was an intelligence agent."

* * *

Arriving in Los Angeles on January 15, 2000, neither Khalid al Mihdhar nor Nawaf al Hazmi spoke English very well. Without a family or a place of residence, one would assume that they were going to struggle to assemble any stability, especially in such a high-cost location as Southern California.

What luck for these wayward travelers that on February 1, as they were having lunch in a Middle Eastern restaurant in Los Angeles, Omar al Bayoumi would enter and strike up a conversation with them. Bayoumi was two hours from his home in San Diego, and he had just wrapped up a one-hour meeting with a Saudi consulate official named Fahad al Thumairy. Out of the kindness of his heart, as he told investigators later, Bayoumi suggested to Mihdhar and Hazmi that they move to San Diego and he would help them get established. Three days later, they were living in Bayoumi's apartment complex, after Bayoumi cosigned their lease and gave them $1,500 for their first two months of rent. Bayoumi seemed quite a generous guy.[10]

Of course, that is Bayoumi's account of the events. Senator Bob Graham would later assess, "That a suspected Saudi spy would drive 125 miles to a meeting with a consular officer with suspected terrorist ties, and then drive another seven miles to the one Middle Eastern restaurant—out of more than 134 Middle Eastern restaurants in Los Angeles—where he would happen to sit next to two future terrorists, to whom he would happen to offer friendship and support, cannot credibly be described as a coincidence."[11] In fact, the timeline is dubious as Mihdhar and Hazmi arrived in Los Angeles two weeks prior to this supposed surreptitious meeting, and early FBI reports on their residency have them living in Bayoumi's apartment complex since the day they arrived in country. Apparently, they claimed this themselves on their rental applications.[12]

For his part, Bayoumi had been living in San Diego for half a decade by the time Mihdhar and Hazmi arrived. It was suspected by many in the Saudi community there that Bayoumi was actually a Saudi spy. He did not have a job to speak of, and told different stories as to how he made money, including that he worked for Dallah Avco, the Saudi aviation firm that D'Amuro's team discovered had connections to the Saudi Ministry of Defense and Aviation.[13] Even Nawaf al Hazmi supposedly began to suspect that Bayoumi was a Saudi spy. He had apparently confessed this unknowingly to Abdussattar Shaikh, the FBI informant he had accidentally moved in with after moving out of Bayoumi's apartment complex. That same FBI asset, charged with feeding information about the San Diego Muslim community to the Bureau, had claimed after the attacks that he simply had not realized his two tenants were al Qaeda members and never reported about them to FBI supervisors in southern California.[14]

Bayoumi's wife was given money by a woman named Majeda Dweikat, who was married to a man named Osama Basnan. Basnan was good friends with Omar al Bayoumi. The source of the money given to Bayoumi's wife was none other than Princess Haifa bint Faisal, the wife of the Saudi ambassador to the United States, Prince Bandar.

"There was a lot of smoke coming out of Saudi Arabia, and everyone assumed there was fire," says John Kiriakou. "No one was ever really able to prove anything." He took notice when the address book recovered from Abu Zubaydah's possessions in Pakistan included two princes. "They both later died very mysteriously," he points out. "One in a single-car accident in the desert, and the other of thirst in the desert. He was an accomplished camper, and he died of thirst."

Kiriakou says he never saw any evidence that funding of Al Qaeda was provided as official Saudi government policy. He adds, "But you know the Saudi royal family has around twenty thousand members, and certainly there were some who were very close to Al Qaeda and wanted to fund it."

"Just listening to the conversations day after day after day," says Larry Wilkerson, "listening to [Colin Powell] come back from National Security Council meetings, and in fact sitting down to the table with Bandar myself . . . my distinct impression was that the Saudis knew quite a bit that they didn't share with us." Wilkerson goes on, "It was also my distinct impression that Bandar knew a whole lot more than he was letting on about Bin Laden's activities and about those people, within particularly the royal family, but also elsewhere within the 'Saudi complex,' that probably were sympathetic to, and probably giving money to, Bin Laden and Al Qaeda. Bandar is in my mind the guy who could tell all regarding all of this."

The CIA wanted sources inside Al Qaeda. At first they reportedly tried to turn a man on the periphery, the jolly Iraqi, Ahmed Shakir. When he apparently turned them down, they saw that Mihdhar was coming to the United States and decided to see if they could make a play for him and his associate Hazmi. Recognizing the need to approach them with someone with which they could identify, possibly, they used Saudi intelligence agents like Omar al Bayoumi and others. That was the idea in a nutshell.

For this theory to make sense, the NSA must have, at some level, been allowed into the operation. They were known to be monitoring the Yemen hub, after all, and would certainly begin picking up calls from Mihdhar in the United States to his wife in Yemen that would raise obvious questions. The Chop Chain had to be made aware so they would not inadvertently alert John O'Neill. Analysts at the NSA like "Bob" would have to remain perplexed as to why relevant law enforcement was not informed. Could this explain why it appears no FISA warrant was sought, despite so many "pings" alerting analysts like "Becky" working counterterror at the NSA over 2000 and 2001?

If the NSA had to be made aware of this operation, why was the White House kept in the dark? Larry Wilkerson, former deputy to Secretary of State Colin Powell, speculates, "What Clinton did with things like that was basically, 'Do it. Don't tell me.'"

Presumably, the understanding between George Tenet and Bill Clinton would have been that Clinton wanted plausible deniability, and thus an operation like this would be run "off the books," utilizing proxies. Richard Clarke could not know because he would be obligated to tell the president. He also was friends with John O'Neill, who it may have been assumed would "flip out" if such an operation were underway within US borders, and would possibly have moved to arrest the Al Qaeda operatives and Saudi spies before all pertinent information had been gleaned.

It may rightly be asked, then: what happened when Bush became president in 2001? Insofar as the record seems to state, Tenet and certain CIA staffers, and likely NSA executives, who may have been aware of this ongoing operation, never briefed the new president or his cabinet. If they never told Clinton, because they knew he did not want to know, how could they justify not telling Bush?

From what he saw, Wilkerson believes the situation that Richard Clarke described—that Tenet and the CIA never told him about Mihdhar and Hazmi until after 9/11—extended to the rest of the White House, presumably both under Clinton in 2000 and then Bush in 2001. "I think so," he asserts. "You kept that [kind of thing] as 'close hold' as you possibly could. I don't doubt that a bit."

* * *

On June 24, 2004, Tom Pickard, acting FBI director during the summer before 9/11, wrote a letter to the Kean Commission. That letter was intended for commissioner eyes only. Years later, as documents began to be released by the National Archives, Pickard's letter became public.[15]

Writing about what he did or did not brief Bush's attorney general John Ashcroft about in the summer of 2001—and why—he volunteered a strange line of text that seemed to come out of nowhere. Pickard wrote, "I had not told [Ashcroft] about the meeting in Malaysia since I was told by FBI assistant director Dale Watson that there was a 'close hold' on that info. This means that it was not to be shared with anyone without the explicit approval of the CIA. I then strongly suggested that [the attorney general] meet with George Tenet to get a full briefing on the matter."

When Dale Watson agreed to interview with us in 2011, we had high hopes that we might finally learn what he had told Pickard about the CIA's "close hold."

"Close hold what? What did he say?" asked Watson.

"He said a 'close hold,' and he put it in quotes, like it's an official term or something. Close. Hold."

"Right, I understand what that is."

"Well what is a 'close hold'?" we asked.

"It's just a term you use for 'not to disseminate.' It's not a classification, but you know, 'This is a close hold.' Information means 'Don't talk about it to anybody.'"

We inquired further, "So what did you tell Pickard about a 'close hold'?"

"Ya know, I do not know the answer to that," he demurred. "If Pickard says that, I don't know where he got that from. I'm not going to dispute and say, 'That's not true.' I don't recall it."

A non-denial denial? Either Watson was passing the buck, or Pickard told the Kean Commission something that was not true about the Malaysia meeting. Only Pickard was now in a position to clarify, but he ignored our 2011 message requesting an interview. He did the same again in 2016.

Mark Rossini wrote with his opinion on the matter in 2015. "What was Dale [Watson] actually told and by whom, and from whom did that person learn it from? I am sure you will find," he speculated, "that George Tenet told FBI director Louis Freeh at some point in 2000 or 2001 that the agency was developing something regarding a terrorist cell which had a meeting in [Kuala Lumpur], and that 'we (the agency) will keep you apprised.' Ergo, whatever Tenet told Freeh, who told Dale, who told Pickard, is [do not pass] CIA information that the FBI was expected to have acted upon. Moreover," he continued, "it is logical to conclude that whatever Tenet told Freeh, it did not contain any information about terrorists in [Kuala Lumpur] having US visas, since if it did the FBI would have acted upon it."

In other words, FBI leadership may have known something was being "held closely" by the CIA without knowing precisely what, and without letting this knowledge filter down to agents in the FBI who might have done something about it. Agents like Ali Soufan, who three times requested information from the CIA about a meeting of terrorists in Malaysia, knew a meeting took place. They could have answered his question directly, but didn't.

\* \* \*

If the CIA was running an operation to try to flip Khalid al Mihdhar and/or Nawaf al Hazmi, the obvious question becomes why Al Qaeda's 9/11 plot succeeded. One would assume that either the CIA's operation was successful in some regard, and thus they should have had the relevant intelligence in order to prevent the attacks, or that the operation was not successful, and at some point CIA operators should have recognized this and pulled the emergency brake, as it were. What do we see happening amid this cluster of activity in August 2001? If a CIA operation existed, do we see evidence of one whose operators were under the impression that it was succeeding as planned, or an operation that was having its plug pulled? And what does the highly suggestive timing of the resignation late that month of Saudi Arabia's long-time spy chief tell us? Prince Turki Al Faisal, after all, had left his position suddenly after twenty-two years, only weeks before the attacks. Was this a coincidence? They do happen. Or was something more going on behind the scenes?

If George Tenet believed his highly secretive operation to flip Mihdhar or Hazmi was not successful, and as a search had begun in the United States to find the men, could he not have claimed he was made aware of their presence at the same time as the rest of Alec Station? Could he not have warned Richard Clarke on September 4, at the Principals Meeting, and at least given the impression that Maggie Gillespie's discovery of Mihdhar and Hazmi was what had brought them to his attention? Seemingly, he had an out.

Was Tenet under the impression that his daring operation to get sources inside Al Qaeda was working? Does his silence on the matter up to and beyond 9/11 suggest that perhaps he had been double-crossed by his Saudi partners but did not know until it was too late? What are we to make of the fact that the CIA finally made the FBI aware of the presence of Mihdhar and Hazmi in the United States in late August but did not mention them to Richard Clarke's counterterror team?

Further, how does the theory of an ongoing surveillance operation square with the fact that Mihdhar, Hazmi, and seventeen other Al Qaeda operatives all had purchased tickets to fly the same morning? One would hope that, if the CIA were to undertake such a risky operation, they would be monitoring it with the utmost attention and care, lest it go horribly awry.

* * *

Richard Clarke's allegations made a small splash in August 2011 when they became public upon our online video release of our interview with him, as well as the rebuttal letter sent to us by George Tenet. Two news articles attributed to our investigation came out in the *Daily Beast* and *Truth-out*. This was the first time we had seen our work published in well-read outlets. The story was picked up by several more news sites, including that of the *Washington Post*.[16]

The title of our forthcoming audio documentary was announced in that moment, called *Who Is Rich Blee?* We found it unreasonable that, despite his important role as chief of the Al Qaeda station in the lead up to Al Qaeda's attacks, his identity had never been released to the public. It was Kevin Fenton, a British amateur contemporary historian transplanted to the Czech Republic, who first lifted the veil. Fenton had pored over the paperwork generated by various government reports and came across the name Rich Blee in the margins. Cross-referenced against what little public information was available about the Alec Station manager, Fenton believed Blee was the one alluded to vaguely in reports.[17] We reached out to him and struck up a friendship.

At some point, one of our interviewees made us aware that one of Blee's key managers was the same woman responsible for the high-profile kidnapping of an innocent German, Khaled el Masri.[18] We took a look at a story about Masri published that year by the Associated Press headlined "CIA Officers Make Grave Mistakes, Get Promoted."[19] That article by Adam Goldman and Matt Apuzzo blamed Masri's rendition on a woman they called "Frances," clarifying, "The AP agreed to the CIA's request to refer to Frances by her middle name because her first is unusual."

Soon after, Fenton let us know that he had searched public postings of State Department nominations,[20] often cover for CIA employees working abroad, and had found a name that seemed to fit the bill: Alfreda Frances Bikowsky. Unusual first name? Check. Middle name Frances? Check.

Following his lead, we did our own search through State postings looking for one of Bikowsky's employees who had allegedly ordered an FBI agent working inside their office to withhold key intelligence.[21] This young woman, sources told us, had older family in important places inside the agency. We searched for last names that matched prominent CIA figures of recent years, including "Casey," that of Ronald Reagan's agency director.

She was referred to in government reports by the name "Michelle," but sources said she actually had a "man's name." One person we saw on the diplomatic role was Michael Anne Casey. A posting for a charity 6K in Fairfax, Virginia,[22] just down the road from CIA headquarters, placed a twenty-something Michael Anne Casey there in 1999, one or two years after our sources believed the mysterious brunette had started her employment. It would later turn out that Michael Anne was actually no relation to Reagan's CIA director.[23]

As we continued interviewing insiders, we casually used the names Rich Blee, Alfreda Bikowsky, and Michael Anne Casey while describing actions alleged to have been taken by figures fitting their descriptions in articles and reports. For all we knew, we had the wrong names entirely. The first few times we dropped those names, we did so nervously, knowing there was a good possibility that our interviewees might chastise us for our incorrect information. No one, however, corrected us. We became more confident.

It feels naive, looking back, but we felt we had a duty to allow Bikowsky and Casey, along with others like Blee and Wilshere, the opportunity to respond to the allegations contained in our forthcoming podcast, to set the record straight. Another new ally we had begun speaking with, Jason Leopold—who would go on to great success at *VICE News* and *Buzzfeed*—advised us to expect a quick response after we sent a message through the CIA's online portal. That message detailed the story we intended to release and our knowledge of the two names, Blee and Bikowsky.

Leopold was right. The response was almost immediate. Our phone rang, and at the other end of the line was an agency spokesperson, Preston Golson, who would become head of their public communications branch to the present day. A succession of phone calls and emails followed over several days, each initiated by the spokesperson. He began multiple emails to us with the words, "What follows is *off the record*,"[24] as if he were our journalistic source. During the calls, he attempted to engage in long conversations about the ethics and legality associated with naming the individuals.

We argued the press had a duty to report without censorship on matters of public interest, particularly when they included allegations of abuse, waste of tax dollars, or incompetence. Golson argued, paraphrased, that a number of reporters for major news organizations had previously felt satisfied referring to Bikowsky by middle name, alias, or pronoun. He mentioned Apuzzo, Goldman, and the *New Yorker*'s Jane Mayer.

We later spoke with Mayer. She had been talked out of using the name of a red-haired woman working in the CIA's Al Qaeda office while writing her excellent book *The Dark Side*. The agency had told her Bikowsky was at risk in an undercover assignment. When this was told to Mayer, in 2008, it may have been the only time in Bikowsky's career it was true, as according to John Kiriakou she was headed to a new position at the London office. On the weight of Mayer withholding the name, Apuzzo and Goldman had similarly been convinced to call her solely by her middle name.

During conversations with Golson, we could not shake the feeling that we were being steered into using language that might be harmful to us if the matter went to court. It was not outside the realm of possibility that the calls were being recorded. We had little understanding at the time of other possible means of acquiring our communications, the NSA program still not understood in detail by the public. At one point, a casually worded verbal threat surfaced, a statement along the lines that the agency might choose to see the publishing of our story as written as a prosecutable crime. This was cemented in writing in an email soon after, then another.

We were alarmed, and forwarded the CIA email to our allies. Author Ray Nowosielski wrote, "I have to admit I'm spooked but still willing to proceed if it's correct. Thoughts?"

Author John Duffy replied:

The CIA man says we could be violating the intelligence identities protection act. http://www.fas.org/irp/offdocs/laws/iipa.html

Haven't fine-tooth combed it, but this seems to be the relevant portion:

SEC. 601. [50 U.S.C. 421] (a) **Whoever, having or having had authorized access to classified information** that identifies a covert agent, intentionally discloses any information identifying such covert agent to any individual not authorized to receive classified information, knowing that the information disclosed so identifies such covert agent and that the United States is taking affirmative measures to conceal such covert agents intelligence relationship to the United States, shall be fined under title 18, United States Code, or imprisoned not more than ten years, or both.

(b) **Whoever, as a result of having authorized access to classified information,** learns the identity of a covert agent and intentionally discloses any information identifying such covert agent to any individual not authorized to receive classified information, knowing that the information disclosed so identifies such covert agent and that the United States is taking affirmative measures to conceal such covert agents intelligence relationship to the United States, shall be fined under title 18, United States Code, or imprisoned not more than five years, or both.

(c) **Whoever, in the course of a pattern of activities intended to identify and expose covert agents and with reason to believe that such activities would impair or impede the foreign intelligence activities of the United States,** discloses any information that identifies an individual as a covert agent to any individual not authorized to receive classified information, knowing that the information disclosed so identifies such individual and that the United States is taking affirmative measures to conceal such individuals classified intelligence relationship to the United States, shall be fined under title 18, United States Code, or imprisoned not more than three years, or both.

(d) A term of imprisonment imposed under this section shall be consecutive to any other sentence of imprisonment.

Looking at all of the bolded portions, we have never had authorized access to classified information, so it doesn't seem to apply to us. Crafty searching of public documents does not seem to apply. The only portion that may apply is under section C, as "pattern of activities" is very vague.

Also, it seems to only apply to covert agents. We are talking about analysts. Correct? People stationed in Langley are not covert, are they?

—Duff

## Kyle Hence [coproducer of *Press For Truth*] responded:

But let us not forget the context: We have pursued this story because there is good reason with bolstering evidence that these individuals may have broken the law and at the very least been grossly (again, possibly criminally) negligent.

Malfeasance: The commission of an act that is unequivocally illegal or completely wrongful. Malfeasance is a comprehensive term used in both civil and Criminal Law to describe any act that is wrongful. It is not a distinct crime or tort, but may be used generally to describe any act that is criminal or that is wrongful and gives rise to, or somehow contributes to, the injury of another person. Malfeasance is an affirmative act that is illegal or wrongful.

That Richard Clarke went so far as to suggest malfeasance and that these individuals are still within the CIA where they've been promoted puts us all in jeopardy and thus we are merely acting in defense of our country to safeguard our lives. We are not safer with such persons on the front lines after 9/11 given what they did. In other words we are telling this story and revealing their identity because the lack of accountability and their obvious incompetence or possible corruption put us on jeopardy, not their continuing to serve in their present capacities!

But I'm not a lawyer.

Kevin Fenton added his two cents:

Guys,

The IIPA problem is section (c), pattern of activities. They can't get you or me under (a) or (b). I guess [Lawrence] Wright was in the same situation in 2006 and he went for it. Thing is, he was a big fish and then it was hard to go after him. Maybe they would take you/us on now. I am on the other side of the pond, I doubt they would do a rendition from the Czech Republic.

One issue is not that one might eventually be found guilty. It is that one's ass may be hauled through pre-trial stages and then the courts, if the agency so chooses. It might be a sort of Thomas Drake situation.

Maybe you should reach out to Scooter Libby? I wonder what he would do in this situation.

Guys, it is your call. If you don't want to do it, don't. If you want to go for it, tell Bradley and Khalid that Kevin says hi when you see them.

Nowosielski picked it up:

Guys,

I've instructed our webmaster to take down the site and replace it with just this message:

"On Thursday, the CIA threatened the journalists behind Who Is Rich Blee? With a possible federal prosecution if the investigative podcast is released in its current form. We are delaying that release while we consult with others and weigh our options. A press statement with a fuller explanation will be made available at this site soon."

We'll be drafting a press release with the help of Kyle Hence to go out Monday morning. We have not made a final decision on which version of the investigative podcast we plan to release but will likely put it out Tuesday or Wednesday. Kyle had suggested that anyway, to get more traction. And the Truthout piece will be ready around then as well.

—Ray

An ally connected us with Ben Wizner, founder of the ACLU's National Security Project, soon to be a principal legal adviser to Edward Snowden. Wizner explained by phone that the IIPA was created to go after government employees who had knowledge of classified information as part of their jobs and released the names of undercover intelligence agents. By precedent, it had never been applied to journalists. *But*, Wizner continued, paraphrased, it was clear the Obama administration was working to extend precedent in that area. When they did, he warned, it would not be Bob Woodward they went after. It would probably be nobodies like us.

Running on financial fumes after weeks of unpaid work, we asked about the likelihood of free representation, updating the others by email with Wizner's response.

Nowosielski wrote:

> They assure me that they will connect us to the best lawyers if we go ahead with this (though not for free) and that we will be supported by a groundswell of civil liberties people, much like WikiLeaks. When I pressed about whether anyone would do pro bono, the guy suggested that a lot of state-appointed defense lawyers are really good. So that doesn't make me feel much better. . . ..

—Ray

Wizner already knew Bikowsky's name. He imparted to us that she had become an "open secret" in Washington among human rights advocates, national security attorneys, reporters, and others. Some of these sources began reaching out to us. We learned then that she was responsible for more than "just" the 9/11 failure and the mistaken rendition of Masri. We were told she was in charge of the drone assassinations program and had more or less been the number two running the War on Terror for the CIA.

It was information from another government source that brought into sharp focus for us the hornet's nest we were presently kicking. Alfreda Bikowsky had been the person most credited internally at the Obama White House with the successful assassination of Usama Bin Laden only months prior. The greatest PR coup of Barack Obama's presidency belonged to her. Her agency would probably prefer her old skeletons not be unearthed.

The CIA's media rep called us several more times in a period of days to ask if we had made a decision. Each conversation added a sense of pressure as we tried to decide the right course of action. "Ray," Golson insisted, "you said in your first email that we should take appropriate steps to ensure their safety. You know you would be endangering them by releasing their names."

"Don't put words in my mouth, Preston," was our attempt to keep from getting pushed into affirmation by failure to deny. "I don't know that. I have been told these two have spent the bulk of their careers working safely from Langley headquarters. Based on everything they have been accused of, I have a real fear that you all are leaving Americans in danger by keeping these people in their positions."

The back and forth ended suddenly on September 10, 2011, when we replied to the latest email, which had again begun with the words, "All of the following is off the record." We decided to correct this notion:[25]

Preston,

We do not acknowledge "off the record" in our dealings with the CIA on an official level, particularly when you are threatening journalists with criminal prosecution. All messages you send are on the record.

In precedent the law you cited, the Intelligence Identities Protection Act, has never convicted a journalist. It is used for government workers who have clearance to access classified information, who access the names of covert agents via that clearance, and then go on to divulge those names to people without that clearance. We believe that attempting to prosecute journalists based on its language would be a perversion of the law and violation of the first amendment. It would also have a dangerous frightening effect on working journalists, which would seem to be the intention of attempting to expand that precedent.

As our entire story surrounds the documented repeated bungling perhaps worse of these agents before and after 9/11, we can only believe that revealing their identities would IMPROVE the United States' foreign intelligence efforts, as retaining and promoting employees with a list of documented failures, to the logical mind, could only have an overall negative effect on the work of the CIA and the safety of the American people whom they are employed to protect.

We need you to tell us, officially, whether the two agents whose names we have mentioned, are currently covert. You should know that we plan to delay the release of our audio documentary and written story until we have sorted out a proper, ethical decision on this matter, and we intend to inform our audience of the reason for the delay.

We never received a reply, nor the promised "on the record statement lodging [CIA's] complete disagreement with [our] account." We were left in the silence to make our decision.

\* \* \*

As we saw it, we were being put in an unfair position by even being made to consider whether reporting the truth was the right thing to do. We had created a website to promote our belief that an atmosphere of extreme secrecy had taken hold in Washington. We knew the names we intended to release had been gleaned from open-source materials. We had done nothing wrong, in our minds, while the two individuals in question had been accused of wrongs that had led to thousands of deaths. How could we live with ourselves if we caved?

After twelve days of consideration, the plan we came up with was simple. We would censor the names in our audio documentary, replacing each mention of Bikowsky and Casey with a robo-voice calling them "Frances" and "Michelle," so audiences would know precisely where information was being withheld. We would release the documentary immediately so the public could understand the issues at stake. Then, we would announce a campaign to pressure the US government to themselves reveal the two employees. We thought we could use the CIA's threats against us to generate more attention for our podcast, and ultimately the issues it exposed.

Fate, apparently, had other intentions. Fate, or dumb luck.

On the morning of September 21, 2011, we emailed our webmaster with final instructions for the "go-live" of *Who Is Rich Blee?* In addition to the censored podcast, we asked him to place the correspondences with CIA, including George Tenet's people, on a section of the website. Our webmaster had been aware of the issue regarding naming Bikowsky and Casey and our ultimate decision to hold off on releasing them, but in the midst of prepping multiple documents for the site, one letter he posted remained unredacted.[26]

Ironically, this was the original email we had sent to the CIA asking them to provide an official response. We should note here our belief that the job

THE WATCHDOGS DIDN'T BARK

of keeping the CIA's secrets should not be a communal effort, should not be the responsibility of every citizen. Since when did we all go to work for them? It is the other way around, correct? The job of guarding their info belongs to the managers of the CIA, not a freelance webmaster, nor even reporters.

We were not immediately aware of what had happened. Our work on the piece was finished and released, and we spent the day at our jobs. That afternoon Sibel Edmonds, a former FBI translator running a muckraking blog called *BoilingFrogsPost*, emailed us that she had obtained the name Alfreda Bikowsky, and she also had "four outside confirmations; including current CIA folks." She informed us that she was going to publish the breaking news within the next hour. She concluded with a line that caused us to raise an eyebrow, writing, "I just visited your site: Thank you for all you do, all you have been doing. You are heroes; at least mine:-)"

Stepping away to do a Google search for the name "Alfreda Bikowsky," we discovered it, freshly posted along with Michael Anne Casey's, on the transparency website Cryptome.[27] The page linked back to our own site, where we saw the accidentally posted email to CIA. Shortly thereafter came a second posting on *BoilingFrogsPost*, also attributing our site.[28] We felt the blood rush to our heads.

At that moment, our phone again rang. At the other end was Jason Leopold, just checking in. The situation was quickly explained. Leopold was in disbelief. "I don't buy it. You did this on purpose," Leopold stated bluntly, caught in the moment. "I hope you know what you're in for here. If Alfreda Bikowsky so much as stubs her toe, get ready to be blamed for it."

We emailed both the webmaster of Cryptome and Sibel Edmonds explaining the mistake and asking them to take down the attributions to our site. Both obliged.

The next day we returned to our day jobs, and Leopold called the CIA for comment. He was told "this is now a legal matter." Leopold's sources inside the Justice Department informed him an investigation had been opened. Such matters were often de facto after events like these. We were worried nonetheless. As we each arrived at our homes that evening, we half expected federal agents waiting to question us. That moment never came.

\* \* \*

A little over a week after our own moment with the CIA, the experience was put into perspective by that of two other American citizens. While living in San Diego, hijackers Nawaf al Hazmi and Khalid al Mihdhar had attended a mosque run by an imam named Anwar al Awlaki. The apartment of Ramzi bin al Shibh in Hamburg, Germany, had been raided after the attack. They had found Awlaki's phone number among the possessions.[29]

It was clear to investigators and commissioners that Awlaki had some level of involvement in 9/11, even if just by way of having had foreknowledge. He was followed after the attacks and even arrested. Without a hard case to prosecute, he was allowed to walk free. In 2002, Awlaki left the United States and moved to England, where he stayed until 2004, when he then headed to Yemen.[30] With ties to a garden variety of successful and would-be terrorists, coupled with his participation in a variety of crimes and supposed joining with Al Qaeda figures in Yemen, Obama's White House began internally debating the legality of killing him. The debate hinged on a particular fact: Anwar al Awlaki was an American. Would the agency's assassination efforts turn inward, toward suspected terrorists who were US citizens?

On September 30, 2011, while he and his travel mates stopped to eat lunch, Awlaki was killed by a Hellfire missile fired from a Predator drone.[31] The Justice Department would provide a legal memo effectively claiming that Awlaki was highly dangerous and very unlikely to be captured. Therefore, they argued, the killing was justified. The ACLU would respond to this memo, claiming that it was "ultimately an argument that the president can order targeted killings of Americans without ever having to account to anyone outside the executive branch."

If the White House, the CIA, and the Justice Department could justify the killing of an American citizen on the president's say-so, simply because his words were inflammatory and gave aid to terrorists, they would at least struggle to justify the killing of Awlaki's sixteen-year-old son. Two weeks after killing Anwar, his son Abdulrahman was in an open-air café in Yemen, when he too, was executed by a Predator drone.[32] Abdulrahman was also an American citizen, having been born in Denver. He had no connections to terrorism. Nine other people sitting near Abdulrahman were also killed. The CIA, meaning likely Alfreda Bikowsky, was behind both of these killings, and in the case of Abdulrahman, they ultimately claimed it was a mistake, that they were trying to assassinate somebody else.

Ten lives lost as they sat eating lunch at a café, one an American citizen. This tragedy seemingly gave little pause to the CIA or the White House. Neither institution dared call the act what it was, murder. While keeping track of civilians killed by US drone strikes is exceedingly difficult, estimates typically range in the hundreds, with some estimates claiming more. Of course, it must be noted that, as the *New York Times* reported, the US government "counts all military-age males in a strike zone as combatants, according to several administration officials, unless there is explicit intelligence posthumously proving them innocent."[33]

A sixteen-year-old boy killed by a drone is automatically considered a "combatant," instead of a civilian, and with this Orwellian twist of language the government can claim its civilian casualties are low, when they likely rival the number of people killed in the 9/11 attacks. It's no wonder that John Kiriakou once said of Alfreda Bikowsky, carefully avoiding using her name, "If an honest investigation were to take place, this person would be found guilty of crimes against humanity."

\* \* \*

After watching the government maneuver aggressively to prosecute Tom Drake despite his having provided only nonclassified material to a reporter, the young NSA contractor Edward Snowden figured it did not matter if he differentiated between classified and nonclassified. Leaks were leaks, and if the truth about domestic wiretapping was going to be told, he was going to make damn sure that it was the whole story, backed by any and every document he could get his hands on.

Snowden was possessed by no delusions that his whistle-blowing would in any way be received positively by the American state. He was not quaint in the way Drake was. Snowden was shrewd, and after contacting *Guardian* reporter Glenn Greenwald, he was able to convince both Greenwald and his associate Laura Poitras to meet him in Hong Kong. There, he would give them the story of their lives. On the flight over, where they felt secure that their laptops could be severed from the Internet and its many spies, they reviewed the contents of thumb drives Snowden had provided them. They were blown away. The source was the real deal.

The interview that Edward Snowden gave to Greenwald and Poitras, and the mass of documents he had to back up his claims, sent shock waves around the world. The NSA was spying on everyone. Not only was there warrantless wiretapping of US citizens being perpetrated by the intelligence apparatus, but the NSA also had the capability to hack into essentially any system around the globe. Further, they were doing so with the cooperation of the major telecommunications and tech companies, as well as foreign governments.[34]

Snowden had no intention of suffering the same fate as Tom Drake. If Drake's media leaks were a bunt, Snowden's were an out-of-the-park grand slam that landed in the next time zone over. Fleet-footed and ready to evade capture, Snowden made his way to Moscow where he still retains asylum. Knowing that leakers who came before him who tried to blow the whistle on criminal activity within government had had their lives destroyed for the effort, Snowden chose a more rogue path. Regarding the "proper channels" for reporting government abuse, he would lament the obvious flaw in hierarchical systems to the *New York Times*, saying, "You have to report wrongdoing to those most responsible for it."

\* \* \*

After all the hoopla surrounding the CIA's threat to us, *Gawker* and *Salon* had turned out to be the only mainstream outlets that would run a story about Alfreda Bikowsky after her name was revealed. The *New York Times* never picked it up, nor CNN or MSNBC.[35] Over the following three years, only Adam Goldman had mentioned her, in passing, in a *Washington Post* piece about her CIA lawyer.[36]

It was the release of Congress's "torture report" that knocked something loose. Matthew Cole of ABC News wrote, "US officials who spoke with NBC News on condition of anonymity confirmed that [one female CIA manager's] name was redacted at least three dozen times in an effort to avoid publicly identifying her. In fact, much of the four-month battle between Senate Democrats and the CIA about redactions centered on protecting the identity of the woman, an analyst and later 'deputy chief' of the unit devoted to catching or killing Usama bin Laden."[37]

After explaining how central this woman was to the report and that she was still working in an important position, Cole added, "NBC News is withholding her name at the request of the CIA, which cited a climate of fear and retaliation in the wake of the release of the committee's report in asking that her anonymity be protected."

Jane Mayer brought further attention to Cole's story with a brief piece in the *New Yorker* entitled "The Unidentified Queen of Torture."[38] When Bikowsky's name had first emerged on *Gawker*, writer John Cook contacted Mayer about it, and she had responded, "I identified everyone I felt was appropriate in my book, and am sorry not to be of more help but need to leave it at that."

Mayer, whose journalism is phenomenal, and who was the first to uncover the seeds of what would become several portions of this book, continued in step with Cole's decision to withhold a name that was at the center of wrongdoing alleged by Congress. Finally, along came Glenn Greenwald and Peter Maass, whose piece at *The Intercept* was aptly named, "Meet Alfreda Bikowsky."[39]

They explained, "*The Intercept* is naming Bikowsky over CIA objections because of her key role in misleading Congress about the agency's use of torture, and her active participation in the torture program (including playing a direct part in the torture of at least one innocent detainee). Moreover, Bikowsky has already been publicly identified by news organizations as the CIA officer responsible for many of these acts."

Consider this: Prior to her naming, there were subtle references to Bikowsky in the reports of Graham-Goss, Kean, Fine, and Helgerson, as well as CIA IG torture reports, Lawrence Wright's *The Looming Tower*, and several other news stories. Despite this reality, her name was always withheld, preventing readers from tracking her story across multiple media.

Eleven years and ten months. That is the amount of time that passed between Bikowsky's first alleged act of criminality—the potential for obstruction of justice charges over her involvement in the December 2000 withholding of information requested by FBI criminal investigations into the bombing of the USS *Cole*—until the date the public could identify her. A number of America's finest journalists, several government investigation reports, and yet it took a random miscommunication with a webmaster working for unpaid amateurs to turn this around. Were eleven years, ten months, and some blind circumstance really the best we as a country could expect?

Bikowsky is not "the answer" to any question. She is one of many, a symbol of sorts, a poster child for a bigger problem. Where were all the people who were supposed to ensure oversight and accountability? Several CIA directors, three presidents, the Senate and House intelligence committees, the offices of inspectors general, and a host of federal and local prosecutors? How had they all failed in her case?

Of course, we all know the answer, don't we? Those who do wrong *for* the empire will be covered, hidden, secreted through the loopholes and back doors in the system. That is why Tenet could perjure himself and then retire to his comfortable life. That is why Michael Hayden could chortle about the NSA being essentially ignored by the 9/11 investigations and then go on to be promoted. That is why the management of the CTC and Alec Station could hide a domestic spying operation that resulted in the largest terrorist attack in US history, provably lie to investigators about it, and then see their eventual tepid reprimands softened and accountability boards never drafted.

\* \* \*

At the end of 2015, some national security journalists were at a party when they noticed Mike Scheuer, now a professional pundit, seated affectionately close to a woman they recognized to be Alfreda Bikowsky.

"What's going on with them?" asked one.

"You haven't heard?" another answered. "They got married."[40]

The journalist was in disbelief. The woman Jane Mayer had dubbed "the Queen of Torture" had wed the self-described "Architect of Renditions." A match made in Washington. The journalist joked, "What do you think they sacrificed on their altar?"

Today the pair lives in a house in the suburbs of Virginia, on a block that comes up blurry on GoogleMaps. Bikowsky continues to go to work at Langley where she is in executive management, helping run the "war on terror."[41] Her reported allies Mike D'Andrea and Gina Haspel are still there too. The man known as "The Undertaker" and "The Dark Prince" has returned from retirement to run the Iran operations for today's White House.[42] On May 21, 2018, "Bloody Gina," Rodriguez's one-time protegé, achieved the dream that had eluded Jen Matthews, nominated by the president and, after confirmation hearings before the congress, sworn in as the first female Director of the CIA.

# AFTERWORD

During the writing of this book and the intermittent ten-year investigation behind it, we often worried about the consequences that might befall us or the people with whom we were speaking. This fear, whether justified paranoia or not, leads to the same outcome: an information blackout.

The incentivizing of self-censorship by would-be journalists and the discouraging of reporting unvarnished truths has become a political policy of the people who have been running the US government, one of the many dark outcomes of the "war on terror." Thus far, it has primarily shown itself within matters related to counterterror and national security, but as we have seen, the slope is often slippery.

A number of journalists working the national security beat have stated that they often feel like drug dealers while doing their jobs, particularly since Edward Snowden provided us evidence definitively proving that the most paranoid suspicions regarding government collection of digital information from its own populace had actually been underestimated. Consequently, people start treating every email, every text, every conversation as if a third party could theoretically learn what is communicated. Ironically, Snowden's revelations served both to inform the public but also allowed citizens to accept and adapt to the new reality. The knowledge that the digital information exists, that it is *collectable*, and quite probably *collected*, leads to a fundamental change in society.

It does not particularly matter whether some bureaucrat *right now* is following your story because you might be a threat of some kind. The fact is that if the wrong guy ends up in the White House, now, ten years from now, if someone decides that the activities you have engaged in, the ideas you have espoused, the causes you have advocated for are suddenly politically a target, all the evidence anyone would need to mount a case against you is sitting on a hard drive somewhere. Everyone commits three felonies a day, claims Kiriakou. A digital dossier potentially exists on everyone, should it become relevant at some point down the line. Do such things really happen? Do not ask us. Ask Tom Drake, John Kiriakou, Mark Rossini, and too many others.

Those in power have made a mantra for the times. If you are not doing anything wrong, you have nothing to hide. Unfortunately, the less savvy among us repeat this line. Of course, the logic of the mantra only travels one way. Absolute transparency is demanded of the citizen, and ironclad secrecy is reserved for the state.

It may never have been the intention of any particular person in Washington to see authoritarian policies and techniques come to dominate the country. Nonetheless, is it extreme to declare that the outcome has taken on a decidedly authoritarian flavor? Power moves in one direction, always growing, always seeking more terrain, always declaring that with a bit more flexibility, a bit more range, that the lurking dangers ever set on seizing away our freedom can finally be slain. The power to read every American's email, record every phone call, monitor every financial transaction, track a human carrying a phone in real time; it was already there, idly waiting for the day when people in power would flip the switch and turn it on. We can only wonder as to what schemes the intelligence agencies are currently engaged in that have not yet become public, like so many in this book that remained hidden for years.

A people should not be so sentimental, so set in their ways, so sure that previous generations got it right, so comforted by the images of wise and just sages sitting atop the pyramid that have been sold to them, that they refuse to consider that maybe, just maybe, other ideas and political formats might allow us to live better lives.

Perhaps we should again consider the question posited to George Tenet in that auditorium in Ann Arbor back in 1997. Does America still need the CIA? Or the NSA? Or the myriad offices operating the terror wars?

Surely within a democratically inclined system, the citizen's need for knowledge is at least equivalent to that of their elected leadership. Better put, there should be no competition. The People should be as informed as their representatives, those at the top of the bureaucracies, and the president, and they should be actively questioning and debating the policies that result from that information. Is that thought really now radical?

Everything in this book was drawn from reports in sound documents, vetted news stories, and first-person accounts, their trustworthiness to be weighed by the reader. Even if only half of the events recounted in this book were true, would it be fair to say we have a significant problem regarding the governance of this nation? If nothing else, there is clearly a pathway for the well-connected to dance between the raindrops of investigative bodies to avoid accountability. Those who do the dirty work of the empire know how to come out clean on the other side, well-intentioned democratic mechanisms be damned, while those who try to shine a little light on that dirty work suffer the devastating weight of the empire crashing down upon their heads.

Whether by design or by the unintended outcome of system operation, it is inescapable. We have a problem.

# BIBLIOGRAPHY

## BOOKS AND NEWS ARTICLES

Allen, Michael. *Blinking Red: Crisis and Compromise in American Intelligence After 9/11.* Dulles Virginia: Potomac Books, 2016.

Arena, Kelli. "Bush Says He Signed NSA Wiretap Order." CNN, December 17, 2005.

Bamford, James. *A Pretext for War: 9/11, Iraq and the Abuse of America's Intelligence Agencies.* New York: Anchor Books, 2004.

_____. *The Puzzle Palace: Inside the National Security Agency America's Most Secret Intelligence Organization.* New York: Penguin Books, 1983.

Barry, John. "A Tortured Debate." *Newsweek*, June, 20, 2004.

Barzilai, Yaniv. "How Bin Laden Escaped in 2001—The Lessons of Tora Bora." *The Daily Beast*, December 15, 2013.

Bergen, Peter. "The Account of How We Nearly Caught Osama bin Laden in 2001." *The New Republic*, December 30, 2009.

Berntsen, Gary and Ralph Pezzullo, *Jawbreaker: The Attack on Bin Laden and Al-Qaeda.* New York: Broadway Books, 2006.

Bikowsky, A. F. "A Comparative Study of US vs. Israeli Counterterrorism Policy: Implications for U.S. Policy,'" Master's Thesis (unpublished), The Fletcher School of Law and Diplomacy, Medford, Mass., 1988.

Binney, William and Thomas Drake and Edward Loomis and J. Kirk Wiebe, "Memorandum For: The President," Open Letter, 2014.

Braun, Stephen and Bob Drogin and Mark Fineman and Lisa Getter and Greg Krikorian and Robert Lopez. "Haunted by Years of Missed Warnings." *Los Angeles Times*, October 14, 2001.

Breitweiser, Kristen. "Enabling Danger." *Huffington Post*, May 25, 2011.

_____. *Wake Up Call: The Political Education of a 9/11 Widow.* New York: Warner Books, 2006.

Brill, Klaus and John Goetz and Frederik Obermaier. "Inside a Secret CIA Prison in the Polish Countryside." *Süddeutsche Zeitung*, February 8, 2013.

Bumiller, Elisabeth. "Saudi Prince Bluntly Tells Bush to Temper Support for Israel." *The New York Times*, April 25, 2002.

Burke, Jason. "Dead Man Walking." *The Observer*, August 5, 2001.

Clarke, Richard A. *Against All Enemies: Inside America's War on Terror*. New York: Free Press, 2004.

_____. "Behind the 28 Pages: Questions About an Alleged Saudi Spy and the CIA." abcnews.go.com, July 19, 2016.

Cole, Matthew. "Bin Laden Expert Accused of Shaping CIA Deception on 'Torture'Program." nbcnews.com, December 16, 2014.

_____ and Richard Esposito. "U.S. Mulls Legality of Killing American al Qaeda 'Turncoat.'" ABC News, January 25, 2010.

Coll, Steve. *Ghost Wars: The Secret History of the CIA, Afghanistan, and Bin Laden, From the Soviet Invasion to September 10, 2001*. New York: Penguin Books, 2004.

Cook, John. "Chief of CIA's Global Jihad Unit' Revealed Online." *Gawker*, September 22, 2011.

_____. "Why Won't the Post Name Counterterrorism Chief Michael D'Andrea?" *Gawker*, March 26, 2015.

Corera, Gordon. "Bin Laden's Tora Bora Escape, just months after 9/11." BBC, July 21, 2011.

Crovitz, L. Gordon. *Three Felonies a Day: How the Feds Target the Innocent*. New York: Encounter Books, 2009.

Crumpton, Henry A. *The Art of Intelligence: Lessons From a Life in the CIA's Clandestine Service*. New York: Penguin Books, 2012.

Edmonds, Sibel. "BFP Breaking News: Confirmed Identity of the CIA Official behind 9-11, Rendition & Torture Cases is Revealed." boilingfrogspost.com, September 21, 2011.

Eggen, Dan and Peter Slevin. "FBI Nominee Lauded for Tenacity." *The Washington Post*, July 31, 2001.

Fenton, Kevin. "Identity of CIA Officer Responsible for Pre–9-11 Failures, Tora Bora Escape, Rendition to Torture Revealed." 911blogger.com, September 11, 2009.

Filkins, Dexter. "The New CIA Deputy Chief's Black-Site Past." *The New Yorker*, February 3, 2017.

Forman, Bill. "Covert Intelligence." *MetroActive*, March 1, 2006.

Freeh, Louis J. with Howard Means. *My FBI: Bringing Down the Mafia, Investigating Bill Clinton, and Fighting the War on Terror*. New York: St. Marks Griffin, 2005.

Gates, Robert. *From the Shadows: The Ultimate Insider's Story of Five Presidents and How They Won the Cold War*. New York: Simon & Schuster, 2006.

Glasser, Susan. "The Battle of Tora Bora." *The Washington Post*, February 9, 2002.

Goldman, Adam and Matthew Rosenberg. "CIA Names the 'Dark Prince' to Run Iran Operations, Signaling a Tougher Stance." *The New York Times*, June 2, 2017.

# BIBLIOGRAPHY

_____ and Matt Apuzzo. "CIA officers make grave mistakes, get promoted." Associated Press, February 9, 2011.

_____ and Kathy Gannon. "Death shed light on CIA 'Salt Pit' near Kabul." NBC, Mar. 28, 2010.

_____ and Matt Apuzzo. "Destruction of Torture Videotapes Documented in CIA Email." Associated Press, April 16, 2010.

_____. "The Hidden History of the CIA's Prison in Poland." *The Washington Post*, January 23, 2014.

_____ and Greg Miller. "Spy Agencies' Attorney Has Fiercely Defended Surveillance Programs Revealed By Snowden." *The Washington Post,* January 12, 2014.

Gorman, Siobhan. "Management shortcomings seen at NSA." *The Baltimore Sun*, May 6, 2007.

_____. "Second-Ranking NSA Official Forced Out of Job By Director." *The Baltimore Sun*, May 31, 2006.

Graham, Sen. Bob with Mark Nussbaum. *Intelligence Matters: The CIA, the FBI, Saudi Arabia, and the Failure of America's War on Terror.* New York: Random House, 2004.

Graham, Duncan and Iain Hollingshead. "The Bin Laden Hunter." *The Telegraph*, May 21, 2011.

Greenburg, Jan and Howard Rosenberg and Ariane De Vogue. "Bush Aware of Adviser's Interrogation Talks." ABC News, April 11, 2008.

Greenwald, Glenn and Peter Maass. "Meet Alfreda BIkowsky, the Senior Officer at the Center of the CIA's Torture Scandals." *The Intercept*, December 19, 2014.

Griffen, Jennifer. "Two US-Born Terrorists Killed in CIA-Led Drone Strike." Fox News, Sep. 30, 2011.

Hagan, Joe. "The United States of America vs. Bill Keller." *New York Magazine*, September 18, 2006.

Hayden, Michael V. *Playing to the Edge: American Intelligence in the Age of Terror.* New York: Penguin Books, 2016.

Hayes, Stephen. "The Connection." *The Weekly Standard*, June 7, 2004.

Henderson, Simon. "The Saudis: Friend or Foe?" *Wall Street Journal*, Oct. 22, 2001.

Henry, Ed. "McCain, Bush Agree on Torture Ban." CNN, December 15, 2005.

Herridge, Catherine. "Mueller Grilled on FBI's Release of Awlaki in 2002." Fox News, March 8, 2012.

Hersh, Seymour. "The General's Report." *The New Yorker*, June 25, 2007.

Hirschkorn, Phil. "Shattered Diplomacy." CNN.com, April 16, 2001.

Hoffman, David E. *The Billion Dollar Spy: A True Story of Cold War Espionage and Betrayal.* New York: Anchor Books, 2016.

Hosenball, Mark and Caren Bohan and Tabassum Zakaria and Missy Ryan. "The Bin Laden Kill Plan." *Reuters*, May 12, 2001.

Horton, Scott. "When Does an FBI Investigation Look Like an Omertà?" harpers.org, December 21, 2007.

Isikoff, Michael. "The Hijackers We Let Escape." *Newsweek*, June 9, 2002.

_____ and David Corn. *Hubris: The Inside Story of Spin, Scandal, and the Selling of the Iraq War*. New York: Three Rivers Press, 2006.

_____ and Tamara Lipper and Even Thomas. "The Insider; the Town Crier." *Newsweek*, April 5, 2004.

_____ "The Interrogation Tapes." *Newsweek*, December 10, 2007.

_____ and John Barry and Michael Hirsch. "The Roots of Torture." *Newsweek*, May 24, 2004.

_____ and Evan Thomas. "The Saudi Money Trail." *Newsweek*, December 2, 2002.

_____. "The White House Is Battling To Keep a Report on the Terror Attacks Secret." *Newsweek*, April 29, 2003.

Jehl, Douglas. "CIA Chief Seeks Change in Inspector's 9/11 Report." *The New York Times*, January 7, 2005.

_____. "High Qaeda Aide Retracted Claim of Link With Iraq." *The New York Times*, July 31, 2004.

_____. "Review at CIA and Justice Brings No 9/11 Punishment." *The New York Times*, September 14, 2004.

_____ and David Johnston. "Within CIA, Worry of Prosecution for Conduct." *The New York Times*, February 27, 2005.

Karl, Jonathon. "'High-Value' Detainees Transferred to Guantanamo." ABC News, September 6, 2006.

Kean, Thomas and Lee Hamilton. "Stonewalled by the CIA." *The New York Times*, January 2, 2008.

Kinzer, Stephen. *The Brothers: John Foster Dulles, Allen Dulles and Their Secret World War*. New York: Times Books, 2013.

Kocieniewski, David. "A Nation Challenged: A Funeral." *The New York Times*, September 29, 2001.

Lauter, David and Timothy Phelps. "Memo justifying drone killing of American Al Qaeda leader is released." *Los Angeles Times*, June 23, 2014.

Lelyveld, Joseph. "The Director: Running the CIA." *The New York Times*, January 20, 1985.

Lengel, Allan and Rachel Leven. "The Raven Haired Actress and the Fall of a Dapper FBI Agent." ticklethewire.com, September 14, 2009.

Leopold, Jason. "Former Counterterrorism Czar Accuses Tenet, Other CIA Officials of Cover-Up." *Truth- Out*, August 11, 2011.

Linzer, Dafna and R. Jeffrey Smith. "Dismissed CIA Officer Denies Leak Role." *The Washington Post*, April 25, 2006.

_____. "Secret Surveillance May Have Occurred Before Authorization." *The Washington Post*, January 4, 2006.

# BIBLIOGRAPHY

Macaskill, Ewen and Dominic Rushe. "Snowden document reveals key role of companies in NSA data collection." *The Guardian*, November 1, 2013.

Mak, Tim. "Inside the CIA's Sadistic Dungeon." *The Daily Beast*, December 9, 2014.

Mavadiya, Madhvi. "Who Is Gina Hapsel? Trump's CIA Director Nominee Revealed." *The Daily Mail*, May 10, 2018.

Mayer, Jane. *The Dark Side: The Inside Story of How the War on Terror Turned Into a War on American Ideals*. New York: First Anchor Books, 2009.

_____. "Outsourcing Torture." *The New Yorker*, February 8, 2005.

_____. "The Secret Sharer." *The New Yorker*, May 23, 2011.

_____. "The Unidentified Queen of Torture." newyorker.com, December 18, 2014.

Mazzetti, Mark and Matt Apuzzo. "Deep Support in Washington for CIA's Drone Missions." *The New York Times*, April 25, 2015.

_____ and David Johnston. "A Window Into CIA's Embrace of Secret Jails." *The New York Times*, August 12, 2009.

Mekhennet, Souad and Don Van Natta Jr. "German's Claim of Kidnapping Brings Investigation of US Link." *The New York Times*, January 9, 2005.

Miller, Greg. "In Zero Dark Thirty, She's the Hero." *The Washington Post*, December 10, 2012.

_____. "Legal Memo Backing Drone Strike that Killed American Anwar al-Awlaki is Released." *The Washington Post*, June 23, 2014.

Miller, John C. and Michael Stone. *The Cell: Inside the 9/11 Plot, and Why the FBI and CIA Failed to Stop It*. New York: Hyperion, 2002.

Miller, Judith. "Dissecting a Terror Plot From Boston to Amman." *The New York Times*, January 15, 2001.

Morrell, Michael. *The Great War Of Our Time: The CIA's Fight Against Terrorism—From al Qa'ida to ISIS*. New York: Grand Central Publishing, 2015.

Mowbray, Joel. "Foggy Bottom's Friends." *The Wall Street Journal*, October 13, 2003.

Natsios, Deborah and John Young. "CIA Officer Alfreda Frances Bikowsky." Crytocomb, January 19, 2014.

Nowosielski, Ray and Rory O'Connor. "Insiders Voice Doubts About CIA's 9-11 Story." *Salon*, October 14, 2011.

Pincus, Walter and Dana Linzer. "CIA Rejects Discipline for 9/11 Failures." *The Washington Post*, October 6, 2005.

_____ and Barton Gellman. "Depiction of Threat Outgrew Supporting Evidence." *The Washington Post*, August 10, 2003.

_____. "Negroponte's First Job is Showing Who's Boss." *The Washington Post*, March 1, 2005.

_____. "Newly Released Data Undercut Prewar Claims." *The Washington Post*, November 6, 2005.

_____ and Joby Warrick. "Station Chief Made Appeal to Destroy CIA Tapes." *The Washington Post*, January 16, 2008.

Posner, Gerald. *Why America Slept: The Failure to Prevent 9/11*. New York: Ballantine, 2003.

Priest, Dana. "CIA Avoids Scrutiny of Detainee Treatment." *The Washington Post*, Mar. 3, 2005.

_____. "Forgotten Briefings of August 2001." *The Washington Post*, April 15, 2004.

_____ and Joe Stephens. "Secret World of US Interrogation." *The Washington Post*, May 11, 2004.

Quraishi, Ahmed. "America's and Pakistan's Joint Defeat in Afghanistan." *Daily Pakistan Global*, May 13, 2018.

Rangeman, Eric. "Ex-AT&T employee: NSA snooping Internet traffic too." *Ars Technica*, Nov. 11, 2007.

Reuters Staff. "Factbox: Has Obama delivered on his 2008 campaign promises?" Reuters, October 28, 2011.

Risen, James. "David H. Blee, 83, CIA. Spy Who Revised Defector Policy." *The New York Times*, August 17, 2000.

_____. *State of War: The Secret History of the CIA and the Bush Administration*. New York: Free Press, 2006.

Rodriguez Jr., Jose A. *Hard Measures*. New York: Threshold Editions, 2012.

Rosenberg, Matthew. "New CIA. Deputy Director, Gina Haspel, Had Leading Role in Torture." *The New York Times*, February 2, 2017.

Ross, Brian and Richard Esposito. "CIA's Harsh Interrogation Techniques Described." ABC News, November 18, 2005.

_____ and Richard Esposito. "CIA Efforts to Prosecute Whistle- Blower Spy Stopped." ABC News, December 11, 2007.

Roston, Aram. "The Gay Terrorist." *The Observer*, March 17, 2010.

Savage, Charlie. "Ex-CIA Officer Charged in Information Leak." *The New York Times*, January 23, 2012.

Schoenfeld, Gabriel. "What Became of the CIA." *Commentary*, March 1, 2005.

Schou, Nicholas. "Outing the CIA's 'Undertaker' Michael D'Andrea." *Newsweek*, June 28, 2016.

Scott, Peter Dale. "Intelligence Cooking By the Deep State." Voltairenet.org, October 4, 2012.

Shane, Scott and David Johnston. "CIA Employee Fired for Alleged Leak." *The New York Times*, April 21, 2006.

_____ and Souad Mekhennet "Imam's Path From Condemning Terror to Preaching Jihad," *The New York Times*, May 8, 2010.

_____ and Jo Becker. "Secret Kill Lists Test Obama's Principles and Will." *The New York Times*, May 29, 2012.

Shelby, Ted. "NSA Employment Cuts Will Hurt Maryland Economy, But Exactly How Much?" *The Baltimore Sun*, December 6, 1991.

Shenon, Philip. *The Commission: The Uncensored History of the 9/11 Investigation*. New York: Twelve, 2008.

_____ and David Johnston. "Preventative Steps." *The New York Times*, October 9, 2001.

_____. "September 11th Anniversary: Richard Clarke's Explosive CIA Cover-up Charge." *The Daily Beast*, August 11, 2011.

Silverstein, David. "An American Strategy Against Terrorism." The Heritage Foundation, August 23, 1991.

Silverstein, Ken. "Baghdad Chief Out." *Harper's*, February 2, 2007.

_____. "Meet the CIA's new Baghdad Station Chief." *Harper's*, January 28, 2007.

_____. "Missed Appointments: The CIA Responds." *Harper's*, April 16, 2007.

_____. "Next Stop: Baghdad Station." *Harper's*, March 23, 2007.

Simon, Richard and Peter Wallsten. "Bush's Prewar Funding is Criticized." *The Los Angeles Times*, April 20, 2004.

Singh, Amrit. "Globalizing Torture." Open Society Justice Initiative, 2013.

Skalka, Jennifer. "Silent Stars." *Washingtonian*, December 17, 2010.

Soufan, Ali with Daniel Freedman. *The Black Banners: The Inside Story of 9/11 and the War Against al-Qaeda*. New York: W.W. Norton, 2011.

Stein, Jeff. "FBI Agent: The CIA Could Have Stopped 9/11." *Newsweek*, June 19, 2015.

_____. "FBI Prevents Agents from Telling 'Truth' About 9/11 on PBS." *Congressional Quarterly*, October 1, 2008.

Summers, Anthony and Robbyn Swan. "Richard Clarke 9/11 Interview." *The Daily Beast*, August 12, 2011.

Suskind, Ron. *The One Percent Doctrine: Deep Inside America's Pursuit of Its Enemies Since 9/11*. New York: Simon & Schuster, 2007.

Taddonio, Patrice. "Why You Never Saw the CIA's Interrogation Tapes." pbs.org, May 19, 2015.

Tenet, George J. with Bill Harlow. *At the Center of the Storm: My Years at the CIA*. New York: HarperCollins, 2007.

_____. and Cofer Black and Richard Blee, "Joint Statement from George J. Tenet, Cofer Black and Richard Blee," August 3, 2011.

Truman, Harry S. "Limit CIA Role to Intelligence." *The Washington Post*, December 22, 1963.

Unknown. "CIA Director Tenet to Stay on With Bush Administration," CNN.com, January 16, 2001.

_____. "Frances D. Bikowsky," Obituary, Dallas Morning News, October 21, 2004.

_____. "Interrogation." *The Washington Post*, January 21, 1968.

_____. "Saudi Prince Found Dead in Desert." *Dawn*, July 31, 2002.

Vest, Jason. "Pray and Tell." *The American Prospect*, June 19, 2005.

Warrick, Joby and Peter Finn. "Harsh Tactics Readied Before Their Approval." *The Washington Post*, April 22, 2009.

_____. *The Triple Agent: The al-Qaeda Mole Who Infiltrated the CIA*. New York: Vintage Books, 2012.

Weiner, Tim. "CIA Severs Ties to 100 Foreign Agents." *The New York Times*, March 3, 1997.

_____. *Legacy of Ashes: The History of the CIA*. New York: First Anchor Books, 2008.

Whitlock, Craig. "Al Qaeda Detainee's Mysterious Release." *The Washington Post*, January 30, 2006.

_____. "US airstrike that killed American teen in Yemen raises legal, ethical questions." *The Washington Post*, October 23, 2011.

Wilber, Del Quentin. "Ex-FBI Agent Mark Rossini Sentenced for Using Bureau Computers in Pelicano Case." *The Washington Post*, May 15, 2009.

Wise, Mike. "The Spy Who Loved Rooney." *The Washington Post*, November 3, 2008.

Woodward, Bob and Dan Balz. "America's Chaotic Road to War." *The Washington Post*, January 27, 2002.

_____ and Dan Balz. "At Camp David, Advise and Dissent." *The Washington Post*, January 31, 2002.

_____. *Bush at War*. New York: Simon & Schuster, 2002.

_____. "CIA Led Way With Cash Handouts." *The Washington Post*, November 18, 2001.

Wright, Lawrence. "The Agent." *The New Yorker*, July 10, 2006.

_____. "The Counter-Terrorist." *The New Yorker*, January 14, 2002.

_____. *The Looming Tower: Al-Qaeda and the Road to 9/11*. New York: First Vintage Books, 2007.

Young, John. "CIA Officers Alfreda Frances Bikowsky and Michael Anne Casey." cryptome.org, September 21, 2011.

## GOVERNMENT DOCUMENTS

9-11 Commision Memorandum for the record: Interview with Abdussattar Shaikh.

9-11 Commission Staff Statement No. 2, National Commission on Terrorist Attacks Upon the United States.

Alleged Secret Detentions in Council of Europe Member States, Council of Europe, Committee on Legal Affairs and Human Rights, January 22, 2006.

A Review of the FBI's Handling of Intelligence Information Related to the September 11 Attacks, Office of the Inspector General, November 2004.

CIA Log Entries from 9/11 and Related Documents, 9/11 Commission, March 24, 2004.

Committee Study of the CIA's Detention and Interrogation Program, US Senate Select Committee on Intelligence, December 9, 2014.

# BIBLIOGRAPHY

Congressional Record S4849—United States Senate, "Executive nominations received by the Senate," May 22, 2008.

Congressional Record Volume 149, Number 7, "Executive nominations received by the Senate," January 15, 2003.

Counterterrorism Detention and Interrogation Activities (September 2001–October 2003), CIA Inspector General, May 7, 2004.

Document no. 17, 9-11 Commission, June 6, 2003.

Dulles-Jackson-Correa Report, Intelligence Survey Group, 1949.

Federal Bureau of Investigation, Overview of the 9/11 Investigation Slide Show, 2014.

Federal Bureau of Investigation, Working Draft Chronology of Events for Hijackers and Associates (Part A), November 14, 2003.

Final Report of The National Commission on Terrorist Attacks Upon the United States, July 22, 2004.

Final Report of The Joint Inquiry into Intelligence Community Activities before and after the Terrorist Attacks of September 11, 2001, Senate Select Committee on Intelligence, December 2002.

Inquiry Into the Treatment of Detainees in US Custody, Senate Armed Services Committee, November 20, 2008.

Joint Response To OIG Report "Accountability Regarding Findings And Conclusions Of The Joint Inquiry Into Intelligence Community Activities Before & After 9/11/2001." December 8, 2008.

Khaled Shaikh Mohammed interview by the International Committee of the Red Cross, "ICRC Report on the Treatment of Fourteen 'High Value Detainees' in CIA Custody," 2007.

Letter from Thomas J. Pickard to the 9-11 Commission, June 24, 2004.

Miscellaneous 9/11 Commission Staff Notes about Drafting the Final Report, published on scribd.com by 9-11 Document Archive.

OIG Vaughn Index of OLC Remand Documents, ACLU v. DOD, No. 1:04-CV-4151 (S.D.N.Y. Sept. 21, 2009).

Report On Central Intelligence Agency Accountability Regarding Findings And Conclusions Of The Report Of The Joint Inquiry Into Intelligence Community Activities Before And After The Terrorist Attacks Of September 11, 2001, Office of the Inspector General, June 1, 2005.

Requirements for the TrailBlazer and ThinThread Systems, Department of Defense Inspector General Audit Report, December 15, 2004.

Task Force Report on National Security Organization, First Hoover Commission, 1948-1949.

The Downing Street Memo, July 23, 2002, published by The Sunday Times on May 1, 2005.

The Intelligence Community's Knowledge of the September 11 Hijackers Prior to September 11, 2001, Eleanor Hill, Staff Director Congressional Joint Inquiry, September 20, 2002.

Tora Bora Revisited: How We Failed To Get Bin Laden and Why it Matters Today, Majority Committee on Foreign Relations, US Senate, Nov. 30, 2009.

Twenty-eight pages declassified, Congressional Joint Inquiry 9-11 Report, August 5, 2016.

Unclassified Report on the President's Surveillance Program, Offices of the Inspectors General, DOD, DOJ, CIA, NSA, Office of the Director of National Intelligence, July 10, 2009.


## MOTION PICTURES/TELEVISION/RADIO/AUDIO BLOG POSTS

Bamford, James (Writer, Producer), Paula S. Apsell (Senior Executive Producer), & C. Scott Willis (Director, Producer). (2009). *NOVA: The Spy Factory* [Motion Picture]. United States: PBS, WGBH.

Barker, Greg (Director, Producer), Peter Bergen and Sheila Nevins (Executive Producers), & John Battsek and Julie Goldman (Producers). (2013). *Manhunt: The Inside Story of the Hunt for Bin Laden* [Motion Picture]. United States: HBO.

Collins, Peter B. "September 28, 2011." [Audio Blog Post]. *Podcast Show*, BoilingFrogsPost.com, September 28, 2011.

Endsor, David (Correspondent). (2001). *Sunday Morning News* [Motion Picture]. United States: CNN.

Kirk, Michael and Scott Willis (Senior Producers), David Fanning (Senior Executive Producer) & Burry, Chris (Correspondent). (2001). *Frontline: The Clinton Years* [Motion Picture]. United States: PBS, WGBH.

_____, David Fanning (Executive Producer), & Jim Gilmore (Co-Producer, Reporter). (2002). *Frontline: The Man Who Knew* [Motion Picture]. United States: PBS, WGBH.

_____, David Fanning (Executive Producer), Jim Gilmore (Producer), & Dana Priest (Reporter). (2011). *Frontline: Are We Safer?* [Motion Picture]. United States: PBS, WGBH.

_____, Mike Wiser (Writer, Producer), David Fanning (Executive Producer), & Jim Gilmore (Reporter, Producer). (2014). *Frontline: United States of Secrets* [Motion Picture]. United States: PBS, WGBH.

_____, David Fanning (Executive Producer), & Jim Gilmore (Reporter, Producer). (2006). *Frontline: The Dark Side* [Motion Picture]. United States: PBS, WGBH.

Kroft, Steve (Correspondent). (November 12, 2004.) "Bin Laden Expert Steps Forward," *60 Minutes* [Television/Radio]. United States: CBS.

Moser, Friedrich (Director, Writer, Producer), & Michael Seeber (Senior Producer). (2015.) *A Good American* [Motion Picture]. Austria: El Ride Productions.

# BIBLIOGRAPHY

Nowosielski, Ray and John Duffy. "Who Is Rich Blee?" [Audio Blog Post]. Amazonaws. com, September 21, 2011.

_____ ("FF4Films"). (August 11, 2011). *Interview #07 (Washington D.C.)* [Video file]. Retrieved from https://www.youtube.com/watch?v=bl6w1YaZdf8.

Olbermann, Keith (Host). (April 24, 2006). *Countdown with Keith Olbermann* [Television/ Radio]. United States: MSNBC.

Ross, Brian (Interviewer). (December 10, 2007). "Interview with John Kiriakou," ABC News [Television/Radio]. United States: ABC.

# ENDNOTES

## CHAPTER 1

1. Interview with Richard Clarke.
2. Interviews with Richard Clarke and Col. Lawrence Wilkerson; Michael Isikoff, Tamara Lipper and Even Thomas, "The Insider; the Town Crier," *Newsweek*, April 5, 2004.
3. Interview with Col. Lawrence Wilkerson; David Gergen interview by Michael Kirk, "The Clinton Years," *Frontline*, January 16, 2001.
4. Annual budget number comes from "Statement by the Director of Central Intelligence Regarding the Disclosure of the Aggregate Intelligence Budget For Fiscal Year 1998," CIA press release in response to a Freedom of Information Act lawsuit from Federation of American Scientists, March 20, 1998. The half million contractors and employees number estimated by a source who worked with the intelligence services may be a significant underestimation for the year in question, given that after the DCI's office was reorganized into the Director of National Intelligence office post-9/11, the DNI released a report in 2011 revealing many "more people than had previously been speculated by the Government Accountability Office." 701,142 federal employees held a "top secret" clearance, along with another 536,637 contractors. It is not known how many of these would have fallen under Tenet's purview. These numbers had also risen in the years since the attacks.
5. "Number of employees at ExxonMobil from 2001 to 2016," Statista.com.
6. Michael Allen, *Blinking Red*, 21.
7. "CIA Director Tenet to Stay on With Bush Administration," CNN.com, January 16, 2001; George Tenet, *At the Center of the Storm*, 136.
8. George J. Tenet, Cofer Black, and Richard Blee, "Joint Statement from George J. Tenet, Cofer Black and Richard Blee," August 3, 2011, written to the authors and provided via email by Bill Harlow. After we responded detailing a number of inaccuracies in the statement, Tenet et al provided an altered joint statement to Philip Shenon, who was first to publish any version of it: "September 11th Anniversary: Richard Clarke's Explosive CIA Cover-up Charge," *The Daily Beast*, August 11, 2011.

9. Richard A. Clarke, "Behind the 28 Pages: Questions About an Alleged Saudi Spy and the CIA," abcnews.go.com, July 19, 2016.

## CHAPTER 2

1. Interview with John Kiriakou; Joby Warrick, *The Triple Agent*, 102; audio interview of Joby Warrick by Peter B. Collins, *Boiling Frogs Post*, September 28, 2011. Kiriakou recalled Matthews in his CIA new-hire class and "the redhead," as he and other sources referred to Bikowsky, as having arrived roughly six months before them. This aligns with Bikowsky's birth date from public records and known graduation years.
2. Interview with John Kiriakou; Jennifer Skalka, "Silent Stars," *Washingtonian*, December 17, 2010; obituary of Frances D. Bikowsky, *Dallas Morning News*, October 21, 2004.
3. Interview with John Kiriakou; Jennifer Skalka, "Silent Stars," *Washingtonian*, December 17, 2010; Barbara Bikowsky, public records; Frances D. Bikowsky, public records.
4. Bikowsky family, public records.
5. Barbara Bikowsky, public records; Alfreda F. Bikowsky, public records.
6. Jennifer Skalka, "Silent Stars," *Washingtonian*, December 17, 2010; Joby Warrick, *The Triple Agent*, 103.
7. Interview with John Kiriakou.
8. Barbara Bikowsky, public records. Barbara Bikowsky, death certificate; obituary of Frances D. Bikowsky, *Dallas Morning News*, October 21, 2004.
9. Interview with John Kiriakou.
10. Jennifer Skalka, "Silent Stars," *Washingtonian*, December 17, 2010.
11. Interview with former South Garland High School teacher. Bikowsky's attendance at South Garland H.S. was discovered by Deborah Natsios and John Young of *Cryptome* through a "SGHS Class of 1983" reunion posting dfwretroplex.com and a SGHS yearbook.
12. Jennifer Skalka, "Silent Stars," *Washingtonian*, December 17, 2010.
13. Interview with John Kiriakou.
14. Joby Warrick, *The Triple Agent*, 103.
15. Interview with John Kiriakou.
16. Deborah Natsios and John Young, "CIA Officer Alfreda Frances Bikowsky," *Crytocomb*, January 19, 2014, confirmed by authors via Alfreda F. Bikowsky, public records.
17. Alfreda F. Bikowsky, public records.
18. Alfreda F. Bikowsky, unpublished master's thesis "A Comparative Study of US vs. Israeli Counterterrorism Policy"; Alfreda F. Bikowsky, public records.
19. Joby Warrick, *The Triple Agent*, 103.
20. Interview with John Kiriakou.
21. Interview with John Kiriakou.

# ENDNOTES

22. Descriptions from multiple employees who worked at CIA's headquarters.
23. "According to one government official, as many as one thousand foreign agents—*somewhere between one-quarter and one-third* [emphasis ours] of all the agents on the CIA's payroll in 1995—failed to meet this test [regarding the scrub of assets with criminal or human rights problems.]," Tim Weiner, "CIA Severs Ties to 100 Foreign Agents," *The New York Times*, March 3, 1997.
24. Interview with John Kiriakou; Joby Warrick, *The Triple Agent*, 102; audio interview of Joby Warrick by Peter B. Collins, *Boiling Frogs Post*, September 28, 2011; "SGHS Class of 1983" reunion posting at dfwretroplex.com, listing Alfreda Bikowsky Silverstein. David Silverstein, fellow Fletcher School alumni, knew of Bikowsky as early as 1991, suggesting they met in college, as evidenced by a reference to her thesis in his article, "An American Strategy Against Terrorism," *The Heritage Foundation*, August 23, 1991. Neighbors of Bikowsky from the period in question spoken to by the authors recognized Silverstein as a regular presence at her home.
25. Michael Scheuer interview by Steve Kroft, "Bin Laden Expert Steps Forward," *60 Minutes*, November 12, 2004.
26. Interviews with multiple employees who worked at CIA's headquarters, who referred to Bikowsky as "the redhead."
27. Richard A. Clarke, *Against All Enemies*, 144.
28. Interview with John Kiriakou; Richard A. Clarke, *Against All Enemies*, 144–145; United States of America v. Fawaz Yunis, A/k/a Nazeeh, Appellant, 924 F.2d 1086 (DC Cir. 1991).
29. Richard A. Clarke, *Against All Enemies*, 144–145.
30. Jane Mayer, "Outsourcing Torture," *The New Yorker*, February 8, 2005; Michael Scheuer testimony before House of Representatives, US Congress, April 17, 2007.
31. Online comment by Michael Scheuer below article by Apostolou, "Michael Scheuer's Bloody Logic," *TCS Daily*, March 17, 2005.
32. Gabriel Schoenfeld, "What Became of the CIA," *Commentary*, March 1, 2005.
33. Interview with John Kiriakou; Jane Mayer, "Outsourcing Torture," *The New Yorker*, February 8, 2005; Michael Scheuer testimony before House of Representatives, US Congress, April 17, 2007.
34. Jane Mayer, "Outsourcing Torture," *The New Yorker*, February 8, 2005; Michael Scheuer testimony before House of Representatives, US Congress, April 17, 2007.
35. Steve Coll, *Ghost Wars*, 15.
36. Interviews with John Kiriakou and Mark Rossini. Neither source used Bikowsky's name, referring to her as "the redhead."
37. Multiple sources who worked at CIA headquarters remember that Tom Wilshere went back to the original formation of Alec Station.
38. Interview with Mark Rossini.
39. Joby Warrick, *The Triple Agent*, 104.
40. Interviews with multiple sources who worked at CIA's headquarters.

41. Interview with Lawrence Wright and multiple sources who worked at CIA's headquarters; Lawrence Wright, *The Looming Tower*, 313.
42. Twenty thousand was the number reported to be Maryland-based NSA employees five years earlier, by Ted Shelby, "NSA Employment Cuts Will Hurt Maryland Economy, But Exactly How Much?" *The Baltimore Sun*, December 6, 1991. This number aligns both with an estimate made by a source who worked at NSA's headquarters and with the square footage of NSA's space at Fort Meade. James Bamford reported the total collecting checks from NSA to be 68,203 in 1978 and at the time "more than all of the employees of the rest of the intelligence community put together," *The Puzzle Palace*, 18.
43. Interviews with multiple sources who worked at NSA headquarters, talking about projected SIGINT numbers for the year 2001.
44. Interview with Thomas Drake.
45. Interviews with Thomas Drake and multiple sources who worked at NSA's headquarters.
46. Phil Hirschkorn, "Shattered Diplomacy," CNN.com, April 16, 2001; Michael Isikoff, "The Hijackers We Let Escape," *Newsweek*, June 9, 2002; Lawrence Wright, "The Agent," *The New Yorker*, July 10, 2006.
47. Interview with Thomas Drake.
48. Interviews with James Bamford and Thomas Drake.
49. Interview with James Bamford; Michael Scheuer, letter to the House and Senate Intelligence Committees, US Congress, published as "How Not to Catch a Terrorist" by *The Atlantic*, December 2004.
50. Transcript, Gerald Ford Library Conference, Ann Arbor, Michigan, November 11, 1997.
51. Tim Weiner, *Legacy of Ashes*, 23, 467–468.
52. Harry S. Truman, "Limit CIA Role to Intelligence," *The Washington Post*, December 22, 1963.
53. Interview with Fulton Armstrong.
54. Harry S. Truman, "Limit CIA Role to Intelligence," *The Washington Post*, December 22, 1963.
55. Eberstadt Report, First Hoover Commission, 1948.
56. Dulles-Jackson-Correa Report, 1949.
57. President Eisenhower created the President's Board of Consultants on Foreign Intelligence Activities.
58. Stephen Kinzer, *The Brothers*, 303.
59. Robert Gates, *From the Shadows*, 60.
60. Joseph Lelyveld, "The Director: Running the CIA," *The New York Times*, January 20, 1985; Tim Weiner, *Legacy of Ashes*, 376.
61. "Senate Select Committee on Intelligence Questionnaire (Mr. George J. Tenet)," US Senate, March 25, 1997.

ENDNOTES

62. George Tenet began his US government career as a legislative assistant, then legislative director to Senator Henry John Heinz III, one of the original cosponsors of the IIPA.

## CHAPTER 3

1. Jason Burke, "Dead Man Walking," *The Observer*, August 5, 2001.
2. Interview with Jack Cloonan.
3. Jason Burke, "Dead Man Walking," *The Observer*, August 5, 2001; United States of America v. Usama Bin Laden, et al., Defendants, S(7) 98 Cr. 1023 (US District Court Southern District of New York 2001).
4. Gen. Michael Hayden, *Playing to the Edge*, 9.
5. Mike Wise, "The Spy Who Loved Rooney," *The Washington Post*, November 3, 2008; Gen. Michael Hayden, US Air Force biography; Gen. Michael Hayden, *Playing to the Edge*, 9.
6. Gen. Michael Hayden interview by David Ensor, *Sunday Morning News*, CNN, March 25, 2001.
7. Interview with Mark Rossini.
8. Michael Kirk, *The Man Who Knew*, *Frontline*, October 3, 2002.
9. Interview with Mark Rossini.
10. CIA Inspector General 9-11 Accountability Report, 301–302, declassified as the result of a Freedom of Information Act lawsuit by Jason Leopold.
11. Michael Scheuer testimony before House of Representatives, US Congress, April 17, 2007.
12. Interview with Mark Rossini. Rossini referred to Casey by her pseudonym from government reports, "Michelle." Casey's name was deduced by the authors as detailed in piece by Ray Nowosielski and Rory O'Connor, "Insiders Voice Doubts About CIA's 9-11 Story," *Salon*, October 14, 2011.
13. CIA Inspector General 9-11 Accountability Report, 54–57; DOJ Inspector General 9-11 Intelligence Report, 231–233.
14. Interview with Mark Rossini.
15. Interview with Richard A. Clarke.
16. Interview with Mark Rossini.
17. Interview with Fulton Armstrong and multiple sources who worked at CIA's headquarters.
18. Rich's father David Blee was reported to be chief of station for Pretoria in 1957, David E. Hoffman, *The Billion Dollar Spy*, 24.
19. Richard Blee, public records; James Risen, "David H. Blee, 83, CIA. Spy Who Revised Defector Policy," The *New York Times*, August 17, 2000.
20. American Embassy School, yearbook; James Risen, "David H. Blee, 83, CIA. Spy Who Revised Defector Policy," *The New York Times*, August 17, 2000.

21. "Key Officers of Foreign Service Posts," State Department, 1984–86.
22. "Key Officers of Foreign Service Posts," State Department, 1989–91.
23. Steven Coll, *Ghost Wars*, 456. Coll referred to Blee only by his first name.
24. Interview with source who worked at CIA's headquarters.
25. "CIA to Mark 50th Anniversary, Honor 'Trailblazers,'" CIA press release, September 10, 1997.

**CHAPTER 4**

1. Judith Miller, "Dissecting a Terror Plot From Boston to Amman," *The New York Times*, January 15, 2001.
2. Judith Miller, "Dissecting a Terror Plot From Boston to Amman," *The New York Times*, January 15, 2001; 9/11 Commission Report, 174–176.
3. United States v. Ressam, No. 07-455 (US Supreme Court 2008).
4. 9/11 Commission Report, 174-180.
5. Interview with Thomas Drake; 9/11 Commission Report, 181.
6. Interview with Mark Rossini; 9/11 Commission Report, 181.
7. Interview with Mark Rossini. Rossini referred to Casey by her government report pseudonym "Michelle."
8. Congressional Joint Inquiry 9/11 Report, 156; 9/11 Commission Report, 502.
9. Interview with Richard A. Clarke; James Bamford, *A Pretext for War*, 225.
10. The CIA Inspector General 9-11 Accountability Report includes six individuals at Alec Station who recur throughout the surveillance operation and Mihdhar visa story, calling them COS, DCOS for CIA, DCOS for FBI, Operations Branch Chief, Targeting Branch Chief, and a targeting officer or analyst. Based on known information, backed by details obtained through interviews with multiple employees who worked at CIA's headquarters, the figures can be deduced to be, in order, Richard Blee, Tom Wilshere, Ed Goetz, Alfreda Bikowsky, Jen Matthews, and Michael Anne Casey. References to Alec's "COS" from mid-2000 onward in the report refer to Hendrik Van Der Meulen. The "worldwide network" comes from 9-11 Commission Staff Statement No. 2, 4.
11. Interview with Lawrence Wright; Lawrence Wright, *The Looming Tower*, 311.
12. 9/11 Commission Report, 502.
13. CIA Inspector General 9-11 Accountability Report, 76, "The DCOS accessed 217 documents, including [REDACTED] which he had open for seventeen seconds early in the morning." From the context of the report, it is clear that REDACTED refers to the January 6, 2000, CIA cable with Mihdhar's US visa information.
14. DOJ Inspector General 9-11 Intelligence Report, 240.
15. DOJ Inspector General 9-11 Intelligence Report, 241.
16. CIA Inspector General 9-11 Accountability Report, 53; DOJ Inspector General 9-11 Intelligence Report, 250.

# ENDNOTES

17. DOJ Inspector General 9-11 Intelligence Report, 240.
18. DOJ Inspector General 9-11 Intelligence Report, 241, 243, 245-247; 9/11 Commission Report, 502.
19. Interview with Mark Rossini.
20. CIA Inspector General 9-11 Accountability Report, 56–57.
21. Stephen Braun, Bob Drogin, Mark Fineman, Lisa Getter, Greg Krikorian, and Robert Lopez, "Haunted by Years of Missed Warnings," *Los Angeles Times*, October 14, 2001; "Statement by the Treasury Department Regarding Today's Designation of Two Leaders of Jemaah Islamiyah," January 24, 2003.
22. 9/11 Commission Staff Statement #2.
23. Lawrence Wright, "The Agent," *The New Yorker*, July 10, 2006; 9/11 Commission Report, 159.
24. Interview with Thomas Drake.
25. CIA Inspector General 9/11 Accountability Report, 56.
26. DOJ Inspector General 9/11 Intelligence Report, 241.
27. 9/11 Commission Report, 354.
28. James Bamford, *A Pretext for War*, 229–230.
29. Stephen Braun, Bob Drogin, Mark Fineman, Lisa Getter, Greg Krikorian, and Robert Lopez, "Haunted by Years of Missed Warnings," *Los Angeles Times*, October 14, 2001.
30. Congressional Joint Inquiry 9/11 Report, 147.
31. George Tenet testimony before Joint Intelligence Committees, US Congress, October 17, 2002; 9-11 Commission Report, 502; DOJ Inspector General 9-11 Intelligence Report, 247–248.
32. DOJ Inspector General 9/11 Intelligence Report, 248.
33. Interview with Mark Rossini.
34. Interviews with multiple sources who worked at CIA's headquarters.
35. Joby Warrick, *The Triple Agent*, 104. A source who worked at CIA's headquarters confirms she was the individual referred to by the CIA Inspector General 9-11 Accountability Report as "the Station's Targeting Branch Chief."
36. Interview with Robert Baer.
37. Interview with John Kiriakou.
38. Interview with John Kiriakou. George Tenet named a "Hendrik V." as the next station chief in his book *At the Center of the Storm*. Van Der Meulen's last name emerged online years later in the context of his work with CIA and counterterror. The authors used it during interviews and were never corrected.
39. Background on the third Alec Station chief was provided by an employee who worked at CIA's headquarters.
40. 9/11 Commission Report, 218–219.
41. Interview with Thomas Drake.
42. Michael Leiter, director of National CounterTerrorism Center, testimony before House of Representatives, US Congress, October 21, 2009.

43. Interview with Thomas Drake.
44. Interview with J. Kirk Wiebe; J. Kirk Wiebe interview by director Friedrich Moser, *A Good American,* February 3, 2017.
45. 9/11 Commission Report, 222.
46. Interview with Robert McFadden; Lawrence Wright, "The Agent," *The New Yorker,* July 10, 2006.
47. Interview with Ali Soufan.
48. Interview with Ali Soufan; DOJ Inspector General 9-11 Intelligence Report, 264–269.
49. Interview with Ali Soufan; DOJ Inspector General 9-11 Intelligence Report, 267–271; 9-11 Commission Report, 267–268, 537.
50. Eleanor Hill, Staff Director, Joint Inquiry Staff, "The Intelligence Community's Knowledge of the September 11 Hijackers Prior to September 11, 2001," Congressional Joint Inquiry, September 20, 2002.
51. Interview with Ali Soufan; DOJ Inspector General 9-11 Intelligence Report, 272–274; 9-11 Commission Report, 267-268, 537.
52. Interview with William Binney; William Binney interview by director Friedrich Moser, *A Good American,* February 3, 2017.
53. Interview with William Binney.
54. Interview with J. Kirk Wiebe.
55. Interview with William Binney; William Binney interview by director Friedrich Moser, *A Good American,* February 3, 2017.
56. Maureen Baginski, NSA biography.
57. Interview with Thomas Drake.
58. Interview with Diane Roark.
59. Interviews with William Binney and J. Kirk Wiebe.
60. Interviews with William Binney, Diane Roark, and J. Kirk Wiebe; "Requirements for the TrailBlazer and ThinThread Systems," Department of Defense Inspector General Audit Report, 2004, obtained through the Freedom of Information Act by the Project on Government Oversight, June 27, 2011.
61. William B. Black Jr., NSA biography.
62. Interview with William Binney; "Requirements for the TrailBlazer and ThinThread Systems," Department of Defense Inspector General Audit Report, 2004.
63. Interviews with William Binney, Diane Roark, and J. Kirk Wiebe.
64. Interviews with John Crane, Thomas Drake, and J. Kirk Wiebe; William Binney, Thomas Drake, Edward Loomis, and J. Kirk Wiebe, "Memorandum For: The President," January 7, 2014; "Requirements for the TrailBlazer and ThinThread Systems," Department of Defense Inspector General Audit Report, 2004.
65. Interview with Thomas Drake.
66. Congressional Joint Inquiry 9/11 Report, 150. Lawrence Wright revealed Wilshere to be the figure mentioned in the Inquiry 9/11 Report in his book *The Looming Tower.*

67. Interview with Mark Rossini.
68. Michael Rolince, personal correspondence.
69. DOJ Inspector General 9-11 Intelligence Report, 282; Substitution for testimony of "Mary," United States of America v. Zacarias Moussaoui, Cr. 01-455-A (US District Court Eastern District of Virginia 2006), July 31, 2006. Shannon was called "Peter" in the DOJ Report and "Dave" in the 9-11 Commission Report, confirmed by sources working at CIA's headquarters to be the individual in question.
70. CIA Inspector General 9-11 Accountability Report, 65.
71. DOJ Inspector General 9/11 Intelligence Report, 284.
72. DOJ Inspector General 9/11 Intelligence Report, 286–7, 293–4. Corsi is called "Donna" and Wilshere "John" by the DOJ Report but has been confirmed by sources working at the FBI as the persons in question.
73. United States of America v. Zacarias Moussaoui, Cr. 01-455-A (US District Court Eastern District of Virginia 2006), Defense Exhibits, Phase 1. Corsi is called "Donna" and Wilshere "John" by the Defense Exhibits but has been confirmed by sources working at the FBI as the persons in question.
74. Interview with Robert McFadden.
75. DOJ Inspector General 9-11 Intelligence Report, 289.
76. Interview with Mark Rossini.
77. DOJ Inspector General 9-11 Intelligence Report, 290.
78. John C. Miller, Michael Stone, *The Cell*, 304; DOJ Inspector General 9-11 Intelligence Report, 291–293.


## CHAPTER 5

1. 9/11 Commission Report, 255–260.
2. Producer/writer James Bamford, "The Spy Factory," *NOVA*, February 3, 2009.
3. 9/11 Commission Report, 237–240.
4. DOJ Inspector General 9-11 Intelligence Report, 298.
5. Interview with Richard A. Clarke; George Tenet, *At the Center of the Storm*, 151–154.
6. CIA Inspector General 9-11 Accountability Report, 67; DOJ Inspector General 9-11 Intelligence Report, 298.
7. Substitution for testimony of "Mary," United States of America v. Zacarias Moussaoui, Cr. 01-455-A (US District Court Eastern District of Virginia 2006), July 31, 2006; CIA Inspector General 9-11 Accountability Report, 67–68.
8. Ron Suskind, *The One Percent Doctrine*, 2; 9-11 Commission Report, 261.
9. Cofer Black testimony before Joint Intelligence Committees, US Congress, September 26, 2002.
10. Dana Priest, "Forgotten Briefings of August 2001," *The Washington Post*, April 15, 2004; George Tenet, *At the Center of the Storm*, 159.

11. 9/11 Commission Report, 275, 541.

12. George Tenet, *At the Center of the Storm*, 201.

13. "The Hijackers We Let Escape," *Newsweek*, June 9, 2002.

14. 9/11 Commission Report, 274.

15. Interview with Thomas Kean.

16. Interviews with William Binney, John Crane, and J. Kirk Wiebe; "Requirements for the TrailBlazer and ThinThread Systems," Department of Defense Inspector General Audit Report, 2004.

17. Interview with Mark Rossini.

18. Lawrence Wright, "The Counter-Terrorist," *The New Yorker*, January 14, 2002.

19. Michael Kirk, *The Man Who Knew*, Frontline, October 3, 2002.

20. Ali Soufan, *The Black Banners*, 249.

21. Interview with Mark Rossini.

22. Interview with Jack Cloonan.

23. Lawrence Wright, *The Looming Tower*, 354–355.

24. Substitution for testimony of "Mary," United States of America v. Zacarias Moussaoui, Cr. 01-455-A (US District Court Eastern District of Virginia 2006), July 31, 2006; DOJ Inspector General 9-11 Intelligence Report, 300–303.

25. DOJ Inspector General 9/11 Intelligence Report, 140–141.

26. DOJ Inspector General 9-11 Intelligence Report, 150.

27. Government Exhibit OG000020.10, United States of America v. Zacarias Moussaoui, Cr. 01-455-A (US District Court Eastern District of Virginia 2006).

28. Simon Henderson, "The Saudis: Friend or Foe?" *Wall Street Journal*, Oct. 22, 2001.

29. 9/11 Commission Report, 262.

30. Interview with Richard A. Clarke.

31. George Tenet testimony before 9-11 Commission, April 14, 2004.

32. Bob Woodward, *Bush at War*, 4.

33. Interview with Thomas Drake.

34. Interview with John Kiriakou.

35. "CIA Log Entries from 9/11 and Related Documents," 9/11 Commission; Blee's presence in Afghanistan is based on a report by Ahmed Quraishi, "America's and Pakistan's Joint Defeat in Afghanistan," *Daily Pakistan Global*, May 13, 2018, and the purpose of Blee's visit there is from Peter Dale Scott, "Intelligence Cooking By the Deep State," Voltairenet.org, October 4, 2012.

36. Interview with Mark Rossini. Rossini referred to Bikowsky as "the redhead."

37. George Tenet, *At the Center of the Storm*, 163. Authors have made inferences regarding the sources in the room who stated the "plane into CIA headquarters" and the "fourth plane" information.

38. George Tenet, *At the Center of the Storm*, 164.

39. "CIA Log Entries from 9/11 and Related Documents," 9/11 Commission.

40. Interview with Richard Clarke; George Tenet, *At the Center of the Storm*, 164–165.

# ENDNOTES

41. Interview with Mark Rossini.
42. Interview with John Kiriakou.
43. Testimony of Steve Bongardt to the Joint Inquiry, US Congress, September 20, 2002.
44. Testimony of Steve Bongardt to the Joint Inquiry, US Congress, September 20, 2002.
45. Interview with Mark Rossini.
46. George Tenet, *At the Center of the Storm*, 167; Anthony Summers and Robbyn Swan, "Richard Clarke 9/11 Interview," *The Daily Beast*, August 12, 2011.
47. Interview with Col. Lawrence Wilkerson.
48. Bob Woodward, *Bush at War*, 33; Richard Clarke, *Against All Enemies*, 21–22.
49. Richard Clarke, *Against All Enemies*, 23–24.
50. Handwritten notes by Stephen Cambone obtained by Thad Anderson through US Freedom of Information Act, September 3, 2002.
51. Richard Clarke, *Against All Enemies*, 24.
52. Handwritten notes by Stephen Cambone obtained by Thad Anderson through US Freedom of Information Act, September 3, 2002.
53. Interview with Richard Clarke.
54. Interview with Robert McFadden; Ali Soufan, *The Black Banners*, 286.

## CHAPTER 6

1. Interviews with William Binney and Thomas Drake; William Binney interview by director Friedrich Moser, *A Good American*, February 3, 2017.
2. Interview with Pasquale D'Amuro; "The FBI's 9/11 Role by the Numbers," FBI website.
3. Interview with Pasquale D'Amuro; "Facts and Figures 2003: Counterterrorism," FBI website.
4. Interview with Pasquale D'Amuro.
5. Interview with Thomas Drake.
6. Witnessed by NSA employee Karen Stewart, interview. The spirit of the encounter she describes that morning was seconded by those of two employees at NSA's headquarters who were interviewed.
7. Interview with Thomas Drake.
8. Remarks by Gen. Michael Hayden, National Press Club, January 23, 2006.
9. Interview with Thomas Drake.
10. In *Playing to the Edge,* Gen. Michael Hayden wrote, "My first encounter with the president was that September 2001 morning when George Tenet ushered me into the Oval to discuss what more NSA could do." Hayden's use of the words "what more" is telling here, as during his nomination hearings for CIA director before the House Intelligence Committee on May 18, 2006, he was asked by Senator Feinstein, "What was your role in *the initiation* [emphasis ours] of the program at issue, the Terrorists Surveillance Program?" There, he explained, "I was asked by Director

Tenet, 'Could you do more?' I said, 'Not within current law.' He says, 'Well, *what could you do more?*' [emphasis ours] And I put it together with, as I said, technologically possible, operationally relevant, now the question of lawfulness."

11. Dan Balz and Bob Woodward, "America's Chaotic Road to War," *The Washington Post*, January 27, 2002; George Tenet, *At the Center of the Storm*, 176.

12. Michael Hayden, *Playing to the Edge*, 371.

13. Michael Hayden testimony before House of Representatives, US Congress, May 18, 2006; Michael Hayden interview by Dana Priest, produced and directed by Michael Kirk, *Are We Safer?*, *Frontline*, January 18, 2011.

14. George Tenet, *At the Center of the Storm*, 237.

15. Michael Hayden interview by Mark Mansfield, "Reflections on Service," CIA website, June 2010.

16. Remarks by Gen. Michael Hayden, National Press Club, January 23, 2006.

17. Keynote address by Gen. Michael Hayden, Washington and Lee University, January 28, 2015.

18. Interview with Col. Lawrence Wilkerson; Dan Balz and Bob Woodward, "At Camp David, Advise and Dissent," *The Washington Post*, January 31, 2002; George Tenet, *At the Center of the Storm*, 177.

19. Interview with Col. Lawrence Wilkerson.

20. Interview with Col. Lawrence Wilkerson; Dan Balz and Bob Woodward, "At Camp David, Advise and Dissent," *The Washington Post*, January 31, 2002; George Tenet, *At the Center of the Storm*, 177; 9/11 Commission Report, 332.

21. Testimony of George Tenet to 9-11 Commission, March 24, 2004.

22. Interview with Col. Lawrence Wilkerson; Dan Balz and Bob Woodward, "At Camp David, Advise and Dissent," *The Washington Post*, January 31, 2002; Dan Eggen and Peter Slevin, "FBI Nominee Lauded for Tenacity," *The Washington Post*, July 31, 2001; George Tenet, *At the Center of the Storm*, 178.

23. George Tenet, *At the Center of the Storm*, 178.

24. Interview with Col. Lawrence Wilkerson; Dan Balz and Bob Woodward, "At Camp David, Advise and Dissent," *The Washington Post*, January 31, 2002.

25. Caren Bohan, Mark Hosenball, Tabassum Zakaria, and Missy Ryan, "The Bin Laden Kill Plan," Reuters, May 12, 2001; 9/11 Commission Report, 333.

26. Interview with Mark Rossini; David Kocieniewski, "A Nation Challenged: A Funeral," *The New York Times*, September 29, 2001.

27. Interviews with multiple employees at CIA's headquarters; "President George W. Bush's Remarks CIA Workforce," CIA website.

28. Interviews with multiple employees at CIA's headquarters; "President George W. Bush's Remarks CIA Workforce," CIA website.

29. "Flashback: Sept. 26, 2001—CIA is 'First In' after September 11th Attacks," CIA website.

30. Interview with Mark Rossini.

31. Michael Morrell, *The Great War Of Our Time*, 73.

32. Interview with Fulton Armstrong; Duncan Graham, Iain Hollingshead, "The Bin Laden Hunter," *The Telegraph*, May 21, 2011.

33. Interviews with multiple sources who worked at CIA's headquarters.

34. Interviews with John Kiriakou and Mark Rossini; Ali Soufan, *The Black Banners*, 484.

35. Federal Bureau of Investigation (FBI), "Overview of the 9/11 Investigation Slide Show," 2014; twenty-eight pages declassified on August 5, 2016, from Congressional Joint Inquiry 9-11 Report.

36. Interview with Pasquale D'Amuro.

37. Interview with Thomas Drake.

38. Interview with "Nicholas," NSA CounterTerror Shop employee.

39. Interview with Thomas Drake.

40. Interviews with William Binney, Edward Loomis, and J. Kirk Wiebe; J. Kirk Wiebe interview by director Friedrich Moser, *A Good American*, February 3, 2017.

41. Interviews with William Binney and J. Kirk Wiebe.

42. Interview with Thomas Drake.

43. Interviews with Pasquale D'Amuro and Jack Cloonan.

44. David Johnston and Philip Shenon, "Preventative Steps," *New York Times*, October 9, 2001.

45. Interview with Thomas Drake.

46. "Unclassified Report on the President's Surveillance Program," July 10, 2009.

47. Interview with J. Kirk Wiebe; J. Kirk Wiebe interview by director Friedrich Moser, *A Good American*, February 3, 2017.

48. Dafna Linzer, "Secret Surveillance May Have Occurred Before Authorization," *The Washington Post*, January 4, 2006; Michael Hayden, *Playing to the Edge*, 77–79.

49. Sen. Mark Kirk interview by director Michael Kirk, *United States of Secrets*, *Frontline*, May 13, 2014; "Unclassified Report on the President's Surveillance Program," July 10, 2009.

50. "Unclassified Report on the President's Surveillance Program," July 10, 2009.

51. Interviews with William Binney and J. Kirk Wiebe.

52. Interviews with Pasquale D'Amuro, Mark Rossini, and Lawrence Wright.

53. Philip Shenon, *The Commission*, 139–140.

54. CIA Inspector General 9-11 Accountability Report, 53.

55. CIA Inspector General 9-11 Accountability Report, 53.

## CHAPTER 7

1. Interview with Pasquale D'Amuro.

2. Yaniv Barzilai, "How Bin Laden Escaped in 2001—The Lessons of Tora Bora," *The Daily Beast*, December 15, 2013; Peter Bergen, "The Account of How We Nearly Caught Osama bin Laden in 2001," *The New Republic*, December 30, 2009; Susan Glasser, "The Battle of Tora Bora," *The Washington Post*, February 9, 2002.

3. Peter Bergen, "The Account of How We Nearly Caught Osama bin Laden in 2001," *The New Republic*, December 30, 2009; Gordon Corera, "Bin Laden's Tora Bora escape, just months after 9/11," BBC, July 21, 2011; Craig Whitlock, "Al Qaeda Detainee's Mysterious Release," *The Washington Post*, January 30, 2006.

4. Peter Bergen, "The Account of How We Nearly Caught Osama bin Laden in 2001," *The New Republic*, December 30, 2009; Craig Whitlock, "Al Qaeda Detainee's Mysterious Release," *The Washington Post*, January 30, 2006.

5. Ron Suskind, *The One Percent Doctrine*, 74; Peter Bergen, "The Account of How We Nearly Caught Osama bin Laden in 2001," *The New Republic*, December 30, 2009.

6. Ron Suskind, *The One Percent Doctrine*, 74.

7. Peter Bergen, "The Account of How We Nearly Caught Osama bin Laden in 2001," *The New Republic*, December 30, 2009; Ron Suskind, *The One Percent Doctrine*, 58; "Tora Bora Revisited: How We Failed To Get Bin Laden and Why it Matters Today," report by majority staff of the Committee on Foreign Relations, US Senate, November 30, 2009.

8. Bob Woodward, "CIA Led Way With Cash Handouts," *Washington Post*, November 18, 2001; Gary Berntsen interview by director Michael Kirk, *The Dark Side, Frontline*, June 20, 2006.

9. Peter Bergen, "The Account of How We Nearly Caught Osama bin Laden in 2001, *The New Republic*, December 30, 2009; "Tora Bora Revisited: How We Failed To Get Bin Laden and Why it Matters Today," report by majority staff of the Committee on Foreign Relations, US Senate, November 30, 2009.

10. Gary Berntsen and Ralph Pezzullo, *Jawbreaker*, 296–297.

11. Gary Berntsen and Ralph Pezzullo, *Jawbreaker*, 296–297.

12. Henry A. Crumpton, *The Art of Intelligence*, 261; Gary Berntsen and Ralph Pezzullo, *Jawbreaker,* 296–297.

13. Peter Bergen, "The Account of How We Nearly Caught Osama bin Laden in 2001," *The New Republic*, December 30, 2009. Greer wrote under the pseudonym "Dalton Fury," and his real name has been revealed since his death.

14. Interview with Pasquale D'Amuro.

15. Interview with Pasquale D'Amuro; Ali Soufan, *The Black Banners*, 450–451.

16. Jason Vest, "Pray and Tell," *The American Prospect*, June 19, 2005. An employee who worked at CIA's headquarters stated the person in the Vest article was Blee.

17. Interview with Robert McFadden; John Barry, "A Tortured Debate," *Newsweek*, June 20, 2004; David Corn and Michael Isikoff, Hubris, 121; James Risen, *State of War*, 29.

18. Dan Eggen and Peter Slevin, "FBI Nominee Lauded for Tenacity," *The Washington Post*, July 31, 2001.

19. Interview with Mark Rossini.

20. Interview with Pasquale D'Amuro.

21. Director Michael Kirk, *The Dark Side, Frontline*, June 20, 2006.

22. Interview with a source who had worked with Casey.

23. Interviews with two sources who worked at CIA's headquarters.

24. Douglas Jehl, "High Qaeda Aide Retracted Claim of Link With Iraq," *The New York Times,* July 31, 2004.

25. Walter Pincus, "Newly Released Data Undercut Prewar Claims," *The Washington Post*, November 6, 2005.

26. Douglas Jehl, "High Qaeda Aide Retracted Claim of Link With Iraq," *The New York Times*, July 31, 2004.

27. Interview with Robert McFadden; Ali Soufan, *The Black Banners*, 445.

28. James Risen, *State of War*, 28.

29. John Barry, Michael Hirsch and Michael Isikoff, "The Roots of Torture," *Newsweek*, May 24, 2004; Dana Priest and Joe Stephens, "Secret World of US Interrogation," *The Washington Post*, May 11, 2004.

30. Interview with John Kiriakou.

31. Amrit Singh, "Globalizing Torture," Open Society Justice Initiative, 2013.

32. Brian Ross and Richard Esposito, "CIA's Harsh Interrogation Techniques Described" ABC News, November 18, 2005; Tim Mak, "Inside the CIA's Sadistic Dungeon," *The Daily Beast*, December 9, 2014.

33. Matthew Cole, "Bin Laden Expert Accused of Shaping CIA Deception on 'Torture' Program," nbcnews.com, December 16, 2014.

34. "Counterterrorism Detention and Interrogation Activities (September 2001–October 2003)," CIA Inspector General.

35. "Inquiry Into the Treatment of Detainees in US Custody," Senate Armed Services Committee, 2008, xiii, 6–7; Peter Finn and Joby Warrick, "Harsh Tactics Readied Before Their Approval," *The Washington Post*, April 22, 2009.

36. Interview with John Kiriakou.

37. Interviews with William Binney and Diane Roark.

38. Jane Mayer, "The Secret Sharer," *The New Yorker*, May 23, 2011.

39. Diane Roark interview by director Michael Kirk, *United States of Secrets, Frontline*, May 13, 2014.

40. Interviews with William Binney, Diane Roark, and J. Kirk Wiebe.

41. Interviews with William Binney and Diane Roark.

42. Interview with Diane Roark.

43. Interview with John Kiriakou.

44. Interview with John Kiriakou; Ali Soufan, *The Black Banners*, 383.

45. Interview with John Kiriakou; Michael Jacobson and Dana Lesemann, "Document no. 17," 9-11 Commission, June 6, 2003, found and posted to 28pages.org by Brian McGlinchey, April 19, 2006; Federal Bureau of Investigation (FBI), "Overview of the 9/11 Investigation Slide Show," 2014; twenty-eight pages declassified on August 5, 2016, from Congressional Joint Inquiry 9-11 Report.

46. Gerald Posner, *Why America Slept*, 208–209.

47. Gerald Posner, *Why America Slept*, 208–209.

48. Interview with John Kiriakou.

49. Interview with Mark Rossini.

50. Ali Soufan, *The Black Banners*, 495. Soufan never referred to the woman as "Jennifer Matthews." Other sources say Matthews was a key leader of the HVTU at this time, and she has been reported to have been present at the Zubaydah site.

51. Jennifer Matthews, public records.

52. Interview with employee who worked with Bikowsky and Matthews at Alec Station.

53. Interviews with Pasquale D'Amuro and John Kiriakou.

54. Interview with Pasquale D'Amuro; Ali Soufan, *The Black Banners*, 376–378.

55. Ali Soufan, *The Black Banners*, 386–387.

56. Ali Soufan, *The Black Banners*, 394. Soufan refers to Mitchell as "Boris."

57. Dexter Filkins, "The New CIA Deputy Chief's Black-Site Past," *The New Yorker*, February 3, 2017; Madhvi Mavadiya, "Who Is Gina Hapsel? Trump's CIA Director Nominee Revealed," *The Daily Mail*, May 10, 2018; Matthew Rosenberg, "New CIA. Deputy Director, Gina Haspel, Had Leading Role in Torture," *The New York Times*, February 2, 2017.

58. David Johnston and Mark Mazzetti, "A Window Into CIA's Embrace of Secret Jails," *The New York Times*, August 12, 2009.

59. Ali Soufan, *The Black Banners*, 394–395.

60. Interview with Pasquale D'Amuro.

61. Ali Soufan, *The Black Banners*, 398–422.

62. Interview with Pasquale D'Amuro; Ali Soufan, *The Black Banners*, 422–423.

63. Elisabeth Bumiller, "Saudi Prince Bluntly Tells Bush to Temper Support for Israel," *The New York Times*, April 25, 2002; Joel Mowbray, "Foggy Bottom's Friends," *The Wall Street Journal*, October 13, 2003; Michael Isikoff and Evan Thomas, "The Saudi Money Trail," *Newsweek*, December 2, 2002.

64. Michael Jacobson and Dana Lesemann, "Document no. 17," 9-11 Commission, June 6, 2003; Federal Bureau of Investigation (FBI), "Overview of the 9/11 Investigation Slide Show," 2014; twenty-eight pages declassified on August 5, 2016, from Congressional Joint Inquiry 9-11 Report; Michael Isikoff and Evan Thomas, "The Saudi Money Trail," *Newsweek*, December 2, 2002.

65. Interview with John Kiriakou.

66. Interview with Col. Lawrence Wilkerson.

67. Jan Greenburg, Howard Rosenberg, Ariane De Vogue, "Bush Aware of Adviser's Interrogation Talks," ABC News, April 11, 2008.

68. Interview with Pasquale D'Amuro.

69. "Counterterrorism Detention and Interrogation Activities (September 2001–October 2003)," CIA Inspector General, 36–37.

70. "Interrogation," *The Washington Post*, January 21, 1968.

71. Michael Jacobson and Dana Lesemann, "Document no. 17," 9-11 Commission, June 6, 2003; Federal Bureau of Investigation (FBI), "Overview of the 9/11 Investigation Slide Show," 2014; twenty-eight pages declassified on August 5, 2016, from Congressional Joint Inquiry 9-11 Report.

72. Richard Simon and Peter Wallsten, "Bush's Prewar Funding is Criticized," *The Los Angeles Times*, April 20, 2004; "The Downing Street Memo," July 23, 2002, published by *The Sunday Times* on May 1, 2005.

73. Interviews with multiple employees at CIA's headquarters; "Saudi Prince Found Dead in Desert," *Dawn*, July 31, 2002.

74. Barton Gellman and Walter Pincus, "Depiction of Threat Outgrew Supporting Evidence," *The Washington Post*, August 10, 2003.

75. Michael Jacobson and Dana Lesemann, "Document no. 17," 9-11 Commission, June 6, 2003; Federal Bureau of Investigation (FBI), "Overview of the 9/11 Investigation Slide Show," 2014; twenty-eight pages declassified on August 5, 2016, from Congressional Joint Inquiry 9-11 Report.

76. CNN/*USA Today*/Gallup poll, March 24, 2003.

77. Interview with John Kiriakou.

78. Michael D'Andrea was revealed publicly by Matt Apuzzo, Mark Mazzetti, "Deep Support in Washington for CIA's Drone Missions," *The New York Times*, April 25, 2015; interview with John Kiriakou, who referred to D'Andrea as "the Wolf."

79. Interview with John Kiriakou.

80. Interview with Ken Silverstein; Ken Silverstein, "Next Stop: Baghdad Station," *Harper's*, March 23, 2007; Ken Silverstein, "Missed Appointments: The CIA Responds," *Harper's*, April 16, 2007.

81. Interview with John Kiriakou. Marty Martin first named himself as a source to Mark Apuzzo and Mark Mazzetti, the Associated Press, May 2, 2011. Martin later appeared in the documentary *Manhunt*.

82. Interview with John Kiriakou. Marty Martin first named himself as a source to Mark Apuzzo and Mark Mazzetti, the Associated Press, May 2, 2011. Martin later appeared in the documentary *Manhunt*.

83. Interview with an employee at CIA's headquarters.

84. Interview with Col. Lawrence Wilkerson.

## CHAPTER 8

1. Interview with Eleanor Hill.

2. Interview with Thomas Kean.

3. Footnote 44, chapter 6, *9-11 Commission Final Report*, 502.

4. Interview with Thomas Drake.

5. Interview with Thomas Drake.

6. Interview with Thomas Drake.

7. Interview with Diane Roark.

8. Interview with Sen. Bob Graham; Gen. Michael Hayden testimony to Joint Intelligence Committees, US Congress, October 17, 2002.

9. Interview with Sen. Bob Graham; Bob Graham, Mark Nussbaum, *Intelligence Matters*, 139.

10. Interviews with Eleanor Hill and Mark Rossini.

11. Interview with Eleanor Hill.

12. Testimony of Steve Bongardt and Thomas Wilshere to the Joint Inquiry, US Congress, September 20, 2002.

13. Testimony of Steve Bongardt and Thomas Wilshere to the Joint Inquiry, US Congress, September 20, 2002.

14. Testimony of Steve Bongardt and Thomas Wilshere to the Joint Inquiry, US Congress, September 20, 2002.

15. Lawrence Wright, "The Agent," *The New Yorker*, July 10, 2006.

16. Testimony of Steve Bongardt and Thomas Wilshere to the Joint Inquiry, US Congress, September 20, 2002.

17. Testimony of Michael Hayden, Robert Mueller, and George Tenet to the Joint Inquiry, US Congress, June 18, 2002.

18. Testimony of Michael Hayden, Robert Mueller, and George Tenet to the Joint Inquiry, US Congress, June 18, 2002.

19. Michael Hayden, *Playing to the Edge*, 44.

20. Interviews with William Binney, Edward Loomis, and J. Kirk Wiebe.

21. Interview with Thomas Drake.

22. "Bush says he signed NSA Wiretap Order," CNN, December 17, 2005; Eric Rangeman, "Ex-AT&T employee: NSA snooping Internet traffic too," *Ars Technica*, November 11, 2007; Hepting v. AT&T (US 9th Circuit 2006).

23. Interviews with William Binney, John Crane, Thomas Drake, Edward Loomis, Diane Roark, and J. Kirk Wiebe; "Requirements for the TrailBlazer and ThinThread Systems," Department of Defense Inspector General Audit Report, 2004, obtained through the Freedom of Information Act by the Project on Government Oversight, June 27, 2011.

24. Interview with Thomas Drake.

25. Interview with Diane Roark.

26. Interview with Mark Rossini; Jeff Stein, "FBI Agent: The CIA Could Have Stopped 9/11," *Newsweek*, June 19, 2015.

27. "Counterterrorism Detention and Interrogation Activities (September 2001-October 2003)," CIA Inspector General, 1.

28. James L. Pavitt, Patriot Defense Group biography.

29. "Counterterrorism Detention and Interrogation Activities (September 2001-October 2003)," CIA Inspector General.

30. Dana Priest, "CIA Avoids Scrutiny of Detainee Treatment," *Washington Post*, March 3, 2005; Adam Goldman and Kathy Gannon, "Death shed light on CIA 'Salt Pit' near Kabul," NBC, March 28, 2010.

31. Multiple sources who worked for the CIA state that Blee left his chief of station position in Afghanistan in 2002 prior to Rahman's death, though the black site itself and its operations would have been created while he was in charge of the area. One source in a position to know claimed Blee next briefly became chief of station in Pakistan before taking the liaison job at FBI headquarters. Multiple sources who worked at FBI's headquarters recall Blee working there by mid-2003.

32. Interview with John Kiriakou.

33. Dana Priest, "CIA Avoids Scrutiny of Detainee Treatment," *The Washington Post*, March 3, 2005; Adam Goldman and Kathy Gannon, "Death shed light on CIA 'Salt Pit' near Kabul," NBC, March 28, 2010.

34. The report of the CIA Inspector General, "Counterterrorism Detention and Interrogation Activities (September 2001-October 2003)," mentions that outside of the Pavitt information, "Separately, OIG received information that some employees were concerned that certain covert Agency activities at an overseas detention and interrogation site might involve violations of human rights." An OIG Vaughn index released in response to a Freedom of Information Act request by the ACLU on October 7, 2003, and May 25, 2004, revealed a "Spot report discussing interrogation of al-Nashiri" as early as November 20, 2002.

35. Jane Mayer, *The Dark Side*, 272–273. Mayer did not name Bikowsky in the account, but multiple sources who worked with Bikowsky allege she is the individual described.

36. Interview with John Kiriakou.

37. Jane Mayer, *The Dark Side*, 272–273.

38. Interview with former employee of Alec Station.

39. "Alleged Secret Detentions in Council of Europe Member States," Council of Europe, 2006; Jane Mayer, *The Dark Side*, 272–273; Klaus Brill, John Goetz, and Frederik Obermaier, "Inside a Secret CIA Prison in the Polish Countryside," *Süddeutsche Zeitung*, February 8, 2013.

40. Adam Goldman, "The Hidden History of the CIA's Prison in Poland," *The Washington Post*, January 23, 2014.

41. Khaled Shaikh Mohammed interview by the International Committee of the Red Cross, "ICRC Report on the Treatment of Fourteen 'High Value Detainees' in CIA Custody," 2007; "Committee Study of the CIA's Detention and Interrogation Program," US Senate, 2014; "Alleged Secret Detentions in Council of Europe Member States," Council of Europe, 2006.

42. Jane Mayer, *The Dark Side*, 273.

43. "Counterterrorism Detention and Interrogation Activities (September 2001-October 2003)," CIA Inspector General; "Committee Study of the CIA's Detention and

Interrogation Program," US Senate, 2014, 44; Patrice Taddonio, "Why You Never Saw the CIA's Interrogation Tapes," pbs.org, May 19, 2015.

44. Interview with Thomas Kean; Thomas Kean, and Lee Hamilton, "Stonewalled by the CIA," *The New York Times*, January 2, 2008.

45. Interview with Mark Rossini.

46. DOJ Inspector General 9/11 Intelligence Report, 226.

47. DOJ Inspector General 9/11 Intelligence Report, 241–255; CIA IG 9/11 Accountability Report, 53–54.

48. Michael Isikoff, "The White House Is Battling To Keep a Report on the Terror Attacks Secret," *Newsweek*, April 29, 2003.

49. "Improving Intelligence," *PBS Newshour*, December 11, 2002.

50. CIA Inspector General 9/11 Accountability Report, 53–54.

51. DOJ Inspector General 9-11 Intelligence Report, 227.

52. Louis J. Freeh, Howard Means, *My FBI*, 297.

53. Testimony of George Tenet before the 9/11 Commission, April 14, 2004.

54. Philip Shenon, *The Commission*, 360.

55. Interview with Thomas Kean; Philip Shenon, *The Commission*, 360.

56. Testimony of George Tenet before the 9/11 Commission, April 14, 2004.

57. Souad Mekhennet and Don Van Natta Jr., "German's Claim of Kidnapping Brings Investigation of US Link," *The New York Times*, January 9, 2005.

58. Matt Apuzzo and Adam Goldman, "CIA officers make grave mistakes, get promoted," *Associated Press*, February 9, 2011.

59. European Court of Human Rights, "CASE OF EL-MASRI v. THE FORMER YUGOSLAV REPUBLIC OF MACEDONIA," December 13, 2012.

60. Souad Mekhennet and Don Van Natta Jr., "German's Claim of Kidnapping Brings Investigation of US Link," *The New York Times*, January 9, 2005; Jane Mayer, *The Dark Side*, 282; European Court of Human Rights, "CASE OF EL-MASRI v. THE FORMER YUGOSLAV REPUBLIC OF MACEDONIA," December 13, 2012.

61. Interviews with multiple employees of CIA's Alec Station.

62. Jane Mayer, *The Dark Side*, 283; Matt Apuzzo and Adam Goldman, "CIA officers make grave mistakes, get promoted," Associated Press, February 9, 2011. Apuzzo and Goldman did not name Bikowsky, but multiple sources who worked with Bikowsky allege she is the individual described.

63. Jane Mayer, *The Dark Side*, 283–284; European Court of Human Rights, "CASE OF EL-MASRI v. THE FORMER YUGOSLAV REPUBLIC OF MACEDONIA," December 13, 2012.

64. Jane Mayer, *The Dark Side*, 283–284.

65. Jane Mayer, *The Dark Side,* 285; Matt Apuzzo and Adam Goldman, "CIA officers make grave mistakes, get promoted," Associated Press, February 9, 2011. Apuzzo and Goldman did not name Bikowsky, but multiple sources who worked with Bikowsky allege she is the individual described.

66. Jane Mayer, *The Dark Side*, 286; European Court of Human Rights, "CASE OF EL-MASRI v. THE FORMER YUGOSLAV REPUBLIC OF MACEDONIA," December 13, 2012.

67. Jane Mayer, *The Dark Side*, 286.

68. Interview with Thomas Drake.

69. Philip Shenon, *The Commission*, 156.

70. "Joint Response to Draft IG 9/11 Report," declassified by the CIA on June 12, 2015, in response to a Freedom of Information Act lawsuit by Jason Leopold, signed by seventeen former or current CIA employees; Dafna Linzer and Walter Pincus, "CIA Rejects Discipline for 9/11 Failures," *The Washington Post*, October 6, 2005. "Seventeen officers mentioned in the OIG 9-11 report, including all 16 of the current or former CTC officers cited by the IG, have signed the above response," "Joint Response to OIG Report," July 4, 2005.

71. George Tenet, *At the Center of the Storm*, 481–482.

72. George Tenet, *At the Center of the Storm*, 478.

73. "Counterterrorism Detention and Interrogation Activities (September 2001–October 2003)," CIA Inspector General; Jane Mayer, *The Dark Side*, 288–289.

74. "Counterterrorism Detention and Interrogation Activities (September 2001–October 2003)," CIA Inspector General.

75. Transcript of White House Medal of Freedom ceremony, December 14, 2004.

## CHAPTER 9

1. Interview with John Kiriakou; Jose A. Rodriguez Jr., *Hard Measures*, 2012.

2. Gina Haspel was named publicly by CIA director Mike Pompeo on February 2, 2017; interview with John Kiriakou, who referred to Haspel by her first name.

3. Interviews with multiple employees of CIA's headquarters; John Cook, "Chief of CIA's 'Global Jihad Unit' Revealed Online," Gawker.com, September 22, 2011.

4. Interview with former employee at CIA's headquarters.

5. Interview with John Kiriakou.

6. Interview with Mark Rossini.

7. Walter Pincus, "Negroponte's First Job is Showing Who's Boss," *The Washington Post*, March 1, 2005.

8. Interview with Mark Rossini; "FBI Announces New Role for Maureen A. Baginski," FBI press release, August 11, 2005.

9. Ewen Macaskill and Dominic Rushe "Snowden document reveals key role of companies in NSA data collection," *The Guardian*, November 1, 2013.

10. Maureen Baginski, National Security Partners biography.

11. Siobhan Gorman, "Second-Ranking NSA Official Forced Out of Job By Director," *The Baltimore Sun*, May 31, 2006.

12. Interview with Mark Rossini.

13. Steve Bongardt, LinkedIn profile.
14. Interview with Pasquale D'Amuro; Ali Soufan, *The Black Banners*, 515–516.
15. Interview with Pasquale D'Amuro.
16. Seymour Hersh, "The General's Report," *The New Yorker*, June 25, 2007.
17. "Joint Response to Draft IG 9/11 Report," January 13, 2005.
18. Douglas Jehl "Review at CIA and Justice Brings No 9/11 Punishment," *The New York Times*, September 14, 2004.
19. Douglas Jehl "CIA Chief Seeks Change in Inspector's 9/11 Report," *The New York Times*, January 7, 2005.
20. CIA Inspector General 9-11 Accountability Report, vi; "Joint Response to OIG Report," July 4, 2005, declassified by the CIA on June 12, 2015.
21. Porter J. Goss, "Statement on CIA Office of the Inspector General Report," CIA press release, October 5, 2005; "CIA Releases Declassified Documents Related to 9/11 Attacks," CIA press release, June 12, 2015.
22. Joby Warrick, *The Triple Agent*, 23–24.
23. "Joint Response to Draft IG 9/11 Report," January 13, 2005, declassified by the CIA on June 12, 2015.
24. "Joint Response to Draft IG 9/11 Report," January 13, 2005, declassified by the CIA on June 12, 2015.
25. "Joint Response to Draft IG 9/11 Report," January 13, 2005, declassified by the CIA on June 12, 2015.
26. "Joint Response to OIG Report," July 4, 2005, declassified by the CIA on June 12, 2015.
27. Interview with employee who worked at CIA's headquarters.
28. Douglas Jehl and David Johnston, "Within CIA, Worry of Prosecution for Conduct," *The New York Times*, February 27, 2005.
29. Interviews with multiple employees at CIA's headquarters.
30. Interview with Mark Rossini, who referred to Bikowsky as "the redhead."
31. Interviews with multiple sources who worked at CIA's CTC; Michael D'Andrea was revealed publicly by Matt Apuzzo, Mark Mazzetti, "Deep Support in Washington for CIA's Drone Missions," *The New York Times*, April 25, 2015.
32. Interviews with multiple sources who worked at CIA's CTC.
33. Interview with former employee of CIA's Alec Station. "The Wolf" was the nickname of the character based on D'Andrea in the movie *Zero Dark Thirty*, according to John Cook, "Why Won't the Post Name Counterterrorism Chief Michael D'Andrea?", *Gawker*, March 26, 2015. "The Undertaker" nickname was reported by Nicholas Schou, "Outing the CIA's 'Undertaker' Michael D'Andrea," *Newsweek*, June 28, 2016. "The Dark Prince" nickname comes from Adam Goldman and Matthew Rosenberg, "C.I.A. Names the 'Dark Prince' to Run Iran Operations, Signaling a Tougher Stance," *The New York Times*, June 2, 2017.
34. Bill Forman, "Covert Intelligence," *MetroActive*, March 1, 2006.

35. Jonathon Karl, "'High-Value' Detainees Transferred to Guantanamo," ABC News, September 6, 2006.

36. "McCain, Bush Agree on Torture Ban," CNN, December 15, 2005.

37. Joby Warrick and Walter Pincus, "Station Chief Made Appeal to Destroy CIA Tapes," *The Washington Post*, January 16, 2008.

38. Joby Warrick and Walter Pincus, "Station Chief Made Appeal to Destroy CIA Tapes," *The Washington Post*, January 16, 2008.

39. Joby Warrick and Walter Pincus, "Station Chief Made Appeal to Destroy CIA Tapes," *The Washington Post*, January 16, 2008.

40. Michael Isikoff, "The Interrogation Tapes," *Newsweek*, December 10, 2007.

41. Matt Apuzzo and Adam Goldman, "Destruction of Torture Videotapes Documented in CIA Email," Associated Press, April 16, 2010.

42. Joe Hagan, "The United States of America vs. Bill Keller," *New York Magazine*, September 18, 2006.

43. Transcript of George W. Bush address to the media, December 17, 2005.

44. Transcript of Hayden comments at National Press Club, "Balancing Intelligence, Security, and Privacy," January 23, 2006.

45. Jane Mayer ,"The Secret Sharer," *The New Yorker*, May 23, 2011.

46. David Johnston and Scott Shane, "CIA Employee Fired for Alleged Leak," *The New York Times*, April 21, 2006.

47. David Johnston and Scott Shane, "CIA Employee Fired for Alleged Leak," *The New York Times*, April 21, 2006.

48. Andrea Mitchell on *Countdown with Keith Olbermann*, April 24, 2006.

49. Interview with John Kiriakou.

50. R. Jeffrey Smith and Dafna Linzer, "Dismissed CIA Officer Denies Leak Role," *The Washington Post*, April 25, 2006.

51. Interview with Ken Silverstein; Ken Silverstein, "Meet the CIA's new Baghdad Station Chief," *Harper's*, January 28, 2007; Ken Silverstein, "Baghdad Chief Out," *Harper's*, February 2, 2007; Ken Silverstein, "Next Stop: Baghdad Station," *Harper's*, March 23, 2007; Ken Silverstein, "Missed Appointments: The CIA Responds," *Harper's*, April 16, 2007.

52. Interview with former coworker of Richard Blee; Ken Silverstein, "Baghdad Chief Out," *Harper's*, February 2, 2007.

53. Siobhan Gorman, "Management shortcomings seen at NSA," *The Baltimore Sun*, May 6, 2007.

54. Interview with Thomas Drake.

55. Jane Mayer, "The Secret Sharer," *The New Yorker*, May 23, 2011.

56. Interview with Thomas Drake.

57. Interview with Diane Roark.

58. Interviews with William Binney, Edward Loomis, and J. Kirk Wiebe.

59. Interview with John Crane.

60. Interview with Thomas Drake.
61. Interview with John Kiriakou; President George W. Bush comments to the press, Oval Office, October 5, 2007.
62. Interview with John Kiriakou.
63. Interview with John Kiriakou; John Kiriakou interview by Brian Ross, ABC News, December 10, 2007; Brian Ross and Richard Esposito, "CIA Efforts to Prosecute Whistle-Blower Spy Stopped," ABC News, December 11, 2007.
64. Scott Horton, "When Does an FBI Investigation Look Like Omertà?" harpers.org, December 21, 2007.
65. L. Gordon Crovitz, *Three Felonies a Day: How the Feds Target the Innocent.*
66. Interview with John Kiriakou.
67. Press release, "Obama Pledges Most Transparent and Accountable Administration in History," August 15, 2007; Reuters, "Factbox: Has Obama delivered on his 2008 campaign promises?" October 28, 2011.
68. Interview with John Kiriakou.
69. Interview with John Kiriakou, who referred to Bikowsky as "the redhead"; claim that she was placed in cover status to be sent overseas is confirmed by others who worked with Bikowsky.
70. Interview with John Kiriakou.
71. Interview with multiple employees at CIA's headquarters; Joby Warrick, *The Triple Agent,* 24–25; Warrick does not mention Bikowsky by name, but his descriptions of a CIA manager who joined Jennifer Matthews in London align with accounts by the previously mentioned employees of CIA.
72. Joby Warrick, *The Triple Agent,* 6–8.
73. Interview with employee at CIA headquarters.
74. Interview with employee who worked at CIA's headquarters, who referred to Bikowsky as "the redhead."
75. Interview with person present at memorial service; Greg Miller, "In Zero Dark Thirty, She's the Hero," *The Washington Post,* December 10, 2012.
76. Interview with employee who worked at CIA's headquarters, who referred to Bikowsky as "the redhead."
77. Interview with employee who worked at CIA's Alec Station, who referred to Bikowsky as "the redhead."
78. Interview with John Kiriakou.
79. Charlie Savage, "Ex-CIA Officer Charged in Information Leak," *The New York Times,* January 23, 2012.
80. Interview with John Kiriakou.
81. Interview with Mark Rossini.
82. Interview with Mark Rossini; Allan Lengel and Rachel Leven, "The Raven Haired Actress and the Fall of a Dapper FBI Agent," ticklethewire.com, September 14, 2009; "Former Federal Bureau of Investigation (FBI) Supervisory Special Agent Mark

Rossini Sentenced for Criminally Accessing FBI Database," FBI press release, May 14, 2009.

83. Interview with Mark Rossini; interview with James Bamford; Jeff Stein, "FBI Prevents Agents from Telling 'Truth' About 9/11 on PBS," *Congressional Quarterly*, October 1, 2008.

84. Interview with Mark Rossini; "The Spy Factory," *NOVA*, PBS, February 3, 2009.

85. Interview with Mark Rossini; Del Quentin Wilber, "Ex-FBI Agent Mark Rossini Sentenced for Using Bureau Computers in Pelican Case," *The Washington Post*, May 15, 2009.

## CHAPTER 10

1. Email from Preston Golson, office of CIA public affairs, "Re: Your Podcast," to Ray Nowosielski, September 8, 2011, 3:39PM CDT.

2. Email from Ray Nowosielski to Preston Golson, office of CIA public affairs, "Re: Your Podcast," September 8, 2011.

3. Email from Preston Golson, office of CIA public affairs, "Re: Your Podcast," to Ray Nowosielski, September 9, 2011.

4. Kristen Breitweiser, "The Mystery in Footnote 44," *Wake Up Call: The Political Education of a 9/11 Widow*. Breitweiser would later expand on this chapter on her *Huffington Post* blog in a piece entitled "Enabling Danger," May 25, 2011, in which she concluded, "There exist at least seven instances between January 2000 and September 11th, 2001, that the CIA withheld vital information from the FBI about these two hijackers who were inside this country training for the attacks."

5. John Cook, "Chief of CIA's 'Global Jihad Unit' Revealed Online," Gawker.com, September 22, 2011.

6. Interview with Dale Watson.

7. Michael Rolince, personal correspondence.

8. Stephen Hayes, "The Connection," *The Weekly Standard*, June 7, 2004.

9. Aram Roston, "The Gay Terrorist," *The Observer*, March 17, 2010.

10. 9/11 Commission Report, 217–218. One source who worked inside CIA's headquarters claims Bayoumi met Mihdhar and Hazmi at the moment of their arrival in Los Angeles, and that the driver for this meeting is the key to proving the Saudi sponsorship/Bayoumi allegation.

11. Interview with Sen. Bob Graham; Bob Graham, Mark Nussbaum, *Intelligence Matters*, 12–13.

12. Federal Bureau of Investigation, *Working Draft Chronology of Events for Hijackers and Associates* (Part A), 52.

13. Michael Jacobson and Dana Lesemann, "Document no. 17," 9-11 Commission, June 6, 2003, found and posted to 28pages.org by Brian McGlinchey, April 19, 2006; Federal Bureau of Investigation (FBI), "Overview of the 9/11 Investigation Slide

Show," 2014; twenty-eight pages declassified on August 5, 2016, from Congressional Joint Inquiry 9-11 Report.

14. 9/11 Commission Memorandum for the record: Interview with Abdussattar Shaikh.

15. Letter from Thomas J. Pickard to the 9-11 Commission, June 24, 2004.

16. Philip Shenon, "September 11th Anniversary: Richard Clarke's Explosive CIA Cover-up Charge," *The Daily Beast*, August 11, 2011; Jason Leopold, "Former Counterterrorism Czar Accuses Tenet, Other CIA Officials of Cover-Up," *Truth-Out*, August 11, 2011.

17. Interview with Kevin Fenton; "Miscellaneous 9/11 Commission Staff Notes about Drafting the Final Report," published on scribd.com by 9-11 Document Archive; Kevin Fenton, "Identity of CIA Officer Responsible for Pre–9-11 Failures, Tora Bora Escape, Rendition to Torture Revealed," 911blogger.com, September 11, 2009.

18. Interview with employee at CIA's headquarters.

19. Matt Apuzzo and Adam Goldman, "CIA officers make grave mistakes, get promoted," Associated Press, February 9, 2011.

20. Congressional Record S4849—United States Senate, "Executive nominations received by the Senate," May 22, 2008.

21. Interview with multiple employees at CIA headquarters; Congressional Record Volume 149, Number 7, "Executive nominations received by the Senate," January 15, 2003; Casey's name was deduced by the authors as detailed in piece by Ray Nowosielski and Rory O'Connor, "Insiders Voice Doubts About CIA's 9/11 Story," *Salon*, October 14, 2011.

22. "Nortel Networks Cherry Blossom 10-mile Run," April 11, 1999.

23. Interview with employee at CIA's headquarters.

24. Emails from Preston Golson, CIA public affairs, to Ray Nowosielski, were sent from September 8 to September 10, 2011.

25. Email from Ray Nowosielski to Preston Golson, CIA public affairs, sent on September 10, 2011, TIME.

26. The email posted unredacted on SecrecyKills.org was from Ray Nowosielski to Preston Golson, CIA public affairs, sent on September 8, 2011, 10:00 a.m.

27. John Young, "CIA Officers Alfreda Frances Bikowsky and Michael Anne Casey," cryptome.org, September 21, 2011.

28. Sibel Edmonds, "BFP Breaking News: Confirmed Identity of the CIA Official behind 9-11, Rendition & Torture Cases is Revealed," boilingfrogspost.com, September 21, 2011.

29. Catherine Herridge, "Mueller Grilled on FBI's Release of Awlaki in 2002," Fox News, March 8, 2012.

30. Scott Shane and Souad Mekhennet, "Imam's Path From Condemning Terror to Preaching Jihad," *The New York Times*, May 8, 2010; Matthew Cole and Richard Esposito, "US Mulls Legality of Killing American al Qaeda 'Turncoat,'" ABC News, January 25, 2010.

31. Jennifer Griffen, "Two US-Born Terrorists Killed in CIA-Led Drone Strike," FOX News, September 30, 2011; Greg Miller "Legal Memo Backing Drone Strike that Killed American Anwar al-Awlaki is Released," *Washington Post*, June 23, 2014; David Lauter and Timothy Phelps, "Memo justifying drone killing of American Al Qaeda leader is released," *LA Times*, June 23, 2014.

32. Craig Whitlock, "US airstrike that killed American teen in Yemen raises legal, ethical questions," *Washington Post*, October 23, 2011.

33. Jo Becker and Scott Shane, "Secret Kill Lists Test Obama's Principles and Will," *The New York Times*, May 29, 2012.

34. Barton Gellman, Glenn Greenwald, Ewen MacAskill, and Laura Poitras, in-depth reporting on Edward Snowden's revelations about the National Security Agency and its vast global surveillance network, in the *Guardian* and *The Washington Post*.

35. John Cook, "Chief of CIA's 'Global Jihad Unit' Revealed Online," Gawker.com, September 22, 2011; Ray Nowosielski, Rory O'Connor, "Insiders Voice Doubts About CIA's 9/11 Story," *Salon*, October 14, 2011.

36. Adam Goldman, Greg Miller, "Spy Agencies' Attorney Has Fiercely Defended Surveillance Programs Revealed By Snowden," *The Washington Post*, January 12, 2014. This article was about the attorney who was "serving as the point person in defending the massive surveillance program" after Edward Snowden first revealed it, Robert S. Litt, strangely adding a line in paragraph eighteen that reads, "Litt, 64, did not disclose the names of [CIA] clients. But current and former US officials said they included a CIA analyst, Alfreda Frances Bikowsky . . ."

37. Matthew Cole, "Bin Laden Expert Accused of Shaping CIA Deception on 'Torture' Program," nbcnews.com, December 16, 2014.

38. Jane Mayer, "The Unidentified Queen of Torture," newyorker.com, December 18, 2014.

39. Glenn Greenwald, Peter Maass, "Meet Alfreda Bikowsky, the Senior Officer at the Center of the CIA's Torture Scandals," *The Intercept*, December 19, 2014. They further explained, "Back in 2011, John Cook, the outgoing editor of *The Intercept*, wrote an article at Gawker, based on the reporting of Ray Nowosielski and John Duffy, naming Bikowsky and pointing to extensive evidence showing that she 'has a long (if pseudonymous) history of being associated with some of the agency's most disastrous boondoggles . . .'"

40. A composite of two different accounts given to us by prominent American journalists.

41. According to multiple employees at CIA's headquarters.

42. Adam Goldman and Matthew Rosenberg, "CIA Names the 'Dark Prince' to Run Iran Operations, Signaling a Tougher Stance," *The New York Times*, February 2, 2017.

# INDEX

# INDEX

# INDEX